# *Total* GUITAR TUTOR

THIS IS A CARLTON BOOK

Copyright © Carlton Books Ltd, 1999

CLD 21307
This edition published in 1999 for
Colour Library Direct
Godalming Business Centre
Woolsack Way
Godalming, Surrey, GU7 1XW

10 9 8 7 6 5 4 3 2

First edition 1998

A CIP catalogue record for this book is available from the British Library

ISBN 1-84100-123-6

Editorial Manager: Julian Flanders
Design Manager: Zoë Maggs
Edited and designed by The Design Revolution
Production: Sarah Schuman
Photographs by Paul Mattock
CD Produced by The Orgone Company

Printed and bound in Dubai

TERRY BURROWS

# *Total*
# GUITAR
# TUTOR

Colour
Library
Direct

# CONTENTS

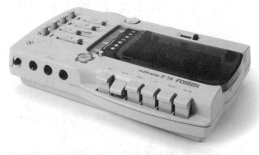

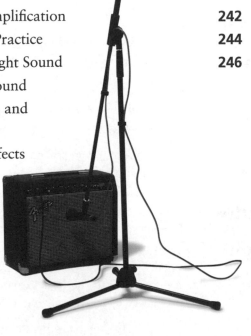

# A FEW WORDS...

As a beginner taking your first tentative steps into a typical music store you might well find the wide-ranging paraphenalia which is now commonly associated with the guitar somewhat overwelming. Besides having to choose from a wealth of nylon-string classical, steel-string, solid-body electric, semi-acoustic, and electro-acoustic guitars, there is also a bewildering array of electronic hardware with which you have to contend—valve and solid-state amplification, not to mention all manner of inscrutably named sound processing effects. Don't be alarmed: the *Total Guitar Tutor* is on hand to guide you through this daunting maze.

Let's begin with a few words on what the *Total Guitar Tutor* is all about. *Here is* a flavor of what you should be able to achieve if you work carefully through the book:

- A good understanding of the history and evolution of the guitar and some of its greatest exponents.

- Knowledge of the different types of guitar and those that are best suited to specific kinds of music.

- An understanding of the fundamentals of music theory, sight-reading standard musical notion and tablature.

- Your chord vocabulary should be sufficiently developed to enable you to play pretty well every popular song that's ever been written, and in any key.

- You should be able to play moderately demanding blues- and rock-based guitar solos using the most commonly heard playing effects.

- You should be able to perform rudimentary country and folk picking styles, as well as alternative tuning systems.

- You should be able to work your way through some simple classical pieces, and master some very basic flamenco and latin-American rhythms.

- You should be able to string together some moderately demanding jazz sequences.

- You will understand the different types of amplifier and sound processing effects that can be used to color the sound of your playing.

- You will have a good understanding of how to record the guitar and operate both in live and studio situations.

You may like to view that as our general manifesto, but I can't stress strongly enough that the *Total Guitar Tutor* is in no way about didacticism. Our true aim is to provide the basic ingredients to let YOU think, act, and play for yourself. Everyone of you will have different needs, goals, dreams, and musical aptitudes. Your reasons for wanting to play will be equally varied. For some, being able to strum the chords of few songs will be more than enough; others may strive to play heavy metal solos as fast as is earthly possible. But no

matter how satisfying it can undoubtedly be, playing the guitar—in my opinion at least—is less an effective means in itself that a truly great musical tool for expressing and communicating your own creativity.

It wouldn't be fair of me, though, to get through this introduction without uttering the dreaded "P-word." As with any learning process, you only get to be good by PRACTISING. The finest musicians combine a mental facility—an understanding of WHAT they are trying to play— with the motor skills necessary to carry out their "commands." The acquisition of the latter will only come about by repetition. Sadly there is no short-cut to having your fingers "learn," for example, chords and scales—and unless you are planning a radical overhaul of the basic principles of music you're going to need both of these. There will be times when this can be frustrating, especially on those occasions that your hands fail to live up to the expectations of your mind. The only advice I can give here is to take it slowly and try to keep yourself mentally focused on your ultimate aim. Work methodically through each lesson and don't move on until you have mastered the last one. If you want to get "new agey" about it, visualization can help: try to hear and see yourself in your mind playing the way you really want to. Keep things in perspective, though: whether you aspire to be a Segovia, a Wes Montgomery, a Chet Atkins or a Johnny Thunders, remember that every novice has had to pass through the same learning experience, so you're in good company. But no matter how great the challenge, never let it become torture. You only live once—the precious time you spend doing anything should be enjoyable, otherwise it's just not worth bothering. As the legendary Les Paul told me a few years ago: "You Don't WORK the guitar, you PLAY it." So with those wise words in mind, get ready to have some fun!

**Terry Burrows**
*London, July 1998*

# CHAPTER 1
# The Guitar

## INTRODUCING THE GUITAR

**The true origin of the guitar remains one of music's great mysteries, and is still the subject of dispute among music historians. For although the guitar as we know it dates back to the Renaissance period, we can reasonably guess from artefacts unearthed in the Middle East that related stringed instruments existed almost four thousand years ago—long before the pre-Christian era. However, the story is made more complex in that although many of these instruments bear a superficial resemblance to the guitar, we can only guess as to the the way in which they were used. Indeed, the main point of disagreement among experts would seem to be a question of what exactly constitutes a guitar?**

Narrowing down the list of possible relatives, the earliest evidence can be traced back to Babylonian clay reliefs found in Asia Minor, dating back as far as 1900 BC, that clearly show images of musicians playing instruments from which the guitar may well have evolved. The identifiable elements include a resonating body, fingerboard, frets, and the use of more than two strings. Similar instruments were shown on carvings found in the same region, although these have been dated to around 1300 BC and attributed to the Babylonians' Hittite conquerors. From this point onward, the volatile cultural shifts within the region, as well as the movements of the early merchants and traders, would seem to have been largely responsible for spreading the use and popularity of these mysterious early instruments.

Probably the earliest surviving relative of the guitar was discovered in an Ancient Egyptian tomb. It is thought to date from between 1500 and 2000 BC, although it shows a closer resemblance to other stringed instruments, such as the harp. In the same region, a Coptic instrument from around a thousand years later shows the early beginnings of the familiar shape and construction, the body and neck being carved separately using different types of wood.

The direct precursors to the guitar are thought to have found their way into Europe from Spain. The development of the instrument in the south of the country resulted from the Moorish invasions of AD 800. A Muslim people of mixed Berber and Arab descent, the Moors introduced stringed instruments such as the ud. During the same period, the ud and the pandoura—a tall, stringed instrument found in Ancient Greece and Rome—began to find their way to the north of

**The guitar has many distant relatives throughout the world.**

## THE VIHUELA

During the 16th century, another important Spanish instrument was also at the peak of its popularity. The vihuela bore a closer resemblance in size to the modern guitar. A flat-backed instrument, the vihuela had a shallow body, a narrow fingerboard with 10 frets, and a headstock which was bent back at an angle, with tuning pegs inserted from the rear. There were three distinct types of instrument: the *vihuela de arco* was played with a bow; the *vihuela de péola* was played with a plectrum; and the *vihuela de mano* was plucked with the fingers. Eventually, it was the latter which came to be known as the vihuela. The instrument's popularity also spread to Italy, where it was known as the viola da mano.

The vihuela was usually found with six pairs of gut strings, although five- and seven-course versions are known to have existed. Like the early lute, the six-course vihuela was mainly tuned to the notes G-C-F-A-D-G. However, significant variations in size meant that this was not always the case. Luis de Milán, a prolific composer of music for the vihuela, went as far as to suggest that the cantino—the top course—be tuned as high as possible without them breaking; the lower strings would then be tuned relative to that note.

The growing popularity of the five-course guitar by the start of the 17th century was partially responsible for the demise of the vihuela. And yet within 200 years, the guitar had assumed the proportions of its elder relative. In spite of its former popularity, the Jacquemart-André Museum in Paris houses the only surviving vihuela. Although the instrument is "extinct", a considerable body of music dating as far back as back to 1536 still exists for the vihuela.

**The lute was extremely popular during the Middle Ages.**

Europe. Here, at the hands of the indigenous European instrument makers instruments such as the lute and gittern—perhaps the closest we have to a true precursor of the modern guitar—gradually evolved. Until well into the 16th century, the lute was the dominant musical instrument throughout Middle Europe and Great Britain.

Renaissance Europe saw the birth of an early lute known as the *guitarra moresca*. References to another relative of the lute—the *guitarra latina* or Latin guitar—can also be found during the same period. The earliest true guitars, which appeared at the end of the 15th century, were closer in size to a lute, and used gut "courses"—pairs of strings tuned in unison, rather than individual strings. Until the late 16th century, the guitar was viewed very much as a poor relation to "nobler" stringed instruments, such as the lute and vihuela. The guitar quickly found itself divergent roles in music. Whilst four-course instruments were generally used to perform self-contained pieces, a five-course guitar soon became more popular as a means of providing accompaniment to a vocalist. The tuning during the 16th century was C-F-A-D—this represents the top four strings on a modern guitar tuned a tone lower.

# THE FIRST GUITARS

**Although they bore a clear visual resemblance to their modern counterparts, the first guitars exhibited very different hardware. Apart from the use of courses rather than individual strings, the most dramatic difference was that the fingerboards did not have fixed metal frets, but were made from pieces of gut tied around the neck. The specific number of frets depended on the nature and complexity of the music. This made the musician's job considerably more difficult. Before performing, not only would each pair of strings have to be tuned, but he would have to ensure that the frets were positioned for correct intonation.**

Although Spain is without question the home of the modern guitar, very little is known about Spanish makers of the period. In fact, of the few 16th-century models known to exist, most emanated from France. Lyons, in particular, was famed for the prowess of its guitar makers, one of the most noted of whom was Gaspard Duyffoprucgar. In fact, legal records from the end of the century indicate that a lesser craftsman named Benoist Lejeune was imprisoned for selling replicas of models by Duyffoprucgar. This is the first documented occurrence of a problem that plagued guitar makers right up to recent times.

The scarcity of early models makes it difficult to judge how instruments from this period were styled. One of the oldest models in existence is a five-course guitar built in Portugal by Belchior Dias in 1581. Although it is restrained in appearance, many other instruments of the period show a tendency towards lavish decoration, featuring inlays and engravings from ebony, ivory, and mother-of-pearl, although this may simply indicate that greater lengths were taken to protect these works of art than more everyday musical instruments.

The 17th century found the guitar popular in Central European court circles. The two main centers of activity were Italy and France. Venice was home to Giorgio and Matteo Sellas. The hallmark of their instruments was ornate fingerboard inlays in ivory and mother-of-pearl. Instruments by the Paris-based

Voboam family—René, Alexandre, and Jean—are also among the most prized models of the period. The only existing example of René's work can be found in Oxford's Ashmolean Museum. Built in 1641, it measures almost 94 cm in length—25% longer than the Dias instrument built 80 years earlier. The guitar had now assumed similar dimensions to the vihuela. Toward the end of the 17th century, the great Antonio Stradivari of Cremona in Italy—probably history's noted maker of musical instruments—also began producing guitars.

The 17th century also produced the first enduring composer of pieces for the guitar. Although little of the classical repertoire for the instrument predates the 20th century, the works of Spaniard Gaspar Sanz are still performed. *Instrucción de Mœsica sobre la Guitarra Española* first appeared in 1674, and was a considerably influential collection of pieces. Unlike his French and Italian counterparts, who produced elegant pieces intended for performance in courts, the work of Sanz reflected a more down-to-earth upbringing, and included Spanish folk dances.

During the first half of the 18th century, the guitar became less fashionable, but it was in the 1780s that the instrument began a crucial period of transition. The mid-18th century saw the development of six-course guitars in Spain, with a lower E-course being added to the other five. However, at the same time in France and Italy, players began to use single strings instead of pairs. It

**The vihuela was gradually overshadowed by the popularity of the guitar.**

would appear that a combination of precise tuning difficulties, and problems related to playing the strings of each course in exact unison, led to the widespread adoption of single strings in most European countries outside of Spain. By the early 19th century, however, the Spaniards had also followed suit.

Another important development was the introduction of fan bracing in the construction of the instrument. Two of the pioneers of this system were José Pagés and Josef Benedid, both luthiers working in the southern Spanish city of Cadiz. The system meant that fan-shaped struts were fixed to the underside of the soundboard, providing the necessary support for the bridge. Previously, the bridge had been held in place by a firm transverse bar. However, this created sound problems. In short, fan bracing produced an improved sound and greater volume.

The late 18th century also saw the frets being fixed to the fingerboard. The early instruments were invariably fretted from ivory, and later on, brass. Because the length of the neck in relation to the body was shorter than at present, there were usually 11 frets, making it as yet impossible to play a single octave on any one string.

# THE CLASSICAL TRADITION

**The middle of the 19th century saw the birth of what we now know as the classical guitar. In Spain, the revolutionary work of Antonio de Torres Jurado (1817–92) was crucial in turning the guitar into a serious and credible instrument. It was Torres who experimented with the existing construction and dimensions, and created the template for an instrument which exists to this day. The first prominent player to use his new design was Francisco de Tárrega (1852–1909)—the man in whose hands the guitar was first treated as a serious musical proposition to rival the established orchestral instruments. Without the work of these two men, the evolution of the classical guitar tradition would have been very different.**

Antonio de Torres Jurado was born in Almeira, Spain, in 1817. After moving to Seville in 1840, he set up a workshop and began his experimentation with new dimensions and production techniques that would revolutionize the future of the instrument. Torres increased the width of the neck to 5 cm at the nut, making the instrument easier to fret accurately. He also standardized the string length to the greater 65 cm. He redesigned the outline and proportion of the body, and further developed the bracing ideas introduced by Pagés, laying out seven struts in the shape of a fan behind the sound hole. Torres also introduced a bridge saddle to which the strings were tied after passing over the bridge. The instruments built by Torres in decade up to his death in 1892 created a template for the modern classical guitar.

Torres became the maker of choice for the finest classical players of the second half of the 19th century. In particular, it was Francesco de Tárrega who, more than any other, brought respectability to the guitar. A classically trained pianist at the Madrid Conservatorio, Tárrega was the instrument's first great virtuoso. He also composed a number of popular romantic pieces, and transcribed a number of popular piano pieces for the guitar. However, it is perhaps as a teacher that his influence can be felt most strongly—single-handedly, Tárrega created the foundations of the modern classical technique. His era saw the standardization of posture—the increase in body size brought about by Torres made positioning of the guitar on the left leg more comfortable. He also altered the manner of right-hand playing, encouraging the abandoning of the practice of supporting the right hand by resting the fourth finger beneath the bridge in favor of having the entire hand poised above the bridge.

The early part of the 19th century was notable for the work of Fernando Sor (1778–1839). A virtuoso player who toured Europe widely, in 1830 Sor produced his famous *Méthode pour la Guitarre*. During an eventful lifetime, he composed over 60 pieces for the instrument. In contrast to the often facile works of the early guitar composers, many of Sor's compositions continue to be performed in modern-day concert halls.

Although some of the finest players of the early 20th century had been pupils of Tárrega, it was a self-taught

**Torres provided a blueprint for the modern classical guitar.**

**Fernando Sor: virtuoso guitarist, and the first great composer for the instrument.**

musician named Andrés Segovia who established the guitar firmly as an international instrument. Refining Tárrega's playing techniques, Segovia's achievements as a performer on the international stage attracted a worldwide following. His popularity brought about an increase in the instrument's repertoire as major 20th-century composers, such as Roussel, Rodrigo, Ponce, and Castelnuovo-Tedesco created works especially for him. Segovia also influenced a new generation of classical guitarists, such as John Williams, through his master classes held at Siena in Italy.

The guitar's 20th-century renaissance has also seen the formalization of study. An indication of how recently the guitar has been accepted by the classical fraternity can be seen in the fact that London's prestigious Royal College of Music found no formal place in its curriculum for the instrument until 1960.

# GUITARS IN AMERICA

**The guitar is without question the instrument at the heart of most of the popular music of the 20th century—from folk and country and western to rock and pop. The roots of the guitar in popular music can largely be traced back to the way in which the guitar developed in the United States. While a classical revolution was taking place in Spain, history was also being forged in America, where two distinct styles were developed by two of the most significant figures in guitar history: C.F. Martin's "flat-top" guitar designs, and Orville Gibson's "arch-top" models.**

## THE MARTIN TRADITION

Hailing from a long line of violin makers, Christian Frederick Martin was born in 1796 in Mark Neukirchen, Germany. At the age of 15 he left home for Vienna, where he became an apprentice to the noted luthier Johann Stauffer. Returning to Germany to open up his own shop, he found himself embroiled in a legal battle between rival guilds. His family had been long-standing members of the Cabinet Makers' guild, who had traditionally made guitars. Looking to restrict competition, the Violin Maker's guild sought to prevent other craftsmen from making musical instruments. Although Martin won his battle to stay in business, he was shaken by the experience and decided that greater opportunities for growth were possible in America.

On arrival in New York in 1833, Martin quickly set up his business, opening a modest music store which housed

**Christian Frederick Martin (1796–1867).**

a small guitar production set-up in the back room. His early instruments were often bartered for other goods. Unhappy with life in New York, in Martin sold his store in 1838 and bought eight acres of land on the outskirts of Nazareth, Pennsylvania, where he concentrated on the production of musical instruments.

Early Martin guitars were hand-crafted to order, and showed little standardization, apart from the unusual Stauffer-style headstock design, which had all the tuning keys on one side. Another unusual feature of the early Martin guitars was the use of an adjustable neck, which was used until the 1890s, when steel strings began to replace those made from gut, exerting greater stress on the joint between the neck and body. The 1850s saw one of C. F. Martin's major design innovations—the "X" bracing system fitted to the underside of the guitar top to provide a distinctive treble tone.

After C.F. Martin died in 1867, the company continued under the guidance of successive generations. It was under the presidency of Martin's grandson, Frank Henry, that some of the company's most innovative products were designed. In 1916, the large-bodied "Dreadnought" style was developed. Intended to produce greater volume and bass response, it was seen as an ideal accompaniment for vocalists. Although it did not go into general production until the 1930s, it would soon become extremely popular among folk and country singers. In 1929, Martin also introduced the 14-fret neck, intended to increase the guitar's range and make it a more versatile instrument. Dubbed the "Orchestra Model," it quickly became a standard design feature among American guitars.

From the 1930s onwards, Martin enjoyed continued prosperity, establishing a world-wide reputation for its flat-top acoustic instruments. Indeed, by the early 1960s demand for Martin guitars was so great that there was a waiting list of three years for new models. Although other US manufacturers, such as Gibson and Guild, have produced fine flat-top acoustic guitars, Martin remains the name with which these instruments are most strongly associated.

**Gibson L-5 arch-top guitar.**

## ORVILLE GIBSON AND THE ARCH-TOP TRADITION

The other great name in the early history of the American guitar is Orville Gibson. Born in 1856, the son of a British immigrant, Gibson was not only a skilled woodcarver but also an accomplished mandolin player. During the 1890s, he brought together these two very different skills to produce a new breed of guitar, that used the methods of construction more usually applied to violins. These instruments had curved, arched tops, and (at first) featured oval-shaped soundholes. In 1902, backed by a group of businessmen in Kalamazoo, Michigan, the Gibson Mandolin-Guitar Manufacturing Company was founded. By the time of Gibson's death in 1918, his company enjoyed a reputation second only to Martin.

In spite of the death of the company's founding father, the business continued to thrive and played an active role in a number of developments that took place in the 1920s, and would have a significant impact on the future of the guitar. A key figure thoughout this period was engineer Lloyd Loar. To begin with, Loar was one of the first to experiment with electronic pickup devices—even if this development would not make an impact until the following decade. In 1924, he was also actively involved in the first of many legendary production guitars—the Gibson L-5. Replacing the oval soundhole with two violin-style "f-holes," the L-5 also featured an adjustable truss rod to give added strength to the neck. It was so successful that by the end of the decade it had all but replaced the banjo as a rhythm instrument in dance bands.

Further innovations followed, as Gibson launched electrified versions of their standard arch-tops, beginning with the single-pickup ES-150 in 1935. At the end of the decade, in the response to the growing use of the guitar as a solo instrument, the L-5 and dreadnought-bodied Super 400 models were issued with a cutaway lower body, allowing easy access to 17 or 18 frets.

## COUNTRY MUSIC AND THE GUITAR

The guitar has always been at the very heart of American country and folk music. The first guitar player to bring country music to a large radio audience was Jimmie Rodgers. As a youth, he had been taught to play guitar by black railroad workers. Although he died in 1933, aged 36, in a short time he created a legacy that would be carried by a new generation of popular guitarists. At the same time, "singing cowboy" stars like Gene Autrey and Roy Rogers glamorized the instrument among young movie-goers. Woody Guthrie introduced politics and social commentary, and in doing so created a songwriting tradition that has passed through to the modern day.

Various styles of country music, such as bluegrass and Western swing, found themselves reaching national audiences through the Grand Ole Opry shows. These introduced great country stars, such as pioneering pickers like Merle Travis and Chet Atkins, who helped to establish the Nashville Sound. Modern-day country stars, such as Garth Brooks and Dwight Yoakum, are now among the most popular artists in the world.

# How an Acoustic Guitar Works

All acoustic stringed instruments use a similar principle to create and project sound. By striking the string the vibrations disturb the surrounding airwaves. By passing this energy into the soundbox via the bridge saddle (the point where each string comes into direct contact with the body) an audible sound sound is created, as it vibrates in sympathy with the strings.

## FACTORS AFFECTING SOUND

The sound produced by any acoustic guitar depends both on the materials used and design of the instrument. These elements play a crucial role in both the volume projected and quality of tone.

There is no definitive formula for the perfect guitar design—for one thing, not all players favor the same kind of sound; equally, some instruments are better suited to certain styles of music. A more complex factor is the nature of wood. No matter what practical steps a luthier takes to standardize methods of production, no two pieces of wood—even if they have come from the same tree—have identical characteristics. Therefore, no two guitars will ever be exactly the same.

During the 1920s guitar makers expended great energy in developing instruments capable of producing a higher volume. This was largely achieved by increasing the body shape and size. However, the tone of an instrument will also be affected by

## THE MODERN ACOUSTIC GUITAR

There can be no doubt that Ovation is the most significant acoustic guitar manufacturer to emerge over the past 50 years. Founded in early 1960s by aerospace engineer Charles Kaman, Ovation guitars have revolutionized the world of the steel-string acoustic guitar.

The fundamental design principle replaced the back and sides of the traditional guitar with a one-piece fiberglass rounded bowl. With no corners or struts, the soundwaves were no longer trapped in the corners of the soundbox allowing more of the natural sound to be heard. Following these first experiments, Ovation went on to experiment with a variety of synthetic materials, as well as combinations of fiberglass and wood.

The Balladeer was Ovation's first production guitar, launched in 1966. Four years later an electro-acoustic version was launched, with a piezo-electric transducer pickup fitted on the underside of the bridge saddle. This system created a more natural acoustic guitar sound than could ever be achieved by fitting a pickup across the soundhole of an a regular acoustic instrument.

It's not much of an exaggeration to suggest that the name Ovation is now pretty well synonymous with the term "electro-acoustic."

---

the bracing used on the underside of the soundboard and on the back. Bracing not only gives strength to the body, but also prevents the wood distorting. However, by their very existence, the bracing struts exert an impact on the soundwaves that move around within the body—this naturally has an impact on the guitar's tonal characteristics.

A variety of materials can be used in the construction of acoustic guitars. However, the most important consideration is that whatever wood is used must have been allowed to settle, losing most of its natural moisture—after all, if the timber was used straight from the tree, it would lose its shape as it dried out naturally. This process can be achieved naturally so that the wood is stored and allowed to dry out over a very long period of time—the top-quality luthiers generally insist on using woods treated in this way. A common (and cheaper) alternative, is to use kiln-dried timbers which can be dried it out within a matter of weeks.

Different types of wood have different tonal characteristics, therefore all acoustic instruments are built from a combination of timbers. The soundboards found on most quality instruments are crafted from European or Canadian spruce. Budget models are generally made from laminated timbers or plywood, which often results in lack of tonal definition. For the backs and sides, rosewood, maple or mahogany are most commonly used. Struts and bracing are generally carved from spruce.

A wider variety of materials has been applied in the construction of the guitar neck. Brazilian mahogany is rated by many luthiers as the best, although as a protected wood it is increasingly difficult to obtain. A cheaper alternative is maple. Fingerboards are commonly carved from rosewood, although on the more expensive models ebony is prized as a more attractive, dense and hard-wearing wood.

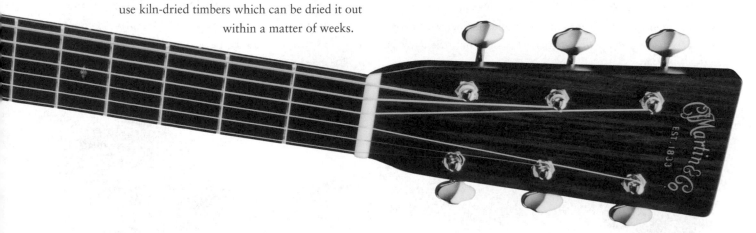

# THE ELECTRIFICATION OF THE GUITAR

**By the 1920s guitars were commonly used in jazz and dance bands, models like the Gibson L5 having usurped the traditional role of the banjo. However, during this time the guitar's naturally low volume, compared to the other acoustic instruments, meant that in most circumstances its use was restricted to providing a rhythmic backing. The answer came with the development of the magnetic pickup.**

In an attempt to solve the guitar's volume problem, one of Gibson's engineers, Lloyd Loar, began to experiment with magnetic coils, and in 1924 developed a very basic pickup that could be fitted to a standard six-string acoustic guitar. Gibson failed to pick up on the potential of this innovation, and Loar eventually left to form his own Vivitone company, which during the 1930s began to produce usable electronic pickup systems. However, before doing this, Loar played an active role in the development of the remarkable Gibson L-5.

The most significant breakthrough came in 1931, when Paul Barth and George Beauchamp, two employees of the California-based National company who had also been developing pickups, joined forces with Adolph Rickenbacker to form the Electro String Company. Together they produced the A22 and A25 cast-aluminum lap-steel guitars. Known as the "Frying Pan" because of their shape, they were the first commercially produced electric instruments.

## THE FIRST "TRUE" ELECTRIC GUITARS

In 1932, Rickenbacker applied their new development to the guitar, producing the first production electric guitar—the "Electro Spanish." This was a basic arch-top design fitted with the same horseshoe magnet pickup used on the Frying Pan. However, it was the famous Gibson ES-150 (see across the page), launched in 1935, that captured the imagination of jazz guitarist Charlie Christian. More than any other single musician, it was Christian who was largely responsible for establishing the electric guitar as a serious musical proposition.

### THE JAZZ AGE

At the beginning of the jazz era the guitar played a low-key role. It was simply not loud enough to compete with the conventional solo instruments. Nonetheless, a tradition gradually emerged during the 1920s, New York guitarist Eddie Lang generally being credited for having pioneered the idea of the guitar as an instrument for playing solos in the 1920s. In spite of his benchmark recordings with violinist Joe Venuti, the role of the guitar was still largely restricted to rhythm work. Django Reinhardt progressed the cause during the 1930s, playing the revolutionary Selmer Maccaferri guitar, whose enlarged body and specially designed D-shaped soundhole made the instrument capable of far greater volumes than regular guitars.

It was Charlie Christian who revolutionized not only jazz but guitar playing. Using the Gibson ES-150 (an electrified version of the standard L-50 arch-top), he made massive strides forward with a style that perhaps owed more to the soloing of saxophonist Lester Young than any other guitarist. A genuine virtuoso, whose recording career lasted barely four years, he helped shape the sound of bebop in the early 1940s. His work cast a long shadow over those that followed, and it took almost 20 years for the next significant influence to arrive in the world of jazz guitar—Wes Montgomery.

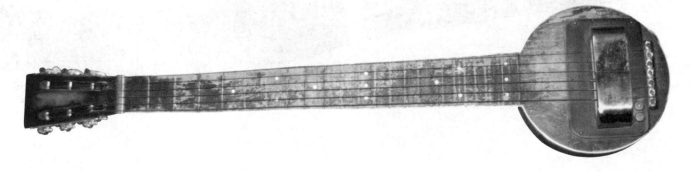

The Rickenbacker "Frying Pan"—although not technically a guitar, it was the first production instrument to be fitted with a pickup.

**GIBSON ES-150**
Launched in the mid-1930s, the ES-150 was Gibson's first production electric guitar.

Modelled on the budget L-50, the ES-150 does not have the same degree of ornamentation as some Gibsons of the period.

The neck joins the body at the 14th fret.

The Gibson bar pickup is also known as the "Charlie Christian"—named after the most famous player of this type of guitar.

This kind of body is known by Gibson as the "Cremona."

Raised pick guard

"F"-HOLE
The ES-150 evolved from Lloyd Loar's designs for the famed L-5, and the cheaper L-50. Among his innovations was the replacement of a central soundhole with two "f" holes.

"Trapeze" tailpiece

# THE SOLID-BODY ERA

**During the 1940s, a number of unrelated parties set about designing and building a solid-body electric guitar. Although Les Paul and Paul Bigsby are credited as being the true pioneers, no-one can say beyond doubt who got there first. There is, however, no question that it was Leo Fender who was responsible for popularizing the idea.**

### DEVELOPMENT BACKGROUND

One fundamental problem that resulted from fitting pickups to an acoustic guitar was that if the amplifier volume was too great, the sound from the loudspeaker would cause the body of the guitar to vibrate. This creating a howling noise referred to as "feedback". The logical solution to this problem was to increase the body mass of the instrument, to reduce its capacity for vibration. Hence, in the 1940s, the first solid-body electric guitars appeared.

Les Paul holding the famed guitar that bears his name.

There is no definitive agreement as to who produced the first genuine solid-body guitar. In the early 1940s, country-jazz guitarist Les Paul created his own "Log" guitar, using a Gibson neck attached to a solid piece of pine, on which the pickups and bridge were mounted. He tried to sell the idea to Gibson, but they were not impressed at the time. Another claimant to the title was engineer Paul Bigsby, who produced an instrument designed in conjunction with country guitarist Merle Travis. An important development, the shape of the instrument clearly influenced some of the early Fender designs. Since around a dozen were produced, it could just about lay claim to being the first production solid-body electric guitar.

### A NEW ERA BEGINS

The single most important name in the history of the solid-body electric guitar is Leo Fender. Formerly the owner of an electrical repair shop, in 1946 he founded the Fender Electrical Instrument Company to produce electrified lap-steel guitars and amplifiers. Two years later, with one of his employees, George Fullerton, Fender set about creating a production-line solid-body electric guitar. Their design first saw the light of day in 1950. It was the groundbreaking Fender Broadcaster. A year later—forced by the Gretsch company who produced "Broadcaster" drums—Fender re-christened his instrument the Telecaster.

Panicked by the success of Fender's first solid-body instrument, Gibson recalled Les Paul—the man whose "broomstick with pickups" they had laughed at only a few years earlier. He was invited to take part in the development of a rival instrument. The resulting guitar launched in 1952 bore his own name—the Gibson Les Paul Standard. Fender replied two years later with the Stratocaster, perhaps the most famous guitar of them all. The two Fenders have been in production ever since, and remain two of the most popular electric guitars ever made. The Les Paul was dropped between 1961 and 1967, but demand for vintage models led to a successful relaunch. It, too, has been in production ever since, although late-1950s originals are now such prized collector's pieces that they are now more likely to be found in bank vaults than at rock concerts.

Although Fender and Gibson are the best-known makers of electric guitars, there have been many other fine American

manufacturers over the years—classic names such as Gretsch, Rickenbacker, Epiphone, and Kramer in the 1970s, as well as Jackson and Paul Reed Smith in the 1980s. European makers such as Selmer, Vox, Hofner, and Burns have also left their own distinct marks on guitar history.

During the 1980s the issue of cheap imitations became a problem. Japanese manufacturers had long since been producing low-cost copies of most of the classic Fender and Gibson designs. At first these guitars had been of too poor quality to pose any serious threat. That was until companies such as Tokai began producing cheap copies that came close to matching the originals. This led to the start of Fender's multi-tiered production system, whereby they began to ship in alternative versions of their own guitars, built in territories like Korea and Mexico. This was a popular move, as it allowed novices or those with little money to own genuine well-made Fender guitars—just not the top-quality models built in the USA.

At the same time, however, some of the better-known Japanese companies began to build up a reputation for their own designs. Ibanez, for example, who linked up with Steve Vai to produce the Jem and Universe models, are now a highly respected maker, whose top instruments can outrank their US counterparts, both in quality and cost.

## BLUES AND ROCK

Although country musicians were the pioneers of the solid-body electric guitars, it was the R&B boom of the 1950s which helped to establish their role in modern music. The sounds of the great electric bluesmen, like Muddy Waters, B.B. King, and Howlin' Wolf, had a major impact on the young blues and rock players of the early 60s, especially the first wave of British R&B bands such as the Yardbirds, who had Eric Clapton, Jeff Beck, and Jimmy Page passing through their ranks.

The first great star of the solid-body electric guitar was Jimi Hendrix. In his short life he gave a glimpse of the potential for the instrument in rock music. An electrifying showman (his years "serving time" with the likes of Little Richard becoming evident), his live performances and first three albums made him every bit as influential as Charlie Christian was at the end of the 1930s.

The past two decades has seen the emergence of pyrotechnicians such as Eddie Van Halen, Steve Vai, and Joe Satriani, although many viewed the late Stevie Ray Vaughan as the greatest post-Hendrix player.

# ANATOMY OF THE ELECTRIC GUITAR

In spite of considerable variations in the production techniques favored by different manufacturers, the majority of electric guitars feature the same types of component. However, the woods used can differ greatly. Most bodies are made from kiln-dried hardwoods, such as mahogany, ash, maple, walnut, or alder. The other major area of contention revolves around fixings. Some manufacturers, such as Fender, prefer bolt-on necks, which can be tilted to the player's preferred angle, whereas Gibson Les Pauls have the necks glued permanently to the body. Other manufacturers favor "straight-through" necks, where the neck and the body that holds the bridge are carved from a single piece of wood.

Strap Button

UPPER BOUT

NECK

Lead (back) pickup

Rhythm (front) pickup

BODY

Scratch plate

Volume Control

Tone control

Output socket

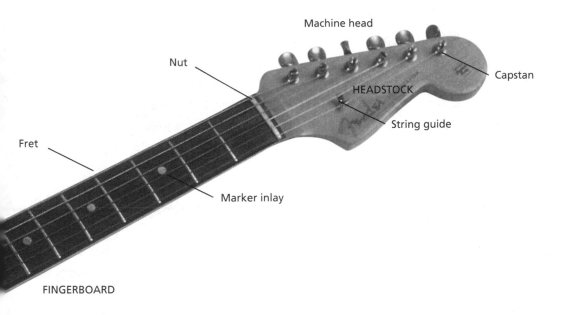

Machine head

Nut

Capstan

HEADSTOCK

String guide

Fret

Marker inlay

FINGERBOARD

## THE FUTURE OF THE GUITAR

It has to be admitted that over the past 40 years, there have been very few radical developments in the guitar world. Makers have experimented with new shapes: the Steinberg "headless" guitar became briefly popular in the 1980s, and the Ovation round-backed acoustic guitars, developed at the end of the 1970s, have remained a popular standard of their type. Manufacturers have also tried out new materials: Dan Armstrong produced instruments with plastic bodies, and Kramer used aluminum necks—both claimed improved levels of sustain, and yet players preferred their instruments to be made of the traditional wood. Radical approaches to playing have been offered: twin-necked guitars found their followers in the 1970s, but are now all but extinct; George Van Eps and Steve Vai championed the seven-string guitar, but to little avail. Alternative electronics have been tried: guitars with in-built effects have come and gone, some making concessions to simple active on-board circuitry to boost the output of the pickups.

In the early 1980s, many felt certain that some kind of hybrid instrument involving the synthesizer was the next stage in the guitar's evolution. Instruments like the Synthaxe and Stepp were certainly impressive, but costly. Japanese manufacturer Roland produced the more flexible idea of MIDI pickup systems that could be fitted to standard guitars, and could control external MIDI devices with great accuracy. Despite the doggedness with which they've pursued this goal, synth-guitarists continue to make up only a tiny minority of the guitar fraternity.

In peripheral areas, such as guitar hardware, effects, and amplification, ingenious design (the Floyd Rose locking tremolo, for example) and digital technology have brought about major advances, but it seems that as far as the instrument is concerned, for the vast majority of players the perfect format has already been established.

Perhaps the guitar-buying population is particularly ultra-conservative, but it does seem somewhat strange that the most popular and desirable solid-body instruments remain among the first production models, launched almost half a century ago. Some of this could possibly be attributed to nostalgia—those people for whom a smoke-green Gretsch Double Anniversary is an attainable alternative to a vintage Coupe de Ville—but the truth might be more simple: maybe the likes of Leo Fender, Paul Bigsby, Merle Travis, and Les Paul just got it right first time.

# CHAPTER 2
## Playing the Guitar

## HOW TO USE THIS BOOK

At the very least, the only things you will need to use this book are an acoustic guitar and a pick. If you want to play an electric guitar, you will also need an amplifier and a lead to plug in the guitar. A strap will come in handy if you want to stand up while you're playing. Apart from that, all that's left is a CD player, and you're ready to go.

### CHOOSING EQUIPMENT

If you are just beginning, choosing a guitar or amplifier can be a nerve-wracking experience. It can be a good idea to try to involve someone who has experience in these matters, especially if you intend buying secondhand equipment. Indeed, as far as guitars are concerned, buying a used model can be an ideal way of starting out with a high-quality instrument, even if, in some cases, you'll find that classic "vintage" equipment can, in fact, appreciate in value. The next four pages spell out some guidelines that you should look out for when buying either a guitar or an amplifier.

### THE 10 COMMANDMENTS OF BUYING A GUITAR

#### RULE 1 – BUY QUALITY

A quality product will be both playable and reliable, so buy the best guitar that you can afford. Any compromise here is guaranteed to be a false economy—it is easy to find something that is cheap but that is ultimately hard to play.

#### RULE 2 – CHECK FOR FINGERBOARD WARPING

If the fingerboard is severely curved or warped, the intonation will be poor and the guitar will be difficult to play. To test the neck, hold the guitar as if you were aiming a rifle, and align your eye with the top surface of the neck. It should appear perfectly even. If the top of the fingerboard appears to be twisted, DON'T BUY IT—the intonation will be poor, and repair work is likely to be costly. If you align your eye with the side of the neck, you are likely to notice a very slight curvature halfway down the neck, around about the 7th to 9th frets. This is normal, and can be controlled using the truss rod.

#### RULE 3 – CHECK INTONATION

The note on the 12th fret should ALWAYS be exactly one octave higher that the open string. A more direct comparison can be

**RULE 5 – CHECK THE MACHINE HEADS**

The machine heads are the mechanisms on the headstock at the top of the neck which control the tension of each string. If they turn too easily, the strings may slip, making the guitar difficult to keep in tune. This is not so important if you are buying an instrument fitted with a locking tremolo unit.

**RULE 6 – CHECK SUSTAIN**

The quality of sustain—the length of time a note rings naturally before it fades out—is governed by the design and construction of the instrument. Play every note on the fingerboard, to ensure that all notes sustain equally. Avoid acoustic instruments on which "dead" notes can be heard—this sometimes occurs as a result of a guitar's natural frequencies.

**RULE 7 – CHECK THE PICKUPS**

Plug an electric guitar into an amplifier. Check the relative volume of each string. If there are significant variations, the height of the pickups need to be adjusted. If each pole of the pickup (the node beneath each string) has an individual height adjustment, then this can be done easily. If not, the whole pickup may need to be replaced.

**RULE 8 – CHECK FOR NOISE**

With the guitar still plugged in, stand it close to the amplifier and listen to the sound. It should be silent. Unpleasant, whistling feedback may indicate that the pickups are not well isolated—this may pose problems when playing at high volumes.

**RULE 9 – KNOW WHAT YOU'RE HEARING**

Make sure that the amplifier in the store is not enhancing the quality of the guitar. Ask for any effects to be switched off so that you hear only the amplified guitar.

**RULE 10 – ENJOY**

Every guitar has a sound and feel of its own. Just as two people are sometimes drawn together for seemingly intangible reasons, if you are lucky you will find a guitar that produces a similar kind of magnetism. It's important that you feel happy with the instrument—this relationship will play a major part in your development as a guitarist.

made between the note and harmonic on the 12th fret. If the notes do not match, then the guitar will gradually go out of tune the further you play along the neck. Although this can easily be rectified, ask someone in the shop to do it for you—setting up should NOT be your first encounter with the guitar!

**RULE 4 – CHECK THE ACTION**

Look at the distance between the top of the 12th fret and the bottom of the string. This height is known as the "action." A low action means that the strings are closer to the frets, so that your fingers don't have to press hard to play a note. This is important for fast solo work. Also, play every note on the fingerboard, to check that the frets are all the same height. If they are not, it will result in buzzing or rattling sounds when some notes are played.

# CHOOSING THE RIGHT HARDWARE

## THE 10 COMMANDMENTS OF CHOOSING AN AMPLIFIER

### RULE 1 – POWER

Before you choose an amplifier, think ahead about what you may want to do with it ultimately, or how loud you want to be able to play. If you intend playing in a live venue, you are likely to need between 50 and 100 watts of power. Bear in mind, though, that a high output is not necessarily a sign of quality in an amplifier.

### RULE 2 – COMPATIBILITY WITH YOUR GUITAR

Any amplifier will work with any guitar, in as far as it will amplify the signal, but it's always a good idea to take in your own instrument when you test an amplifier. This is the only way you will really know if it's the right piece of equipment for your sound. You will find that some combinations unquestionably work better than others.

### RULE 3 – KNOW WHAT YOU NEED

Take care with amplifiers that offer a lot of additional effects. Make sure that you really need them. Like their guitar counterparts, some of the best and most popular amplifiers are very simple models designed in the 1950s. It's usually a good idea to start out with a pared-down system, and then build it up as new requirements emerge.

### RULE 4 – SIZE MATTERS

Amplifiers can vary greatly, both in size and weight. If you are buying an amplifier "head" with a large independent speaker cabinet, make sure that you have sufficient room to store it in your home. Damp basements or garages are not ideal places to keep delicate electrical equipment. Similarly, lugging a "four-by-twelve" cabinet up and down eight flights of stairs is also guaranteed to dampen your enthusiasm.

### RULE 5 – WHERE HAS IT BEEN?

If you are buying a secondhand amplifier, take care when you encounter models that seem to have taken a battering.

This may indicate that the amplifier has been heavily used, is very widely traveled, or has been badly treated, all of which might affect its longevity.

### RULE 6 – SILENCE IS GOLDEN

Listen out for excess buzzing or hiss, both before you plug the guitar in, or when you are not playing. This may mean that some of the circuitry is worn or damaged.

### RULE 7 – SPEAKER CONDITION

If at all possible, remove the grille that covers and protects the loudspeaker. Check the cone, and ensure that it is not torn or dented. Also check the periphery of the cone—this is where natural wear occurs. All of these elements can adversely affect the sound.

### RULE 8 – ELECTRICS

Test all of the switches, and the volume and tone controls. Make sure that they all do as they are supposed to, without making clicks or crackling noises. These things are generally fairly straightforward to repair, so if you're being offered a real bargain, you should still consider it—a simple service by a qualified technician is not likely to break the bank.

### RULE 9 – STAMP YOUR FEET

With the amplifier switched on, but not connected to a guitar, stamp your foot on the ground next to the model. If you hear any electrical noise as a result, there may be loose valves or other circuitry. This is likely to cause you problems eventually.

### RULE 10 – DON'T UNDERESTIMATE THE IMPORTANCE OF AMPLIFICATION

Some guitarists are a little blasé about the subject of amplification. An amplifier not only boosts the guitar's volume, it colors your sound, so don't just take the first model that you see. Try out a variety of different types—the differences will quickly become apparent.

## EFFECTS AND THE NOVICE

When you first get your system up and running, avoid the temptation to add the latest in electrical gadgetry to your newly acquired armory. Believe me, you'll have your work cut out just getting your fingers to obey your instructions, without the added distraction of worrying about strange and exotic sounds coming out of the loudspeaker. If you simply HAVE to get hold of an effect, though, choose something simple, classic, and versatile, such as reverb or delay (or distortion, if you don't have an amplifier that can produce such sounds).

When you practice your basic playing techniques, it's always a good idea to use the cleanest sound possible. Although heavily processed sounds can be used to mask poor or imprecise playing, it can also be a hindrance, preventing you from evaluating your own technical development.

# BASIC MUSICAL PRINCIPLES

**If you are completely new to the idea of written music, this spread should give you a brief overview of what it's all about. If it seems a bit mysterious at first, don't panic: the mechanics of music are EXTREMELY logical—indeed, Pythagoras saw music, mathematics, and philosophy as part of the same system. This book uses several different methods to get across its musical ideas. Most of the exercises are shown using standard music notation (the five-line treble staff) and the alternative, guitar tablature. Visual diagrams looking onto the fingerboard from above are used as a convenient way of showing chord positions. Photographs are also used to show some examples.**

## NAMING THE NOTES

In Western musical systems there are 12 different notes—12 fixed pitches. These are best viewed as the notes of a piano keyboard. The interval between each note is called a "half-step" (or "semitone" in Europe). The white notes on the keyboard are named from A to G. Each of the black notes can have two possible names, depending on their musical context. Sometimes they can be seen as a "sharpened" version of the note to their immediate left. In such cases they take that note name, followed by a "sharp" symbol (♯). In other cases they may be seen as a "flattened" version of the note to the immediate right, in which case they take that note name followed by a "flat" symbol (♭). These notes with dual identities are known as "enharmonic." After every 12 notes, the sequence of lettering repeats itself; if you find the note C on a piano keyboard, the same note can be heard 12 half-steps either side of that note, albeit in a different register. An interval of 12 half-steps is referred to as an "octave."

### STANDARD MUSIC NOTATION

Music is traditionally written out on a five-line grid known as a "staff" (sometimes "staves" in the plural form). There are

a variety of symbols that can be placed on and between the lines of the staff, to indicate both the pitch and duration—how long the note should be held.

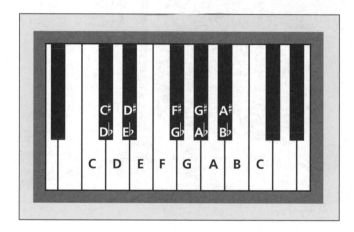

Musical instruments such as the piano have a wide range of notes—a concert grand piano can encompass over seven octaves. As such, all of these notes cannot be fitted within a single staff, therefore a staff can be given its own range of notes by positioning a symbol at the start of the music. Notes that are predominantly above "middle C" on a piano are positioned on a "treble" staff, which is prefixed by a treble clef (𝄞); notes

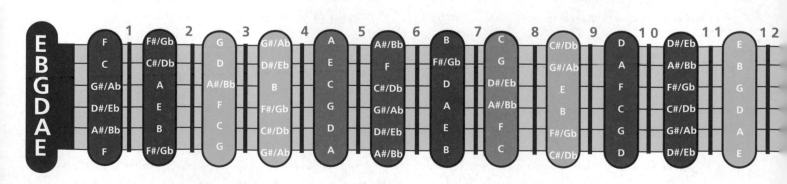

predominantly below middle C are positioned on a staff prefixed by a bass clef (𝄢). For this reason alone, piano music has to be written over two concurrent staves—treble notes are usually played by the right hand; bass notes by the left.

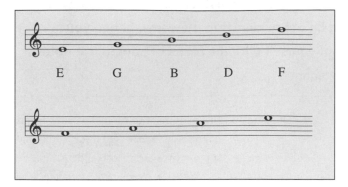

However, the guitar has a range limited to a maximum of four octaves, which, if written correctly, would also have to be split over two registers—therefore, for convenience, guitar music is written an octave higher that the actual pitch, which allows it to be written on a single treble staff.

The clef defines the notes on and between each line on the staff. For a treble clef, the notes on the lines are E, G, B, D, and F. The notes between the lines are F, A, C, and E. If a note extends beyond the range of a staff, additional "ledger" lines can be added above or below for each single note. Enharmonic notes appear on the line after which they are named, with either a flat or sharp symbol appearing alongside.

### GUITAR TABLATURE

A complementary form of written music is the tablature system, which is often used for the guitar and other fretted instruments. Tablature (or "TAB" for short) is quite simply a six-line grid in which each line represents a string, from top to bottom. A number written on a line is an instruction to play a specific fret. This has the advantage over conventional musical notation in that it provides very specific playing instructions. As you can see from the example on the left, the note E positioned on the top space of the staff can be played in the same register on every string of a 24-fret guitar.

The full range of notes along the fingerboard are shown on the diagram below.

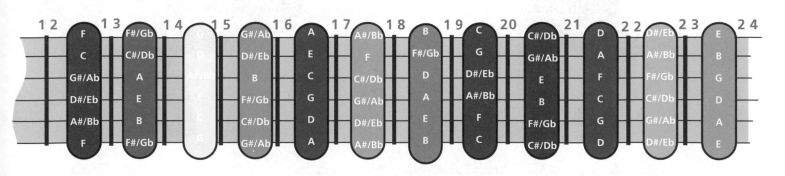

# GETTING STARTED

# Lesson 1

Before you start to play it's important that you feel relaxed and comfortable holding your instrument. The exact posture you choose can to some extent depend on the type of music you play. In general terms, classical, folk and flamenco players are invariably seen seated, whereas most rock and country players perform in a standing position with the guitar supported by a shoulder strap. However, before you actually begin to play the guitar you also need to acquaint yourself with the basics of how to fret notes with the left hand and, of course, how to tune your instrument.

## THE SITTING POSITION

There are two independent approaches to playing the guitar in the sitting position. The "classical" method, which largely came about as a result of developments originated by guitar maker Antonio de Torres and virtuoso musician Francesco Tarrega in the 19th century, demands that the "waist" of the guitar is placed between the legs, resting on the left thigh. The neck should be held at an angle of about 45°—an adjustable footstool can be used to allow people of different heights to achieve this position. As an alternative, a solid box around 6 inches (150mm) in height could be used. Holding the neck at the correct angle allows for the optimum positioning of the left hand for movement along the fingerboard, and the right hand above the strings.

Although this posture can be seen in other forms of music, it is most commonly restricted to those with a classical background. It is more usual simply to rest the guitar on the right thigh, supporting the neck with the left hand so that it maintains a broadly horizontal angle. The body of the instrument is held in place by the inside of the right arm. This position is the one which most novices find the most natural for playing an acoustic instrument. Playing a solid-body electric guitar when sitting can sometimes cause problems. These instruments have primarily been designed for playing in the standing position—their shape and balance of weight can cause the instrument to tilt awkwardly. If this happens you can get find additional support by wearing a shoulder strap.

A brief note for left-handers: although most of the classic guitars are available in mirror-image left-handed models, some players find it easier—or more economical—to buy a standard model and re-string it in reverse. Whilst this is fine as far as the fingerboard goes, you may find that shape of the body, or the positioning of the controls on electric models, now affects the positioning of your left hand around the bridge area. As a result you may need to modify your posture. Getting hold of a left-handed model is generally more desirable, although Jimi Hendrix managed to cope well enough on a right-handed one!

Classical posture.

Informal sitting posture.

## OTHER MATTERS TO CONSIDER

Take care about the kind of clothing you wear when you play the guitar. Bulky clothing can easily restrict your movement. If your sleeves are too loose they can easily drag against the strings, muting the sound. Metal buttons, jewelry, or zippers can catch the body of the guitar—as well as making an unpleasant noise, this can also scratch or damage the instrument.

Not every seating surface is appropriate for playing the guitar. You should choose a sturdy stool or upright chair, and the floor on which the left-foot support is positioned also needs to be firm. Desk chairs are of little use since the arms will just get in the way. Nor is soft seating, such as a sofa or bed, ideal for learning—it becomes difficult to hold the guitar in the correct position, and this can encourage bad habits.

## THE STANDING POSITION

To play the guitar in the standing position you will need a shoulder strap. Almost any strap you see in a music store will be perfectly adequate, although those without reinforced strap holes will always be liable to snap at inopportune moments. Paying a little more money for a good-quality leather strap is usually a worthwhile investment—and it should last a lifetime.

With a shoulder strap in place, the guitar should hang naturally against your body, leaving both arms free to move comfortably. Ideally, the neck of the guitar should be held at an angle of between 30° and 45°. It is also important that the strap is adjusted so that the guitar is held at the correct height—a good rule for a beginner is to ensure that the bridge of the guitar hangs at approximately the same height as your waist.

When you become more experienced you are likely to find a height and neck angle that works best for you. Of course, it is not unusual to see some rock musicians performing on stage with extremely low-slung instruments. While this may look cooler than the standard

**Standing posture.**

posture, it will make learning more difficult—the further away the guitar neck is held from the body, the more pronounced the angle of the left hand has to become. You will quickly find yourself exercising hitherto unknown muscles in your wrist, which can be extremely painful. You've been warned!

## PARANOIA

There can few things more terrifying for the performing guitarist than having your instrument come adrift from the shoulder strap—the guitar can easily be damaged, and it can also be extremely embarrassing. Whilst most shoulder straps are perfectly adequate to support any guitar, some professionals choose to use locking straps. These are small metal fixtures which are clamped onto the shoulder strap and can then be "clicked" into place on the body of the guitar. In fact, it's rather like belting yourself into a car seat.

The strap lock is secured to the holes on either end of the strap by a simple nut, washer, and bolt mechanism. Manufacturers usually supply their own strap buttons, which must be fitted to the guitar.

# LEFT-HAND TECHNIQUES

Notes are played when the fingers of the left hand force the strings down between the frets on the fingerboard. Achieving the correct left-hand posture is crucial, especially for playing with more complex techniques. As with any skill, if you adopt bad habits to begin with, they can be doubly hard to turn around or change, even slightly, later on.

## BASIC PRINCIPLES

There are two distinct left-hand techniques used by players of all styles of music: the classical, and—for want of a better description—the "alternative." The classical left-hand technique has the thumb held against the back of the neck at all times. This tension allows the neck to be clasped firmly, providing additional pressure when fretting notes along the fingerboard. For correct classical posture the thumb must be kept perfectly straight.

However, many self-taught players can be seen sliding the left hand thumb around the neck so that it rests along the edge of the fingerboard. This is an easy habit to acquire when learning, but is positively frowned upon by classical teachers. However, it is not necessarily

a bad habit—some players find it more comfortable, and if you a have a wide enough fingerspan it can allow the thumb to fret notes on the 5th and 6th strings, which can be useful when playing certain chords. If you rely too heavily on this method, there is no doubt that it can restrict agility. All in all, though, there are virtues in both systems.

### FRETTING A NOTE

Acquiring a good fretting technique is an equally important part of developing your left hand. The tip of the finger should fall immediately behind the fret. If it is held too far back the string is likely to buzz against the fret; if it is too close to the fret, the string will be muted.

To avoid accidentally muting the other strings all of the fingers should be kept as vertical as possible when held

The pad on the tip of the finger holds the string down against the fret.

against the fretboard. This is one of the clearest benefits of using the classical left-hand technique—if your thumb is resting on the edge of the fingerboard, it becomes extremely difficult to keep the fingers vertical.

### WORKING THE LEFT HAND

The two exercises shown across the page are intended merely to get you used to the idea of fretting notes with the different fingers of your left hand. You should notice that the notes in each of the exercises are the same notes played on different strings: in exercise 1 you are always playing the note C; in exercise 2, the note G.

In each case you must press the finger between the frets and sound the string with your right hand—it doesn't matter for now whether you use your fingers or a plectrum. You need to ensure that you exert just

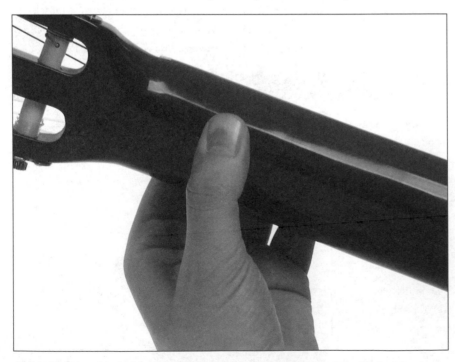

Classical left-hand technique requires the thumb to be held against the back of the neck.

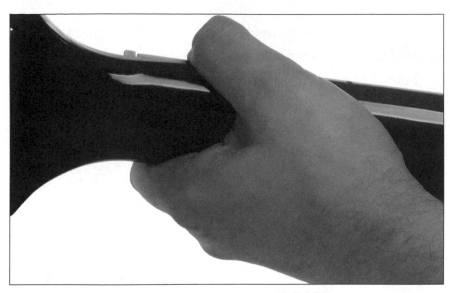

Some players prefer to bring the thumb over the side of the fretboard.

enough pressure on the fingerboard so that the note can be sounded clearly. If you press too lightly the sound will be muted; too hard and your fingers will tire, and at worst you can develop unpleasant blisters.

Stop playing as soon as your fingers get tired or become painful. Remember, the tips of your fingers are rarely used for anything more demanding than holding a pen—it will take a little time before they become hardened to persistent pressure on nylon or metal strings.

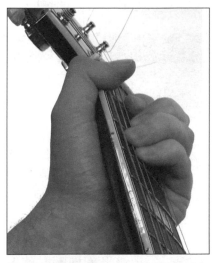

The thumb can also be used to fret notes.

### FINGERNAILS

Satisfactory fretting will be quite impossible if your fingernails are too long. Test their length by bringing them down vertically onto any firm horizontal surface—if the tip of the nail touches the surface before the pad of the finger, the nails should be cut. Guitarists who play without a pick, such as classical players, often deliberately grow the nails of their right hand long enough for them to be able to strike the strings. Next time you see someone with short nails on one hand and long nails on the other you can probably have a good guess as to the reason why.

### Exercise 1

| String | Fret | Finger |
|--------|------|--------|
| 1 | 8 | 1st |
| 2 | 1 | 1st |
| 3 | 5 | 2nd |
| 4 | 10 | 3rd |
| 5 | 3 | 4th |
| 6 | 8 | 4th |

### Exercise 2

| String | Fret | Finger |
|--------|------|--------|
| 1 | 3 | 1st |
| 2 | 8 | 1st |
| 3 | 12 | 2nd |
| 4 | 5 | 3rd |
| 5 | 10 | 4th |
| 6 | 3 | 4th |

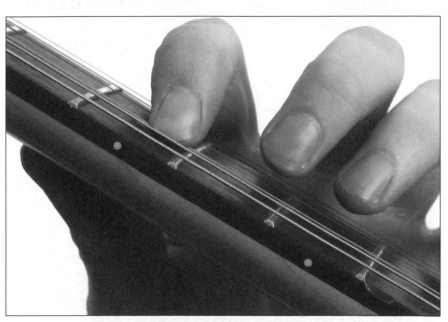

When fretting a note, ensure that redundant fingers are held clear of the strings.

# TUNING THE GUITAR

Making no apologies for stating the obvious, the first and most fundamental rule of playing the guitar—whatever your style of music—is to get your instrument in tune. One of the most difficult aspects of learning any instrument is developing a facility for hearing tiny variations in pitch and being able to recognize when intonation is correct. It is fair to say that not everyone is gifted with a "musical ear", but it *is* something that can be learned and improved just like any other skill, so don't be alarmed if it's something that doesn't come naturally to you.

## BASIC PRINCIPLES

The pitch of any note, whatever instrument has produced it, is determined by the frequency of sound waves travelling through the air, and is measured in hertz, or cycles per second. The frequency of a note produced by striking a guitar string is dependent on three factors—length, thickness, and tension of the string. Although guitar strings are always the same length in relation to one another, each open string is of a different gauge, or thickness. The fattest strings give the lowest notes and the thinnest strings the highest. The pitch of a string is altered by turning the machine head. This increases or reduces the tension and thus allows you to create different notes.

There are a number of different techniques you can use to tune a guitar. Ensuring that all of the strings are in tune relative to one another will be good enough for you to play on your own. If you want to play with other instruments, however, your guitar ought to be tuned to what is known as "standard concert pitch." This is a reference tone for all instruments which fixes the value of the note A above middle C on a piano keyboard with a frequency of 440 hertz. Therefore, the only surefire way of accurately tuning your guitar is to use an independent reference tone, such as a guitar tuner, tuning fork, or pitch pipes. An electronic keyboard or well-tuned piano will also do the trick. For the moment, however, you don't need to worry about such hardware, as you can tune up to the first six tracks on the accompanying CD.

The different techniques shown on the next four pages will illustrate the most commonly used systems, all of which involve variations on tuning one string for use as a reference point for the other five strings. As you will see as you work through the book, or hear by experimenting for yourself, the standard tuning shown here is by no means the only way in which a guitar can be tuned. This subject is looked at in greater depth on pages 130–133.

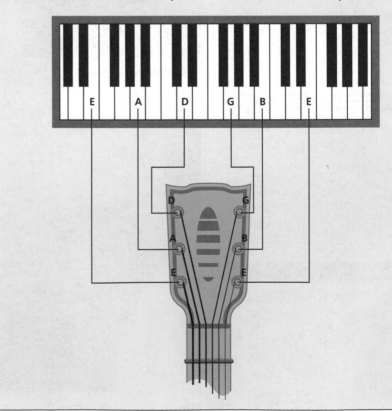

### THE NOTES

The six guitar strings are tuned according to specific musical intervals. From top to bottom, the string notes are E, B, G, D, A, and E. 12-string guitars also use the same intervals, but whereas the top two pairs of strings are tuned in unison, the bottom four pairs are usually tuned at octave intervals. This diagram shows the relationship between the strings of the guitar and the notes of a keyboard.

## TUNING TO A REFERENCE POINT

The first technique tunes the 1st string (top string) to a reference point. You can then tune the other five strings relative to that note. To check that your tuning is correct as you go through, play the string along with the tracks of the CD, as shown below. Some players also use this method in reverse, tuning the 6th string to a reference tone and working back up to the top string.

**Hand turning machine head.**

### 1ST STRING—OPEN E

Play track 1/1 of the CD. At the same time, play the top string. Turn the machine head until the notes ring together. Repeat this process until you are happy that the string is in tune. **1/1** ▶

### 2ND STRING—OPEN B

Place your index finger on the 5th fret of the 2nd string. Play the note followed by the open 1st string. Adjust the machine head of the 2nd string until the top two strings are in tune. Compare your open B to track 1/2 of the CD.

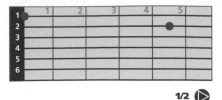

**1/2** ▶

### 3RD STRING—OPEN G

Play the 4th fret of the 3rd string along with the open 2nd string. Adjust the machine head which controls the 3rd string until it is tune. Compare your open G to track 1/3 of the CD.

**1/3** ▶

### 4TH STRING—OPEN D

Play the 5th fret of the 4th string along with the open 3rd string. Adjust the machine head on the 4th string until it is in tune. Compare your open D with track 1/4 on the CD.

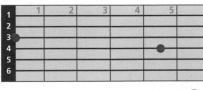

**1/4** ▶

### 5TH STRING—OPEN A

Play the 5th fret of the 5th string (this is the note D), and at the same time, play the open D on the 4th string. Now adjust the machine head that controls the pitch of the 5th string until it is in tune. To check your tuning, compare the open A (the open 5th string) with track 1/5 on the CD.

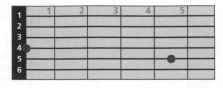

**1/5** ▶

### 6TH STRING—OPEN E

Play the 5th fret of the 6th string along with the open 5th string. Adjust the machine head on the 6th string until it is in tune. Compare this with track 1/6 on the CD.

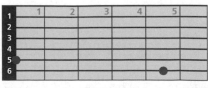

**1/6** ▶

# TUNING WITH OCTAVES AND HARMONICS

Different guitarists favour different methods of tuning their instruments. A common alternative to the techniques shown on the previous pages involves comparing octave intervals or harmonics. Once they have their first reference note, some players find it preferable to hold down a chord with the left hand, and tune the other five strings accordingly.

## OCTAVE INTERVALS

This method compares the same notes played on different strings at octave intervals. Begin by tuning the 5th string—open A—to a reference tone.

- Play the 7th fret of the 5th string—the note E—and use this to tune the 1st and 6th strings.
- Play the 7th fret of the 1st string (B) and tune the open 2nd string to that note.
- Play the 8th fret of the 2nd string (G) and tune the open 3rd string to the same note.
- Play the 7th fret of the 3rd string (D) and tune the open 4th string to that note.

## MIXED TUNING METHOD

You can also tune your guitar using the top string and the lower frets. Begin by tuning the 1st string to a reference tone.

- Play the 7th fret of the 1st string—the note B—and use this to tune the 2nd string.
- Play the 3rd fret of the 1st string (G) and tune the open 3rd string to that note.
- Play the 3rd fret of the 2nd string (D) and tune the open 4th string to the same note.
- Play the 2nd fret of the 3rd string (A) and tune the open 5th string to that note.
- Play the 2nd fret of the 4th string (E) and tune the open 6th string.

Traditionally, classical guitarists use a piano keyboard to provide reference tones that enable them to tune their instruments to concert pitch. Many players still prefer this method, and the keys you need to find are shown on the diagram on page 34.

If you don't have access to a piano or electronic keyboard, you can use alternative sources. A tuning fork can be used to provide a single tone—usually the note A below middle C. The fork is struck, and by holding it against the body of the guitar a tone can be heard clearly. Similarly, pitch pipes can be used to produce tones for all six strings.

Nowadays it is more common to use an electronic medium. For the past two decades, many cheap and reliable electronic tuners have been produced. To use one of these, the guitar is plugged into the unit and the pitch is monitored on a VU meter. Some tuners can also be used "in-line," connected between the guitar and amplifier, so that the guitar can be retuned on stage without having to disconnect. These days, many multi-effects units also come with built-in tuning facilities. If you are an acoustic guitarist, ensure that before you buy an electronic tuner it has a built-in microphone, otherwise it will not be able to do the job for you.

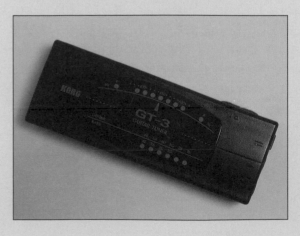

## TUNING WITH HARMONICS

When you strike a guitar string, the sound produced is the result of a complex set of components known as the "harmonic series". The dominant sound is known as a "fundamental". However, if you position your finger gently on any of the strings directly over the 12th fret, instead of hearing the fretted note you will hear a bell-like tone. This sound is a harmonic, which can also be generated by playing above other frets on the fingerboard. The subject of harmonics is covered in greater depth on pages 104–105, but for now all you need to know is that they can be used effectively to tune the guitar.

Begin by tuning the tuning the 6th string to concert pitch. The other five strings can now be tuned by matching the harmonics as demonstrated below.

• Play the harmonic on the 5th fret of the 6th string followed by the harmonic on the 7th fret of the 5th string. Adjust the 5th string machine head until it is in tune.
• Tune the 4th string by comparing harmonics on the 5th fret of the 5th string and the 7th fret of the 4th string.
• Tune the 3rd string by comparing harmonics on the 5th fret of the 4th string and the 7th fret of the 3rd string.
• Tune the 2nd string by comparing the harmonic on the 7th fret of the 6th string with the open 2nd string.
• Tune the 1st string by comparing harmonics on the 5th fret of the 2nd string and the 7th fret of the 1st string.

| 4 | 5 | 6 | 7 | 8 | 9 | 10 | 11 | 12 |
|---|---|---|---|---|---|---|---|---|
|   |   |   | B |   |   |    |    | B |
|   | B |   | D |   |   |    |    |   |
|   | D |   | A |   |   |    |    | D |
|   | A |   | E |   |   |    |    | A |
|   | E |   |   |   |   |    |    | E |

### TREMOLO UNITS

Tremolo units can be a nightmare for tuning. The old Bigsby or Fender mechanisms developed in the 1950s were notorious for not only going out of tune during playing, but while going through the initial tuning process. Sanity came in the 1980s with the Floyd Rose locking nut system, variations on which are now standard on most models. Whilst they can make your instrument seem indestructible, they do provide a number of problems for initial tuning.

Begin by unlocking the nut with an Allen key and then tuning the guitar in the standard way, using the machine heads to alter the string tension. When each string is approximately in tune, lock the nut. Thereafter, the strings can be fine-tuned using the hand-adjustable screws on the bridge.

Fine-tune using the screws on the locking bridge unit.

Turn the Allen key anticlockwise to unlock the nut unit.

# PICKING

# Lesson 2

For the guitar string to make a sound, it has to be struck by the right hand. This can be done in a number of different ways. Whereas classical and flamenco players—and other musicians who favor nylon-string guitars—invariably pluck the strings with the individual fingers (or fingernails), most players in other genres use a pick. This is a triangular object, usually made from plastic or tortoiseshell, which is held between the first finger and the thumb of the right hand. As you can see from the picture below, plectra—also known as "plectrums" or "flatpicks"—can been found in many different shapes, sizes, and materials.

## PICK BASICS

When it comes to choosing a pick, the size and thickness is largely a matter of personal taste. Nonetheless, the type you choose can have a significant effect the tone of your playing; using a small, heavy-gauge pick is ideal for fast solo work, whereas something thinner and more flexible is better suited for strumming. An alternative approach is used by some country and folk musicians who use picks which slide over each of the right-hand fingers, thus effectively extending the fingernails. As a novice, it's a good idea to get hold of a large selection as possible—you'll quickly find yourself gravitating towards one particular type.

## HOLDING THE PICK

Take the pick between the thumb and the top joint of the 1st finger. Hold it at an angle of 90° to the body of the guitar and parallel to the strings. The finger grip should be quite relaxed but tight enough so that it doesn't move around while you are playing. As you strike the string you should swivel the wrist and forearm, moving the joints of the thumb and fingers. It's important that this should be a flowing movement.

## DIRECTIONAL PICKING

There are two distinctly different ways to strike a string with a pick, commonly referred to as "downstrokes" and "upstrokes." A downstroke is made by taking the tip of the pick above the string and pushing down. The upstroke is the reverse—the tip is placed below the string and pulled up. Each method has its own symbol, making it possible to indicate in written music the type of stroke that should be played. This notation is usually found above the notes on the staff.

Downstroke

Upstroke V

When used exclusively, each type of stroke creates a unique type of sound. However, if you are to truly master this technique you must become well-acquainted with mixing strokes: this means making an upstroke after a downstroke in a single movement is the most effective way of playing. This is really the only way you can play fast lead passages.

The exercises across the page will set you on your way to mastering the pick. The first four of these examples concentrate on picking open strings. This will allow you to concentrate fully on the right-hand technique without having to worry about fretting notes with the left hand. Try to keep the speed at which you play the notes and the strength with which you hit the strings consistent. The remaining two exercises include some simple fretting on the same string.

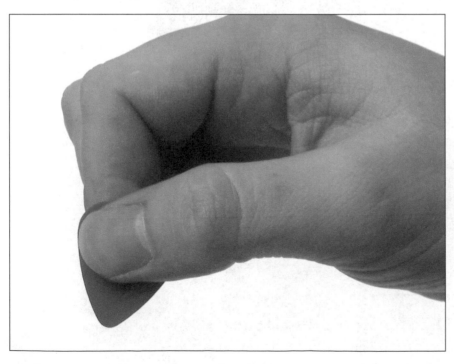

**EXERCISE 1** 2/1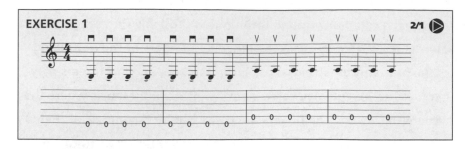

**EXERCISE 2** 2/2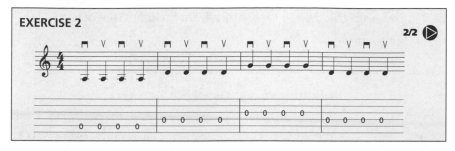

**EXERCISE 3** 2/3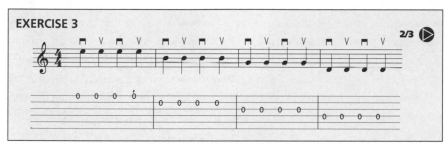

**EXERCISE 4** 2/4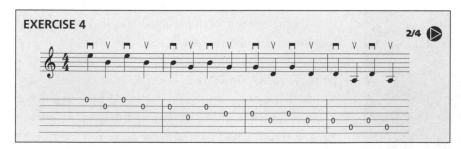

**EXERCISE 5** 2/5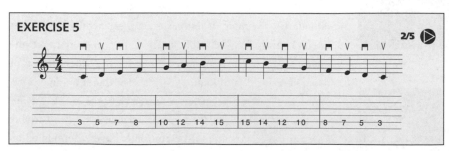

**EXERCISE 6** 2/6

## DICK DALE

<u>Born:</u> 1937, Beirut, Lebanon (Richard Monsour)
<u>Equipment:</u> Fender Stratocaster and Twin Reverb amplifier
<u>Recorded Highlights:</u> *The Best Of Dick Dale and the Deltones*

In the early 1960s, Dick Dale was the undisputed king of surf guitar. A left-handed guitarist, Dale alternated his pick strokes at a lightning speed to produce a unique staccato sound that simulated the rhythms of riding the surf.

Although he retired from music in the late 1960s, his career enjoyed an unexpected revival in 1995 when the track 'Miserlou' was used as the main theme for the film *Pulp Fiction*. The song became one of the most heavily-played instrumentals of the period, and Dale was lured out of retirement. Even at the age of 60, Dale proved that he could still put on a riveting show and, more significantly, that his pick was still firing as fast as ever.

# FINGERPICKING

Fingerpicking is used in classical, flamenco, and a wide variety of folk styles. Whilst there are a great many variations used within different genres, the most commonly found technique is probably that taught to classical players. This method—often referred to as "PIMA"—uses the individual fingers of the right hand to play specific strings. The thumb plays the bass strings (strings 4 to 6); the 1st, 2nd, and 3rd fingers play each of the treble strings respectively (strings 1 to 3). You may come across printed guitar music where the fingering is shown on the manuscript. Where this occurs, the fingers are identified by the initials of their Spanish names. The thumb is "P" (pulgar), the 1st finger is "I" (indice), the 2nd finger is "M" (medio), and the 3rd finger is "A" (anular). Use of the 4th finger in this way is rare, but where it occurs it is often referred to as "C" (meñique), or sometimes "X" or "E."

## RIGHT-HAND POSITION

Although there have been some notable exceptions, classical guitarists are trained to strike the strings with their fingernails rather than the pads of the fingers. This is fairly uncommon in other genres of music. The most common alternative is the "clawhammer" style used by steel-string players. As you can see from the photographs below, the positioning of the right hand differs greatly between the techniques. The classical position rests the inside of the forearm at the upper edge of the guitar's body; the clawhammer method rests the palm of the hand on the bridge.

Classical hand position.

Clawhammer position.

## FINGERPICKING EXERCISES

Work through the exercises shown across the page. Once again, they are largely based on playing the open strings, so that you can concentrate on the right hand. The first two exercises use just the thumb playing the three bass strings. It is important that you remember to keep the thumb straight at all times—the playing action should come from the thumb joint rather than the knuckle. Exercises 3 and 4 feature the first, second, and third fingers playing the treble strings. Try to strike the notes evenly, playing through with a smooth, flowing motion. The final two exercises bring the thumb and fingers together. You'll notice that to play exercise 6 you have to pick two strings simultaneously. Where fingering instructions are shown for such written music, the PIMA notation is usually stacked above the note.

### PICKS, FINGERS, OR BOTH?

The decision as to whether you play with a pick or the fingers may be dictated by the type of music you play. In classical or flamenco music, you have little choice—picks are rarely used. However, in other styles of music, as genres cross over, blurring their respective boundaries, the choice is less clear-cut. It's generally agreed that direct contact between the finger and string, without the intermediary piece of plastic, allows for a greater degree of dynamic control, although playing fast passages on an electric guitar with low-gauge strings is hard to achieve in this way. In country and jazz, the most accomplished guitarists are invariably adept at either technique. Rock music is largely dominated by pick-oriented players—and it's reasonable to say that the use of some heavy-duty electronic effects, such as distortion and compression, reduces the impact of dynamic nuance by their very nature. However, in a largely self-taught field, where techniques are often born out of taking short cuts, many players have found that it's easier to pick the notes of a chord (called an "arpeggio") accurately with the fingers than a pick.

**EXERCISE 1**    2/7

**EXERCISE 4**    2/10

**EXERCISE 2**    2/8

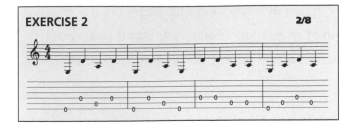

**EXERCISE 5**    2/11

**EXERCISE 3**    2/9

**EXERCISE 6**    2/12

## HYBRID TECHNIQUE

An interesting hybrid technique, used mostly by country musicians, integrates playing with the fingers and a pick. It is extremely demanding, and is also highly unorthodox in that it uses the "little" finger to play the top strings. To try out this method, the plectrum is held in the conventional way between the index finger and thumb—the remaining three fingers are then free to play each of the treble strings respectively.

One of the most demanding aspects of this mode of playing is in getting the 3rd and 4th fingers of the right hand to operate independently. As you will find with the left hand when you start to play demanding chords, there are small muscles in the fingers that get very little exercise away from playing a musical instrument.

Although the exercise shown below on the left is similar to exercise 5 above, the fingering instructions shown above the staff are different. In each case, the notes on the bass strings are played using downstrokes.

Don't worry unduly about this technique. It's extremely difficult, and is best approached once you have become adept at playing both with the fingers and pick independently. It does illustrate, however, as you will realise as you work through the book, that hard-and-fast rules for playing the guitar are surprisingly thin on the ground.

Hybrid technique.

# PLAYING CHORDS

# Lesson 3

Whether we talk about pop, rock, country, classical, jazz, or flamenco, chords are a central part of all guitar-based music. A chord is the effect of three or more notes being played at the same time. Chords are formed on the guitar by pressing the fingers of the left hand onto specific positions on the fingerboard. Once you get started you will quickly become familiar with the basic chord shapes, and understand how they sound in relation to one another. The nine examples shown over the next four pages are the simplest and yet the most commonly used chords. It's not too much of an exaggeration to say that if you learn to play these chords with a degree of fluency, you will probably be able to play many of your favorite songs.

## TRIADS

The chords shown in this section are known as "triads". This is because they are made up of three different notes, although you will notice that as you are playing six strings of the guitar, some notes are repeated in different registers. For example, the open E major chord shown below features the note E played over three different octaves.

It is also possible to achieve a chordal effect by playing just two different notes—this is technically an "interval" rather than a chord. The note intervals used by every triad are always the same in relation to the chord's "root —the note by which the chord's key is identified. For a major triad, the sequence of intervals are named root, major 3rd and perfect 5th. For example, a C major triad uses the notes C (root), E (major 3rd), and G (perfect 5th). Don't worry too much about this technical detail for the moment—it will all become clear soon enough. For the moment, concentrate on playing your first chords.

## YOUR FIRST CHORD

You're now ready to make what (hopefully) will be your first recognisably musical sound—an E major chord.

The easiest chords to learn are known as "open-string" chords. They are called this because they can be formed by using a combination of open (unfretted) strings, and the first two or three frets along the fingerboard. The E major chord is particularly significant, since the basic shape can be moved along the fingerboard to create a wide range of alternative chords.

### FRETTING THE CHORD

Here are four easy steps to playing an open E major chord. Take it slowly, one step at a time. Your fingers are likely to feel extremely uncomfortable to begin with. Don't worry—this is quite normal.

- Place the 2nd finger of your left hand behind the 2nd fret of the 5th string.
- Place the 3rd finger of your left hand

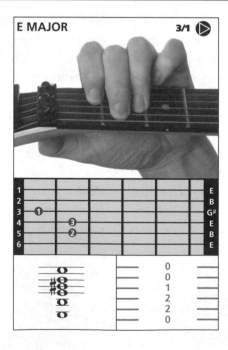

**E MAJOR** 3/1

on the 2nd fret of the 4th string.
- Place the index finger of your left hand on the 1st fret of the 3rd string.
- With a pick in your right hand, strum across all six strings.

Congratulations–you've just played your very first chord.

**READING CHORD DIAGRAMS**

The chord diagrams shown throughout the book are simple to understand. Think of each diagram as a if you were looking over the fretboard of a guitar. The dots placed between frets on the strings represent the positions where your fingers should go. The number on each dot tells you which finger you should use (1 through 4 represent the index finger to the little finger). If no number is shown, fretting the note is optional. Beside the chord chart you will find the note names of each string. If the note is marked "X", then the string should not be played. A note name shown in brackets also indicates that the note is optional.

# THREE-CHORD TRICKS

The next two chords you will learn about are A major and D major. These chords are closely related to E major, which you have just played. All three chords are related by the intervals of their root notes. Many of the greatest rock, pop, blues, and country songs have comprised only this "three-chord trick." Such chord structures are also sometimes known as "one-four-fives." They are written down using Roman numerals (I-IV-V).

### A MAJOR

When you play the A major chord, the 6th string is optional—the note is shown alongside the chord diagram in brackets. This "bottom E" is a musically correct element of an A major triad, but because it is lower in pitch than the chord's root note, in can create an imbalance to the overall sound. In some situations, playing this note simply makes the chord sound wrong.

### D MAJOR

There are several alternatives you can choose from when playing a D major chord. One approach is to ignore the bottom two strings, only playing the notes of the other four. More common,

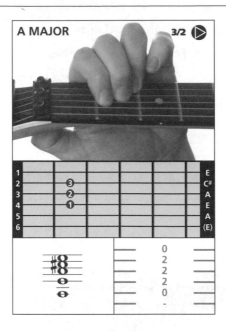

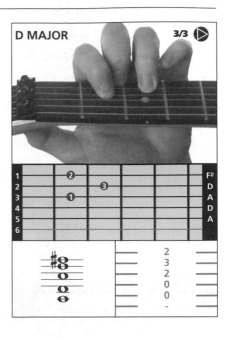

perhaps, is to include the 5th string—even though the note A is lower in pitch than the root D, the chord still generally sounds good played this way. These approaches can be difficult when strumming quickly in both directions with a pick. As a consequence, some players prefer to bring the thumb around the back of the neck to play the F♯ on the 2nd fret of the 1st string. This approach is not at all popular with classical tutors, but has nonetheless been widely used by such luminaries as Jimi Hendrix, which surely must make it worthy of at least some consideration.

### CHANGING CHORDS

The exercises shown below will help you to get used to the idea of moving around between the three chord shapes you have just learnt. Don't worry about keeping time for the moment, just concentrate on fretting the notes correctly. If you are an absolute beginner, THIS WILL BE A TOUGH EXERCISE. It's well worth concentrating on this section for a while before you move on to the other chords. Try not to be discouraged, everyone from Segovia to Satriani has been here at some stage. And you can bet that they found it just as difficult.

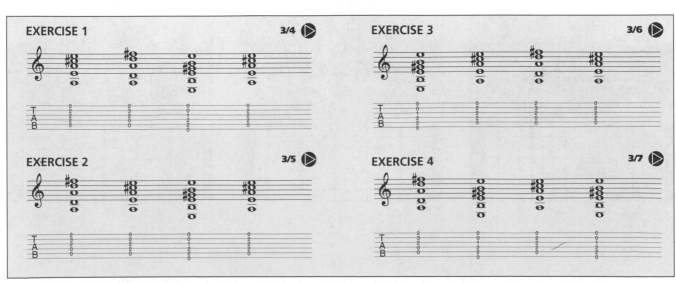

# MORE OPEN-STRING CHORDS

Here are another six open-string chords. You will notice that three "minor" chords have been included this time. A minor chord is created by "flattening" the third note of a major triad—that means reducing it by a semitone, or one fret on the fingerboard. For example, a C minor triad consists of the notes C (root), E♭ (minor 3rd), and G (perfect 5th). To hear the dramatic difference between major and minor chords, alternate the E major and E minor chords simply by removing the 1st finger.

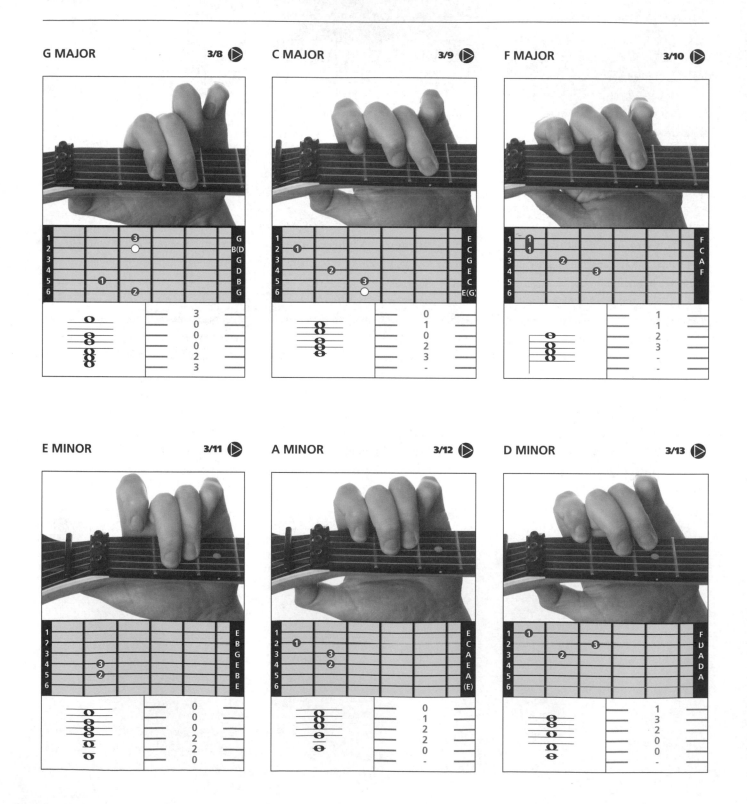

## CHORD FLUENCY

The next set of exercises integrates some of the new chords which you've just seen. Try to play each exercise as smoothly as possible, this time see if you can begin to keep time. As you play, count out aloud "one-and-two-and-three-and-four-and," striking a new chord each time you reach "one." Alternatively, you can play along with a metronome or a drum machine. These four sequences are "turnarounds," which mean that when you get to the end of the sequence you return to the beginning and start over.

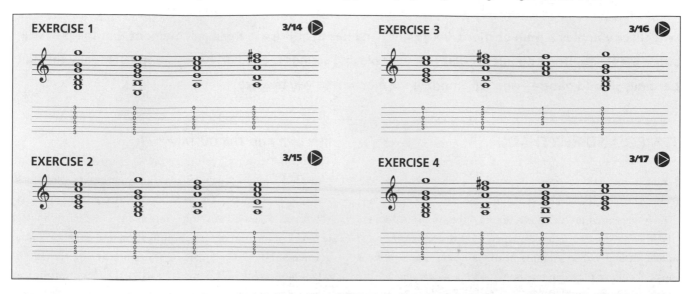

EXERCISE 1 — 3/14

EXERCISE 2 — 3/15

EXERCISE 3 — 3/16

EXERCISE 4 — 3/17

### SOUND AFFECTS

It is sometimes surprising that the sound of a simple open-string chord can alter so dramatically depending on its musical context. Compare, for example, the gentle acoustic minor chords which signal the start of Rodrigo's *Guitar Concerto de Aranguez* with the ringing introduction to 'Venus In Furs' by the Velvet Underground. Although they represent two very different sides of the musical spectrum, they are essentially the same two chords.

Apart from the obvious stylistic differences, sound is clearly a crucial element. For the electric guitarist, the choice of amplification and processing effects can have a radical impact on the way in which a chord sounds. Musical notes, as you have already seen on the tuning pages, are mathematically related by their frequencies. Some of these relationships, such as the 3rds and 5ths which make up a major or minor triad, tend to remain harmonious whatever type of sound is used. Others, especially if they have been heavily treated, can begin to sound discordant .

Perhaps the most commonly heard electric guitar sounds use some form of distortion or "overdrive." If you need further first-hand evidence of the way sound can affect the nature of the music, try playing the set of exercises above through a heavily overdriven amplifier.

Joaquin Rodrigo and Lou Reed: are these two men by any chance related?

# TIMING AND RHYTHM

# Lesson 4

Playing in time is a crucial skill that every musician must develop. Keeping time is the ability to play a piece of music or accompany other musicians at exactly the right speed, without getting faster or slowing down. For many beginners it is one of the hardest skills to master, especially when so much attention is focused on getting the fingers of the left hand in the correct fret positions. The fundamental problem is that whenever you play a note or chord, your right hand has to anticipate the exact moment that the pick will strike the string. Don't be put off if at first your playing sounds ragged or inconsistent. Eventually this skill becomes second nature—and will improve the more often you practice.

## TEMPO AND RHYTHM

Tempo is one of two elements of timing; the other is rhythm. The tempo refers to the specific speed of a piece of music, which is usually measured in "beats per minute" (bpm). Printed guitar music often shows a tempo instruction at the top of the page above the staffs. The example below indicates that a piece of music should be played at a tempo of 120 beats per minute.

$$\quad = 120$$

### CLASSICAL TERMINOLOGY

A good deal of written music is specified only in terms of a general tempo. Such instructions are traditionally indicated by the use of Italian names. The list at the foot of the page shows the approximate range in beats per minute associated with each term (known as a "tempo mark"). As you can see, they give the player or conductor considerable scope for their own interpretation—after all, a piece of music written to be played *Allegro* would sound significantly different played at 120 bpm from at 150 bpm. Tempo marks can also be used to indicate the character of the music being played, and this explains why some of the tempo ranges overlap.

## RHYTHM AND THE GUITAR

The term "rhythm" refers to the way in which notes are played or accented. It is the rhythm that creates the "feel" of a piece of music. The rhythm guitar has played a vital role in all forms of ensemble music since the early days of jazz and blues, and before amplification had given the guitar a voice "above" the music. It was only during the 1930s, when pioneering jazzmen such as Charlie Christian started experimenting with guitars fitted with electronic pickups, that the guitar joined the brass and woodwind instruments capable of having solo or "lead" parts that were audible in a large orchestra or band.

## DEVELOPING TIMING SKILLS

There are many different ways in which you can develop your sense of timing. The most time-honored approach is to play along with records or CDs. However, your favorite music will not necessarily be tuned to concert pitch, so you may have to retune the guitar. Alternatively you can use a traditional metronome—a clockwork device which you can set to "click" at a specific tempo. A drum machine can also fulfill the same kind of function.

## STRICT TEMPO?

If you play with a group of musicians, unless you are playing to a mechanical rhythm, the group will almost invariably create its own feel, periodically pushing and pulling against the basic tempo. Far from being a sign of poor musicianship, the creation of a unique "feel" is the hallmark of a good ensemble. If you doubt this in any way, listen to the house bands of the Motown or Stax labels, who backed some of the greatest soul singers of the 1960s, or James Brown's 1970s backing band, the JBs. The feel and dynamism of these master craftsmen (and women) is something that modern technology, for all of its incredible benefits, can never match.

| Tempo mark | Description | BPM range |
|---|---|---|
| *Grave* | Very slow, serious | Below 40 |
| *Lento* | Slow | 40-55 |
| *Largo* | Broad | 45-65 |
| *Adagio* | Slow (literally, at ease) | 55-75 |
| *Andante* | Walking speed | 75-105 |
| *Moderato* | Moderate speed | 105-120 |
| *Allegro* | Fast (literally, cheerful) | 120-160 |
| *Vivace* | Lively | 150-170 |
| *Presto* | Very fast | 170-210 |
| *Prestissimo* | As fast as possible | Above 210 |

## GETTING A FEEL FOR TEMPO

To put the idea of tempo into a more understandable context, here is a chart that lists the approximate tempos (or tempi, to use the correct plural form) of a number of well-known pieces of music in terms of beats per minute.

With experience it will become possible to give a broad estimate at what tempo a piece of music is being played. Here are few general rule-of-thumb examples: slow soul ballad (80-90 bpm); disco (120 bpm); techno or drum and bass (130-150 bpm); slow rock ballad (100-110 bpm); upbeat country (140 bpm); fast rocker (160 bpm); slow blues (90-100 bpm).

| Song | Artist | Approximate BPM |
| --- | --- | --- |
| Bittersweet Symphony | The Verve | 85 |
| Boom Boom | John Lee Hooker | 135 |
| Born Slippy | Underworld | 140 |
| Devil's Haircut | Beck | 120 |
| Dock of the Bay | Otis Redding | 115 |
| Everybody Hurts | R.E.M. | 95 |
| Firestarter | Prodigy | 140 |
| Jump | Van Halen | 135 |
| Layla | Derek and the Dominos | 130 |
| Liberty | Steve Vai | 150 |
| Nuages | Django Reinhardt | 110 |
| Paranoid | Black Sabbath | 170 |
| Satisfaction | The Rolling Stones | 140 |
| Summertime Blues | Eddie Cochran | 150 |
| What's Going On | Marvin Gaye | 110 |

## KEITH RICHARDS

<u>Born:</u> December 18, 1943, Dartford, England
<u>Equipment:</u> Fender Telecaster
<u>Recorded Highlights:</u> *Beggars Banquet*; *Let It Bleed*; *Exile On Main Street* (all by the Rolling Stones)

In the realm of rock and roll rhythm guitar, Keith Richards has few rivals. Taking a cue from his idol, Chuck Berry, Richards has spent the last 35 years pumping out Telecaster riffs in the engine room of the mighty Rolling Stones. During this time, he has been responsible for immortal guitar phrases like the introductions to classic hits such as "(I Can't Get No) Satisfaction" and "Brown Sugar".

His prodigious intake of drugs throughout the Seventies and the Eighties may have caused critics to wonder at his instinct for survival, but even during his darkest periods "Keef" managed not only to retain an almost child-like enthusiasm for rock and roll, but sought to bring new influences, such as funk, reggae, and country, to the band that many still consider to be the greatest rock and roll act of all time.

Although a more than capable lead player, Richards has always been happiest to view himself as a crucial component of the rhythm team, allowing the likes of Brian Jones, Mick Taylor, and Ronnie Wood to take the solo kudos. As he says, "The whole secret, if there is any secret behind the sound of the Rolling Stones, is the way we work two guitars together."

In fact, no twin-guitar rock band has ever come close to matching the interaction of the Rolling Stones at their best.

# NOTE VALUES

A note played on the guitar has three basic characteristics: pitch, volume, and duration. The pitch is governed by the fret position; the volume by how hard the string has been struck; the duration by how long the note is allowed to sustain. In written music, the overall tempo is governed by how many "beats" should be played every minute—an individual note obtains its value in relation to the length of that beat.

## NOTE DIVISIONS

The longest note value is a "whole note," which is a note sustained for four beats. Subsequent notes may be halved in value until they reach the "sixty-fourth note," whose value is a sixteenth of a beat—in practice, this is very rarely, if ever, used in guitar music.

Each of the different types of note has its own unique symbol as it appears in written music, all of which are shown on the table below. Each note below a quarter note has a series of "flags" attached to the stem. When groups of these notes appear on the staff, the flags are replaced by "beams" which join the notes together.

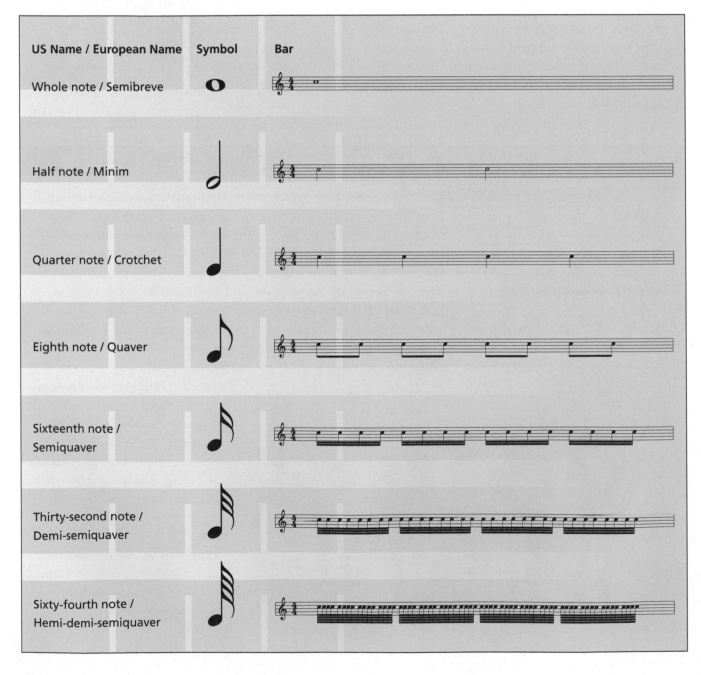

## NOTE VALUES IN PRACTICE

You may find it easier to understand the breakdown of note values by strumming the same sequence using chords with different time values. The following exercises uses the open-string chords C major, A minor, E minor, and G major—if you can't remember the correct finger positions, refer back to pages 42–45. As before, strike the strings of a chord in one sweeping movement, either with a pick or with the fingers of the right hand. Continuously count in seconds from one to four, emphasising "one"—the first beat of the bar—each time. If you have a metronome or drum machine, this will be easier.

## WHOLE-NOTE CHORD

The four chords in this exercise are made up from whole notes.

- Play C major on the first beat of the first bar. Sustain the chord while you count through four.
- Play A minor on the first beat of the second bar. Sustain the chord while you count through four.
- Play E minor on the first beat of the third bar. Sustain the chord while you count through four.
- Play G major on the first beat of the fourth bar. Sustain the chord while you count through four.

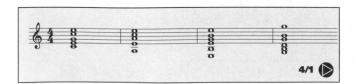

## HALF-NOTE CHORDS

Groups of notes that sustain for two beats are half notes. In this exercise each chord is played twice in every bar, once on the first beat and once on the third.

- Play C major on the first beat of the first bar. Sustain the chord for two beats. On the count of three play the chord again. Sustain the chord while you count through four.
- Play A minor on the first beat of the first bar. Sustain the chord for two beats. On the count of three play the chord again. Sustain the chord while you count through four.
- Play E minor on the first beat of the first bar. Sustain the chord for two beats. On the count of three play the chord again. Sustain the chord while you count through four.
- Play G major on the first beat of the first bar. Sustain the chord for two beats. On the count of three play the chord again. Sustain the chord while you count through four.

## QUARTER-NOTE CHORDS

This exercise halves the note value one stage further so that you play each chord four times, once on each beat. These chords are made up from quarter notes and are sustained for one beat. If you play along with the exercise, you may find that you have difficulty getting your left hand into position quickly enough. If this happens, practice first at a slower speed without the CD. Also, try playing this exercise using different right-hand techniques. If you are using a pick, start by using downstrokes exclusively. After that you can begin to alternate between downstrokes and upstrokes.

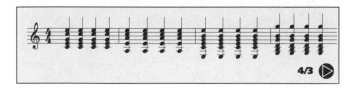

## EIGHTH-NOTE CHORDS

This final exercise uses chords made up from eighth notes—notes that are sustained for half a beat. This time around you must play two chords for each number that you count out. Therefore, to ensure that your strokes are of an equal value, try inserting the word "and" between each number—all you have to do is play on every half beat.

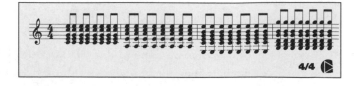

# TIME SIGNATURES

When notes are written down, they are grouped together in small blocks called "bars." Each bar contains a defined number of "beats." It's easiest to explain this idea in terms of counting numbers out aloud: if you slowly and evenly count out "1-2-3-4-2-2-3-4-3-2-3-4-4-2-3-4" you have counted out four bars, with each single bar containining four beats.

## COMMON TIME

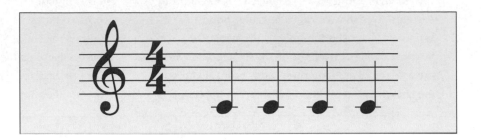

You may have noticed that some of the written music you've seen on previous pages has begun with a pair of numbers, one sitting above the other on the staff to the left of the notes. These two numbers indicate the "time signature" of the piece of music. The number at the top tells you how many beats there are in each bar, and the bottom number tells you the time value of each of those beats.

In the example above there are four beats in the bar; each beat has a value of a quarter note, because it lasts for a quarter of the bar. This can be a slightly confusing notion for beginners—it does not mean that each bar *has* to consist of four quarter notes, but simply that irrespective of how many notes are played in the bar, their total value *must* add up to the top figure, which in this case is four.

A piece of music which has four beats (quarter notes) in the bar is said to have a time signature of "four-four," which is usually written in text as "4/4." Four-four time is far and away the most commonly used time signature, so much so, in fact, that it is also widely known as "common time" and is sometimes abbreviated on the staff as the letter "C," or in its its more stylized form—𝄴.

## SIMPLE TIME

There are three basic time signatures: 2/4, 3/4, and 4/4. These are known as "simple time." Four-bar groupings for each of these time signatures are shown in the examples on the right. Try counting along with each line of music, always accenting the first beat of each bar. The count for the four bars of 2/4, for example, would go "one-two-one-two-one-two-one-two."

With its unique, unmistakable feel, the 3/4 time signature is also known as "waltz time" or "triple" time and has three beats in each bar.

You will probably have noticed that the time signatures in 2/4 and 4/4 are essentially the same. However, the fact that the example in 2/4 would require twice as many bars to produce the same number of notes naturally alters the feel of the way the beats are counted.

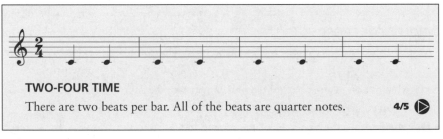

**TWO-FOUR TIME**
There are two beats per bar. All of the beats are quarter notes.    4/5 ▶

**THREE-FOUR TIME**
There are three beats per bar. All of the beats are quarter notes.    4/6 ▶

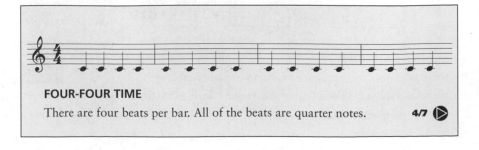

**FOUR-FOUR TIME**
There are four beats per bar. All of the beats are quarter notes.    4/7 ▶

## COMPOUND TIME

The simple time signatures (or "meters" as they are also sometimes known) shown on the previous page can also be grouped into triplets—groups of three. This produces what is known as a "compound" time signature.

Looking at the first example on the right, using 2/4 time, the two beats are played as two groups of three, which creates a bar made up of six beats. This is a time signature of 6/4 (or 6/8 if eighth notes are being used).

In a similar fashion, bars of triple time (3/4) can be played in groups of three, producing a compound time signature of 9/4 or 9/8, both of which have nine beats to the bar.

When bars of 4/4 time are grouped in the same way, a compound time signature of 12/4 or 12/8 is the result, with twelve beats in each bar.

**SIX-EIGHT TIME**

There are six beats per bar. All of the beats are eighth notes.    **4/8**

**NINE-EIGHT TIME**

There are nine beats per bar. All of the beats are eighth notes.    **4/9**

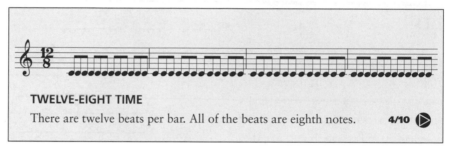

**TWELVE-EIGHT TIME**

There are twelve beats per bar. All of the beats are eighth notes.    **4/10**

## ASYMMETRIC TIME

Less common are time signatures whose number of beats in the bar are not divisible by two or three. The most common of these "assymmetric" times comprise five or seven beats in the bar. Eleven- and thirteen-beat time signatures can also be found. Although the music using such rhythms is generally more complex or esoteric in nature, the rhythms themselves are usually accented in such a way that they can be broken down into groups of two, three, or four. For example, a piece of music in 5/4 can be heard as a group of two beats followed by a group of three beats—the accents falling on beats one and three. Alternatively, they can be heard as a group of three beats followed by a group of two, with the accents falling on beats one and four. The marks above the staff indicate these accent points.

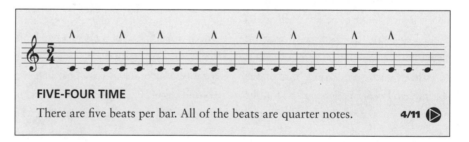

**FIVE-FOUR TIME**

There are five beats per bar. All of the beats are quarter notes.    **4/11**

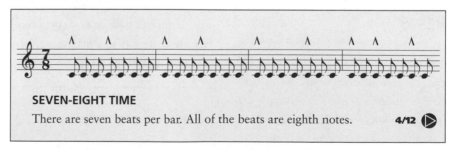

**SEVEN-EIGHT TIME**

There are seven beats per bar. All of the beats are eighth notes.    **4/12**

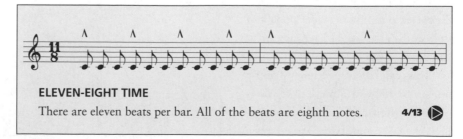

**ELEVEN-EIGHT TIME**

There are eleven beats per bar. All of the beats are eighth notes.    **4/13**

# SUSTAINS AND RESTS

Note values—from the largest (whole note) to the smallest (sixty-fourth note)—can be thought of as your basic units of musical currency. However, a note's core value can also be increased by adding "dot" or "tie" symbols. These effects play a vital role in the creation of rhythm, and in the mood or atmosphere of a piece of music. Dots and ties can be applied to any kind of note.

## DOTS

A note followed by a dot has the effect of lengthening that note by half its value. Take, for example a half note, which has a value of two beats. Placing a dot after the note increases its value to three beats.

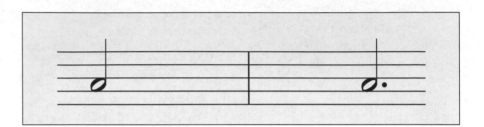

## TIES

The time signature of a piece of music indicates how many beats there are in a bar. Thus, a piece of music written in 4/4 tells you that whatever combination of note lengths exists within that bar, they must total up to the value of a whole note, i.e. four beats. However, it is often necessary for a note to be sustained across a bar line—say, for example, if a chord struck on the fourth beat of bar one has to sustain until the second beat of the second bar. In such cases, the value of the notes in each bar are shown on the staff

"tied" together with a curved bar. This point is important: WHENEVER you see a chord or note tied across a bar line, the second note is NEVER played—it is simply an instruction to sustain the previous note of the last bar for its own value, PLUS the value of the second note. Using the same example as the one shown above, a half note tied across the bar to a quarter note is sustained for three beats.

## RESTS

The final note-value element that plays a crucial part of rhythm is the "rest." Rather unsurprisingly, this is simply an instruction not to play. Each type of note has an associated rest symbol. When this is written on a piece of music, it instructs the player to rest for the same amount of time as the note would have lasted if it had been played.

Rests can have an extremely subtle impact on the way a piece of music is played. Listen to the example shown below. The second two bars inserts a pair of quarter-note rests in the second bar. Note the way in which this affects the sound. To emphasize how ties and rests are counted within the bar, the note values in beats are written beneath the staves.

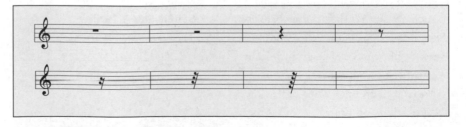

## DYNAMIC EFFECTS

The simple effect of altering the volume of a chord or note within a bar can dramatically change the tone, rhythm and "emotion" of a piece of music. These dynamic effects can be created by either striking the strings harder with the right hand (shown in printed music with an upward-pointing arrow above the note—see below— or by muting them.

There are two techniques you can use to dampen or mute the strings. The tension of the fingers on the left hand can be released as soon as the notes have been played, or you can bring the edge of your right hand down over the strings above the bridge.

Notes can still be picked while the strings are being dampened. In fact, this can be extremely effective technique, especially when played on an electric guitar fed through processing effects such as delay.

4/14

### VOLUME INSTRUCTIONS

In written music, Italian phrases can be used to describe the dynamics of a piece of music (or a passage within a piece of music). Some of these instructions are shown below.

| | | |
|---|---|---|
| *pp* | Pianissimo | Very soft |
| *p* | Piano | Soft |
| *mp* | Mezzo piano | Moderately soft |
| *mf* | Mezzo forte | Moderately loud |
| *f* | Forte | Loud |
| *ff* | Fortissimo | Very loud |

### CRESCENDO AND DIMINUENDO

Gradual changes in volume can be indicated using "crescendo" and "diminuendo" marks. These horizontal arrows are positioned above the staff and indicate that the range of notes beneath should gradually be played louder or softer.

**CRESCENDO**         **DIMINUENDO**

### STACCATO

The Italian word "staccato" literally means "short and sharp." It is an instruction for a note to be played for half its value, but keeping to the overall rhythm. It is shown on the staff with a dot either above or below the note. It is, in effect, shorthand for showing a note followed by a rest of the same value. The opposite of "staccato" is "legato," in which notes are "slurred" together with as small a gap as possible.

# DEVELOPING RHYTHM

Up until now, the exercises have been devised to help you understand how the components of rhythm work on their own. In practice, rhythms are created by mixing the different note lengths. The exercises shown below will help you to put these into some kind of musical context. Each one uses a chord progression that moves through A major, E minor, D major, and returns to A major. Afterwards you can try out the different rhythms over the top of a full-length backing track that also uses these chords.

## MIXING NOTE VALUES

The first two exercises illustrate how you can mix different note values to create rhythmic effects. It will help if you count out the note values as you work through the bars—in the first example, as there are two quarter notes followed by a half note, the count would be "one-one-one-two." You will also notice that each bar starts with a series of sharps preceding the meter. This indicates that the song is in the key of A major, so the music written on the staff may look different to the previous examples, which have all been in the key of C. You don't need to worry about this for now—it will all become clear in the next lesson.

## PLAYING ON THE "OFF" BEAT

Still using the same pattern of chords, the following two exercises place the emphasis on the second and fourth beats of the bar.

This is termed playing on the "off" beat. Although it's an extremely common rhythm-guitar device, and one that is used in all forms of popular music, the effect is an integral, central part of all reggae and ska music.

## ACCENTING

This exercise illustrates how you can create different rhythms—even when playing the same chord—by emphasizing the volume of different notes. The music contains four bars of an A major chord all played as eighth notes. Wherever you see the accent command (the arrowhead) above the note, play it with greater volume. You will notice the difference more effectively if you dampen the strings with your right hand.

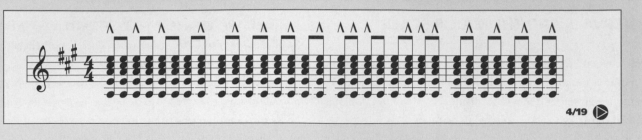

4/19

## USING CHORD TIES

The final three exercises in this lesson show the dramatic effect that can be created by using a tie to pull the chord change into the preceding bar. The final exercise makes slightly more complex use of eighth notes. You may find it easier to deal with if you double up the speed of your count so that you go "one-and-two-and-three-and-four-and."

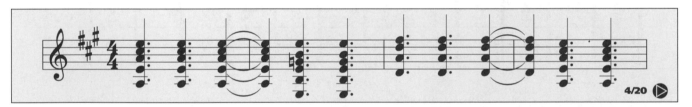

4/20

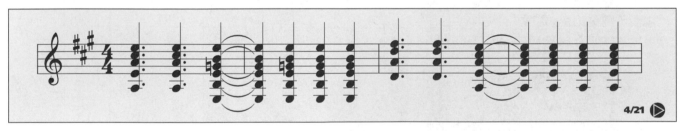

4/21

4/22

## BACKING TRACK

This backing track will help to reinforce the information you've picked up throughout this lesson. It is a simple sequence which uses the chords A major, E minor, D major, and then returns to A major. It repeats this eight-bar cycle continuously, although the dynamic of the piece shifts between soft and loud every 32 bars, creating a typical verse/chorus effect. Try out some of the different rhythmic combinations shown above with this track.

4/23

# SCALES AND KEYS

# Lesson 5

A "scale" is a series of related notes. Each type of scale follows a pattern of intervals played in sequence from a specified note to the octave of that note. The first note of the scale is always called the "root." This indicates the "key" of the scale. The most commonly used scales are the diatonic major and the three relative minors.

## INTERVALS AND THE MAJOR SCALE

An "interval" is the distance in pitch between any two notes. In a major scale, the pattern of intervals that define the scale is made up either of "steps" (a distance of two frets on the fingerboard), which are referred to as "tones" in Europe, or "half-steps" (a distance of one fret), which are called "semitones" in Europe. The major scale progress in the following way from the root: STEP•STEP•HALF-STEP•STEP•STEP•STEP•HALF-STEP. In the key of C, the notes are C, D, E, F, G, A, B, and C—the "white" notes on a piano keyboard.

Once a key has been defined, i.e. the root is known, every note of the scale—referred to as a "degree"—can be named both on its own and in terms of the interval between itself and the root. The diagram below shows how the notes of a C major scale are named in terms of the guitar fingerboard.

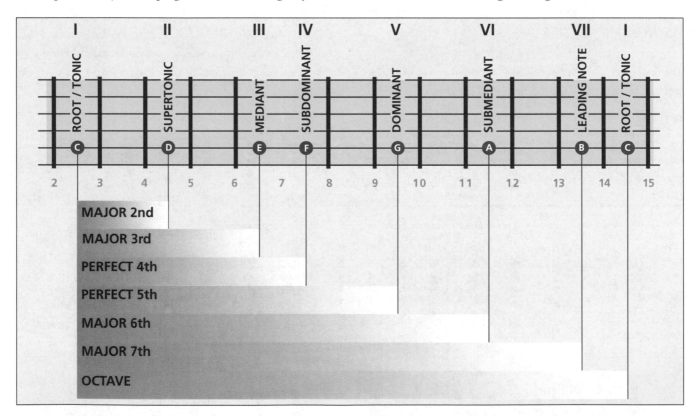

## MAJOR-SCALE FINGERING

Whilst it is possible to play scales along a single string, it's far more sensible to spread the load across the fingerboard. By adopting the correct fingering, you should find yourself able to play all of the notes of the major scale without having to move your left-hand position. Classical training encourages economic use of the fingers by dictating that each fret in the range in which you're playing is covered by just one finger of the left hand.

You can try out this idea for yourself on a C major scale. The range of notes you will be playing are all found within the 2nd to 5th frets on the fingerboard. Irrespective of which strings are being used, the notes played on the 2nd, 3rd, 4th, and 5th frets are ONLY held in position by the 1st, 2nd, 3rd, and 4th fingers respectively. Play each note of the C major scale, paying careful attention to using the correct left-hand fingering. You are likely to find this exercise extremely challenging, since it makes heavy use of the 4th finger. In fact, mastering the interval between the "leading note" and the "octave," which requires the co-ordination of the 3rd and 4th fingers, is likely to be little short of torture. Don't panic! Every guitarist finds this a problem at first — it's just that the muscles in the little finger would seem to get very little exercise away from musical instruments or computer keyboards.

As the major scale, like all scales, follows a precise pattern of intervals, you could easily imagine that once the fingers of your left hand become used to their positions on the fingerboard,

playing scales in other keys simply becomes a matter of sliding your hand along the neck to find a new root-note position. And so it is—this pattern, starting on the 5th string, can be used anywhere on the fingerboard to play a major scale in any key.

Move your entire hand so that the fingers of your left hand cover the 9th to the 12th frets. By repeating the pattern above, but this time starting on the 10th fret of the 5th string, you can play the scale of G major.

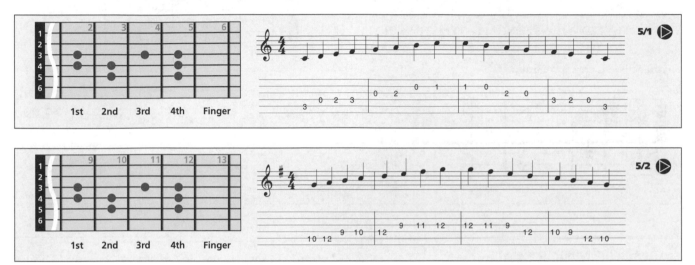

## ALTERNATIVE MAJOR-SCALE FINGERING

Two alternative major-scale patterns are also commonly used. One starts on the 6th string, the other on the 3rd string. Both are shown playing a C major scale below. As before, these can be moved up and down the fingerboard to play in alternative keys. The sixth-string scale positions allow you to play two full octaves straight through from the 1st string to the 6th string.

If you were wondering why there isn't a major scale pattern that starts on the 4th string, the answer is simple:

there is, but because of the interval between the 2nd and 3rd strings differs from the others, it would require a range of five frets, meaning that one of the fingers of the left hand would have to cover two frets. Major-scale patterns played from the 4th string, are, therefore, unecessarily awkward and not really advisable.

It is extremely worthwhile mastering these three fingering patterns—both ascending and descending the scales. The ability to use them with a degree of fluidity will help you to develop your skills as a lead player.

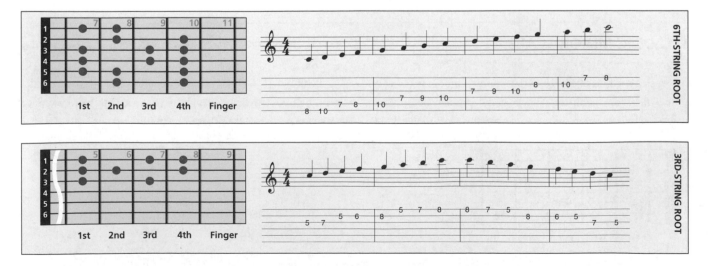

# THE THREE MINOR SCALES

The primary difference between a major scale and a minor scale is the interval between the 1st and 3rd notes. On a major scale the interval is a major 3rd (two steps); on a minor scale it is a minor 3rd (a step and a half-step). There are three distinct types of minor scale: natural minor, harmonic minor, and melodic minor. They differ only in the 6th and 7th degrees of their respective scales.

## NATURAL MINOR SCALE

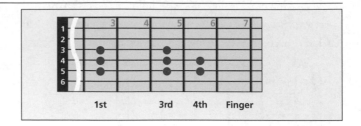

The natural minor scale has the following intervals from the root: STEP•HALF-STEP•-STEP•STEP•HALF-STEP•STEP•STEP. In the key of C the notes are C, D, E♭, F, G, A♭, B♭, and C. The fingering options are shown below.

## HARMONIC MINOR SCALE

The harmonic minor differs from the natural minor in that the 6th note is raised by a half-step. The notes on the harmonic minor scale consist of the following intervals from the root: STEP•HALF-STEP• STEP•STEP•HALF-STEP•STEP PLUS HALF-STEP•HALF-STEP.

In the key of C the notes used are C, D, E♭, F, G, A♭, B, and C.

If you look at the fretboard diagram below, you will see that playing a harmonic minor scale from the 6th string requires you to break the one-finger-per-fret rule. In this instance, the most efficient alternative is to allow the index finger, which is the strongest and most mobile finger, to cover the first two fret positions.

## MELODIC MINOR SCALE

The melodic minor differs from the natural minor in that the 7th note is raised by a half-step. The melodic minor scale is created using the following set of intervals from the root: STEP•HALF-

STEP•STEP•STEP•STEP•STEP•HALF-STEP. In the key of C this uses the notes C, D, E♭, F, G, A, B, and C.

IMPORTANT POINT: this scale differs from the other scales in the minor set, in that when playing a descending melodic minor scale, the notes revert to that of the natural minor scale.

## CONTRASTING THE SCALES

| | I | ii | II | iii | III | IV | V | V | vi | VI | vii | VII | I |
|---|---|---|---|---|---|---|---|---|---|---|---|---|---|
| | ROOT | MINOR 2nd | MAJOR 2nd | MINOR 3rd | MAJOR 3rd | PERFECT 4th | AUGMENTED 4th or DIMINISHED 5th | PERFECT 5th | AUGMENTED 5th or MINOR 6th | MAJOR 6th or DIMINISHED 7th | MINOR 7th | MAJOR 7th | OCTAVE |
| **MAJOR** | ● | | ● | | ● | ● | | ● | | ● | | ● | ● |
| **NATURAL MINOR** | ● | | ● | ● | | ● | | ● | ● | | ● | | ● |
| **HARMONIC MINOR** | ● | | ● | ● | | ● | | ● | ● | | | ● | ● |
| **MELODIC MINOR** | ● | | ● | ● | | ● | | ● | | ● | | ● | ● |

This table shows how the major scale and the three minor scales differ in terms of their intervals.

### CONTRASTING SCALES

To hear the differences between the scales in practice, play through the four scales shown below in the key of A. Use the fingering shown in the examples for the key of C, starting from the 6th string. All you have to do is move the patterns three frets down the fingerboard. Note the "three sharps" at the front of the A major scale are missing from the minor scale. This is because the A natural minor scale has no flats or sharps. It is called the "relative minor" of the C major scale because it shares the same notes, although starting from different roots.

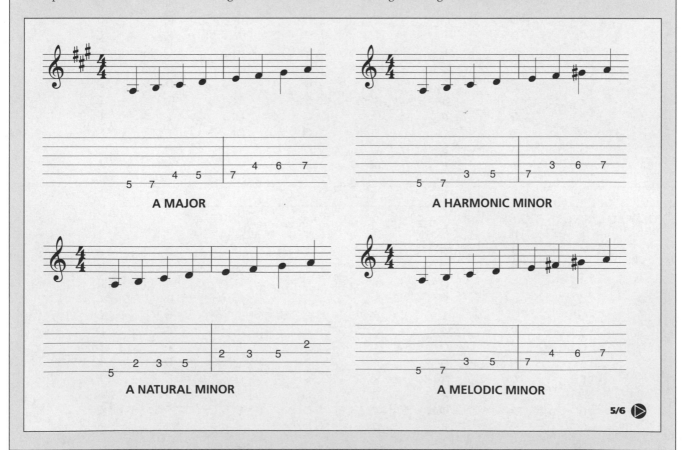

A MAJOR

A HARMONIC MINOR

A NATURAL MINOR

A MELODIC MINOR

**5/6**

# THE SCALE FINDER

It might not look too likely at first, but the information held on these two pages could change your life. The five tables illustrate the notes of the four scale types which you have been shown on the previous pages. Each degree of each scale is shown in all twelve keys. If you treat each scale as a practice exercise, you will quickly become familiar with the characteristics of each type of scale. Play the notes in ascending and descending sequence, not forgetting that when you descend the melodic minor scale you should switch to the notes of the natural minor for each key.

## PRACTICING SCALES

For the novice musician, the process of practicing scales can be one of the least exciting aspects of learning an instrument, but it genuinely does pay. In fact, there are too many reasons why it shouldn't be ignored. Learning scales will bring about a greater understanding of the way notes relate to one another. This will be extremely valuable as your chord vocabulary increases. If you want to write songs, a knowledge of scales will help you develop an ear for melody and understand why certain notes work well with chord sequences.

Scales will also be fundamental to the development of your lead-guitar playing. In fact, you could treat this chapter as your first lesson in playing lead guitar, because, whether conscious or not, a high proportion of the solo work heard in most forms of popular music revolves around the use of a very limited number of scale types—typically, those already covered in this lesson and the major and minor pentatonics, which we'll discuss in a later lesson. A well-developed scale vocabulary will also provide a useful framework from which you will be able to improvise more effectively. In short, the greater your knowledge of scales, the greater your playing options.

**MAJOR**

| I | II | III | IV | V | VI | VII | I |
|---|---|---|---|---|---|---|---|
| A | B | C# | D | E | F# | G# | A |
| B♭ | C | D | E♭ | F | G | A | B♭ |
| B | C# | D# | E | F# | G# | A# | B |
| C | D | E | F | G | A | B | C |
| C# | D# | F | F# | G# | A# | C | C# |
| D | E | F# | G | A | B | C# | D |
| E♭ | F | G | A♭ | B♭ | C | D | E♭ |
| E | F# | G# | A | B | C# | D# | E |
| F | G | A | B♭ | C | D | E | F |
| F# | G# | A# | B | C# | D# | F | F# |
| G | A | B | C | D | E | F# | G |
| A♭ | B♭ | C | D♭ | E♭ | F | G | A♭ |

**NATURAL MINOR**

| I | II | iii | IV | V | vi | vii | I |
|---|---|---|---|---|---|---|---|
| A | B | C | D | E | F | G | A |
| B♭ | C | D♭ | E♭ | F | G♭ | A♭ | B♭ |
| B | C# | D | E | F# | G | A | B |
| C | D | E♭ | F | G | A♭ | B♭ | C |
| C# | D# | E | F# | G# | A | B | C# |
| D | E | F | G | A | B♭ | C | D |
| E♭ | F | G♭ | A♭ | B♭ | B | D♭ | E♭ |
| E | F# | G | A | B | C | D | E |
| F | G | A♭ | B♭ | C | D♭ | E♭ | F |
| F# | G# | A | B | C# | D | E | F# |
| G | A | B♭ | C | D | E♭ | F | G |
| A♭ | B♭ | B | D♭ | E♭ | E | G♭ | A♭ |

Practicing scales also makes a useful warm-up exercise, helping you to improve the agility of the fingers of the left hand and your right-hand plectrum or fingering technique.

A final note on scales: you may come across some music books that discuss what might seem to be impossible note names. This comes about because each scale is a specified pattern of intervals. In the key of E♭, for example, the natural minor flattens the 6th note of the major scale, so to be musically correct a flattened C should be referred to as C♭, even though a flattened C is the same as B. In the tables below, to avoid unnecessary confusion, the notes C♭, B♯, F♭, and E♯ have all been referred to as B, C, E, and F respectively.

**HARMONIC MINOR**

| I | II | iii | IV | V | vi | VII | I |
|---|----|-----|----|---|----|----|---|
| A | B | C | D | E | F | G# | A |
| B♭ | C | D♭ | E♭ | F | G♭ | A | B♭ |
| B | C# | D | E | F# | G | A# | B |
| C | D | E♭ | F | G | A♭ | B | C |
| C# | D# | E | F# | G# | A | C | C# |
| D | E | F | G | A | B♭ | C# | D |
| E♭ | F | G♭ | A♭ | B♭ | B | D | E♭ |
| E | F# | G | A | B | C | D# | E |
| F | G | A♭ | B♭ | C | D♭ | E | F |
| F# | G# | A | B | C# | D | F | F# |
| G | A | B♭ | C | D | E♭ | F# | G |
| A♭ | B♭ | B | D♭ | E♭ | E | G | A♭ |

**MELODIC MINOR**

| I | II | iii | IV | V | VI | VII | I |
|---|----|-----|----|---|----|----|---|
| A | B | C | D | E | F# | G# | A |
| B♭ | C | D♭ | E♭ | F | G | A | B♭ |
| B | C# | D | E | F# | G# | A# | B |
| C | D | E♭ | F | G | A | B | C |
| C# | D# | E | F# | G# | A# | C | C# |
| D | E | F | G | A | B | C# | D |
| E♭ | F | G♭ | A♭ | B♭ | C | D | E♭ |
| E | F# | G | A | B | C# | D# | E |
| F | G | A♭ | B♭ | C | D | E | F |
| F# | G# | A | B | C# | D# | F | F# |
| G | A | B♭ | C | D | E | F# | G |
| A♭ | B♭ | B | D♭ | E♭ | F | G | A♭ |

**MELODIC MINOR (descending)**

| I | vii | vi | V | IV | iii | II | I |
|---|-----|----|---|----|-----|----|---|
| A | G | F | E | D | C | B | A |
| B♭ | A♭ | G♭ | F | E♭ | D♭ | C | B♭ |
| B | A | G | F# | E | D | C# | B |
| C | B♭ | A♭ | G | F | E♭ | D | C |
| C# | B | A | G# | F# | E | D# | C# |
| D | C | B♭ | A | G | F | E | D |
| E♭ | D♭ | B | B♭ | A♭ | G♭ | F | E♭ |
| E | D | C | B | A | G | F# | E |
| F | E♭ | D♭ | C | B♭ | A♭ | G | F |
| F# | E | D | C# | B | A | G# | F# |
| G | F | E♭ | D | C | B♭ | A | G |
| A♭ | G♭ | E | E♭ | D♭ | B | B♭ | A♭ |

# KEY SIGNATURES

Just as the root note of a scale provides that scale with its key, a piece of music can be identified in the same way. If, for example, a melody comprises notes from the G major scale, it is said to be "in" G major. What this means is that it has a "key signature" of G major.

## SHARPS AND FLATS

As you have already seen, the notes as they appear on the lines of a treble staff are E-G-B-D-F; the notes that sit between the spaces are F-A-C-E. This is all well and good if a piece of music is written in the key of C major, which has no flats or sharps. Unfortunately life—or music theory, at least—is not that simple: all of the other major keys contain at least one sharp or flat. It would be possible to indicate sharp and flat symbols alongside each note as they occur, but if you came across a piece written in F♯ (whose scale includes six sharps) it would most likely appear as an illegible blur of sharp symbols. Instead, the practice is to show an instruction at the beginning of the staff that any occurrence of a specific note should be sharpened or flattened, unless specifically shown otherwise. Therefore, the key signature of a piece of written music can always be identified by the number of sharps and flats appearing after the clef at the beginning of a piece of music.

Positioning sharps on the C and F lines of the staff indicates that the piece of music is in D major. Consequently, wherever notes appear on those lines they must be played as C♯ and F♯.

## 4THS AND 5THS

You may have already discovered for yourself that there are certain types of chord sequence that seem to work more harmoniously that others. There is a particularly strong relationship between the chords formed on the root, 4th and 5th degrees of the major scale. Try out the four sequences shown below—see how smoothly they flow together.

| I | IV | V | I |
|---|----|----|---|
| C Major | F Major | G Major | C Major |
| E Major | A Major | B Major | E Major |
| D Major | G Major | A Major | D major |
| G Major | C Major | D Major | G Major |

Now, just as an experiment, sing the root note of the first chord all the way through the entire sequence—in the first example, sing the note C, even while you are playing the F and G chords. You will hear that even when the chords change, the note you're singing still seems to fit. This is because the note C appears in the major scale for all three chords. In fact, if you look at the notes of each scale, you will see precisely how closely the three are related: F major and G major have only one different note to the C major scale.

### THE CIRCLE OF 5THS

This relationship can be seen most effectively in what has become known as the "circle of 5ths." The circle is divided into twelve segments, with the key of C at the top. In a clockwise sequence, key signatures are added to each segment

| CONTRASTING C MAJOR, F MAJOR, AND G MAJOR | | | | | | | | |
|---|---|---|---|---|---|---|---|---|
| | I | II | III | IV | V | VI | VII | I |
| C Major | C | D | E | F | G | A | B | C |
| F Major | F | G | A | B♭ | C | D | E | F |
| G Major | G | A | B | C | D | E | F♯ | G |

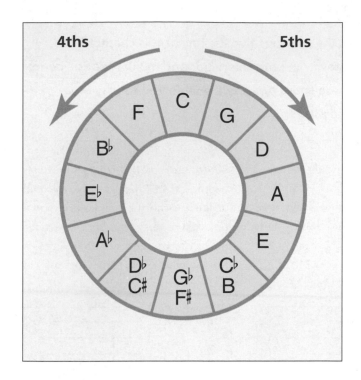

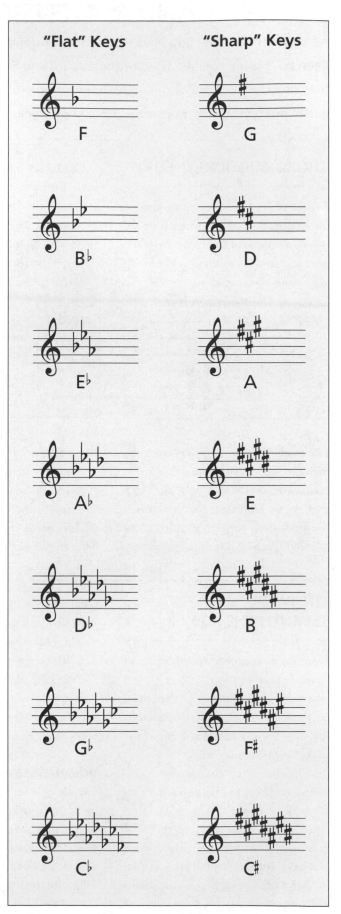

in intervals of a 5th. If you move clockwise in 5ths around the circle, you will find that each major scale differs from the preceding scale by just one note. In each case, the subsequent major scale is formed by raising (sharpening) the note on the 7th degree (the leading note) by a half-step (or semitone). As you can see from the diagram on the right, the scale on each subsequent segment has an additional sharp.

In a similar fashion, by moving counterclockwise around the circle in 4ths there is also just one note difference between each pair of scales. In these cases, the new scale is formed by lowering (flattening) the note on the 4th (subdominant) degree of the previous scale.

### ENHARMONICS

Some notes can have more than one designation. If C is raised by a half-step it becomes C♯; if D is lowered by a half-step it becomes D♭—even though both notes are the same pitch. This is known as an enharmonic relationship. In this case, if the note appears in a "sharp" key it will be known as C♯; if it is a part of a "flat" key it will be known as D♭. There are two other enharmonic keys: F♯/G♭ and C♭/B. Whilst the above rules apply equally to them, in practise—in popular music, at least—the use of G♭ is rare and C♭ almost unknown.

# SEVENTHS AND EXTENSIONS Lesson 6

**All of the chords that you have encountered throughout the previous five lessons of this chapter have been built using combinations of the 1st, 3rd and 5th notes from both the major and minor "triads," hence they have all been major or minor chord types. Whilst these chord types will enable you to play or write a wide variety of songs, numerous other chord types are possible.**

## CHORD-BUILDING THEORY

To understand the way in which some of these "extended" chords work, there are two other forms of triad that you really need to know about: the "augmented" and "diminished" triads.

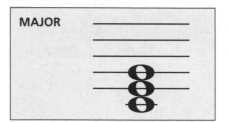

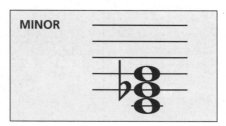

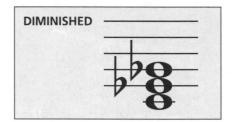

The augmented triad differs from the major triad, in that the 5th note is raised (or sharpened) by a half-step (semitone); similarly, the diminished triad has both the 3rd and 5th notes lowered (flattened) by a half-step.

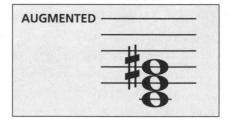

By taking the four triads and notes related to the root, it is possible to create a rich variety of alternative chord types. The families you will meet in this section of the book are the "7ths," "suspended 4ths," "6ths," "9ths," "11ths," and "13ths." Each of these new chord types can be described in terms of a triad with added intervals. If you find this a difficult concept, keep referring to the top section of the table of 7th chords shown across the page. This names the relationship of each

note to the root. It also names the notes for the key of C—the key in which all of the 7th chord examples are shown throughout this section of the lesson.

Before you go any further, here's a brief summary of the four types of triad and how they are constructed.

## THE FAMILY OF SEVENTH CHORDS

Easily the most common family of chord extensions is the "7th." There are ten possible types of 7th chord. All of them are formed by adding either a diminished 7th, a minor 7th, or a major 7th to one of the four types of triad.

The three 7th chords which are most commonly used in popular forms of music are the "dominant 7th," "minor 7th," and "major 7th." The diminished forms are also quite common. Although a full set is shown over the next four pages, it's fair to say that some of the more obscure

members of the 7th family find little use outside of the margins of the jazz world. Nonetheless, these are shown here for completeness.

The table across the page shows the way in which these ten chords are built in terms of the relationship of each of the notes to the root.

### DOMINANT SEVENTH

Usually referred to simply as a "seven" or "7th" chord, the dominant 7th is formed by adding a minor 7th to a major triad. In the key of C, the notes used are C (root), E (major 3rd), and G (perfect 5th) with an added B♭ (minor 7th). Its abbreviation is C7.

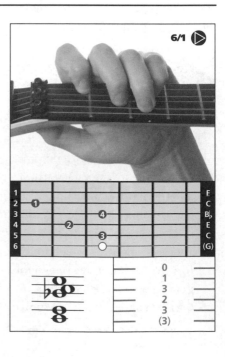

| | ROOT (C) | MINOR 2nd (C#/Db) | MAJOR 2nd (D) | MINOR 3rd (D#/Eb) | MAJOR 3rd (E) | PERFECT 4th (F) | AUGMENTED 4th or DIMINISHED 5th (F#/Gb) | PERFECT 5th (G) | AUGMENTED 5th or MINOR 6th (G#/Ab) | MAJOR 6th or DIMINISHED 7th (A) | MINOR 7th (A#/Bb) | MAJOR 7th (B) |
|---|---|---|---|---|---|---|---|---|---|---|---|---|
| | I | ii | II | iii | III | IV | IV+/V° | V | V+/vi | VI/vii° | vii | VII |
| **Dominant** | ● | | | | ● | | | ● | | | ● | |
| **Minor** | ● | | | ● | | | | ● | | | ● | |
| **Major** | ● | | | | ● | | | ● | | | | ● |
| **Diminished** | ● | | | ● | | | ● | | | ● | | |
| **Diminished 5th** | ● | | | | ● | | ● | | | | ● | |
| **Augmented 5th** | ● | | | | ● | | | | ● | | ● | |
| **Minor/major** | ● | | | ● | | | | ● | | | | ● |
| **Half diminished** | ● | | | ● | | | ● | | | | ● | |
| **Major diminished 5th** | ● | | | | ● | | ● | | | | | ● |
| **Major augmented 5th** | ● | | | | ● | | | | ● | | | ● |

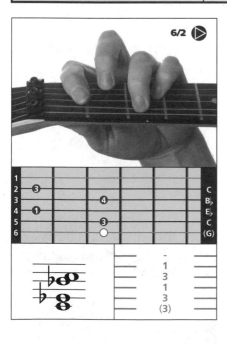

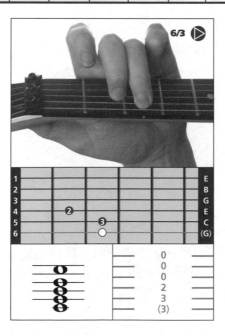

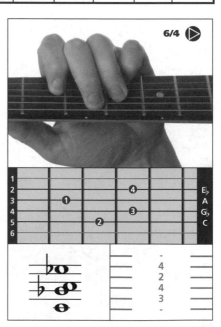

### MINOR SEVENTH

Minor 7th chords are formed by adding a minor 7th note to a minor triad. In the key of C, this chord uses the notes C (root), E♭ (minor 3rd), and G (perfect 5th), with an added B♭ (minor 7th). Its abbreviation is Cm7.

### MAJOR SEVENTH

Major 7th chords are formed by adding a major 7th note to a major triad. In the key of C, the notes used are C (root), E (major 3rd), G (perfect 5th), with an added B (major 7th). Its abbreviation is Cmaj7 or CΔ.

### DIMINISHED SEVENTH

The diminished 7th is usually referred to simply as a diminished. It is formed by adding a diminished 7th note to a diminished triad. In the key of C, this adds the note A to C, E♭, and G♭. Its abbreviation is Cdim or C°.

# MORE SEVENTH CHORDS

### SEVENTH DIMISHED FIFTH

7th diminished 5th chords are usually referred to as "seven flat fives." They are formed by adding a minor 7th to the root, major 3rd and diminished 5th. In the key of C, this adds B♭ to the notes C, E, and G♭. Its abbreviation is C7-5.

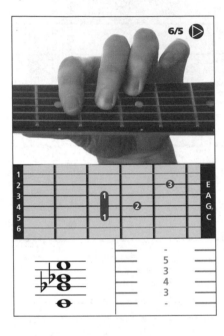

### SEVENTH AUGMENTED FIFTH

7th augmented 5th chords are usually referred to as "seven sharp fives." They are formed by adding a minor 7th to an augmented triad. In the key of C, this adds a B♭ to the notes C, E, and G♯. Its abbreviation is C7+5.

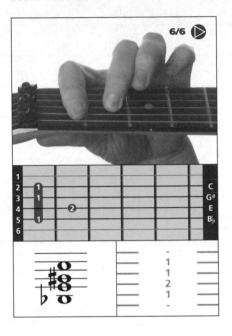

### MINOR/MAJOR SEVENTH

Minor/major 7th chords are formed by combining the root, perfect 5th, major 7th, and minor 3rd notes. In the key of C, the major/minor 7th chord uses the notes C, G, B, and E♭. The abbreviation is Cm/maj7 or Cm/Δ7.

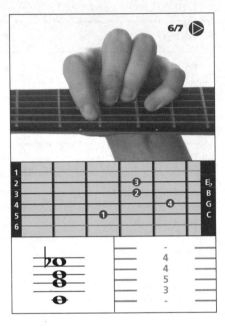

### HALF-DIMINISHED SEVENTH

Half-diminished 7th chords are formed by adding a minor 7th to a diminished triad. Therefore the chord C7 half-diminished uses the notes C, E♭, G♭, and B♭. Its abbreviation is Cm7-5.

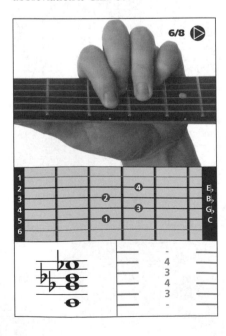

### MAJOR SEVENTH DIMINISHED FIFTH

This chord is formed by combining the root, major 3rd, diminished 5th, and major 7th notes. In the key of C, the notes used are C, E, G♭, and B. Its abbreviation is Cmaj7-5 or CΔ7-5.

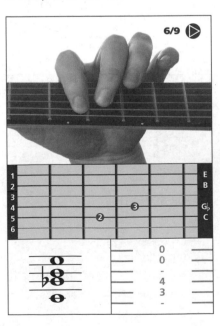

### MAJOR SEVENTH AUGMENTED FIFTH

The major 7th augmented 5th is formed by combining the root, major 3rd, augmented 5th, and major 7th notes. In C, the notes C, E, G♯, and B are used. Its abbreviation is Cmaj7+5 or CΔ7+5.

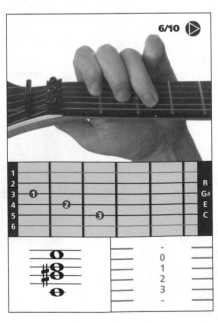

## EXERCISING THE SEVENTH CHORDS

You are likely to find that the ten 7th chords you have just played are the most difficult you have yet come across. One of the reasons for this is that they require some pretty nimble work with the 4th finger. When you first begin playing the guitar, you will probably find that you just can't get your little finger to obey your instructions. Don't be impatient: the muscles in this finger don't usually get too much work, so it's no surprise that they may well be underdeveloped.

The eight-bar exercise shown below will help you to become more fluid in playing the basic 7th chords. Work through them slowly. To start with, don't worry too much about your timing—you'll have your work cut out just getting your fingers in the right position.

The progression of the first three chords — from major to major 7th to dominant 7th—is a very common (almost clichéd) sequence which emphasizes the movement of the three highest notes—in relation to the root, the notes move from the octave, to the major 7th, and then to the minor 7th.

The chords in the key of C are all shown over the previous three pages. As you won't yet have come into contact with open-string voicings for D minor 7th and G dominant 7th, they are both shown below.

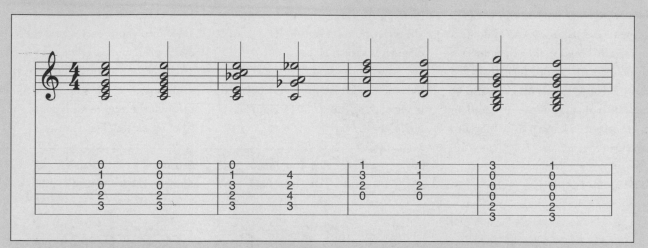

### D MINOR SEVENTH

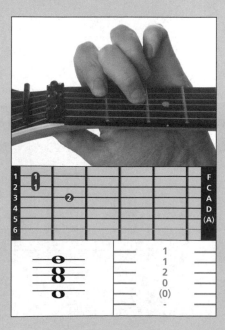

### G DOMINANT SEVENTH

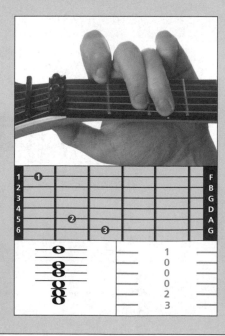

### D MINOR SEVENTH

This chord is formed by adding the minor 7th to a minor triad. In the key of D, the notes used are D (root), F (minor 3rd), A (perfect 5th), and C (minor 7th). This voicing may seem similar to a F major with the 3rd finger released so that the open D can be heard.

### G DOMINANT SEVENTH

This chord is formed by adding the minor 7th to a major triad. In the key of G, the chord comprises the notes G (root), A (major 3rd), C (perfect 5th), and F (minor 7th).

# FOURTH AND SIXTH NOTES

There are seven different notes that make up a major or minor scale. All of the chords shown so far in the book have used the four types of triad (the root, major or minor 3rd, and diminished, perfect or augmented 5th notes). Additionally, the family of 7ths uses all of these triads with an added major or minor 7th note. It is also possible to use the perfect 4th, and major 6th notes of the scales to create further interesting and commonly used chord voicings. When the perfect 4th is used in a chord, it invariably replaces the major 3rd; the major 6th is simply added to the basic triad. Chords using these notes are suffixed "suspended 4ths" and "6ths" respectively.

## SUSPENDED CHORDS

By replacing the major 3rd in a major triad with a perfect 4th, the complexion of a major chord can be radically altered. This produces what is known as a "suspended" chord. Applying this principle to a major chord produces a "suspended 4th" chord (usually called simply a "sus4"). This idea can also be applied to a dominant seventh chord, in which case it is known as a "seventh suspended fourth" (or "7sus4").

### SUSPENDED FOURTH

By replacing the major 3rd in a major triad with a perfect 4th, a suspended 4th chord is created. In the key of E, this uses the notes E (root), A (perfect 4th), and B (perfect 5th). The chord is usually described as "Esus4."

## SEVENTH SUSPENDED FOURTH

7th suspended 4th chords are created by adding a minor 7th to a suspended 4th chord. In the key of E, this comprises the notes E (root), A (perfect 4th), B (perfect 5th), and D (minor 7th). Its abbreviation is E7sus4. The chord diagram is shown below.

An extremely famous example of the use of suspended 7th chords can be heard in the opening chimes to "A Hard Day's Night" by the Beatles.

## SUSPENDED CHORD EXERCISE

Try playing the exercise shown below. Apply the rhythm, which is only shown over the first two bars, to each pair of chords listed directly above the music. In each case, the movement is from the suspended chord back to the equivalent major or dominant 7th in the same key. This kind of progression is known as a "full close," and has been widely used through the ages in all types of music, from classical to heavy metal.

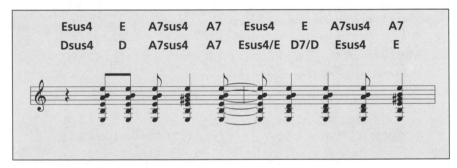

| Esus4 | E | A7sus4 | A7 | Esus4 | E | A7sus4 | A7 |
| Dsus4 | D | A7sus4 | A7 | Esus4/E | D7/D | Esus4 | E |

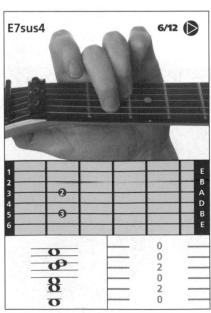

Esus4    6/11

| | | | | | E |
| | | | | | B |
| | | ① | | | A |
| | | ② | | | E |
| | | ③ | | | B |
| | | | | | E |

0
0
2
2
0

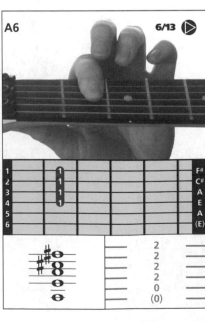

E7sus4    6/12

| | | | | | E |
| | | | | | B |
| | ② | | | | A |
| | | ③ | | | D |
| | | | | | B |
| | | | | | E |

0
0
2
0
2
0

A6    6/13

| | | | | | F# |
| | ① | ① | ① | ① | C# |
| | | | | | A |
| | | | | | E |
| | | | | | A |
| | | | | | (E) |

2
2
2
0
(0)

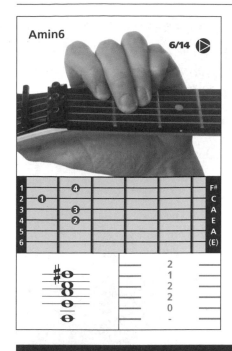

**Amin6**

6/14

F#
C
A
E
A
(E)

2
1
2
2
0
-

## THE SIXTH FAMILY OF CHORDS

When a major triad has the 6th note of the major scale added, it produces what is known as a "6th" chord (usually referred to as a "six"). Similarly, when the 6th note is added to a minor triad, a "minor 6th" chord ("minor six") is created. 6th chords are commonly used in progressions that lead from a major chord to a dominant 7th, passing through the 6th, within the same key.

The two voicings shown in this lesson (E6 at the foot of page 68, and A minor 6, left) are the most basic of the 6th chords. More complex variations can be found in the Chord Finder (see pages 156–191).

### SIXTH

6th chords are formed by adding a major 6th note to a major triad. The chord A 6th uses the notes A (root), C# (major 3rd), E (perfect 5th), and F# (major 6th). Its abbreviation is A6.

### MINOR SIXTH

Minor 6th chords are created by adding the major 6th note to a minor triad. The chord A minor 6th is made up from the notes A (root), C (minor 3rd), E (perfect 5th) and F# (major 6th). Its abbreviation is Am6.

## PETE TOWNSHEND

<u>Born:</u> May 19th 1944, Chiswick, England

<u>Guitars:</u> Rickenbacker 330 and "signature model"; Gibson Les Paul and SG; Fender Stratocaster and Telecaster

<u>Recorded Highlights:</u> *The Who Sell Out*; *Quadrophenia*

Pete Townshend has always been much more than just a great guitarist in one of the greatest British bands of the 1960s—The Who.

Like many British musicians, he was a product of the post-war art-school system. This may have contributed to his restless desire to experiment with the pop format. After early classic singles like "My Generation" and "I Can't Explain," the horizons of his ambition opened up with epics such as "I Can See For Miles" and the concept albums *Tommy* and *Quadrophenia*.

The Who also carved out a reputation as one of the greatest live acts of the period, harnessing the ability to produce an awesome degree of power without resorting to the excessive soloing which was so common in much rock music of the time. Indeed, when the tremors of Punk were felt, Townshend was one an elite number of the "old school" who retained unequivocal respect, and even picked up a new generation of admirers.

Like Keith Richards of the Rolling Stones, Townshend has always defined himself as a rhythm player. And, like Richards, he is likely to be remembered for the sheer power of his playing and the ability to pen some of the most memorable intro riffs of the past 30 years, such as the "sus4" chords which herald the opening of "Pinball Wizard."

# BEYOND THE OCTAVE

The 2nd, 4th, and 5th notes can also be added beyond the octave, creating what is known as an "extended" chord. Playing a 2nd note added above the octave creates a "9th" chord—this is the seven notes of the scale plus the first two notes of the extended scale. Working in a similar fashion, the 4th and 6th notes can be added to produce "11th" and "13th" chords. Some of these chords are among the most difficult to play on the guitar, requiring you to omit certain notes at your own discretion, but still retain the flavor of the extension.

## NINTHS

The "9th" series of chords is created by adding a major 2nd an octave above a chosen 7th chord. In this way, the three principle 7ths—dominant, minor, and major—all have their equivalent 9ths. In the key of C major, the major 2nd note is D—to create a ninth chord, the note D is added ON TOP OF the 7th chord. The music below shows how the chords are formed.

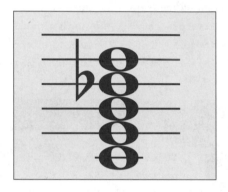

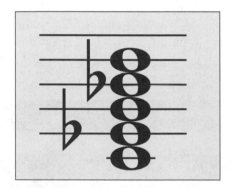

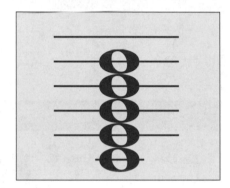

### NINTH

A 9th chord—referred to as a "nine"—is formed by adding the major 2nd above the octave to a dominant 7th chord. In the key of D, the chord comprises the notes D (root), F♯(major 3rd), A (perfect 5th), C (minor 7th), and E (major 2nd/9th). Its abbreviation is D9.

### MINOR NINTH

Minor 9th chords are created by adding a major 2nd above the octave to a minor 7th chord. In the key of D, the chord comprises the notes D (root), F (minor 3rd), A (perfect 5th), C (minor 7th), and E (major 2nd/9th). Its abbreviation is Dm9.

### MAJOR NINTH

Major 9th chords are created by adding a major 2nd above the octave to a major 7th chord. In the key of D, the chord comprises the notes D (root), F♯ (major 3rd), A (perfect 5th), C♯ (major 7th), and E (major 2nd/9th). Its abbreviation is Dmaj9 or D△9.

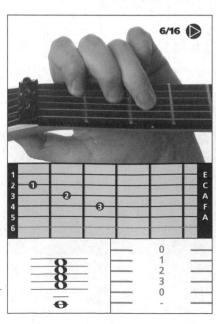

# ELEVENTHS AND THIRTEENTHS

"Eleventh" and "thirteenth" chords are formed using the same principles as the 9th chords shown on the previous page. 11th chords are created by adding a perfect 4th to an existing 9th chord, and similarly, 13th chords are created by adding a major 6th note to the 11th chord.

The two chords on the staff (see right) show how they are built in relation to the 9th chords described on the previous page.

## C ELEVENTH

The chord comprises the root (C), major 3rd (E), perfect 5th (G), minor 7th (B♭), 9th (D), and perfect 4th/11th (F).

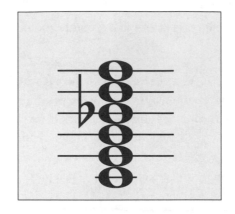

## C THIRTEENTH

Root (C), major 3rd (E), perfect 5th (G), minor 7th (B♭), major 2nd (D), perfect 4th (F), and major 6th/13th (A).

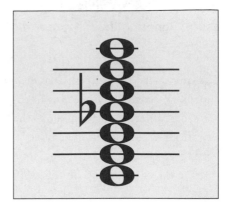

## THE ELEVENTH

In the key of G, the note C (perfect 4th) is added to the 9th chord to form G 11th. Its abbreviation is G11.

The notes required to create a full 11th chord in the key of G are: G (root), B (major 3rd), D (perfect 5th), F (minor 7th), A (major 2nd/9th), and C (perfect 4th/11th).

To play a full 11th chord requires the use of six notes (see the example above for the key of C). However, while it is technically possible to play a full voicing on the guitar, some of the time this will simply be impractical. Certainly, when

you are trying to use open-string voicings, in most cases the notes just won't sit happily together—while it may be possible to play all six notes that form the chord, you are likely to end up with an inscrutable inversion that may well not sound terribly pleasant. To avoid this, the solution is to leave out one or more of the notes. This will often be the 5th and 9th notes, although the voicing on the right omits the 3rd and 5th notes.

It is possible to produce a wide variation of alternative chords that include the extended major 6th—some are shown later in the book.

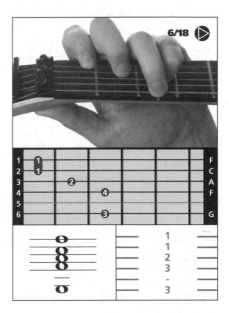

## THE THIRTEENTH

In the key of G, the note E (major 6th) is added to the 11th chord to form G 13th. Its abbreviation is G13.

The notes that are required to create a full 13th chord in the key of G are G (root), B (major 3rd), D (perfect 5th), F (minor 7th), A (major 2nd/9th), C (perfect 4th/11th), and E (major 6th/13th).

Special attention needs to be taken when using 13th chords. As you have already seen from the chord on the staff on the top right-hand corner of the page, to play a full 13th chord

requires the use of seven different notes. This makes it impossible to play on a guitar. The voicing for the guitar shown on the right leaves out the 5th and 9th notes. Another commonly used alternative is to omit the 9th and 11th notes, making the chord in essence a 7th with an added 13th note. In short, as long as the root, 3rd, and 13th notes are sounded, the flavor of the 13th chord will be retained.

It is also possible to create minor and major 13ths by adding the major 6th above the octave on a minor or major 11th chord.

# PLAYING BARRE CHORDS Lesson 7

All of the chords you have encountered so far have been formed around the open strings of the guitar. However, if you restrict yourself to using only these chords, you have little access to playing in many of the sharp or flat keys. Whilst it's fair to say that many pieces of popular music can be played only using open-string chords, ignoring the full range of possibilities is rather like a painter being unable to deal with certain colors.

The answer to this dilemma comes in the form of barre chords. Essentially, these are open-string chord shapes formed at different positions along the fingerboard. To form a barre chord, the index finger is stretched across the width of the fingerboard, and the remaining three fingers are used to form the chord shape. In this way, the index finger acts like the nut when playing open-string chords. This allows open-string chord shapes to be played in any key. The most common barre chords are variations on the E- and A-shaped open-string chords. However, the C and G shapes can also be played as barre chords, although these provide a greater challenge to the fingers of the left hand.

## FORMING AN E-SHAPED BARRE

The E-shaped barre chord is essentially the same as an open-string chord shape. However, as the index finger is now being used as the barre, the 4th finger must be used in the formation of the chord shape.

• Form an open-string E major chord, only this time using the 3rd, 4th, and 2nd fingers to fret the 5th, 4th, and 3rd strings respectively. Keep your index finger well clear of the strings.
• Slide your left hand five frets along the fingerboard.
• Place the index finger firmly behind the 5th fret. Now play across all six strings of the chord. This is an A major played using an E-shaped barre on the 5th fret.

Any major chord can be converted in this way. The chord will take its key name from the note barred on the 1st and 6th strings.

**A MAJOR**     7/1 ▶

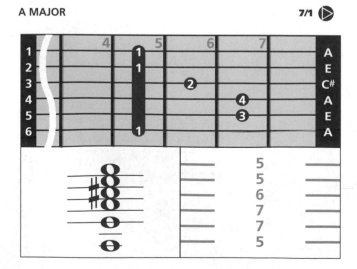

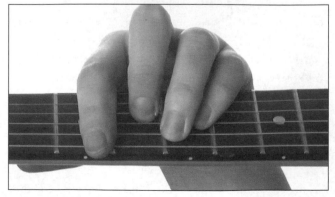

## EXTENDING THE E-SHAPED BARRE

As you have seen on the previous pages, the basic major and minor chords can be "extended" to produce a rich array of alternative sounds. It is also possible to extend barre chords, although in some of the more complex cases you may run out of fingers which may mean that one or more of strings should not be played. Six of the most common extensions are shown below. In all cases they are shown in the key of G, and the barre is held on the 3rd fret.

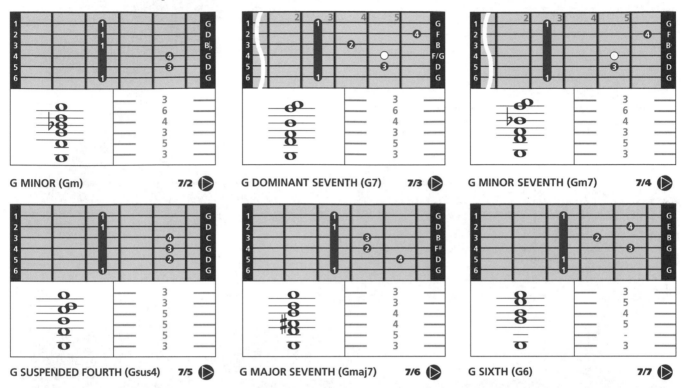

**G MINOR (Gm)**    **7/2** ▶

**G DOMINANT SEVENTH (G7)**    **7/3** ▶

**G MINOR SEVENTH (Gm7)**    **7/4** ▶

**G SUSPENDED FOURTH (Gsus4)**    **7/5** ▶

**G MAJOR SEVENTH (Gmaj7)**    **7/6** ▶

**G SIXTH (G6)**    **7/7** ▶

### BREAKING THE RULES

The "correct" left-hand posture for the E-shape barre shown above gives you maximum flexibility to switch between playing chords and single notes. However, some guitarists can also be seen using an alternative technique; this uses the index finger to barre the top two strings, but has the thumb stretched around the back of the next to fret the 6th string.

Most tutors would consider this to be pretty poor form. However, more creatively-minded people may well take a more lenient attitude. It may make changing chord shapes a little more difficult, but it does allow for the alteration of muting of the 6th string. Also, if your fingerspan is wide enough, you may also be able to reach over to fret the 5th string.

Frankly, the view put forward in this book is that anything goes: if you really think your guitar playing might sound more effective by, for example, rubbing sandpaper up and down the fingerboard, then it's probably worth giving it a try (that's not a recommendation, by the way).

As in many areas of life, progress is often made by those who are prepared to rethink the rules. This is by no means inverted snobbery. Although the classical system provides everything you need to become a good guitarist, if you find other approaches that may be worthwhile, then you should at least try them out.

# OTHER TYPES OF BARRE

## A-SHAPE BARRE CHORDS

Barre chords can also be built using the open-string A major chord shape. Extensions are shown underneath.

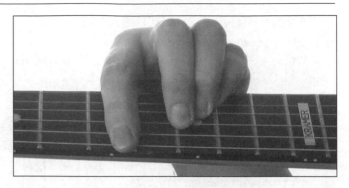

• Form an open-string A major chord using the 2nd, 3rd, and 4th fingers to fret the 4th, 3rd, and 2nd strings respectively.
• Slide your left hand seven frets along the fingerboard, so that the 9th fret is being held on the 4th, 3rd, and 2nd strings.
• Place the index finger firmly behind the 7th fret. Now play across all six strings of the chord. This is an E major played using an A-shaped barre on the 7th fret.

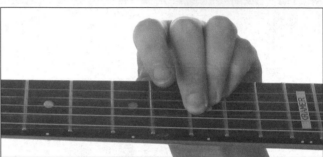

**E MAJOR** 7/8

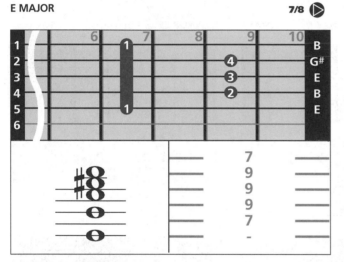

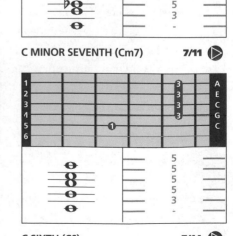

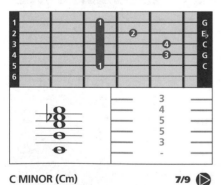
**C MINOR (Cm)** 7/9

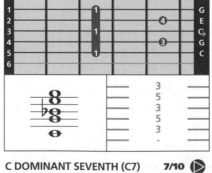
**C DOMINANT SEVENTH (C7)** 7/10

**C MINOR SEVENTH (Cm7)** 7/11

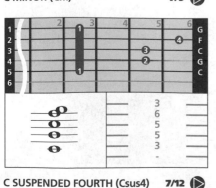
**C SUSPENDED FOURTH (Csus4)** 7/12

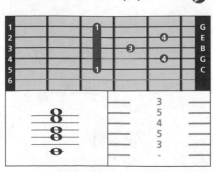
**C MAJOR SEVENTH (Cmaj7)** 7/13

**C SIXTH (C6)** 7/14

## ALTERNATIVE A-SHAPE BARRE

When playing an A-shape barre chord, many modern players find it more convenient to play a kind of double-barre, using the 3rd finger to cover the 2nd, 3rd, and 4th strings. This technique is highly effective, as long as you ensure that the tip of the 3rd finger is bent back at a sufficiently obtuse angle so that the 1st string is not accidentally muted. Alternatively, you can simply not play the 1st string, although that may be tricky if you are strumming.

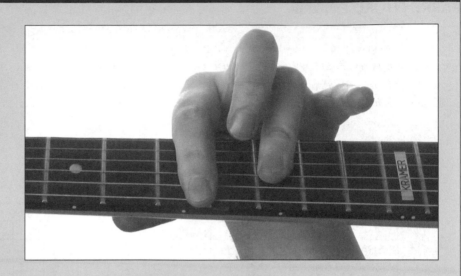

## C-SHAPES AND G-SHAPES

To form the C-shaped barre, play an open C major chord with the 2nd, 3rd, and 4th fingers playing the 2nd, 4th, and 5th strings respectively. Now slide the fingers four frets along the fingerboard and place the index finger behind the 4th fret. This produces an E major chord.

The C-shaped barre places considerable strain on the little finger—it not only has a sizeable stretch, but also has to fret a bass note, which, being of a higher gauge, requires more pressure to hold it down against the fret. As such, practicing the C-shaped barre can help you to strengthen the little finger considerably.

The G-shaped barre is perhaps the least commonly used open-string shape. Because of what would be an unfeasible stretch between the 2nd, 3rd, and 4th fingers, it is not possible to play a complete open-G chord on the barre. Therefore, the 1st string is not used.

Form a partial open-G major chord using the 3rd and 4th fingers to fret the 5th and 6th strings. Slide your hand five frets along and place the index finger behind the 5th fret. This creates a C major chord.

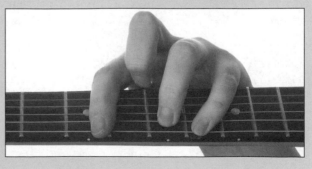

# THE BARRE CHORD FINDER

## BARRE CHORD FINDER

The chart below gives you an at-a-glance reference for playing chord types in any key using the four barre shapes outlined on the previous four pages. The numbers along the top row indicate the fret on which the index finger is positioned to create the barre. The individual cells in each of the four subsequent rows tell you the key of the chords produced by using the various barre shapes. For example, if you want to play A-shaped barre chords in the key of G, look along the second row until you reach the key of G—if you follow the column up to the top row you will see that the barre must be placed on the 10th fret.

With a reasonable knowledge of the notes on the fingerboard, the positioning of the barre for E and A shapes will become second nature—they simply follow the notes of the 6th and 5th strings respectively.

| | OPEN STRING | FRET ON WHICH BARRE SHOULD BE POSITIONED | | | | | | | | | | | |
| --- | --- | --- | --- | --- | --- | --- | --- | --- | --- | --- | --- | --- | --- |
| | | 1 | 2 | 3 | 4 | 5 | 6 | 7 | 8 | 9 | 10 | 11 | 12 |
| E-SHAPED BARRE | E | F | F♯ | G | A♭ | A | B♭ | B | C | C♯ | D | E♭ | E |
| A-SHAPED BARRE | A | B♭ | B | C | C♯ | D | E♭ | E | F | F♯ | G | A♭ | A |
| C-SHAPED BARRE | C | C♯ | D | E♭ | E | F | F♯ | G | A♭ | A | B♭ | B | C |
| G-SHAPED BARRE | G | A♭ | A | B♭ | B | C | C♯ | D | E♭ | E | F | F♯ | G |

## INVERTING CHORDS

By now it will be apparent to you that that the same chords can be played using a wide variety of different finger positions. Reorganizing the register in which one or more of the notes appears (raising or lowering the pitch by an octave) can make the same set of chords played on any instrument sound very different. Play through the exercise shown below, which consists of an open C major chord played as three major triads. Listen to the difference between the three chords.

Each of the chords in the exercise is made up of the notes C, E, and G, hence they are all C major chords.

However, the second and third chords differ in that the lowest pitched notes in either triad are not the root note (C). This principle is known as "inversion." The second chord, whose lowest note is E, is known as a "first inversion." The third chord, whose lowest note is G, is known as a "second inversion."

However, inverting chords on a guitar (or guitar-related instrument) is uniquely complicated by the fact that the same note can be played on different strings. In fact, if your guitar has a two-octave fingerboard, the note E played on the open 1st string can be played on *every* other string. Therefore the choice you have at your disposal is made even greater (and more complex).

Mastering the use of inverted chords is one of the unsung arts of arranging music for the guitar. It really is worth spending time experimenting in this area, especially if you want to write or arrange your own material.

## BARRE PROGRESSIONS

One way of forming an understanding of chord inversions and, at the same time, getting to grips with the different barre shapes is to practice the barre-chord progression exercise shown at the top of the page on the right.

The exercise uses a simple sequence of two alternating chords (E major and

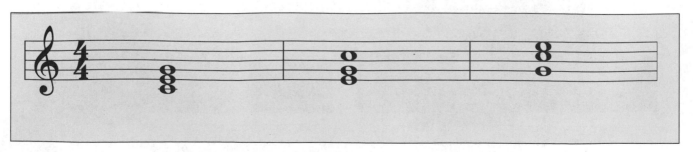

D major), all of which are played using each of the four barre shapes shown on the previous four pages: the E-shape is used in bars one and two; the G-shape in bars three and four; the A-shape in bars five and six; and the C-shape in bars seven and eight. Once you have mastered this exercise you can try a more demanding alternative by using the same chord types with different extensions—for example, try it out using minor voicings and then with sevenths.

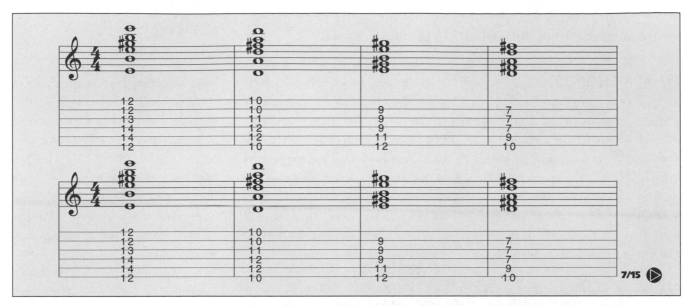

**7/15**

## USING A CAPO

There is no question that for all but the most accomplished guitarists, the tonal difference between playing barre chords and open-string chords can be noticeable. On some kinds of instrument—12-string guitars, for example—barre chords often just don't sound as good. This is largely a result of the index finger failing to exert pressure evenly across the fingerboard, which ends up with some strings partially muted. To overcome this problem, some players use a mechanical device called a capo, which fits around the neck, effectively creating a new zero fret at a different position on the fingerboard. This allows the open-string chords with which you should now be familiar to be played in different keys.

In the photograph below, the capo is fitted behind the 4th fret. The basic open-string fingering now produces the following chords:

| Open String | 4th-fret root |
|---|---|
| Open E major | G♯ major |
| Open A major | C♯ major |
| Open D major | F♯ major |
| Open C major | E major |
| Open G major | B major |

If you use a capo, take care when you fit it around the neck. If it's too tight, it may detune the guitar or damage the strings; if it's too loose, the strings will be able to move across the fret, which is likely to result in an unpleasant scraping noise each time you strum a chord.

Although some musicians may look down on the capo, it is a cheap and useful addition to the guitarist's tool bag—and it can be worth its weight in gold during a long, arduous recording session, where your index finger feels as if it's about to drop off.

# THE ROOT AND THE PERFECT FIFTH

Technically speaking, for a chord to be termed as such, it must contain at least three notes. However, for many years, especially in the field of blues and rock, guitarists have been using "chords" based around only two notes—a pairing of the root with the perfect fifth. Irrespective of whether you refer to these groupings of notes as chords, or use the technically correct terminology and call them "intervals," they have a good deal of useful applications in modern music.

## POWER CHORDS

Chords formed around the root and an interval of a perfect fifth are sometimes known as "fives," "fifths," or simply "power chords." They are very widely used, and can be highly effective.

What makes these chord types particularly problematic for theorists is that they are tonally ambiguous. If you consider the characteristics of a major and minor triad, the fundamental differences revolve around the second note—whether the chord contains a major 2nd or a minor 2nd in this context wholly defines the chord either as a major or a minor. The "five" chord has only the first and third notes of the triad, which could allow both major and minor scales in the same key to be played over the chord. Alternatively, in a group setting, the major 2nd or minor 2nd notes could be played on a different instrument, thereby creating the full triadic effect.

This type of chord is particularly popular in heavy metal and rock precisely because of its simplicity. When played through a heavily distorted amplifier, or using heavy effect processing, "five" chords tend to retain their character and emphasize the harmonious nature of the two closely related notes.

### IMPLIED HARMONIES

In most cases, accompanying instruments or vocals render the chords implicitly "major" in tone. However, if the guitarist were to add the major 2nd, creating the full major triad, the result would sometimes be to "muddy" the overall sound, reducing the "cutting" nature of the guitar chords.

## FROM THE BARRE TO THE FIVE CHORD

Five chords are extremely easy to play—indeed, the simplest examples are those based around the E- and A-shaped barre forms. To get the full effect, try the following examples using both clean and heavily distorted sounds.

### EXAMPLE 1

In the first example shown below, the fingering is taken from a standard E-major barre chord shape. However, in this instance you only need to play the bottom three strings. The chords are A, C, B, and D, and are formed by placing the barres on the 5th, 8th, 7th, and 10th frets respectively.

### EXAMPLE 2

The example at the foot of the page uses the fingering for both an A-shaped barre and an E-shaped barre. Remember that you should only play the 3rd, 4th, and 5th strings when playing the A-shape, so take care to mute the other strings or else you are likely to saddle yourself with unwanted noise.

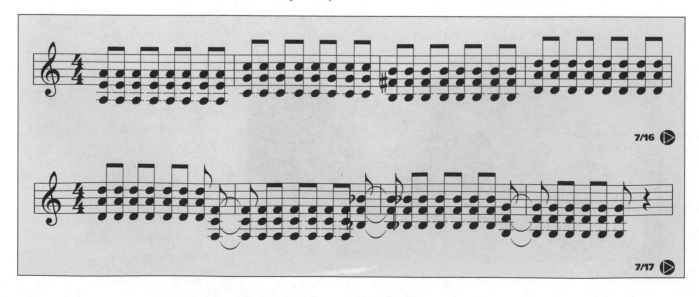

7/16

7/17

## FORMING A SIX-STRING "FIVE" CHORD

Full six-string "open" versions of these five chords can also be created. On the right you can see chord diagrams for the keys of E and A. The example shown below illustrates how these two chords can be used in practice.

### DOUBLING UP

With two different notes played across six strings, some of the notes will be doubled up. If you find the sound this creates attractive, you will probably find the section on alternate tunings (see pages 130–133) of further interest. Similarly, you may also find it worthwhile experimenting with 12-string guitars.

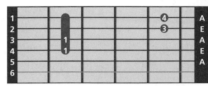 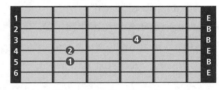

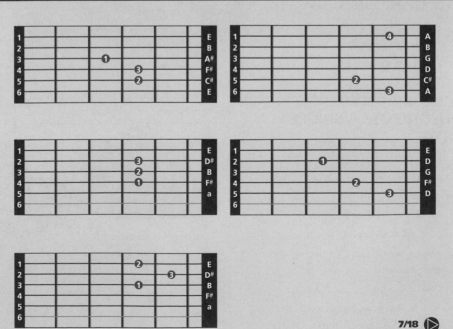

**PLAYING WITH OPEN-STRING CHORD SHAPES**

The final piece in this section is perhaps slightly tangential to the subject of barre chords, but it's included because it nonetheless looks at a different approach to manipulating the basic open-string chord shapes. Here we will be taking the basic finger position and moving it along the fingerboard—rather like playing the barre chord but leaving the barre off. This can allow you to create some interesting new chordal effects, most of which rarely find their way into standard chord books, but which you hear often enough on well-known recordings.

7/18

# LEAD GUITAR EFFECTS    Lesson 8

For many guitarists, playing a solo is the most glamorous aspect of the instrument, giving even the most modest, self-deprecating player a chance to step into the limelight. One way or another, lead playing comes down manipulating scales, although this needn't be restricted to a succession of cleanly played single notes. There are many playing effects, such as hammering, pulling, string bending, or vibrato, which can give a distinctive quality to your playing, or allow you greater freedom of expression and "feel."

## HAMMERING-ON AND PULLING-OFF

The "hammer-on"—or "ligado" as it is called in the classical world—is used in every form of guitar music. It is produced by moving a left-hand finger to another fret further along the fingerboard on the same string, while that string is playing, hence sounding a higher note. It is shown in written music as two notes joined by a slur with the letter "H" placed alongside.

The reverse of the hammer-on is known as a "pull-off"—or "descending ligado." This effect is produced by playing a fretted note and releasing the left-hand finger to sound a lower note. This is shown in written music in a similar way to the hammer-on, only the letter "P" is used instead.

Hammering and pulling techniques can be used effectively for playing both single notes or chords.

## HAMMERING A SINGLE NOTE

You can try out the hammer-on by following the steps shown below.

- Position your 1st finger on the 5th fret of the 3rd string—this is the note C.
- Play the note.
- While the note is still ringing, position the 3rd finger on the 7th fret of the 3rd string—the note D.
- Let the note sustain.

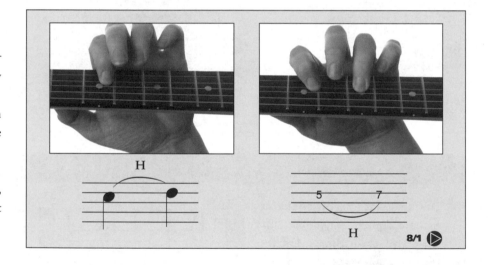

## PULLING OFF A SINGLE NOTE

This example shows you how to execute the pull-off.

- Place the 4th finger on the 10th fret of the 6th string—this is the note D.
- Place the 1st finger on the 7th fret of the 6th string—the note B.
- Play the note.
- While it is ringing, release the 4th finger, allowing the B to sustain.

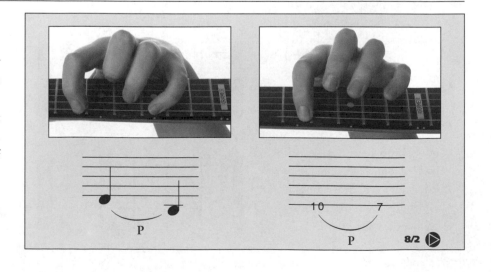

## HAMMERING AND PULLING EXERCISES

The three exercises shown below will get your fingers working across the full width of the fretboard. It is important to master these two effects—they are a central part of ALL guitar playing. Pay careful attention to the letters "H" and "P" on the written music. Also remember the one-finger-per-fret rule—for example, in the first exercise the 1st finger plays ALL the notes on the 5th fret of EVERY string.

# HAMMERING CHORDS

The hammering and pulling technique shown on the previous two pages can also be applied to chords. This often takes the form of using an incomplete open-string chord along the fingerboard. One technique, for example, is to barre the 2nd, 3rd, and 4th strings—forming a partial A-shaped barre—with the 1st finger. A second barre can then be hammered-on with the 3rd finger, two frets along the fingerboard, or, more demandingly, with the 4th finger three frets along.

Here is an example for you to try out for yourself:

- Position the barre on the 7th fret with the 1st finger.

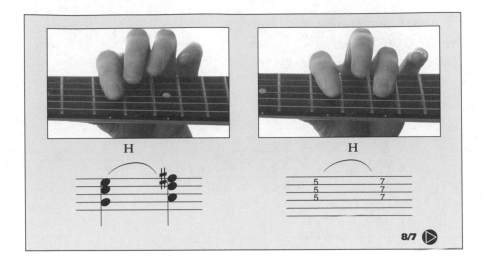

- Play ONLY the 2nd, 3rd, and 4th strings with the right hand—this chord is a D major triad.

- Hammer-on a barre on the 9th fret with the 3rd finger—this is the chord E major.

---

## STEVE VAI

Born: June 6, 1960, Brooklyn, New York, USA

Guitars: Ibanez Jem; Ibanez Universe; Fender Stratocaster

Amplification and Effects: Marshall and Eventide

Recorded Highlights: *Eat 'em and Smile* (1986) (by David Lee Roth); *Passion and Warfare* (1990); *Sex and Religion* (1993)

If there is one man who embodies the art of the modern lead guitarist it is Steve Vai.

Born in Brooklyn, New York in 1960, Vai first played the guitar at the age of 14. His earliest influences included the likes of John Lee Hooker, Led Zeppelin, Jimi Hendrix, Roy Buchanan, and Carlos Santana. A phenomenal student, Vai entered the prestigious Berklee School of Music, where he met teacher and performer Joe Satriani.

Vai first made his mark in the late 1970s as second guitarist in the Frank Zappa band, a perfect home for such a disciplined musician—Vai has in the past applied himself to a rigorous 10-hour daily practice regime. Zappa clearly made an impact as Vai's mid-1980s debut album—the home-recorded *Flex-able*—contains some of the most intricate rock guitar work heard in years.

Vai has also worked widely in the mainstream rock arena, having replaced Yngwie Malmsteen in Alcatrazz, and played with Van Halen's Dave Lee Roth and Whitesnake. His ascension to the status of guitar god became official with the award-winning and technically stunning *Passion and Warfare* album. He followed this up three years later with the more restrained *Sex and Religion*.

Although many younger guitar players worship Vai's undoubted abilities, others are turned off by what sometimes can seem like technique-heavy noodling.

Vai has also actively involved himself in the development of new instruments, helping to design the successful Jem and Universe models for Ibanez. These are highly playable "rock" guitars with a two-octave fretboard and scalloped fingerboard beyond the 20th fret. The seven-string Universe adds a bottom string, which is usually tuned to B. This type of instrument has yet to catch on.

## HAMMERING EXERCISE

Try playing this chord-hammering exercise. The starting position uses an index-finger barre on the 3rd fret. In the first bar, the first movement hammers-on what seems to be an open A minor chord shape, but is in fact an inversion of E♭. This is a commonly used progression in rock music.

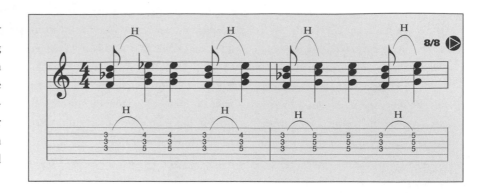

## STRING BENDING

One of the most basic yet effective techniques used by electric guitarists comes from bending the strings. This is usually achieved by playing a note and then bending the string to alter the pitch. It can also be produced mechanically if you have a tremolo arm fitted to your instrument. Originally developed by blues and country players to mimic the sound of a bottleneck guitar or, much later, pedal steel guitar, string bending has become a central part of modern guitar playing, where it can provide greater texture to the sound as well as an added emotional dimension. String bending can also be achieved on steel-string acoustic guitars, but its use is extremely limited on classical or flamenco instruments.

The principal factor which will govern the degree to which you can bend a string is its thickness or "gauge." If your guitar uses light-gauge strings—where the 1st string is no more than 0.10 inches thick (string gauges are always referred to in inches)—the pitch of a note can be altered by at least a step (tone). On the other hand, the heaviest-gauge, or nylon strings may make it almost impossible to reach even a semitone. The treble strings are the most commonly used for bending.

## BENDING A SINGLE NOTE

In this exercise you will play the note F on the 2nd string and bend it up to a G on the same string.

- Play the 6th fret of the 2nd string with your 3rd finger.
- Sound the string with your right hand.
- While the note is sustaining, pull the string downwards until the pitch increases by a whole tone.

- You should now be playing the note G.

At first it may be difficult to stop bending at the correct pitch, but this will come with practice. In fact, in some styles of playing a pitch-perfect bend is not even strictly necessary, or even appropriate—a slight flattening of the second note can be effective in blues-oriented playing. Take care, however, not to push the string too far, otherwise you will make the note sharp.

As an alternative, it is also possible to bend the string by pushing upwards rather than pulling downwards. Which technique you use is is largely a matter of personal preference, although if you bend the top two strings upwards, your fretting fingers can easily slip off the fingerboard. Some players find it easiest to pull the treble strings and push the bass strings. If you try out both methods, you will soon discover which feels the most comfortable.

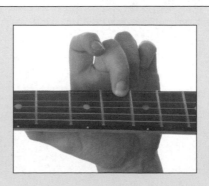

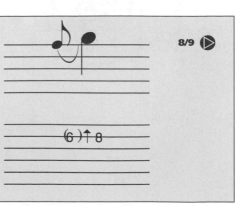

# BENDING WITH A SECOND STRING

The basic bending techniques shown on the previous page can be made even more interesting by playing to, or with, a second string.

A common rock and blues lead guitar cliché—which is nonetheless highly effective—is to bend a note on one string up to the same note played on an adjacent string. The purpose of the exercise shown below is to bend a D to an E, and while that note is still ringing to play an E on an adjacent string. The key to mastering this technique is to have the correct fingering for the second note in place before you actually start to play the first note.

- Place the 1st finger on the 5th fret of the 2nd string (E), and the 3rd finger on the 7th fret of the 3rd string (D).
- Strike the 3rd string and bend the note up by a step (tone).
- While that note is still ringing, play the 2nd string, allowing the two notes to sound together.

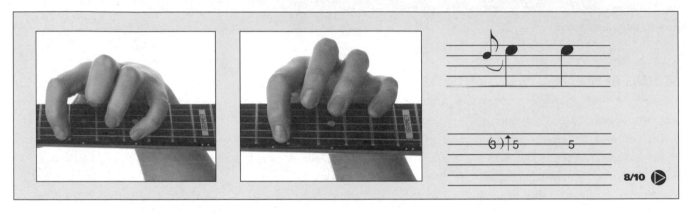

## TWO NOTES BENDING INTO ONE

A variation on the technique shown above is to play the two notes together and then bend the 3rd string. This brings the pitch of the two strings together and produces the same note.

The following exercise will help to get your fingers working and also get you accustomed to bending to the correct pitch. This is a C major scale played by moving the hand along the same two strings (2nd and 3rd) and bending the notes together.

### PROBLEMATIC INTERVALS

Using the 2nd the 3rd strings in this way is a relatively straightforward matter. The interval of a major 3rd between the two strings means that, using the one-finger-per-fret rule, the 3rd string can be bent by the 3rd finger (the original notes are two frets apart).

For other adjacent string combinations, however, the original notes will be three frets apart, meaning that the bend has to be made by the 4th finger—which is considerably more demanding.

String-bending techniques like these are especially effective when played with a distorted sound, where the inevitable variation of pitch can create interesting textures. The effect can be exaggerated by adding vibrato (see page 87).

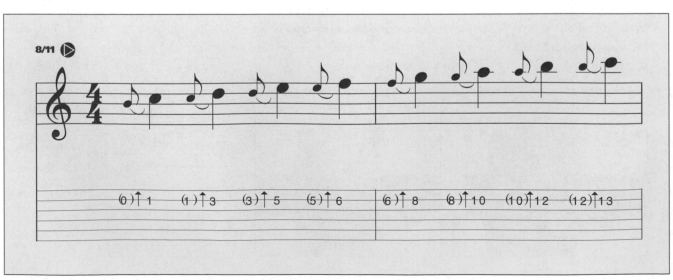

## "PRE-BENDING" THE STRINGS

It is also possible to bend a string to play a note which is LOWER in pitch than the starting note. To do this, the string needs to be bent into position before being struck; when you sound the string, the tension is released, bringing the string back to its natural position.

- Place your 3rd finger on the 7th fret of the 3rd string (the note D), and push the string upwards. As an alternative, you can pull it downwards if you prefer.
- Hold the finger in position and play the note with a plectrum.
- While the note is still ringing slowly release the string allowing it to rest at its natural position.

Because you are not able to hear the first note to judge whether it is at the correct pitch before you strike the string, the pre-bending technique will require considerable practice before you can play accurately. It is also requires a good knowledge of your own instrument—different string brands, gauges and materials will all have an impact on how strings behave when they are bent.

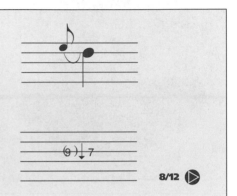

## NOTATING BENDS

The examples demonstrated on the previous few pages show you some of the different ways in which bends are notated in written music.

On the staff the bend is shown as two notes joined together by a line known as a "slur." You will notice that the first of the two notes is much smaller than the second note. This is known as an "appoggiatura," and can be very confusing for beginners struggling to count out note values within a bar.

The main point to remember is that the duration value of the appoggiatura is NOT counted within the bar. As far as bending notes are concerned, it simply indicates the starting pitch. It is the value of the second note that governs the overall duration of the note from the start of the bend to the finish, although the appoggiatura can be seen as "eating into" the value of the second note.

### PRACTICING BENDS

Like every other aspect of playing the guitar, the capacity to bend notes with accuracy will come with practice.

One of the main difficulties is that string bending is often executed at great speed, so in practice rather than being able to listen and modify what you are doing at the time, your fingers almost instinctively need to "know" how far they should go to reach the correct note.

To help you to get a feel for how far your fingers need to push or pull to achieve an accurate bend, here is a useful exercise to try out. You can develop your own variations on this idea and incorporate it into your regular practice regime.

- Play the D on the 7th fret of the 3rd string.
- Bend the string in either direction until it sounds the note E♭.
- Now release the tension

taking the string back until it reaches its original position.

- With the note still ringing, bend the string until it sounds the note E.
- Release the tension, taking the string back to its natural position.
- Alternate between intervals of a half-step and step until the string stops sounding.

# MULTIPLE STRING BENDS

A further interesting set of techniques involves the use of bending more than one string, or one or more of the notes of a chord. Like bending to a second note (see page 85), these playing effects often make use of the 2nd and 3rd strings, where there is a convenient interval of a major 3rd between the two strings. Try out the exercise shown below.

- Place the 3rd finger on the 7th fret of the 3rd string and the 4th finger on the 7th fret of the 4th string.
- Play both notes simultaneously.
- Push both strings downwards while the notes are still ringing.

An alternative approach is to barre the 2nd and 3rd strings with the 3rd finger and push the barre downwards. Using either method, it is hard to control the pitch of both strings accurately. In the example, you bend the 3rd string by a step (tone) and the second string by a half-step (semitone). This is more common than bending both strings by an equal pitch—because of string gauges, bending each string by the same amount will not alter the pitch to exactly the same degree.

## BENDING CHORDS

Bending one or more notes of a chord can provide an interesting country flavor to a solo. The example below is based around fretting the three treble strings of an E-shape chord. In this case, the second note of the chord is bent from a major 2nd up to the major 3rd to create the chord.

- Place the 2nd finger on the 9th fret of the 3rd string.
- Place the 3rd finger on the 10th fret of the 2nd string.
- Place the 4th finger on the 10th fret of the 2nd string.

- Sound the three strings together.
- Bend the 3rd string so that it increases in pitch by a tone.

You could, of course, play this position using the first three fingers—you would probably find it easier to play in this way. However, allowing the 1st finger to "float" above the action will make it easier to integrate this style of playing with using barre chords.

A mechanism which can help to create the same kind of sounds, and found favor with country-rock guitarists of the 1970s, was the Parsons-White system. More often than not fitted to a Fender Telecaster, the 1st and 2nd strings were connected by a strong spring mechanism to the strap buttons. When fitted, it is possible to push the body of the guitar downwards at either end of the strap causing the the pitch of either string to be altered. Although the system is highly effective—especially for imitating pedal steel sounds—it does require the guitar to undergo considerable cosmetic surgery, which is probably not advisable on a vintage instrument.

Another pitch-altering technique which is only possible on guitars without locking nut systems is to press on the treble strings behind the nut. The effectiveness of this technique varies from guitar to guitar.

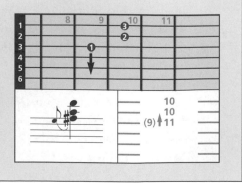

## TREMOLO ARMS

The tremolo arm was developed during the 1940s to produce vibrato effects. At some point during the 1950s the term "tremolo" was applied to these mechanisms, a name which, although technically incorrect, seems to have stuck (although some pedants still insist on calling them vibrato arms).

During the late 1950s, guitarists like Dick Dale, Duane Eddy, and Hank Marvin began integrated them into their playing styles. During the following decade, some guitarists saw the potential to perform string bends that would be impossible to achieve using conventional means.

The original designs produced by Fender and Bigsby were barely changed over the next 30 years. However, tuning problems were common on even the best models, a fact that led, in the 1980s, to the development of the modern locking tremolo, designed by guitarist Floyd Rose.

His system allows strings to be detuned to the point of laying slack on the fingerboard before being brought back to perfect pitch. It has proved to be so effective that every major guitar manufacturer now uses a variation on the Floyd Rose tremolo arm.

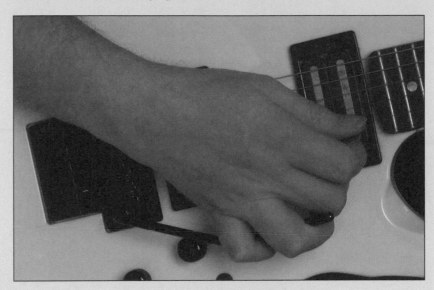

## VIBRATO

One of the most effective and expressive single-note playing devices is "vibrato." Used on all types of stringed instruments, vibrato is a sound created by invoking slight variations in pitch either side of a note. Indeed the word comes from the Latin verb *vibrare*, which literally means "to shake." The effect can be used to intensify the impact of the music.

Vibrato can be executed on the guitar in several different ways. The classical technique, which is also used in many other types of music, sees the finger "rocking" back and forth along the string. The movement of the hand is extremely slight, amounting to little more than a vibration, consequently the variation in pitch is barely perceptible. Alternatively, there are some musicians who prefer to create a fuller-sounding vibrato by moving across rather than along the string. This amounts to a very gentle form of string bending.

### CLASSICAL VIBRATO TECHNIQUE

The example below shows a vibrato effect played on the note D on the 5th fret of the 6th string. Note that the movement comes not from the fingers themselves, but from the entire wrist action. In contrast, when playing vibrato by bending the string, the motion comes entirely from the finger.

The terms vibrato and tremolo are often used interchangeably. This is incorrect, but probably came about during the 18th century, when the latter became widely used to described left-hand vibrato effects on the violin. Although technically a rapidly repeated succession of notes, in practice, tremolo often refers to an exaggerated vibrato.

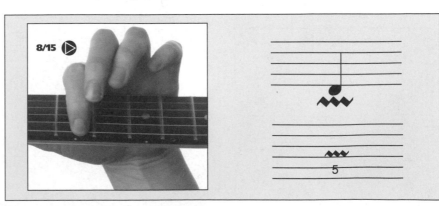

# SLIDES

The term "slide" refers to running one or more of the fingers of the left hand along the length of a string, thereby altering the pitch. There are a number of different types of commonly used slide, all of which produce their own distinct effects. It can also refer to a separate style of guitar playing, which uses a glass or metal tube fitted over one of the fingers of the left hand to achieve the same kind of effect.

The four examples shown below all move between the 3rd and 10th frets of the 1st string—these are the notes G and D. You should also pay special attention to the different ways in which each type of slide is shown in written music. Note that written music doesn't differentiate between using your fingers or using a glass bottleneck to slide—the musical effect is the same.

## SLIDING BETWEEN NOTES

For the most commonly used type of slide, position the 1st finger on the 3rd fret of the 1st string and play the note. While it is still ringing, slide the 1st finger up to the 10th fret. Make sure that you keep the pressure consistent throughout—as with all types of slide, if you release the pressure from the string while you move your hand it will dampen or mute the sound.

## SLIDING TO A STRUCK NOTE

This is essentially the same as the previous exercise, only this time when your 1st finger reaches the 10th fret you should play the note again with the pick. The difference is shown in the written music by the removal of the tie symbol joing the two notes.

## OPEN SLIDE TO A NOTE

It is also possible to make an "indeterminate" slide to or from a note. In this example, place the 1st finger on the 3rd fret of the 1st string. Quickly move your left hand along the fingerboard, but DON'T play the string with your right hand until you reach the 10th fret.

## OPEN SLIDE FROM A NOTE

You can do the same operation in reverse. Place your 1st finger on the 3rd fret of the 1st string and play the note. Move your left hand along the fingerboard, gradually releasing pressure as you go. The sound should gradually fade away, but not on any note in particular.

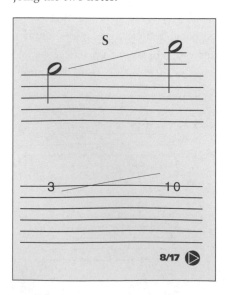

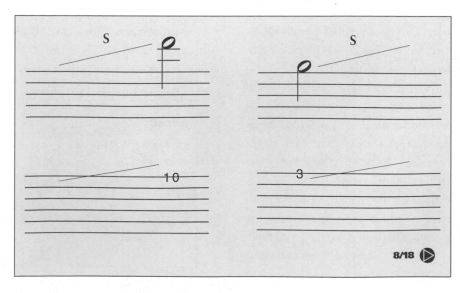

## TRILLS

The trill is a very fast form of hammering and pulling between two different notes. It can be shown in written music in a number of ways (indeed, for some curious reason, the subject of whether the starting note should be considered as the main note or the auxiliary seems to have engaged music scholars in passionate debate for many years). Trills are most commonly shown as a single movement, with the notes sounding almost "blurred" or indistinct. The example below moves between D and E on the 7th and 9th frets of the 3rd string.

- Position the 1st finger on the 7th fret of the 3rd string.
- Play the note and hammer-on the 9th fret with the 3rd finger.
- Immediately pull-off with the 3rd finger.
- Repeat the last two steps any number of times in quick succession.

---

### LEAD GUITAR TIPS

Armed with the scales you encountered between pages 56 and 63—which you have doubtless been learning dilligently—and the playing effects you've seen on the previous few pages, you should now be able to make some noises that sound at least a bit like lead guitar.

Here, then, are a few considerations for you to ponder on the subject of lead playing. Once again, it should be emphasized that there are no hard and fast rules in this territory—what sounds god-like to one set of ears may sound like a hideous row to another.

#### Use your ears
Listen to as many different guitarists as you can. Try to analyse and understand what they are doing, and (of greater importance, perhaps) WHY they are doing it. It's worth listening to soloists on other instruments, too. Pioneering jazz guitarist Charlie Christian's playing technique owed a great deal to saxophonist Lester Young.

#### Use your eyes
No two guitarists employ identical playing techniques. If you get the opportunity, try to WATCH a good guitarist in a live environment. Get as close to the action as you can, and study exactly what's being done.

#### Use your mouth
Without making a nuisance of yourself, if the moment seems right, why not try to talk to musicians you admire? There are players of all levels out there who eat, sleep, and breathe music. They will often be more than happy—even flattered—to pass on their advice to someone less experienced.

#### Use your hands
A worthwhile piece of soloing ought to be more than an excuse to show off your masterful playing technique. Being able to play every scale imaginable in every key at a breakneck speed might be impressive, but unless you place it in an appropriate musical context it remains little more than a technical exercise. Oh, and there's a great deal more to playing with "feeling" than just bending a few strings and giving your audience a tortured grimace!

#### Use your brain
If music is about anything, it's COMMUNICATION. If you're playing with other musicians, listen to THEM as much as you listen to yourself. There are few things more satisfying for a musician than being a part of a group that enjoys playing together. At its best, the musicians operate as components of one enormous intelligence: at its least pleasant, it can become a group of egos battling for attention.

# SYNTHETIC SCALES

# Lesson 9

The diatonic scales that you have seen so far—that's the major and minor series—are by far the most widely used in most forms of music. However, there are a number of other scale types that are made up using different combinations of intervals from the twelve half step (semitone) steps that make up an octave. These are known as "synthetic" scales. The three most common synthetic scale types are pentatonic, augmented ("whole-tone"), and diminished. Pentatonic scales are very widely used in blues, jazz, and rock—in fact the minor pentatonic scale is sometimes known as the "blues" scale. There are many other scale types, many of which are found more commonly in ethnic musics from around the world. Experimenting with these alternative note combinations will help you to avoid continually drawing from the same resources. This will, in turn, enable you to create your own distinctive lead parts.

## PENTATONIC SCALES

Far and away the most widely used type of synthetic scale, pentatonic scales are among the oldest known. Variations have been found in the diverse ethnic musical cultures of Asia, Eastern Europe, the Far East, and Native America.

As the name suggests, pentatonic scales are built using a different five notes from the root to the octave. In Western music, the two most commonly found forms are the major and minor pentatonics. They are the most commonly heard non-diatonic scales, largely because of their strong melodic feel.

## ROCK, BLUES, AND THE PENTATONIC SCALES

Although pentatonic scales have been used in some 20th-century classical works, they are most widely known for their use in popular music forms, especially rock and blues. Indeed, there are numerous classic rock riffs from the past 30 years that have been derived from pentatonic scales. Famous examples include "Layla" by Derek and the Dominos, "Black Night" by Deep Purple or "Whole Lotta Love" by Led Zeppelin.

This is not to say that there are not numerous other uses for pentatonic scales—they are also widely used both in folk and country musical forms.

## THE MAJOR PENTATONIC

The major pentatonic scale draws from the same set of notes as a regular diatonic major scale, with the exception of two notes, which are omitted—these are the fourth and seventh notes of the scale.

With that in mind, the set of intervals that define the major pentatonic scale is as follows: **STEP•STEP•STEP+HALF STEP•STEP•STEP+HALF STEP**. In the key of C, the notes used are C, D, E, G, and A. As with all scales, this set of intervals can be transposed to every other key. The notes of the major pentatonic scale are shown below in the seven principal scales.

| A | • | B | • | C♯ | • | E | • | F♯ | • | A |
|---|---|---|---|----|---|---|---|----|---|---|
| B | • | C♯ | • | D♯ | • | F♯ | • | G♯ | • | B |
| C | • | D | • | E | • | G | • | A | • | B |
| D | • | E | • | F♯ | • | A | • | B | • | D |
| E | • | F♯ | • | G♯ | • | B | • | C♯ | • | E |
| F | • | G | • | A | • | C | • | D | • | F |
| G | • | A | • | B | • | D | • | E | • | G |

## PLAYING THE MAJOR PENTATONIC

To work through the major pentatonic scale, take a look at the fingering patterns shown below. They feature three alternative sets of positions, the first two of which start with the root note played on the 6th string. These extend a full two octaves across the width of the fingerboard. The third pattern (below, right) has the root positioned on the 5th string and covers a single octave. In each case, the scale is played in the key of C, and again in each case, the left-hand finger number is indicated on the diagram.

### SWITCHING TO OTHER KEYS

To play these major pentatonic patterns in other keys, all you have to do is chose a new root note along the fingerboard and move the pattern accordingly.

**ROOT ON THE 6TH STRING**

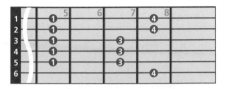

**ROOT ON THE 6TH STRING**

**ROOT ON THE 5TH STRING**

## THE MINOR PENTATONIC SCALE

The minor pentatonic scale uses the same notes as a natural minor scale, but leaves out the second and sixth notes. It is sometimes referred to as the "blues scale". The set of intervals is STEP+HALF STEP•STEP•STEP•STEP+HALF STEP•STEP. The notes for the seven main keys are shown on the right.

| A | • | C | • | D | • | E | • | G | • | A |
| B | • | D | • | E | • | F♯ | • | A | • | B |
| C | • | E♭ | • | F | • | G | • | B♭ | • | B |
| D | • | F | • | G | • | A | • | C | • | D |
| E | • | G | • | A | • | B | • | D | • | E |
| F | • | G♯ | • | A♯ | • | C | • | D♯ | • | F |
| G | • | B♭ | • | C | • | D | • | F | • | G |

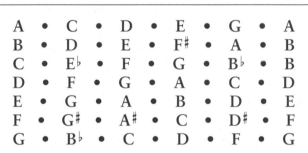

## PLAYING THE MINOR PENTATONIC

Once again, three alternative fingering patterns are shown below, this time for playing the minor pentatonic scale in the key of C. The first two patterns start with the root note on 6th string and extend over two octaves; the third pattern has the root positioned on the 5th string and plays through a single octave. Attaining a good understanding of the minor pentatonic scale is an absolute must for all aspiring blues guitarist—without that scale, it just wouldn't be the blues!

**ROOT ON THE 6TH STRING**

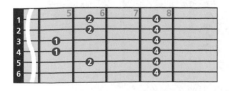

**ROOT ON THE 6TH STRING**

**ROOT ON THE 5TH STRING**

# AUGMENTED AND DIMINISHED SCALES

Although pentatonic scales have come to dominate blues and much of rock music, the augmented and diminished synthetic scales are also widely used in Western music. Melodies created using augmented scales often have a mysterious lilting or floating characteristic; diminished scales are more likely to be used used by jazz musicians than in other forms of popular music.

## AUGMENTED SCALE

The augmented scale is also known as "whole-tone" scale. This is because it moves from the the root to the octave over the course of six steps or tones. The pattern of intervals is therefore **STEP•STEP•STEP•STEP•STEP•STEP**.

Because of the nature of the intervals, the effect of the scale will sound the same whatever note you start from. Consequently, only two different combinations of notes are needed to play an augmented scale in any key. They are C-D-E-F♯-G♯-A♯ and C♯-D♯-F-G-A-B.

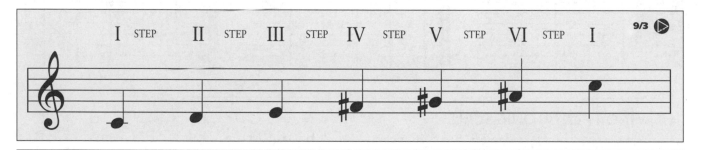

## PLAYING THE AUGMENTED SCALE

A fingering pattern for the augmented scale covering two octaves is shown on the right in the key of C. This position allows you play the scale in half of the possible keys. By shifting the pattern one fret along in either direction, you will be able to play the other half.

## DIMINISHED SCALE

The diminished scale moves from the root to the octave, using a pattern of eight separate intervals. They are: **STEP • HALF STEP • STEP • HALF STEP • STEP • HALF STEP • STEP • HALF STEP**. In the key of C this uses the notes C - D - E♭- F - Gb - G♯ - A - B. The diminished scale has four key centers based around the 1st, 3rd, 5th, and 7th notes. This means that a diminished scale in any key will share the same notes with three other keys. Therefore three scale patterns will cover all twelve keys.

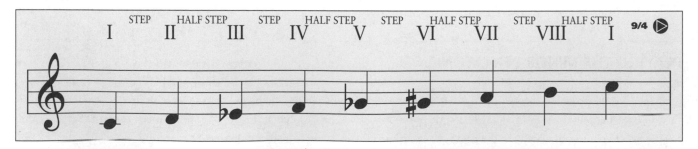

## PLAYING THE DIMINISHED SCALE

A fingering pattern for the diminished scale covering two octaves is shown on the right in the key of C. This position allows you play the scale in four possible keys. By shifting the pattern by either one or two frets in either direction, you will be able to play the eight keys.

## ETHNIC SCALES

These approximations of ethnic scales can be used to create a flavor of the cultures. In their original forms, many of the scales do not use chromatic tuning—that is, they do not necessarily conform to an octave comprising twelve equal parts. Consequently, when the scales are played correctly, they will often sound alien or even out of tune to Western ears.

**PELOG SCALE**     9/5

**INDIAN SCALE**     9/6

**HIRAJOSHI SCALE**     9/7

**KUMOI SCALE**     9/8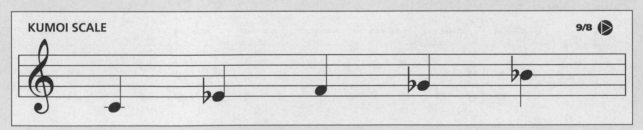

**NEAPOLITAN SCALE**     9/9

**HUNGARIAN SCALE**     9/10

# RHYTHM AND BLUES

**Blues music evolved out of the experience of Black Americans, whose ancestors were transported from their homes in Africa to work as slave labor in the American South. Combining with other folk forms brought to the continent by European migrants, by the beginning of the 20th century it had become a uniquely American folk form. Much of the music of the last 100 years has evolved directly from the blues.**

This exercises shown below aim to get you playing some simple blues guitar over the top of a backing track which you can hear in full on the CD. The structure of a blues song usually is based on a twelve-bar turnaround that uses chords on the first, fourth, and fifth degrees of the major scale. The I-IV-V structure usually follows the form shown in the diagram below. The backing track is played in the key of C, so the chords are C major, F major, and G major.

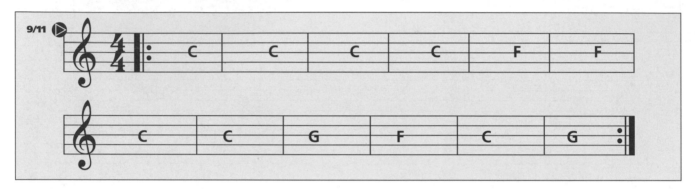

There are four options shown below, each new sequence a little tougher than the one before. In each case you are given two bars of music in C. To play on the other keys, simply move the root so that it starts on fret 13 for F or fret 15 for G, and play the same pattern of notes—alternatively you move across the strings, playing the patterns from frets 8 and 10 of the 5th string.

**1. BOOGIE SEQUENCE**

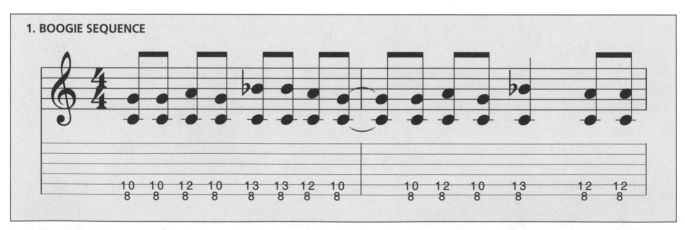

**2. SIMPLE MINOR PENTATONIC LEAD**

### 3. ALTERNATIVE MINOR PENTATONIC LEAD

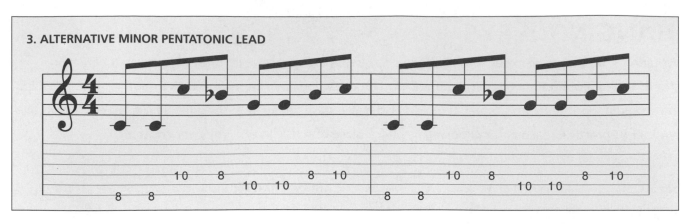

### 4. DOUBLE-SPEED PICKING

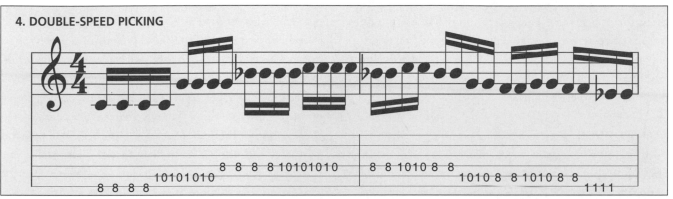

### B.B.KING

<u>Born:</u> 16th September, 1925, Itta Bena, Mississippi, USA (Riley King)
<u>Guitar:</u> Gibson ES-355 ("Lucille")
<u>Recorded Highlights:</u> *Live At The Regal* (1960); *King Of The Blues* (compilation)

Not only one of the greatest blues guitarists of all time, but in a career which has now lasted over half a century B.B.King is perhaps the single most famous blues artist of all time.

His legacy to the modern guitarist has been the extensive use he makes of string bending, both as a playing device and an alternative vibrato technique.

King's first break came in the late 1940s, when he was given a sponsorship on a black radio station in Memphis. Here he became known as the "Pepticom Blues Boy," a name which soon found itself shortened to

"blues boy" and finally just "B.B."

Signing for the RPM label in 1952, King made over 200 recordings over the next ten years, among them seminal electric blues compositions like "Woke Up This Morning" and "You Upset Me, Baby."

In spite of an impressive (and immense) body of recorded work, it is as a live performer that King truly comes to life, as he proved with *Live At The Regal*—perhaps one of the finest concert albums ever made.

During this period, the audience for blues music was largely restricted to Black Americans and the hipper young urban whites. However, in the early 1960s King and fellow blues players like Muddy Waters were surprised to find themselves the subject of veneration by a new young generation of white blues musicians: Eric Clapton, John Mayall,

Keith Richards, and Paul Bloomfield, all of whom started life imitating their heroes. Since that time, King has regularly found himself a muse for successive generations of musician, particularly those in search of that illusive "authenticity."

He found a new lease of life (and an even younger audience) in the late 1980s ,when he scored a hit with Irish band U2 on the track "When Love Comes To Town."

# CHANGING KEYS

# Lesson 10

Wouldn't it be easy if all music was written in one key—C major, for example? If you were only using chords based around the major scale, there wouldn't even be any sharps and flats to bother about. Whilst life would undoubtedly be simpler, it would also make music really dull—besides which, there are also a number of practical reasons for choosing to play a piece of music in one key over another.

The two most common musical terms you are likely to come across in conjunction with key changes are "transposition" and "modulation." You may sometimes come across people using these terms interchangeably, but they are wrong— these are two very distinct concepts. Transposition refers to playing the same piece of music in different keys, whereas modulation refers to a deliberate key change that takes place within a piece of music.

### TRANSPOSITION

There are several reasons why you might want to play the same piece of music in a different key, the most common of which is probably to accomodate a vocalist. Even the best singers have specific note ranges with which they are happiest working, or with which they feel they can give the best performance. Quite simply, if you want to get the best out of a vocalist, you should play in a key that is well suited to their voice.

You may also want to change keys to fit in when playing with other musicians, because using certain voicings on certain instruments can radically alter the mood of a piece of music. Cast your mind back to the exercise on barre chords (see pages 72–79), and remember the different ways that, say, a C major chord could sound, depending on which chord voicing you chose. Additionally, if you ever try arranging for a large ensemble, there are some instruments—especially reeds and brass—which are much harder to play in certain keys or registers.

### TRANSPOSING CHORDS

By now, you should have a reasonable basic understanding of the way in which intervals work—in particular, how the unique relationship between the 1st (I), 4th (IV), and 5th (V) degrees of a scale can be used to create chord progressions which sound harmonious and somehow "right" when played in conjunction with one another. Just as any scale is constructed using its own unique set of intervals, a set of chords can be built on each degree of a scale. Such patterns of chords are referred to as "scale tone" chords. Each of these chords can be given a Roman numeral associated with the degree of the scale on which it falls. The pattern of chords for the key of C major are as follows: C major (I), D minor (II), E minor (III), F major (IV), G major (V), A minor (VI), B diminished (VII), C major (I). Play the three sequences below which show the chords on the major scales in the keys C, F, and G.

The use of these scale degrees can also be used as a form of musical shorthand for playing chords, or notating a song structure. For example, a sequence which progresses from I through IV to V can be identified as a "I-IV-V" sequence. If the I chord is C major, you automatically know that the IV chord is F major, and the V chord is G major. If you become used to thinking in this way, you will gain a natural understanding of the way notes and chords sound in relation to one another. This will make it easier for you play any chord sequence in any key. This approach to notation is popular among jazz musicians, but is worth attention for whatever kind of music you play.

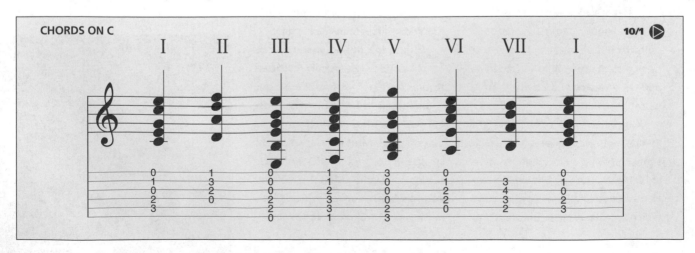

**CHORDS ON F**

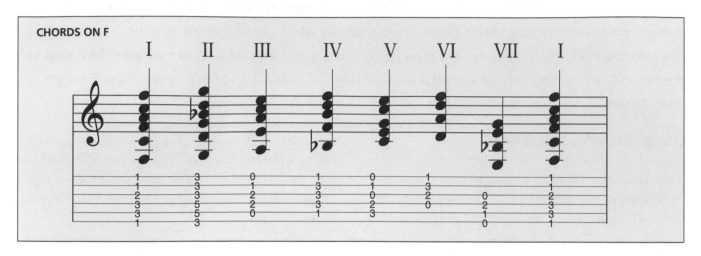

**CHORDS ON G**

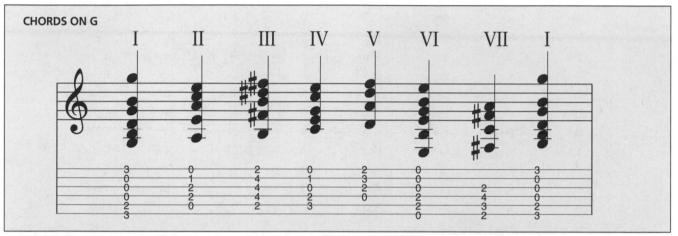

## TRANSPOSITION WITH A CAPO

The capo is a mechanical device which clamps around the guitar's fingerboard, creating a kind of "mobile nut" or zero fret. You've already seen how a capo can be used to create an artificial barre for playing open-string chords along the fingerboard (see page 78). The capo can also be extremely useful when you are transposing chord progressions. Take,

for example, a chord progression that moves from D major to A major, and then to E major, all played as open-string chords. If you wanted to transpose the sequence from D to G, by fixing a capo to the 5th fret, the same open-string voicings could be used to play the chords G major, D major, and A major.

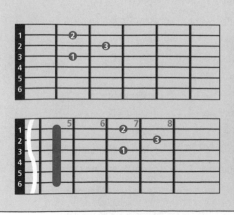

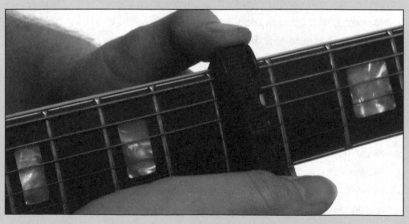

# SCALE DEGREES AND TRANSPOSITION

To transpose a sequence using scale degrees, you first need to write down the chords in terms of their Roman numeral equivalents. Take a simple chord sequence which goes C major–E minor–D minor–G major. The root chord is C major, therefore the progression could be termed "I-III-II-V." To transpose the chords to the key of G, you simply need to work out the chords on the 2nd, 3rd, and 5th degrees of the G major scale. Therefore, the new chord sequence is G major–B minor–A minor–D major.

## USING ROMAN NUMERALS

It should be noted that, in a practical sense, although the chord types built from each degree of the scale are musically correct in their use of major, minor, and diminished voicings, different extensions can also be used. Some people use an alternative method, where each scale degree is simply associated with a note name and NOT a chord type. In such cases, a II chord would automatically be a major chord—if a minor chord was required, this would be denoted as IIm.

| Key | I | II | III | IV | V | VI | VII |
|-----|-----|-----|-----|-----|-----|-----|-----|
| A | A | Bm | C#m | D | E | F#m | Gdim |
| B♭ | B♭ | Cm | Dm | E♭ | F | G | Adim |
| B | B | B♭m | E♭m | E | F# | G#m | A#dim |
| C | C | Dm | Em | F | G | Am | Bdim |
| C# | C# | D#m | Fm | F# | G# | A#m | Cdim |
| D | D | Em | F#m | G | A | Bm | C#dim |
| E♭ | E♭ | Fm | Gm | A♭ | B♭ | Cm | Ddim |
| E | E | F#m | G#m | A | B | C#m | D#din |
| F | F | Gm | Am | B♭ | C | Dm | Edim |
| F# | F# | G#m | A#m | B | C# | D# | Fdim |
| G | G | Am | Bm | C | D | Em | F#dim |
| A♭ | A♭ | B♭ | C | D♭ | Eb | F | Gdim |

By using the table above, you will be able to transpose chord sequences easily from one key into another.

## WEIRD STUFF

If you want to arrange music for other instruments, a facility for transposition is absolutely crucial—never more so than when dealing with brass and reed instruments. For a variety of mysterious and complex reasons, a middle C on some instruments is NOT the same note as concert pitch middle C. This may seem insane, but there are quite a few of these "transposing instruments." The trumpet, for example, transposes down a tone to B♭. Therefore, if you give a trumpet player a piece of music requiring an F to be played, the note you hear will be the equivalent of E♭ on a piano keyboard. If you want to hear concert pitch F, you must write down the note G on the trumpet player's score!

Technically speaking, the guitar is also a transposing instrument, in that music written for the instrument is an octave higher than it actually sounds. This can sometimes be indicated on the staff with a small "8" written below the treble clef. Instruments requiring transposition include:

| | |
|---|---|
| Trumpet | down to B♭ |
| Piccolo trumpet | up to D |
| Flugelhorn | down to B♭ |
| French horn | down to F |
| Cor Anglais (English horn) | down to F |
| Cornet | down to B♭ |
| Clarinet | down to B♭ |
| Soprano saxophone | down to B♭ |
| Alto saxophone | down to E♭ |
| Tenor saxophone | down over the octave to B♭ |
| Baritone saxophone | down over the octave to B♭ |

## CHORD CHARTS

In most forms of music outside of the classical domain, group arrangements are not always notated in full. This leaves the way clear for the players to interpret the music in the way they feel is most appropriate.

In the fields of rock, pop, and jazz, the most common mode of working is probably to use a chord chart. You've already seen how scale tone chords can be used to transpose chord sequences—this is in itself a form of chord chart. However, in practice, chord instructions are far less formal.

### OTHER SHORT CUTS

Chord charts can take many different forms—a scrap of paper with chord names scribbled down being perhaps the most basic (and not entirely uncommon) example. A slightly more sophisticated approach is to provide a time signature and a series of chord names written within the musical bars. Such chord charts are often written out on manuscript paper for convenience. These can be embellished with different types of standard musical notation, such as rests and repeat signs. Although some of these instructions can be rather confusing at first, they are worth getting to know—they can save untold time in the long run.

The simplest embellishment—and one that you have already encountered—is the bar repeat sign. This indicates start and end points surrounding a piece of music which must be repeated. There are also simple instructions for repeating chords and bars. Some of the most commonly found are shown below:

**REPEAT PREVIOUS CHORD WITHIN BAR**

**REPEAT PREVIOUS BAR**

Take a look at the four four-bar examples shown below—they are all showing the same information in differing degrees of complexity. The top line of bars gives the staff with the chord written out. The second line shows just the chord names, which are played on each beat of the bar. The third line shows how the stroke symbol can be used as an instruction to play the same chord as the last within the bar. The fourth line shows the bar repeat symbol, which instructs the player to repeat the previous bar exactly.

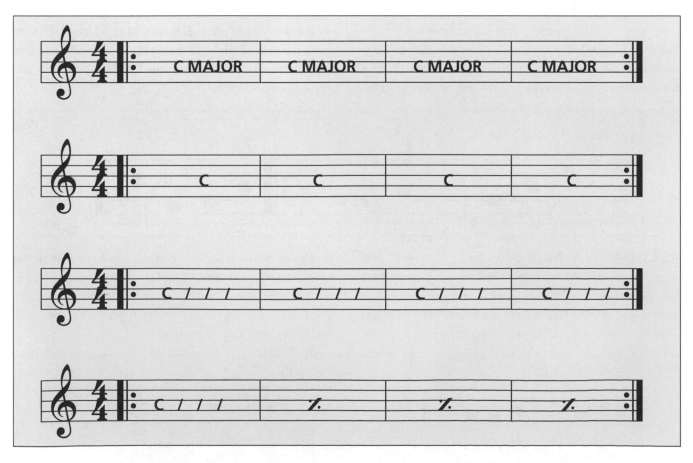

# OTHER REPEATS OR REITERATIONS

**Standard music notation makes allowances for the repetition of pretty well every eventuality. On this and the following page, you can see how these instructions can be used. As with the chord charts shown on the previous page, repeat instructions can be used either formally, or simply as a type of musical shorthand. However you intend to use them, they are well worth familiarizing yourself with, as they can save a good deal of time, both in notating and reading.**

## SEGMENT REPEATS

The "dal segno" and "da capo" symbols show both the start and end points within which a segment of music should be repeated.

Dal segno literally means "from the sign" in Italian. When the instruction "D.S. 𝄋 " appears at the end of a bar, below the staff, it is an instruction to return to a "segno" symbol (𝄋) that will have already been shown in an earlier bar.

Da capo literally means "from the head" in Italian. It is indicated by the symbol "D.C." When you see these letters printed at the end of a bar beneath the staff, it is an instruction to return to the beginning of the music, and begin playing through for a second time.

## ENDING SYMBOLS

The ending direction allows you to play through the same musical sequence, but using alternative ending bars. In the example below, you are instructed to play to the end of the section marked "1," and then return to an "open" repeat symbol earlier in the piece. This time, when you reach the start of the bar marked "1," you don't play it—instead, you move onto the bar marked "2." Any number of such markers can be used in a piece of music.

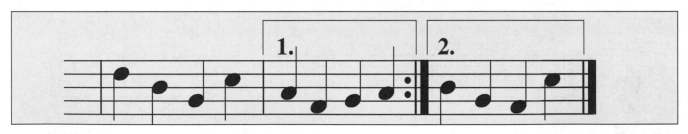

## AL CODA

The end section of a piece of music is called the "coda," or the tail. The al coda symbol (al coda ⊕) instructs the player to go directly to the ending sequence of the piece of music (as shown below left). The end sequence starts with the symbol shown earlier (⊕), and is played through until reaching the leters "fine" (as shown below right). An alternative to using "fine" is the symbol (⌢), although sometimes both are used together.

## WORKING THROUGH AN EXAMPLE

On the right, you can see an example of a complete progression of chords which have been abbreviated with repeat and reiteration symbols. Play through the chords, following the examples below:

- Play the opening four bars
- Play the first eight bars. When you reach the repeat sign (E7), return to first "open" repeat sign (A).
- Play the first seven bars. When you reach the "first time" bar (E7), IGNORE IT and play the "second time" bar.
- Continue playing through until you reach the D.S al coda sign (E7). Return to 𝄋 until you reach the ⊕ sign (E7).
- Go to the coda section and play the final five bars.

## ROUTINING A SONG

Breaking down a song into its constituent parts so that it can be arranged for other musicians is sometimes known as "routining."

To try this idea out for yourself, take any popular song—for convenience, choose one with a four-four beat. Start by playing along with the recording. Once you have worked out the chords that you need to use, you are ready to start working out the structure. If you find there are some "tricky" chords in the song that you can't work out immediately, don't let it slow you down for now—working out its root note will probably do

for now. If you have trouble working out the simpler chords, refer to the key signature of the song and the chords built on the major scale—you're likely to find that most of the chords you need will be in there.

When you are familiar with the song some patterns will emerge quickly, and you will be able to isolate the verses and choruses, for example. You should now be able to write down the overall structure of the song. Wherever something different happens, identify it. A typical structure is shown on the right.

In fact, this piece is composed entirely from five different sections. You can now mark each section with a

| Introduction |
|:---:|
| Verse |
| Chorus |
| Verse |
| Chorus |
| Middle eight |
| Verse (solo guitar) |
| Chorus |
| Chorus (repeat) |
| Ending (to fade-out) |

unique letter, from A to E. If you notate each section individually, it would be possible to provide players with a series of brief chord charts and an overall structure.

A — B — C — B — C — D — B — C — C — E

# COUNTRY GUITAR

# Lesson 11

The guitar has always played a central role in the way country music has evolved. Although country boasts some of the finest guitar soloists to be found playing in any field, it is as an accompanying instrument to vocals that makes the guitar such a crucial ingredient of the country sound. For such purposes, often simple chord sequences are strummed or picked.

## COUNTRY STRUMMING

To get into the swing, begin by strumming out a set of chords. Each of the four bars in the music shown below strums a different kind of rhythm. Pay special attention to the picking instructions—the usual way of strumming involves playing downstrokes on the quarter note and upstrokes on the eighth note, although deviations are possible. The chord sequence passes from G major through D major, and C major, back to D major.

## ADDING A SWING

The country swing is one of rhythms most strongly associated with the genre. To create this effect, each pair of eighth notes is played as a dotted eighth note followed by a sixteenth note. This creates the "boom-chuck-a-boom" kind of sound which is so strongly associated with country artists like Johnny Cash. The four-bar exercise below is quite similar to the one you have just played. This time the chord sequence is D major—A major—G major—A major. Notice the difference in rhythm.

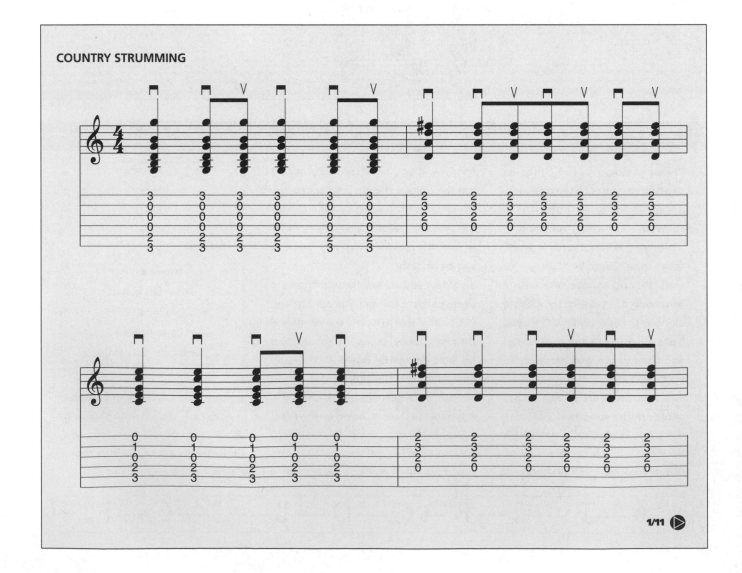

COUNTRY STRUMMING

1/11

**ADDING A SWING**

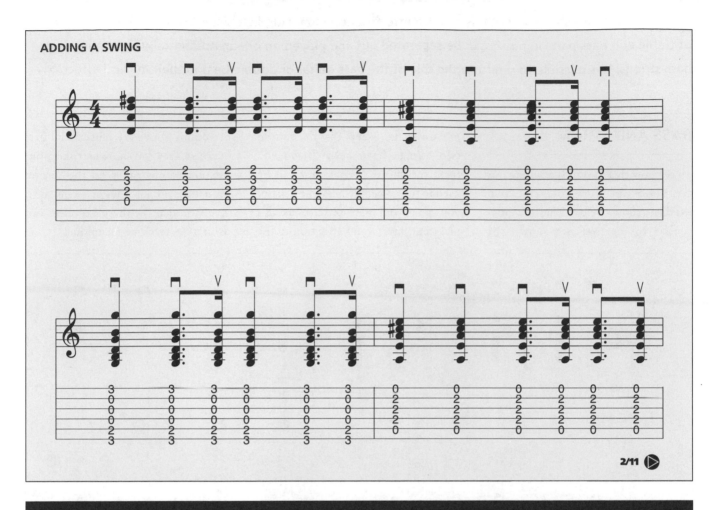

2/11 ▶

## CHET ATKINS

<u>Born:</u> 20th June, 1924, Luttrell, Tennessee, USA

<u>Guitars:</u> Gretsch and Gibson "signature" models

<u>Recorded Highlights:</u> *King Of Country* (compilation)

Country music's greatest virtuoso musician, Chet Atkins could put forward a good case for being the man who invented the legendary Nashville Sound.

A prodigious talent, by the age of 18 Atkins was regularly heard on Tennessee radio, where he had already been christened "Mr Guitar." By his early twenties, with a record deal under his belt, Atkins moved to Nashville, where he found national recognition during the 1950s with his many appearances at the Grand Ole Opry. A hit artist in his own right, much of his finest work can be heard accompanying others. In fact, it's no exaggeration to say that every major Nashville artist of the period—from Jim Reeves to Waylon Jennings—benefitted from the unique Chet Atkins sound.

At the heart of Akins' style lies an awesome fingerpicking technique that incorporates a very sophisticated syncopation of muted bass strings. This sound can be heard to the full on tracks like "One Mint Julep" and "Country Gentleman"—a name also given to his signature series guitars produced by Gretch from the late 1950s, now highly prized by collectors.

In 1973 Atkins was inducted into the Country Music Hall of Fame—at the age of 49, the youngest such country legend. His playing has influenced successive generations on both sides of the country fraternity.

# SEPARATING THE BASS STRINGS

One of the reasons that the guitar is such an effective accompanying instrument is that the differing roles of treble and bass parts in music can be separated out and played on one instrument. By separating the bass strings, it is possible to replicate the role of the bass guitar or double bass in their musical effect.

## BASS AND STRUM

To see how this idea of separating out the notes can work, play the two exercises shown below. They are quite similar to the exercises shown the previous page, except that the bottom two strings have been "removed" from the chord so that they can be used to play a simple bass line. Again, you can try out these exercises using a pick, but pay careful attention to the directions above the music. The first exercise uses only downstrokes, but introduces upstrokes on the second sequence, which adds a swing feel. You can also try these exercises out using fingerpicking techniques.

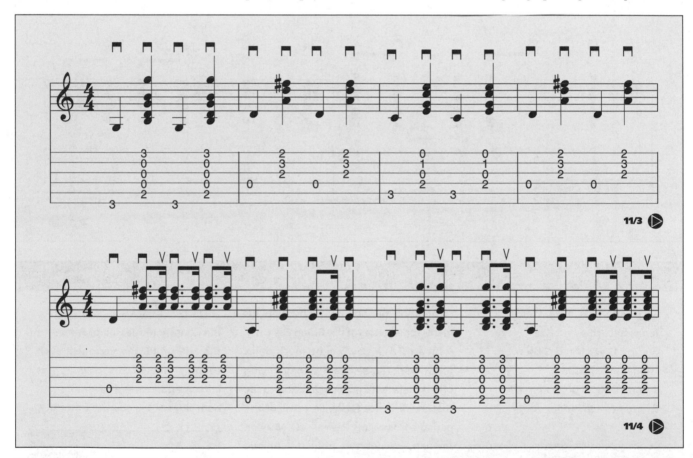

## ALTERNATING THE BASS

We can extend the idea of separating out the bass notes by alternating them with other strings. This creates a "bouncing" bass line played on the bottom strings. Such lines invariably alternate between the root note and the perfect 5th—this means when you are playing a D major chord, the bass line will alternate between D and A.

## ALTERNATING BASS LINES IN OTHER KEYS

The root-5th alternating bass lines are shown for every key in staves on the right. The bass notes are annotated with their names—the root is the larger letter, and the 5th is the smaller letter shown above and below. In most cases it is desirable to move down in pitch to the perfect 5th from the root, however, this is not always going to be possible—chords whose root notes begin on the 6th string must move up in pitch to the perfect 5th.

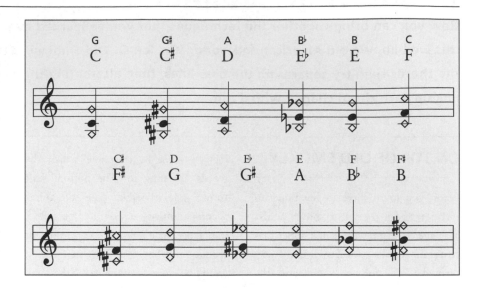

## ADDING A BASS RUN

Having learned how to alternate the bass strings of the guitar when playing chords, you can now take this idea a stage further by linking the bass line with a run of single notes. One of the easiest ways for this to work is to use the last three notes of the major scale—from the perfect 5th right up to the root. The exercise below uses the chords C and G. The run comprises the notes G, A, B before playing the C chord. This idea can be used both to link up to a new chord or link down from a chord. This type of sound is one of the most famous characteristics of country and Western Swing music.

11/6

# PUTTING IT INTO PRACTICE

Now you can bring together the techniques that you've learned over the past few pages to try out this well-known old American folk song, "On Top Of Old Smokey." Start off by just strumming out the chords then try separating the bass lines, then alternating the bass lines, before finally trying to link up each chord change with a run.

## ON TOP OF OLD SMOKEY

Before you go on, there are few things to mention about the music shown across the page. To begin with, you'll notice that two staffs of music are shown all the way through. The top staff indicates the melody—that is, the tune which the words are sung to. The bottom staff shows one possible type of guitar accompaniment—a separated bass note. In practice, such a simple accompaniment would rarely be found written out: it would be more common to see the small chord diagrams above a melody line.

The song is in three-four time, so if you want to count out the beat, remember that it repeats in cycles of three. A cheery set of lyrics are shown below, so you can sing along while you practice your playing if you so wish.

1. On top of old Smokey, all covered with snow, I lost my true lover by courting too slow.
2. Oh courting is pleasure and parting is grief, but a false-hearted lover is worse than a thief.
3. A thief will just rob you of all that you save, but a false-hearted lover will lead to the grave.
4. The grave will decay you and turn you to dust, not one in a million a poor boy

(girl) can trust.
5. They'll kiss you and squeeze you and tell you more lies than the rain drops from heaven or stars from the skies.
6. They'll swear that they love you, your heart for to please, but as soon as your back's turned they'll love who they please.
7. It's raining and hailing this cold stormy night; your horses can't travel, for the moon gives no light.

8. So put up your horses and give them some hay , and come sit beside me as long as you stay.
9. My horses aren't hungry, they don't want your hay, I'm anxious to leave so I'll be on my way.
10. On top of old Smokey, all covered with snow, I lost my true lover by courting too slow.

## FINGERPICKS

Many country guitarists who play fingerpicking styles find that they can get greater clarity by using a special set of fingerpicks. These are in effect false nails that fit over the edge of the finger. It gives a greater level of "attack"—almost a treble clicking sound as the pick hits the string, whereas playing with the pads of the fingers produces a slightly duller, muted effect by comparison.

Whilst these can be extremely effective, they are difficult to master as they require the angle between the hand and wrist to be pulled back. This can be uncomfortable if you are not used to it. It is also not uncommon to see a hybrid form of picking which uses just a thumbpick: contrast this with the pick/fingering crossover style shown on page 41, and you can see that it has certain advantages—namely that the thumbpick does not need the 1st finger for support, therefore the 1st to 3rd fingers can be used to play the treble strings in the usual way.

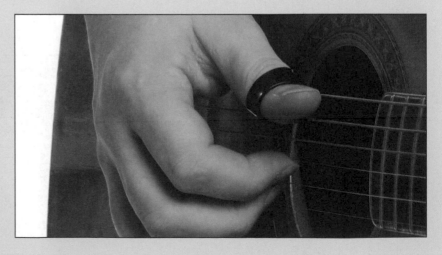

# COUNTRY CHORDS

The final two pages of this section deal with alternative ways in which chords can be played in country and folk music. One of the hallmarks of country guitar accompaniment is the use of chords with hammered notes (see pages 82–83). These work especially well when playing open-string chords with alternating bass lines. You can see the way they work by using a simple G major chord in the example shown below.

## HAMMERING CHORDS

The principle behind the use of hammered chords is relatively simple: you select your chord, fret all the fingers except for one, play the chord with the right hand, and then hammer the remaining finger in place.

The example below uses an open G major chord. To try it out, fret the chord in the usual way and then release the 1st finger, so that only the 2nd and 3rd fingers are pushing the strings down against the frets. Play the chord, and while it is still ringing, bring your 1st finger down onto the 2nd fret.

You can extend this idea and integrate it with picking out alternating bass notes. Try the exercise shown below, alongside the chord. This example uses the same open G major chord.

- First beat—play the note G on the 3rd fret of the 6th string.
- Second beat—strum across the top four strings.
- Third beat—play the open 5th string and hammer on the 2nd fret (B). Each of these notes has a value of an eighth note.
- Fourth beat—strum across the top four strings.

### HAMMERING OTHER OPEN CHORDS

Below and on the opposite page, you will find more open-string chords which have notes that can be hammered-on.

Although it is possible to hammer-on any of the notes, only the most commonly used options are shown. This technique is usually at its most effective when the 3rd note of the chord is used; however, hammering between the 7th and the octave also works well. The same priciples can also be applied to barre chords.

It's also possible when playing some of these chords to pull-off certain notes. To do this, you simply take way the finger after the chord has been played.

In all cases, the colored dots denote the strings that can be hammered. Where more than one note is shown, you have the option of hammering-on one or all of the strings.

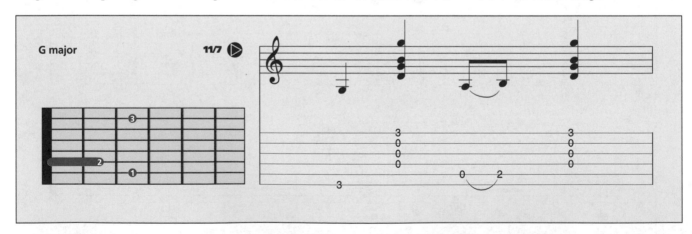

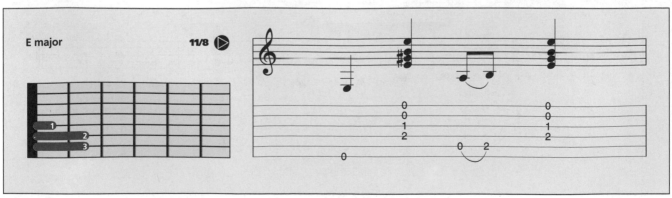

A major  11/9

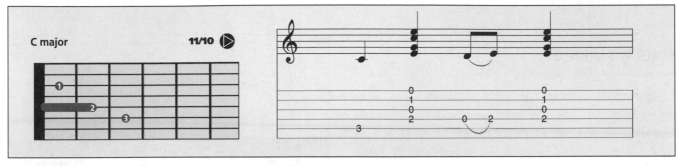

C major  11/10

D major  11/11

## ARPEGGIOS

The effect of playing the notes of a chord one after the other in quick succession is known as an "arpeggio." When played slowly—using notes with a duration of an eighth note or lower, for example, the effect of the arpeggio is such that it can be written out as a sequence of single notes,

even if, in practice, the notes will sustain above one another, creating a chordal effect. When an arpeggio has to be played quickly, the effect is shown as a wavy line

alongside the chord. The first bar of the example below plays the chord as eight eighth notes, and the second bar as a very fast arpeggio.

## COUNTRY BACKING TRACK

Finally, here is a complete sequence you can play through on your own. It uses the chords G major, C major, A minor, and D7. The music is shown below—you can accompany yourself on the backing track on the CD.

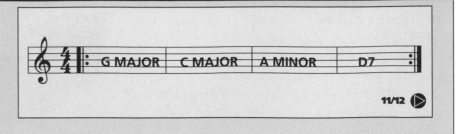

G MAJOR  C MAJOR  A MINOR  D7

11/12

# ADDITIONAL EFFECTS Lesson 12

**You have already seen examples of most common types of lead guitar ornamentation—effects such as hammering-on, pulling-off, string bending—all of which can give character to an individual performance. There are also a number of more advanced techniques which can be integrated to give style and flair to your solo playing. Some of the fastest pyrotechnic soloing can be achieved using a variation of the hammering and pulling effects called "finger tapping." Additionally, you can use string harmonics to provide alternative sound textures.**

## FINGER TAPPING

Finger tapping, or fret tapping as it is sometimes known, is an extension of the single-note technique of hammering-on and pulling-off (see page 80), which also uses the fingers of the right hand to "tap" out notes along the fingerboard. Its prime exponents, including Eddie Van Halen, Steve Vai, and Joe Satriani, use the technique to play solos at a blistering speed. Although finger tapping became prominent during the 1980s, it is not exactly a new idea—session players like jazz-funkster Harvey Mandel could be heard using the effect on albums in the early 1970s. A related technique can also be seen used by jazz musician Stanley Jordan, who places the the guitar in a more or less horizontal position on his lap and plays it rather like a piano keyboard, pressing down on the strings with both hands. Both techniques require not only great skill, but only work effectively on amplified instruments, where notes can be sustained all over the fingerboard. In the case of the rock players, extreme levels of compression and distortion can help to give a consistency of volume to individual notes.

## TAPPING EXERCISE

Tapping technique is not dissimilar to hammering-on and pulling-off—notes are hammered when moving up a scale and pulled off when moving down. The principal difference is that the pull-off played by either hand can be executed with a slight sideways pluck, to give extra volume for the next hammered note. Try this example out for yourself.

- Position the 1st finger of the left hand on the 7th fret of the 1st string. Place the 1st finger of your right hand near to the 11th fret and pluck the note.
- With the note sustaining, hammer-on the 9th fret of the 1st string with the 3rd finger of the left hand.
- Pull-off the 11th fret by plucking the string alongside the fret and releasing the finger. Pull-off with the other two fingers in a similar manner.

## TAPPING ACROSS THE STRINGS

This exercise will help you to achieve a greater degree of fluidity when playing across the strings. Take a look at the music written out on the right. On each string, the first two notes are played by the 1st and 3rd fingers of the left hand respectively. The third note is tapped by the 1st finger of the right hand. The number "3" written alongside the beam in the music indicates that the groups of notes are "triplets." Although each bar contains four groups of eighth notes, three notes must be played in equal time on every beat of the bar. Although this may sound a little complicated, listening to the track played on the CD will make everything immediately clear.

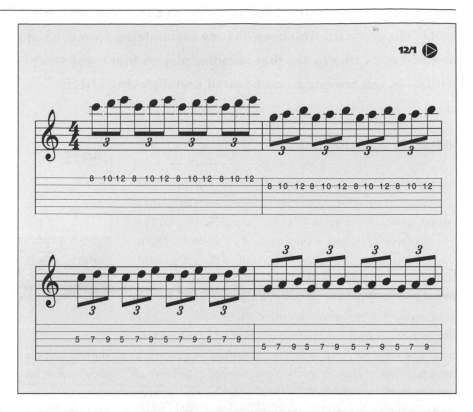

### EDDIE VAN HALEN

<u>Born:</u> January 26th, 1957, Nijmegen, Netherlands
<u>Guitars:</u> Kramer; MusicMan "Signature"
<u>Recorded Highlights:</u> *Van Halen* (1978); "Beat It" (1983 Michael Jackson single); "Jump" (1984 single)

Throughout most of the 1990s, the likes of Joe Satriani and Steve Vai took the plaudits for their awesome displays of sheer technique. However, a decade earlier it was a young Eddie Van Halen who dragged rock music out of the realms of the Spinal Tap parody and made the high-performance guitar solo respectable once more.

Born in the Dutch town Nijmegen in 1957, Van Halen moved to California with his family in the middle of the 1960s. Initially starting life as a drummer, Eddie and his brother Alex formed the band The Broken Combs with a group of school

friends in 1973. Within three years—and changing their name simply to Van Halen—they quickly established themselves as one of the best live bands working on the west coast of America, a reputation forged jointly by Eddie Van Halen's striking finger-tapped soloing and the antics of charismatic frontman David Lee Roth.

The band's 1978 debut album, *Van Halen*, became an instant rock classic, selling well over two million copies and giving heart to a generation of young musicians who felt that they had been marginalized by the "anti-muso" stance of Punk and the New Wave.

Although Van Halen became one of the biggest selling rock bands of the mid-1980s, perhaps more than any other single track, it was Eddie's

finger-tapping solo extravaganza on Michael Jackson's million-selling 1983 hit "Beat It" that had analysts of the guitar solo scratching their heads. Since then, finger tapping (or fret tapping as it is also sometimes known) has become a standard feature of the modern guitarist's armory.

Like many other innovators, Van Halen settled into other areas of interest, leaving a tide of flashy second-rate impressionists in his wake. In spite of his extraordinary technical skills, at its very best, Eddie Van Halen's playing is purposeful, and avoids being showy for its own sake. That is lesson that many a soloist could do well to learn—and one that he could do to remember for himself from time to time.

# HARMONICS

The term "harmonic" refers to the bell-like sounds you can get by damping specific frets on the guitar's fingerboard. You have already encountered harmonics in the tuning section (see page 37), and whilst it's true to say that for some players that is the extent of their knowledge and use, harmonics can provide a good deal of useful playing effects.

## WHAT IS A HARMONIC?

Each time you strike a guitar string, the precise sound you hear is the result of a number of different components which, when taken together, are referred to as the "harmonic series." The dominant sound you hear is known as a "fundamental." This is the string vibrating along the full length of the fingerboard between the bridge and the nut, and consequently the element which defines the pitch of the note. However, there are further components that can also be heard, which result from shorter frequencies vibrating along different parts of the string. These frequencies—known as harmonics or overtones—are always strict multiples of frequency of the fundamental. The balance between the the various harmonics and the fundamental is what creates the tonal characteristics of an acoustic note produced by any musical instrument.

### 1ST TO 5TH HARMONICS

The sound of the harmonic can be heard alone by playing a note muted by the left hand at specified points on the fingerboard— the most commonly used being the 12th fret. When this happens, the fundamental is muted, leaving only the harmonic to sound. The pitch of the note heard depends on the mathematical divisions that are allowed to resonate. By muting the

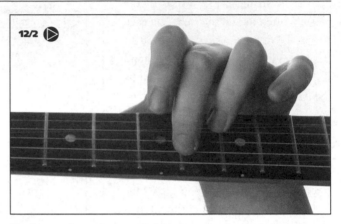

**The harmonic can be heard when the string is gently muted above specific nodes along the fingerboard.**

fundamental at the 12th fret you divide the string in half, causing the string to resonate in two equal measures (the distance between the nut and the 12th fret is identical to the distance between the 12th fret and the bridge saddle). This is known as a 1st harmonic, and creates a note which is the same as the fretted note at the 12th fret.

Other types of harmonic are also possible: the 2nd harmonic divides the string into three equal segments; the 3rd harmonic causes the string to vibrate in four equal lengths; and the 4th harmonic divides the string into five equal lengths.

---

**PLAYING THE HARMONIC**

Different types of harmonic can be played at various points on the fingerboard. The diagram below shows where they can be found.

⬤ **1ST HARMONIC**

Place the finger above the 12th fret, causing the string to vibrate in two equal segments. This creates a note one octave higher than the open string.

⬤ **2ND HARMONIC**

Place the finger above the 7th or 19th fret, causing the string to resonate in three equal segments. This creates a note one octave and a perfect 5th above the open string.

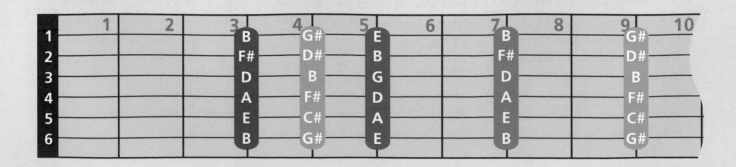

## FRETTED HARMONICS

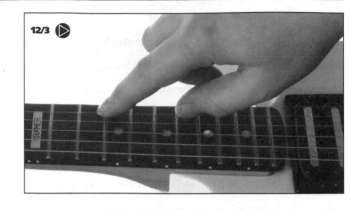

12/3

It is possible to play harmonics for any note on the fingerboard. The left hand frets notes in the conventional way, while the right hand simultaneously mutes the string with the 1st finger of the right hand and plucks the note either with the thumb or 4th finger. To pitch a note in this way requires an excellent knowledge of the fingerboard. By fretting a note you are, in effect, creating a new "nut" position. Therefore harmonics are played relative to the shift between the nut or zero fret and the fretted note.

To see how this works, position the 1st finger on the 2nd fret of the 2nd string. Now place the 1st finger of the right hand lightly on the string above the 14th fret and pluck the note with the thumb of the right hand. This produces a first harmonic of

C♯. Similarly, with the left hand still in position it is possible to hear second harmonics—the note G♯— on the 9th and 21st frets, and a third harmonic (C♯) on the 7th fret.

### FRETTING A CHORD

With skill you should be able to pick out a melody using fretted harmonics. An especially pleasant technique is to pick out the notes of a chord and play them as an arpeggio of fretted harmonics. Try out this example using an open C major chord.

- Hold an open C major chord with the left hand. To remind you, in case you've forgotten, the 1st finger holds the 1st fret of the 2nd string; the 2nd finger

holds the 2nd fret of the 4th string; the 3rd finger holds the 3rd fret of the 5th string.

- Hold the 1st finger above the 15th fret of the 5th string and pluck the note with the thumb.
- In a similar way, play the 14th fret of the 4th string, the 12th fret of the 3rd string, the 13th fret of the 2nd string, and the 12th fret of the 1st string. Try to play the notes of the chord evenly, both in timing and volume.

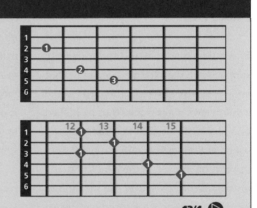

12/4

### 3RD HARMONIC

Place the finger above the 5th (or 24th) fret, causing the string to vibrate in four equal lengths. The note produced is two octaves above the open string.

### 4TH HARMONIC

Place the finger above the 4th, 9th, or 16th frets, causing the string to resonate in five equal lengths. The note is two octaves and a major 3rd above the open string.

### 5TH HARMONIC

The 5th harmonic falls between the 3rd and 4th frets, and produces a note two octaves and a perfect 5th above the open string.

# IMPROVISATION

# Lesson 13

Improvisation can mean many things to many people. At its simplest, it can be playing around with, and extending scales, but it is also at the very heart of some musical cultures, such as Spanish flamenco or the ragas, alapanas, and tanams used in classical Indian music. Improvisation has also had a particularly wide usage in jazz, from the technical wizardry of the stars of bebop to the more controversial "free" musicians, who at their most extreme play without reference to melody, rhythm, or harmony.

It may also come as a surprise to those people who view Western classical musical as an extremely rigid form to know that improvisation has played a significant role in its history and development. Indeed, some of the great musician-composers like Bach and Handel were noted for their organ improvisations; the violinist Paganini is thought of as one of the greatest improvisers of all.

## IMPROVISATION IN PRACTICE

It would be idealistic (and certainly simplistic) in the extreme to imagine that every guitarist who steps forward to take a solo views what is about to be played as a blank canvas, and that the resulting sound is a mystical manifestation of pure inspiration. In fact, in the hands of many musicians improvisation can mean little more than linking together a series of stock musical phrases which, although they might not be identical from one performance to another, amount to minor variations on the same theme. Much soloing in the realms of popular music falls into this category, and it's even true in genres where improvisation has a more traditional role, such as jazz, if to a more technically proficient degree. This is not particularly surprising: if you, as a musician working in a broadly accessible sphere of music, choose NOT to play set-pieces, the possibilities open to you may seem relatively limited in scope.

In fact, the word "limit" is especially apt when discussing improvisation, because at a practical level it generally requires working within a predefined musical framework (see Fred Frith on page 117 for an exception).

Of course, this may seem somewhat theoretical and irrelevant to the majority of guitarists, many of whom pride themselves on being able to replicate identical performances to their recordings, but this is not to say that improvisation is irrelevant in mainstream music. How are new songs composed? More often than not, it is a result of sitting down with an instrument and just playing until something "happens." It is often a similar process with developing solos and band arrangements.

### WHAT IS IMPROVISATION... REALLY?

According to the *Harvard Dictionary of Music*, improvisation is: "The creation of music in the course of a performance." However, this seems far too narrow a definition to do justice to the way in which it has come to be used in most forms of modern music.

Take a typical approach to a jazz solo. Traditionally, the melody is predefined, and the soloist then moves away from the melody, but still (generally) playing around the notes used in the melody. Similarly in blues-based music, soloing often seems to be a case of playing around with the notes of a minor pentatonic scale, frequently based around previously developed motifs.

This all rather begs the question of what actually constitutes improvisation, and in some cases—such as an outstanding jazz soloist—are we simply confusing inspiration with an extraordinarily well-developed musical vocabulary? Or are they part of the same equation?

Those interested in the nature of improvisation should track down a copy of *Improvisation: Its Practice and Nature in Music* by Derek Bailey. One of the most active "free" guitarists of the past 30 years, Bailey discusses the art of improvisation with some of the the finest exponents from musical cultures throughout the world. As he points out: "The word improvization is actually used very little by improvising musicians." Which brings to mind the story of a young musician quizzing Charlie Parker. When asked about his approach, "Bird" replied: "I just play, man!" Perhaps we try too hard to analyse music sometimes.

## JIMI HENDRIX

<u>Born:</u> November 27, 1942, Seattle, USA

<u>Died:</u> September 18, 1970, London, England

<u>Guitars:</u> Fender Stratocaster and Fender Jaguar

<u>Recorded highlights:</u> *Axis: Bold As Love*; *Are You Experienced?*; *Electric Ladyland*

One name towers above all other improvising musicians of the electric era—James Marshall Hendrix.

Hendrix was given his first electric guitar in 1954. He learned to play by listening to the great electric blues players of the time—immortal names like Muddy Waters and Elmore James. After a stint in the US Army, he found work as a back-up player for touring rock and roll and soul artists: among Hendrix's numerous credits were performances with Little Richard, Ike and Tina Turner, The Isley Brothers, B.B. King, and Jackie Wilson.

Brought over to London in 1966, he formed The Jimi Hendrix Experience with drummer Mitch Mitchell and guitarist Noel Redding, who switched over to bass just to get the job. A UK hit for their debut single "Hey Joe" was followed by a sequence of three classic albums all of which featured arguably the most consistently peerless guitar work ever heard in rock.

In 1967 Hendrix returned to his home country, where at that point he still remained a relative unknown. This situation changed following his explosive performance at the Monterey Pop Festival. One of the lesser-known names on the bill, Hendrix gave a performance that defied the eyes and ears of a massive outdoor crowd, ending a high-octane set by setting fire to his guitar.

Towards the end of his life, his never-ending search for artistic development took him into less popular areas. Disbanding the Experience, he formed the Band Of Gypsies with Buddy Miles and Billy Cox. If anything it proved once again that a combination of three virtuoso musicians don't necessarily make for great art or even necessarily a great listening experience.

During the same period, Hendrix seemed to spend most of his waking hours in his owm Electric Ladyland recording studio, improvising alone or with anyone (literally) who happened to walk in. In a career which saw the release of only five "official" albums during his lifetime, these recordings (and endless live tapes) have resulted in approaching 500 releases since his death in 1970.

In the space of barely four years, Jimi Hendrix took the the electric guitar into new territory, setting new standards for rock and blues improvisation. Although at the time of his death he already looked, to some extent, to have turned his back on mainstream rock, he influenced successive generations of musicians more than any electric guitarist since Charlie Christian in the 1940s.

# IMPROVISING AROUND A SINGLE KEY

It is a musical fact that, one way or another, most single-note soloing revolves around playing the notes of an appropriate scale. Let's take the simplest example—a C major scale. If you are playing over the chord of C major, every note of of the C major scale will "work" to a greater or lesser degree. But what about the other five possible notes that exist outside of the scale? Is it wrong to use these notes? This page introduces the concepts of consonance and dissonance—how the notes within a scale sound in relation to one another.

## WHAT WORKS AND WHAT DOESN'T?

It's hard not to sound didactic when describing which notes you should and should not play. The bottom line, of course, is that it really IS up to you—the only rule worth sticking to is if you think it sounds good, play it. However, as you will probably have discovered for yourself in the process of learning the guitar, some combinations of notes sound great; others can sound rather unpleasant. This brings us then to the concept of what are "consonance" and "dissonance." These terms describe the sound characteristic of any two notes when they are played together.

Consonance describes a smooth, harmonious combination—for example, the root note of any key played with the perfect 5th, for example, C and G, F and C, or G and D. These notes will work together in pretty well any context.

The opposite of consonance is dissonance. A sound which is described as dissonant is not usually pleasing to the ear—it can often be heard when a "bum" note is played, for example. The most dramatic of these effects usually takes place if you miss a note by a half-step (semitone).

This is not to say that dissonant notes are by definition wrong or a bad thing—let's just say that "pop" composers making extensive use of such sounds are likely to find themselves with a limited audience. When used in the right context, they can be employed to great dramatic effect.

## TABLE OF EFFECTS

The table at the foot of the page describes the effect of the sound created by each possible interval from a root note of C. The names shown alongside the intervals are alternative descriptions for the notes on any diatonic scale. These are not quite the same as interval descriptions you have seen up until now, as they relate only to the scale degree. For example, the major 3rd in the key of C major—the note E—is described as the "mediant"; the minor 3rd in the key of E natural minor—the note E♭—is the mediant note for that key (E does not appear in that key, so there is no chance to confuse the description).

Once again, you can see the strength of the link between the 1st, 4th, and 5th notes of the scale.

|       | SCALE DEGREE | NOTE INTERVAL | EFFECT |
|-------|--------------|---------------|--------|
| I | TONIC | C to C | Open consonance |
| ii | SUPERTONIC | C to D♭ | Sharp dissonance |
| II | SUPERTONIC | C to D | Mild dissonance |
| iii | MEDIANT | C to E♭ | Soft consonance |
| III | MEDIANT | C to E | Soft consonance |
| IV | SUBDOMINANT | C to F | Consonance or dissonance |
| IV+/V° | TRITONE | C to F♯/G♭ | Neutral |
| V | DOMINANT | C to G | Open consonance |
| V+/vi | SUB-MEDIANT | C to G♯/A♭ | Soft consonance |
| VI/vii° | SUB-MEDIANT | C to A/B♭♭ | Soft consonance |
| vii | SUB-TONIC | C to B | Mild dissonance |
| VII | LEADING NOTE | C to B♭ | Sharp dissonance |

## WORDS OF WISDOM FROM AN EXPERT

Fred Frith is a pioneering guitarist, whose music has never fitted comfortably into convenient musical categories. His musical life started with Henry Cow, a band he formed with drummer Chris Cutler at Cambridge University in the late 1960s. Nominally viewed as a progressive rock band, Henry Cow's left-wing politics and anti-corporate stance may have limited their commercial potential, but they remain one of the most influential "underground" bands of their time.

For the past 25 years Frith has carved a niche for himself as one of the finest improvising guitarists performing in any field. Of one of Frith's most fascinating albums, *Guitar Solos* (1974), the magazine *Guitar Player* described it as being "to mainstream guitar playing what quantum mechanics is to an auto mechanic."

Although his music and playing are approaching as far from the mainstream as you can get, his thoughts on the nature of improvisation illustrate the point that, in many ways, it is more a cerebral process than a "motor" process. I asked Fred some deliberately basic questions about the nature of improvisation and free playing.

*What does the word "improvisation" mean to YOU as a guitarist? Is there really such a thing as "free" playing?*
Improvisation means learning how to listen fast, which is not at all the same as playing fast. Being alert, trusting in intuition as a guide, not being afraid of risks, knowing that if it unravels it doesn't negate the process. "Free" means free of the restrictions of particular musical forms, but that's where the freedom stops, too. "Free" players are sometimes trapped by the rigidity of their reaction to the very forms whose rigidity they are trying to avoid. In any case, you soon find out that "free" doesn't mean you can just do what you want—rather, that you are responsible for your own limits.

*How do you approach an improvised piece?*
It boils down to flexibility. I try not to be closed to any possibility that seems to make sense in a given context, which means I'm as likely to accompany a folk-singer by drumming on the strings with paintbrushes as I am to play lyrical melodies in a "free" performance.

*Do you consciously practice improvising, or work on playing techniques from which you may be able to draw in the future? Can you "learn" to improvise?*

To answer the last question first, yes, of course. As to technique, the only time that I consciously worked on this aspect was while preparing for my *Guitar Solos* record in 1974. Since then, I feel as if I'm in a continuous learning process. Every gig throws up unexpected questions that I have to try and answer, and over a period of years techniques emerge and are refined in the process of performing—so I practice improvising by improvising.

*What advice would you give to the improvising novice?*
Listen to as much improvisation as you can, especially 'live', and figure out for yourself what you like and don't like about what you hear—that'll teach you about your own orientation. Learn to give equal weight to the idea of NOT playing as well as playing. Silence is what gives the music its vital tension. And try and understand the importance to a sound of the gesture that produces it.

# PLAYING WITH SCALES

Although improvisation can't be taught as such, a good way to introduce the idea to the novice is to experiment with the idea of playing variations within a very limited musical spectrum, For example, playing the same sequence of notes, but using different timings or emphases.

Here are eight two-bar examples of playing a C major scale over a single octave. Even within the realms of playing around with the same eight notes, the possibilities for variation are, surprisingly, quite endless.

The fingering is for an open C major scale. You can also try them out an octave above. The fingering for both is shown below—this eliminates the need to show the tablature.

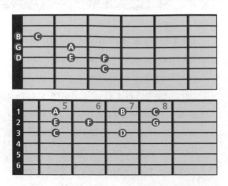

13/5
13/6
13/7
13/8

## PRACTICE AND IMPROVISATION

It may sound like an oxymoron, but you CAN practice improvisation. The facility you develop to improvise will, as much as anything, be down to attitude as technical capability. As Fred Frith says on page 117, the very act of improvisation IS practice for future improvisation—like anything else, the more you do, the better you become.

In fact, the discipline of improvising within a very tight musical framework, as shown in the exercises on the previous page, teaches you how to draw out as much as possible from very little. Try to integrate this approach with your everyday practice of scales—it will also help to improve the fluidity of your single-note work.

# EXTENDING THE PENTATONICS

The minor pentatonic scale is one of the most widely used for improvisation in blues, jazz, and rock. We can further continue the idea of moving notes from a scale around with the following set of exercises, which take the notes from a pentatonic scale and then extend it—adding "unrelated" notes from the scale.

The first two bars show the scale played in the key of C. This scale—like any other—can be extended by adding notes from outside of the scale. These can be used to produce a wider range of melodies, or simply as "passing notes"—notes whose role is simply to connect two notes within a phrase.

**THREE ADDITIONS**

There are three main additions that can be made to the minor pentatonic: the addition of a flattened 5th (this is the note F♯ in the key of C), the addition of a major 3rd (E in the key of C), and the addition of a major 2nd and major 6th (D and A in the key of C). All of these are shown in the exercises below. In fact, the final example converts the minor pentatonic scale into what is known as the Dorian mode. Modes are covered in more detail on pages 126–129.

## MOVING AROUND THE MINOR PENTATONIC

Finally, here is an example of how the notes from a minor pentatonic scale can typically find themselves used in a rock setting. Take it slowly to begin with—the hammered 16th-note runs in bars 5 and 8 are particularly demanding, as they are played at high speed. Notice also the slide between the 3rd and 4th notes of bar 2. This effect is common in rock and blues.

# ALTERING CHORDS

# Lesson 14

So far, all of the chords you have used have been more or less straightforward, in that they are all, one way or another, extensions built onto the four triadic forms—major, minor, augmented, and diminished. However, the definition of these chords can sometimes be more ambigious. "Polytonal" chords, for example, are those which contain the basic elements of two different chords played at the same time. Similar in effect is the sound of a chord when it is played over a bass note which differs from the root. This effect is extremely common both in all types of music.

## ALTERED BASS NOTES

To hear the effect of a chord played over an altered bass note, play a regular open-string D major chord and shift the root note—the open 4th string—up to E on the 2nd fret.

The notes of the D major chord are D (1st), F♯ (3rd), and A (5th).

If we now treat the new chord as having a root of E rather than D, the notes of the chord and their relationship to the root become: E (1st), F♯ (9th), A (11th), and D (flat 7th). These are all notes from the chord E11. By adding an E root to a D major chord, you have created E11.

But compare that first chord with the more conventional E11 voicing shown above. As with any alternative voicings, you will always hear that it sounds a little different; however, there is something more significant going on here. The simple fact of adding the flattened 7th and 11th notes to a root produces the "flavor" of an 11th chord—however, the first

chord you played was missing the 3rd and 5th notes, which give the eleventh its full-bodied sound. Therefore, in such circumstances, it is usually more helpful to refer to the original triad with an altered bass note. As such, the chord would usually be referred to as "D major over E" and would be written simply as "D/E."

Although this distinction may seem a little bogus, it does make good practical sense. For a start, it simplifies matters: it's less cumbersome referring to a chord as "D/C" rather than "C6/9♭5" or "C/6/9♯/11"—not to mention the fact that few amateur guitarists would be able to come up with the fingering without looking at a chord dictionary. But in most practical senses, converting discrepencies between chords and bass lines, whilst musically correct, may not give a true indication of what's really going on. For example, in most cases—in a rock or pop band, at least—such chords would usually be a result of interplay between the the guitar and another instrument, typically a bass guitar. In the

above example, the guitarist would, in almost all cases, NOT be playing either of the C6/9 chords. It is more likely that the guitar would be playing D major, and the bass the note C. In its effect, this is something QUITE different.

**D MAJOR**    14/1

**D MAJOR OVER E**

**E11**

## FULL RANGE OF ALTERED BASS NOTES

The sequence of chord diagrams shown on the opposite page illustrates a full set of altered bass notes. From left to right (from the top of the page), an E major chord is played on the guitar, with the

root note descending in half-step intervals. As you will hear if you try to play them for yourself, some of these sounds are extremely harmonious and commonly used; others create discordant effects. The principle of altered bass notes not only applies to major chords, but can be used with any other chord type.

To play all 12 of these examples, use the fingering for the top four strings of an open E major chord. The root (which starts on the 3rd string) gradually descends over the bottom three strings. Note that you should only ever play four strings—the top three, and whichever string the new root note is on.

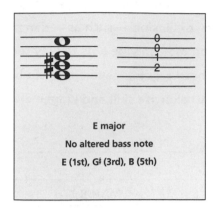

**E major**

No altered bass note

E (1st), G# (3rd), B (5th)

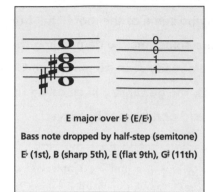

**E major over E♭ (E/E♭)**

Bass note dropped by half-step (semitone)

E♭ (1st), B (sharp 5th), E (flat 9th), G# (11th)

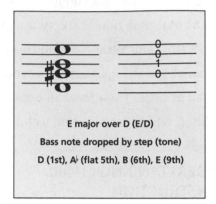

**E major over D (E/D)**

Bass note dropped by step (tone)

D (1st), A♭ (flat 5th), B (6th), E (9th)

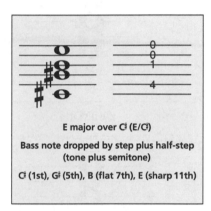

**E major over C# (E/C#)**

Bass note dropped by step plus half-step (tone plus semitone)

C# (1st), G# (5th), B (flat 7th), E (sharp 11th)

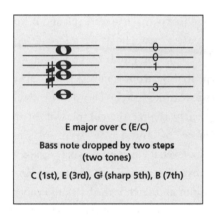

**E major over C (E/C)**

Bass note dropped by two steps (two tones)

C (1st), E (3rd), G# (sharp 5th), B (7th)

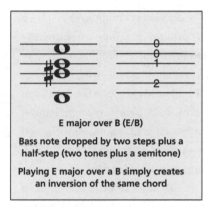

**E major over B (E/B)**

Bass note dropped by two steps plus a half-step (two tones plus a semitone)

Playing E major over a B simply creates an inversion of the same chord

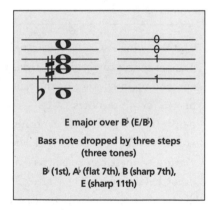

**E major over B♭ (E/B♭)**

Bass note dropped by three steps (three tones)

B♭ (1st), A♭ (flat 7th), B (sharp 7th), E (sharp 11th)

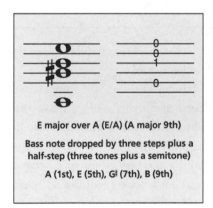

**E major over A (E/A) (A major 9th)**

Bass note dropped by three steps plus a half-step (three tones plus a semitone)

A (1st), E (5th), G# (7th), B (9th)

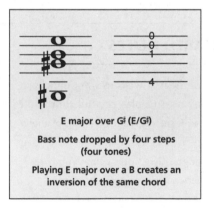

**E major over G# (E/G#)**

Bass note dropped by four steps (four tones)

Playing E major over a B creates an inversion of the same chord

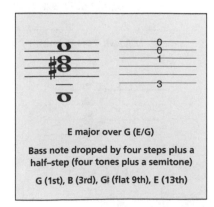

**E major over G (E/G)**

Bass note dropped by four steps plus a half-step (four tones plus a semitone)

G (1st), B (3rd), G# (flat 9th), E (13th)

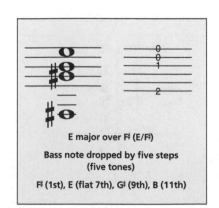

**E major over F# (E/F#)**

Bass note dropped by five steps (five tones)

F# (1st), E (flat 7th), G# (9th), B (11th)

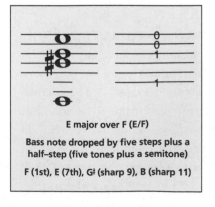

**E major over F (E/F)**

Bass note dropped by five steps plus a half-step (five tones plus a semitone)

F (1st), E (7th), G# (sharp 9), B (sharp 11)

# SUBTRACTING NOTES

The guitar is inherently limited as a chordal instrument, in that that maximum number of strings you can play at the same time is six. When playing some of the more "full-bodied" extensions—such as variants on 9ths, 11ths, and 13ths—the voicings are sometimes so demanding that you may only be able to play four or five of the strings. Indeed, as you've already seen, to play a full 13th chord requires seven notes to be played at once. Therefore, on occasions, the guitarist will be called upon to exercise skill and judgement in deciding which notes within a chord need or need not be played.

## UNDERSTANDING CHORD CONSTRUCTION

For a player to be able to make the best possible decision in omitting notes from a chord requires not only an extremely accomplished understanding of the way chords are constructed—which, if you've worked diligently through the book, you should be well on the way to attaining—but, in ensemble situations, empathy and understanding of what the other instruments are also playing.

Part of this understanding also requires a knowledge of groups of chords or chord types that share the same notes.

Let's look at a simple example. As you already know, the chord C major 7th consists of the notes C, E, G, and B. However, if you leave out the root note and just play the notes E, G, and B, you create a new chord—E minor. If you were playing guitar on your own, you probably would never think of of substituting these chords—it would clearly change the complexion of the piece of music you were playing. However, if you were playing with other musicians, the effect of playing an E minor chord while the bass or keyboard was playing the root note C would still create the C major 7th chord overall.

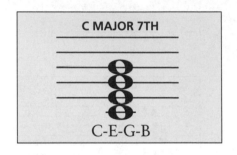

**C MAJOR 7TH**

C-E-G-B

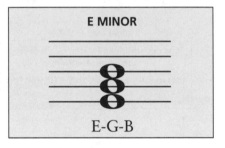

**E MINOR**

E-G-B

## SHARED NOTES

One of the best ways to work out chord synonyms is to play the full chord and then omit the root. This will create a new root, usually starting on the 3rd (although other notes can also be used), and hence a whole new chord type.

This approach can be taken with chords formed on top of the major and minor triads, even if most of the time the

results are likely to produce an unusable level of discord.

Understanding the process of chord synonyms will increase your chord vocabulary and can also be extremely helpful in composition, making the task of moving between chord positions a good deal easier. Essentially, this is just one more step along the road to understanding the way notes relate to one another.

The following examples illustrate how pairs of chords can begin life in one key and end up in another by the removal of one or more notes. All six chord pairings begin in C, and yet create new voicings in the keys of E, E♭, G, and G♭. Naturally, these can be converted into other keys—look at the circle of 5ths diagram (see pages 64–71) to see how the keys relate: for example, Cadd9 to Gsus4 transposes to Gadd9 to Dsus4.

### MINOR NINTH TO MAJOR SEVENTH

Leaving out the root of any minor 9th chord produces a major 7th chord whose root is a minor 3rd higher than that of the original chord. For example, C minor 9th beomes E♭ major 7th by omitting the note C. Similarly, G minor 9th converts to B♭ major 7th by leaving out the note G.

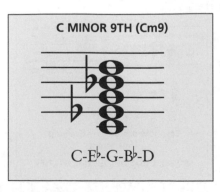

**C MINOR 9TH (Cm9)**

C-E♭-G-B♭-D

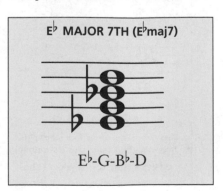

**E♭ MAJOR 7TH (E♭maj7)**

E♭-G-B♭-D

## SEVEN FLAT NINE TO DIMINISHED

Leaving out the root of any 7-9 chord produces a diminished chord whose root is a major 3rd higher than that of the original chord. Because of the nature of diminished chords, the remaining notes can be inverted to create alternatives with ANY of the notes as a root.

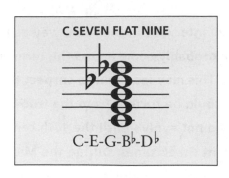

**C SEVEN FLAT NINE**

C-E-G-B♭-D♭

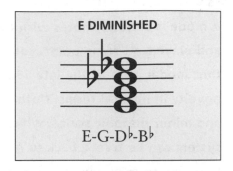

**E DIMINISHED**

E-G-D♭-B♭

## NINTH TO HALF DIMINISHED

Leaving out the root of any 9th chord produces a half diminished chord whose root is a major 3rd higher than that of the original chord. In the key of C, C7-9 becomes E half diminished by leaving out the root (C). Similarly, G7-9 becomes B half diminished by leaving out the note G.

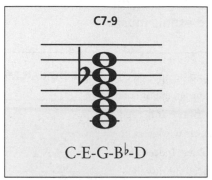

**C7-9**

C-E-G-B♭-D

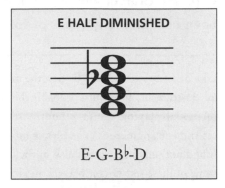

**E HALF DIMINISHED**

E-G-B♭-D

## NINTH DIMINISHED FIFTH TO SEVENTH AUGMENTED FIFTH

Leaving out the root of any 9th diminished 5th chord produces an inversion of a 7th augmented 5th chord whose root is a diminished 5th higher than that of the original chord. In practice, the 3rd of the first chord becomes the flattened 7th of the synonym.

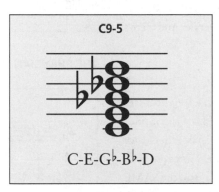

**C9-5**

C-E-G♭-B♭-D

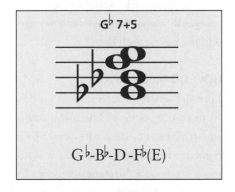

**G♭ 7+5**

G♭-B♭-D-F♭(E)

## MINOR SEVENTH TO SIXTH

The 6th can be viewed as a simple inversion of of a minor 7th whose root is a minor 3rd higher that that of the original chord. The root, minor 3rd, perfect 5th, and minor 7th notes of the minor 7th chord therefore become the major 6th, root, major 3rd, and perfect 5th of the 6th chord.

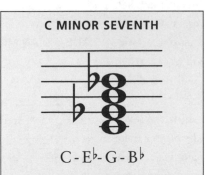

**C MINOR SEVENTH**

C - E♭- G - B♭

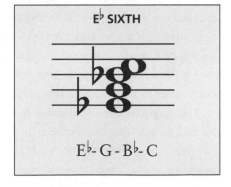

**E♭ SIXTH**

E♭- G - B♭- C

## ADD NINE TO SUSPENDED FOURTH

Leaving out the 3rd from an "add9" chord and inverting the root so that the 5th is the lowest note produces a suspended 4th chord whose root is a perfect 5th higher than that of the original chord. Therefore, Cadd9 becomes Gsus4 when E is not played.

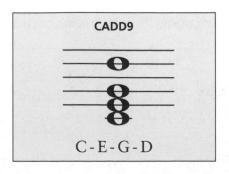

**CADD9**

C-E-G-D

**G SUSPENDED FOURTH**

G-C-D

# MODES

# Lesson 15

**A mode is series of notes with fixed intervals, in the same way as the scales you have already seen and played. At some point, you've probably come across the term "mode"—perhaps in reference to the "modal jazz" of the late 1950s. This may lead you to suspect that modes are something of a novelty in musical terms. Nothing could be further from the truth. In fact, modes pre-date the major and minor diatonic scales, which did not evolve until the 17th century. The history of the modal system can be traced back to Ancient Greek times. During the Middle Ages, it was taken up by the Christian church, where it dominated Western music for several hundred years. Modes have also been used in many types of folk and ethnic music.**

Like other types of music theory, the modes can be applied to any instrument, and whilst probably the best-known exponents of modal playing are jazz improvisers on brass and reed instruments, numerous examples of modal guitar work can be found not only in jazz, but also in rock and blues. Indeed, for some of these self-taught players, modes are used intuitively—the guitarist likes the sound of the notes being played but doesn't necessarily realise that they are from a specific mode. And there's nothing wrong with that!

### HOW DO MODES WORK?

Like the diatonic scales, each mode comprises eight notes from root to octave. The notes used by ALL of the modes equate directly to the white notes of a piano keyboard—hence the equivalent to the notes of a C major scale. However, each mode starts on a different note, even though it uses the SAME eight notes between root and octave. This means that each of the seven modes has a different set of intervals, which means that each also has a unique sound characteristic. Nonetheless, as the notes are the same, if you have learned your major scale fingering thoroughly, you will find it that much easier to play through these modes.

The diagrams here and across the page show the seven different modes. You can hear how they work by playing them over their "tonic" chords—the chords on the major scale. These are shown in their simplest triadic forms—just the three notes.

### THE DORIAN MODE (D TO D PLAYED OVER D MINOR)

### THE PHRYGIAN MODE (E TO E PLAYED OVER E MINOR)

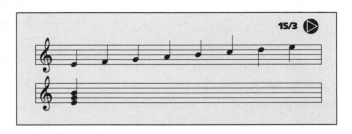

### THE LYDIAN MODE (F TO F PLAYED OVER F MAJOR)

### THE IONIAN MODE (C TO C PLAYED OVER C MAJOR)

### THE MIXOLYDIAN MODE (G TO G OVER G MAJOR)

**THE AEOLIAN MODE (A TO A OVER A MINOR)**

**THE LOCRIAN MODE (B TO B OVER B DIMINISHED)**

## MODAL INTERVALS

Right now, you might be wondering what use any of this is? That's a good question. In their original forms, the modes were viewed as a fixed series of notes, not a set of relative intervals. Before the evolution of key signatures, musicians knew and understood the nature of each mode—pieces of music were written for the mode, which in turn defined the notes used. However, modern usage has reinterpreted each mode as a scale with its own unique set of intervals, rather than specific notes. Therefore it is possible to transpose any of these sets of intervals into any key, effectively creating seven new types of scale, each with its own unique characteristics.

In actual fact, there are only five unfamiliar scales—when you play through the set of modes below and over the page, you should be able to recognize that the Ionian mode is, in fact, a major scale by any other name; similarly, the Aeolian mode uses the same set of intervals as the natural minor scale.

Below and over the page you will see all seven modal types written out in the same key—C. By working through them in turn, you should quickly be able to establish a feel for their different characteristics.

**IONIAN MODE** 15/8

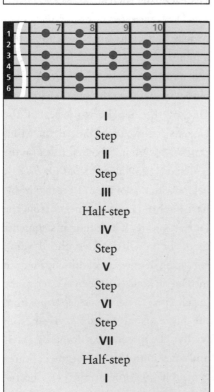

| | |
|---|---|
| I | |
| | Step |
| II | |
| | Step |
| III | |
| | Half-step |
| IV | |
| | Step |
| V | |
| | Step |
| VI | |
| | Step |
| VII | |
| | Half-step |
| I | |

**DORIAN MODE** 15/9

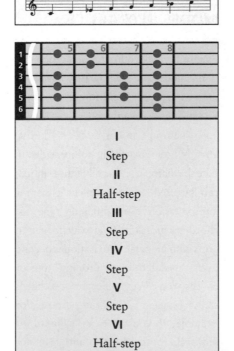

| | |
|---|---|
| I | |
| | Step |
| II | |
| | Half-step |
| III | |
| | Step |
| IV | |
| | Step |
| V | |
| | Step |
| VI | |
| | Half-step |
| VII | |
| | Step |
| I | |

**PHRYGIAN MODE** 15/10

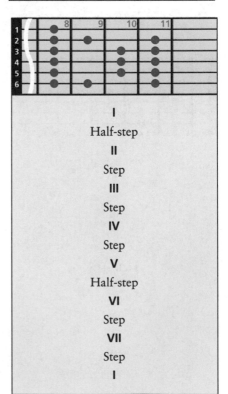

| | |
|---|---|
| I | |
| | Half-step |
| II | |
| | Step |
| III | |
| | Step |
| IV | |
| | Step |
| V | |
| | Half-step |
| VI | |
| | Step |
| VII | |
| | Step |
| I | |

### LYDIAN MODE    15/11 ▶

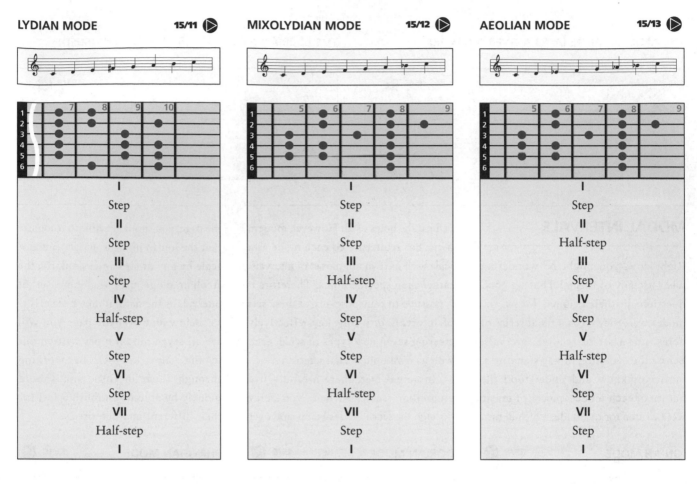

| | |
|---|---|
| I | |
| | Step |
| II | |
| | Step |
| III | |
| | Step |
| IV | |
| | Half-step |
| V | |
| | Step |
| VI | |
| | Step |
| VII | |
| | Half-step |
| I | |

### MIXOLYDIAN MODE    15/12 ▶

| | |
|---|---|
| I | |
| | Step |
| II | |
| | Step |
| III | |
| | Half-step |
| IV | |
| | Step |
| V | |
| | Step |
| VI | |
| | Half-step |
| VII | |
| | Step |
| I | |

### AEOLIAN MODE    15/13 ▶

| | |
|---|---|
| I | |
| | Step |
| II | |
| | Half-step |
| III | |
| | Step |
| IV | |
| | Step |
| V | |
| | Half-step |
| VI | |
| | Step |
| VII | |
| | Step |
| I | |

### LOCRIAN MODE    15/14 ▶

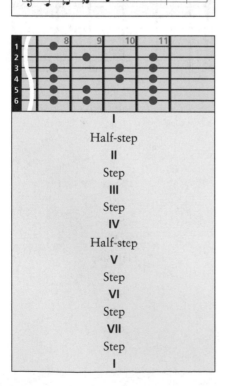

| | |
|---|---|
| I | |
| | Half-step |
| II | |
| | Step |
| III | |
| | Step |
| IV | |
| | Half-step |
| V | |
| | Step |
| VI | |
| | Step |
| VII | |
| | Step |
| I | |

## MODES IN PRACTICE

Finally, let's take a brief look at each one of the modes and see how they have been used in practice. We'll forget about the Ionian and Aeolian modes—the major and natural minor scales—they've already been covered in suffcient detail. Like the diatonic scales, all of these modes can be used as an excellent basis for improvisation over different types of chord progression. One way to get to grips with modal improvisation is playing over a pedal tone—a droning note or chords. You can use the scales and chords shown on page 126 for this purpose. For example, if you have a keyboard or sequencer, program an infinite D minor chord and improvise using only notes from the Dorian scale. This is the fastest way to get a flavor of the different effects you can get from using the modes.

## THE DORIAN MODE

The Dorian mode has been widely used by jazz musicians since the 1950s. It is a minor mode, although it differs from the natural minor scale (or Aeolian mode) in that the 6th note is sharpened. One of the best-known uses of the Dorian scale can be heard on Miles Davis' "So What," the first track on the landmark 1960 album *Kind Of Blue*. It begins with one of the most recognizable bass lines in jazz, using notes from the Dorian mode. The other instruments then cut in with a two-chord vamp consisting of intervals of 4ths, again from the Dorian scale (see the music across the page). This is a harmonic departure from the more usual chords derived from triads. The matchless soloing by Davis and tenorman John Coltrane captures ensemble playing at its very best—virtuoso musicians exploring a new approach to their art, one which changed the face of jazz.

In fact, Coltrane took the form to even higher levels—his later work with pianist McCoy Tyner produced some of the most hypnotic and spiritual music ever heard in jazz. Indeed, Coltrane had devoted years to the study of modal music, both from the early European church and traditional Eastern music.

### THE PHRYGIAN MODE

The Phrygian mode is another minor mode, differing from the natural minor in that the 2nd note is flattened—a note which in practice can be heard as a flattened 9th. A minor mode can be identified by looking at the interval between the 1st and 3rd notes—they are two steps apart on all of the major modes. The Phrygian mode is used extensively in flamenco music (see page 140).

### THE LYDIAN MODE

The Lydian mode differs from the diatonic major scale, in that the 4th note is sharpened. It was the composer George Russell who helped to kick off the modal fashion in the 1950s, with his well-known work *The Lydian Chromatic Concept Of Tonal Organization*.

### THE MIXOLYDIAN MODE

The Mixolydian mode differs from the Ionian (or diatonic major scale) by just one note—the 7th note is a flattened 7th—this creates a mellow, "bluesy" effect, which has made it probably the most widely used mode in all types of modern music. The flattened 7th makes the Mixoldyian mode especially useful in blues playing, where it can be effectively interchanged with a minor pentatonic scale in the same key.

### THE LOCRIAN MODE

As the 7th degree of the scale, the Locrian mode differs from all of the

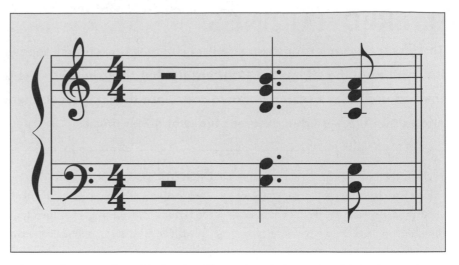

others in that it is a diminished scale. All of the notes except the 1st and 4th degrees are flattened, which creates an unusual and exotic flavor. Widely used in

the ethnic music of Asia, its use is not common in Western music, although it can easily be applied to give a simplistic character of Middle Eastern music.

## LEARNING FROM OTHER INSTRUMENTS

Modal masters Miles Davis and John Coltrane cast a giant shadow over the jazz world of the late 1950s and early 1960s, which can still be heard today. Even though they played trumpet and tenor saxophone respectively, their work transcended their own instruments and influenced both musicians and composers of other instruments.

In fact, you might be surprised at how many guitarists have found inspiration for their own playing in listening to the way other instruments are played. Charlie Christian, the pioneer of electric jazz guitar, is widely held to have drawn his major influence as a jazz musician from the work of saxophonist Lester Young.

Similarly, Ritchie Blackmore, the legendary 1970s guitarist with rock bands Deep Purple and Rainbow, found that his style of soloing was aided by listening to, and copying, jazz and R&B saxophone soloists. As he says: "They're all single notes,

and therefore can be repeated on the guitar." He goes on to add: "If you can copy a sax solo, you're playing very well, because the average sax player can play much better than the average guitarist."

Musicians throughout the ages have also found inspiration in the different musical forms and unusual instruments played in cultures from other parts of the world.

Many musical cultures, for example in parts of Asia and the Far East, do not use standard chromatic systems—that is, their scales cannot be conveniently broken down into intervals of steps (tones) and half-steps (semitones). In such cases, approximations are needed to give a flavor of the sound, rather than an accurate reproduction. Some of these ethnic scales have already been covered on page 93.

In the same way, playing melodies based around the modes shown on this page is likely to give a different slant to your playing.

# ALTERED TUNINGS
# Lesson 16

**The guitar has undergone some radical changes since it first appeared during the Renaissance era. But it wasn't until the end of the 18th century that six strings became the norm and the tuning system that we use today became standardized. Since then, however, there have always been variations—or altered tunings—used in different types of guitar music.**

In classical music, tunings for the lute and vihuela have been adapted for the guitar to allow the performance of pieces written for those instruments. In the realm of blues and folk, there has long since been a tradition for the use of open tunings.

A parallel development came in the jazz age, when banjo players turned to the guitar in order to continue working—they brought their varied tunings with them. A further tangent came when the guitar crossed from America to the island of Hawaii, which saw the birth of the "slack-key" tuning.

It was during the late 1960s that the vogue reached a peak of popularity, primarily championed by country and folk musicians of the period. Some of the most famous musicians of the period— from the Beatles to Led Zeppelin— experimented with this alternative. Joni Mitchell, for example, has used open tuning on ALL of her music—she never learned to play using standard tuning. Recent years have seen a new generation of "ambient" guitarists, for whom altered tunings provide an ideal starting point for some of their "new age" musings.

## USING ALTERED TUNINGS

A wide variety of alternative tunings exist, some of which will be shown in this section. Whilst they are more often than not used with steel-string acoustic guitars, they can equally be applied to electric instruments—although if your guitar is fitted up with a locking tremolo unit, you'll probably wear out a few Allen keys if you take to the style of playing.

### OPEN-STRING TUNING

Open-string tuning is so called because the strings of the guitar are tuned to a chord. The most commonly used system is open G tuning. If the strings are played across the chord G major will be heard. Open D, A, and E tunings are also heard from time to time.

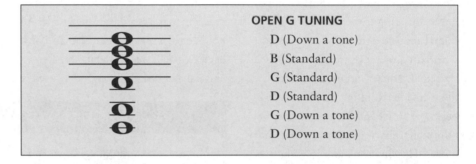

**OPEN G TUNING**

D (Down a tone)

B (Standard)

G (Standard)

D (Standard)

G (Down a tone)

D (Down a tone)

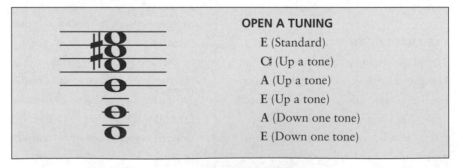

**OPEN D TUNING**

D (Down a tone)

A (Down a tone)

F♯ (Down a half-step)

D (Standard)

A (Standard)

D (Down a tone)

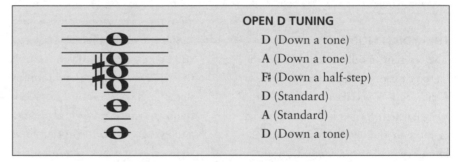

**OPEN A TUNING**

E (Standard)

C♯ (Up a tone)

A (Up a tone)

E (Up a tone)

A (Down one tone)

E (Down one tone)

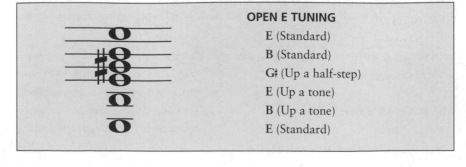

**OPEN E TUNING**

E (Standard)

B (Standard)

G♯ (Up a half-step)

E (Up a tone)

B (Up a tone)

E (Standard)

## OPEN-STRING CHORD EXERCISES

To play the next set of exercises, tune your guitar to an open G—the 1st, 5th and 6th strings all go down by a tone.

The simplest way to use open-string tunings is with a barre. If you play the strings without fingering any frets, you will hear the chord G major. Therefore if you hold a barre over the 2nd fret you will be playing an A major chord. This simple approach to playing full six-string

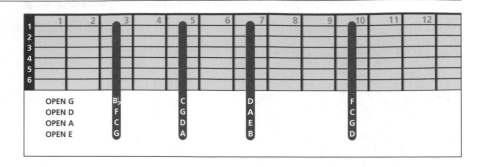

chords makes open-string tuning very popular among slide players (see page 146). The diagram above shows which the major chords you can create at

different points along the fingerboard. Also shown are the chords in the same positions using the other three open tunings shown on the left.

## FINGERING

One of the most enjoyable aspects of using altered tunings is the unexpected chords that can be produced.

Here are two interesting chord positions for use with an open G tuning—Cadd9 and G7. Try playing the following two sequences. For the first (above right), simply strum the chords any way you like; the second (below) uses the same chord sequence, only this time with right-hand fingerpicking.

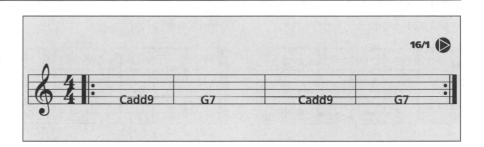

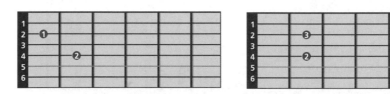

# OTHER ALTERED TUNINGS

**Drop D is one of the simplest tunings. All you do is lower the pitch of the 6th string by a whole tone, taking it down to D. Much less common, but still effective is the Double Drop D tuning, which also takes the 1st string down to D.**

## DROP D TUNING

Many altered tunings have been developed to play in specific keys—indeed, the reason that they have not been more widely adopted is the very fact that standard tuning gives a greater degree of general flexibility. As such, a drop D tuning is excellent for songs which make extensive use of

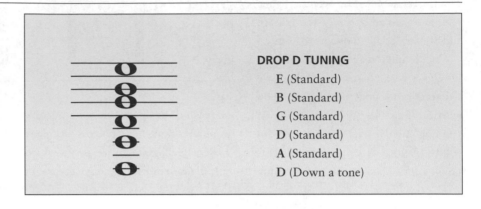

**DROP D TUNING**

E (Standard)
B (Standard)
G (Standard)
D (Standard)
A (Standard)
D (Down a tone)

open D chords. It now allows for a full six-string chord with the root note on the lowest string. Try it out for yourself—there's no better-sounding voicing for a D major chord.

Drop D tuning also works very well for other chords—all you have to remember is that on the 6th string you must position your finger two frets higher than you would with standard tuning. Of course, if you don't want to learn new chord positions you have the option of simply not playing the

**D MAJOR**

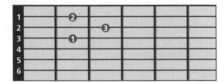

**E MAJOR**

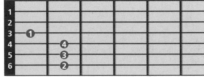

**A MAJOR**

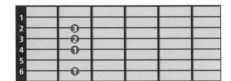

**C MAJOR**

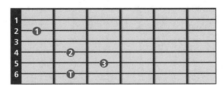

**G MAJOR**

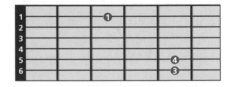

6th string. This is also a good time to deviate from the classical left-hand position and bend the thumb around the back of the neck to fret the 6th string—the alternative may tie your fingers up in knots.

In the chord positions shown above, the dots on the diagrams marked "T" should be played by the thumb. Note, also, the quality of the G major chord—like D, this is another beautiful-sounding alternative.

## DADGAD

The DADGAD tuning first emerged in the 1960s, partially a result of folk guitarist Davey Graham's experiments in playing with ethnic musicians from Morocco. This tuning is especially effective on melodic work where the pedal tones—the droning strings that underpin the sound—can be used to

**DADGAD TUNING**

D (Down a tone)
A (Down a tone)
G (Standard)
D (Standard)
A (Standard)
D (Down a tone)

provide a harmonic framework to accompany tunes played either on single or double strings. Although it is most commonly used by folk players, one of the best known use of the DADGAD tuning is probably Jimmy Page's version of "Blackwater Side."

On the right you will find fingerings for a brief selection of chords you can play using the DADGAD tuning.

The exercise shown beneath illustrates how DADGAD tuning can be used to great melodic effect, and how the pedal tones create an effect not unlike many types of ethnic music heard throughout the world—from Celtic to North Indian.

For the purposes of this exercise, only the tablature is shown—the purpose is for you simply to experiment with the eight chords.

**D MAJOR**

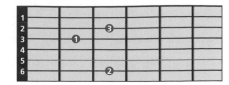

**D 5**

**G MAJOR**    **A MAJOR**

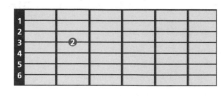

16/3 ▶

| | | | | | | | | |
|---|---|---|---|---|---|---|---|---|
| 0 | 0 | 0 | 0 | 0 | 0 | 0 | 0 | |
| 9 | 7 | 5 | 3 | 0 | 0 | 0 | 0 | |
| 7 | 5 | 4 | 2 | 4 | 2 | 0 | 0 | |
| 0 | 0 | 0 | 0 | 5 | 4 | 2 | 4 | |
| 0 | 0 | 0 | 0 | 0 | 0 | 0 | 5 | |
| 0 | 0 | 0 | 0 | 0 | 0 | 0 | 0 | |

## DROP G (OR G6) TUNING

Drop G tuning is highly effective for playing in the key of G. The bottom two strings are tuned down a whole tone. As these bass notes are G and D, there is rarely any need to fret them with this tuning. A further advantage is that the top four strings still use standard tuning, which means most standard chord voicings can be used or adapted.

**DROP G TUNING**

E (Standard)
B (Standard)
G (Standard)
D (Standard)
G (Down a tone)
D (Down a tone)

### TOO MUCH TENSION

Some of the alternate tunings shown in this lesson require you to tune strings to a higher pitch—for example, open A increases the pitch of the 2nd, 3rd and 4th strings by a tone. Any time you increase the tension of the strings you place a strain on the body and neck of the guitar. If you are already using heavy-gauge strings, this strain could, in extreme circumstances, damage your instrument. For the same reason, string breakage is more likely to happen, so it's a good idea take precautions like muting the fingerboard with a cloth—snapped strings have a nasty habit of flying up towards the face. An alternative course of action is to use lower-gauge strings which can take greater tension.

The converse is also true, though. If you detune a set of the lightest gauge strings by a tone, the slackness is likely to result in the strings hitting against the fingerboard as they vibrate. This will prevent you getting a clean sound. In such situations, you should consider fitting higher-gauge strings.

# JAZZ AND THE GUITAR Lesson 17

Jazz, especially in some of its more contemporary forms, is perhaps the most demanding music for any instrumentalist to play. To be an accomplished jazz musician requires the playing skills of the best classical players, a considerable understanding of technical theory and the ability to put it into a flexible musical context, the technique to deal with demanding rhythms and accenting, and an advanced vocabulary of chords and scales. Above all, however, the jazz musician must be able to harness these considerable skills and bring them together with the imagination necessary to improvise freely and creatively and with "feeling."

## WHERE TO BEGIN

Not only is jazz demanding to play, but it can be one of the most difficult to teach, much formal study being devoted to matters of music theory that would be off-limits to all but the most experienced players.

Perhaps the best starting point for the fledgling jazz guitarist (indeed, for those wishing to learn more about ANY type of music) is to emerse yourself in the work of the experts. In the field of jazz, if you want to move chronologically, begin with Eddie Lang or Django Reinhardt to hear the first significantly advanced jazz soloing during the 1930s. Indeed, Eddie Lang is credited by many as being the first guitar soloist. Later during the same decade, Charlie Christian developed the form to become the first great electric guitarist, and one of the progenitors of bebop.

The post-bop era saw a number of outstanding jazz guitarists come to fore—players such as Joe Pass, Barney Kessell, Howard Roberts, and, perhaps the finest of all, Wes Montgomery. Pass was noteworthy as one of the masters of unaccompanied jazz guitar; Montgomery the most influential post-war jazz guitarist.

Some of the "free" players of the 1960s took technique to new heights, although the lack of structure made it unappealing to most listeners. From this period, players such as Sonny Sharrock and Ornette Coleman's guitarist, James Blood Ulmer, were among the most interesting. A downside of this was, like many modern art forms, the fact that it sounded like a deliberate attempt to distance itself from its past, and thus it attracted those who lacked the technical and musical skills to give depth to their work.

The late 1960s saw the birth of fusion, popularly introduced by the Miles Davis album *Bitches Brew* (although preceded by John McLaughlin's *Extrapolations*). The music moved away from an obvious jazz base, applying the theory and technique to rock and funk rhythms. Major talents such as McLaughlin, Larry Coryell, Al DiMeola, and Pat Metheny emerged during this period. At the same time, jazz started finding its way into mainstream rock music, with popular bands such as Steely Dan making extensive use of chord progressions (and musicians) more commonly associated with jazz. The past decade has seen the emergence of other hybrid forms that link jazz to ethnic folk musics, hip-hop or even "new age" ambience. Among the best-known names to emerge during this period have been Ralph Towner, Bill Frissell, and the late Michael Hedges.

Listening to recordings by the dozen or so guitarists mentioned above will give you a well-rounded potted history of jazz guitar. It will also give you a flavor of the technical expertise needed to play such music. You can also learn a good deal by working through the sheet music for jazz standards.

## JAZZ PROGRESSION

Now have a go for yourself. Although it's hard to give anything more than a flavor of the sound and complexity of jazz in a few pages, across the page you'll find an example of a reasonably demanding jazz chord progression. The chord names are spelled out, but pay careful attention to the tablature, as it doesn't always use conventional chord shapes.

The piece uses pairs of quarter-note chords and should be played quite slowly (*adagio*). You might find that the chord changes are too tricky at first, so you could try treating the 1st and 3rd notes as half notes, and ignoring two beats and ignoring the chord on the 2nd and 4th beats. The final chord of the sequence resolves, so that the piece can played as a turnaround. As you play through, you'll notice that some of the chord voicings almost "imply" a melody—for example, the movements at the end of bars 2 and 8 from a 13th to a 7 sharp 5.

Once you have become accustomed to the chord voicings, you can move on to pages 136–7, which feature the sequence over the page extended in complexity.

# JAZZ UNACCOMPANIED

**Seeing and hearing an unaccompanied jazz guitarist performing a complete piece of music, with no other instruments involved, can be an extraordinary experience. To succeed, the solo player must have a good understanding of the mechanics of music—the chord work is used to create the harmony and rhythm; a melody has to be identifiable (or at least implied) over the top, and the whole thing needs to be underpinned by a shifting bass line. In effect, the "complete" solo player needs to be able to function as a one-man band armed only with a guitar.**

The piece of music on the opposite page is essentially the same set of chords as you just played on page 135. This time, however, the chords have been broken up with a set of four 16th-note runs on the 2nd beat of each bar. Some of these runs draw the notes from the previous chord, in which case no finger positions need changing—others demand that you move your hand from the previous chord position, play the run, and then fret the new chord position, all in successive beats. This is where an intimate knowledge of the fingerboard is essential.

As you play through the piece, you will notice how the bass notes of some of the chords change, creating the impression of a slow, "walking" jazz bass line. The bass notes sometimes move using intervals of a flattened 5th—for example, between the 3rd and 4th beats of bars 2 and 3. This is a commonly used device (indeed, something of a cliché) for introducing each subsequent chord, creating a harmonic and melodic flow. Work through the sequence slowly. It may be a simple and unassuming piece, but it demands some nimble left-hand fingerwork.

## CHARLIE CHRISTIAN

<u>Born:</u> July 29, 1916, Dallas, Texas, USA
<u>Died:</u> March 2, 1942, Staten Island, New York, USA
<u>Guitar:</u> Gibson ES-150
<u>Recorded Highlights:</u> *The Genius of the Electric Guitar*; *Solo Flight* (both compilations)

Considering his crucial role in the development of jazz guitar, Charlie Christian remains a slightly mysterious and even controversial figure. Nonetheless, he was beyond doubt one of the pioneers of the electric guitar—indeed, his sweeping single-note runs and complex use of harmony was responsible for redefining the guitar as a solo instrument. Despite this, for some, the adulation is tempered by a view that, in spite of his technical genius, much of his music was simply an adaptation on the newly electrified guitar of the style of saxophone player Lester Young.

Part of the mystique surrounding Christian is the enormous impact he

made in such a brief playing career. It was seeing Eddie Durham playing an amplified arch-top guitar in the Jimmie Lunceford band during his late teens that aroused Christian to the possibilities of the instrument. In 1938 he obtained a Gibson ES-150, the first production-line guitar produced to be fitted with a pickup. Within a year, Christian had become

a well-established figure in the jazz world, working with Benny Goodman, whose band, legend would have it, he had gatecrashed his way into.

Barely three years later, at the age of 25, Christian was dead, having contracted pneumonia while convalescing from tuberculosis—a victim, it was said, of the stress of the Big City, with which this farm boy from Oklahoma was never really able to come to terms.

Although Christian remained with Benny Goodman until his untimely death, it was his extra-curricular activity during his final years that made him one of the most influential jazz figures of his time. He was a key player in the regular after-hours jam sessions at Minton's in Harlem, New York, that brought together a new generation of gifted young musicians like Charlie Parker, Dizzy Gillespie, and Thelonious Monk. It was the birthplace of bebop.

# ACOUSTIC TECHNIQUES Lesson 18

The playing techniques shown in this section—for classical, flamenco and Latin styles of music—are all traditionally played on nylon-string guitars. This is not to say that if you don't have, or don't intend to use, such an instrument they won't come in useful when playing a steel-string acoustic or electric guitar. All of them abandon the use of a pick in favor of "PIMA" right-hand fingering, which was first shown on page 40. To refresh your memory, in written music "P" is the thumb, "I" is the 1st finger, "M" is the 2nd finger, and "A" is the 3rd finger.

## CLASSICAL TECHNIQUES

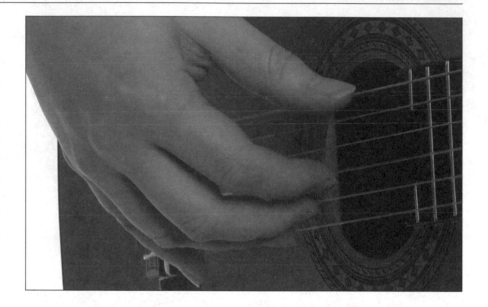

Although the classical left-hand technique is widely used in all types of music, its right-hand uses are largely restricted to nylon-string guitars. There are two principal techniques: the "free stroke" and the "rest stroke." To play the free stroke,. the finger strikes the string with the fingernail in a "pulling" motion and comes to rest ABOVE the adjacent string. The rest stroke is played in the same way, only the finger comes to rest AGAINST the adjacent string.

### SCALES WITH CLASSICAL FINGERING

Playing scales on a clasical guitar is somewhat different to playing with a pick. Sequences of notes are played by alternating different fingers. Here is an open C major scale ascending and descending over one octave. First play it through using just the "I" and "M"

fingers (1st and 2nd) as shown. After you have done that, try the same scale using the "M" and "A" fingers (2nd and 3rd), and finally just the "I" and "A" fingers (1st and 3rd). You should also give equal practice to playing with free and rest strokes.

You can use the same techniques to play this more complex staggered scale. This time the notes of the C major scale are played in a slightly different order: C-E-D-F-E-G-F-A-G-B-A-C-B-D-C. Again, try to practice the full range of right-hand techniques.

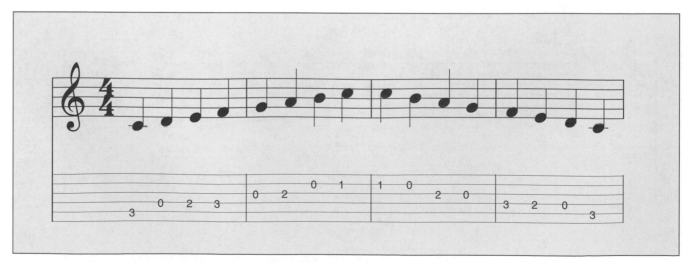

## DIFFERENT VOICES

In some forms of written music you will frequently come across examples where at first glance the duration of the notes in the bar don't seem to add up to the values described by the time signature. This is to allow for circumstances when two are more notes are played together but do not all have identical values. In the first bar shown below, it appears that although the time signature is 4/4 the bar is made up two half notes and six eighth notes, which would not be possible if played in sequence. In fact, the beamed notes indicate that each note is played on the half beat. However, the first and fifth notes both sustain for two beats, WHILE THE OTHER NOTES ARE PLAYING. Where this occurs a note will appear with two stems, or else if two notes are to played at once, they will not be indicated as being joined in the normal but with independent stems pointing in different directions, as shown in the second bar. Each of the notes is referred to as having a separate voice.

## ANDRES SEGOVIA

Born: February 21, 1893, Linares, Spain
Died: June 2, 1987, Madrid, Spain
Guitars: Ramirez and Fleta
Recordings: *Concerto de Aranjuez* (composed by Rodrigo)

More than anyone before or since, it was Andrés Segovia who brought respectability to the guitar and helped the instrument gain acceptance in the often elite world of classical music. Up until that time, in spite of the works of composers and musicians from Tárrega to Sor, the guitar had been considered a rather crude and limited "boudoir" instrument.

Born in 1893, Segovia studied music in Granada, but abandoned all other instruments in favor of the guitar. Under his own tuition, Segovia refined the revolutionary developments in playing that had made by Tarrega during the previous century, especially in the area of the right-hand technique.

Remarkably, by the age of only 14 Segovia had already made his first professional recitals. During the 1920s he toured widely throughout Europe, astounding audiences with an unprecedented virtuosity on the instrument. However, it was his visits to South America that had wider implications for the development of guitar music. It was here that he encountered great composers of the period, such as the Brazilian Villa-Lobos, who began to compose for the instrument.

The importance of Segovia's role as the instrument's greatest ambassador during the first half of the 20th century cannot be overestimated. In making the guitar a truly international instrument, he brought a new repertoire to the classical stage.

It would be no exaggeration to say that without Segovia it is doubtful that such fine composers as Castelnuovo-Tedesco ("Cavatina") and Rodrigo (*Concerto de Aranjuez*) would enjoy the same popularity throughout the world. Equally, with his own transcriptions of works composed for other instruments, he greatly increased the guitar's classical repertoire.

# THREE CLASSICAL PIECES

On these pages you will find three brief classical pieces, all of which were written by the Italian composer Ferdinando Carulli (1770–1853). Although the tunes themselves are quite simple, they will require practice to play accurately. Pay special attention to the PIMA instructions. In some cases, they are shown throughout, where a pattern is repeated only the first line is shown. In all cases, the notes with the downward stems are played by the thumb (P). You will notice that, unlike the rest of the book, these pieces do not show tablature—a system which is less well acknowledged in classical music. Where there are specific left-hand instructions, they are shown alongside the notes with the number of the left-hand finger. Don't confuse these numbers with fret numbers in tablature.

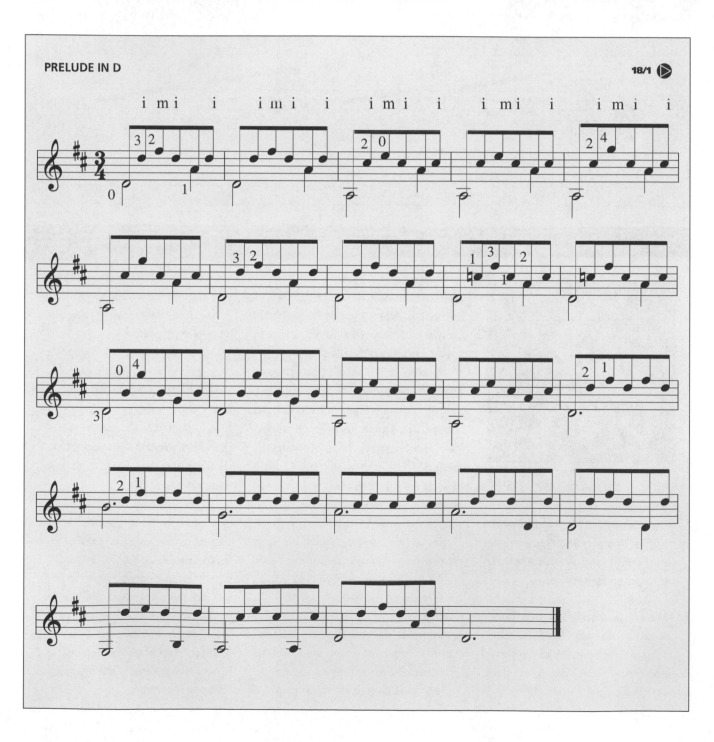

**ENGLISH DANCE** 18/2

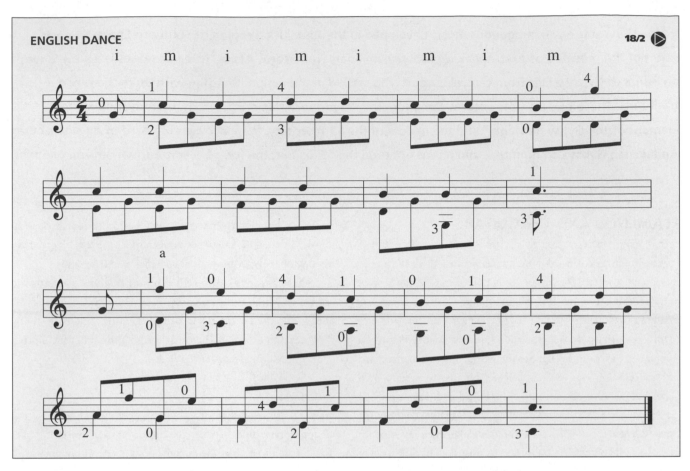

**WALTZ IN A** 18/3

# FLAMENCO

In the 12th century, an indigenous music developed in the Andalusian region of Southern Spain, a direct result of the presence of Arab-speaking Moorish invaders from North Africa. Three centuries later, there was an influx of Gypsy tribes from central Europe who settled in the region, bringing with them their own traditions. These two musical cultures came together to produce flamenco, which has remained a strong element of the Gypsy heritage. Until the middle of the 19th century, flamenco was unheard of outside of the Andalusian Gypsy communities, and it was not until the 1920s that the form became known outside of Spain.

## FLAMENCO AND THE GUITAR

Although flamenco is tied in many people's minds to the guitar, it originally took the form of unaccompanied song (*cante jordan*) and dance. It was in the 19th century that the Spanish guitar was first used in flamenco, as a means of enhancing the human voice (*cante flamenco*). It was this development which helped to popularize the form throughout the world. Since then, flamenco has not only found itself an immensely popular form in its own right, but has crossed over into the classical and jazz fields. The past decade has also seen the development of Flamenco Nuevo in Spain—a new form which puts traditional flamenco in a modern instrumental context. As yet, however, this remains little known outside of Spanish-speaking countries.

## HOW FLAMENCO WORKS

Clearly no single book can hope to pass on the nuances of such a subtle and complex musical form as flamenco within a few pages. Instead of trying, here are some of the most fundamental ideas behing the form. Let's begin with the two essential elements of flamenco music: compás and falsetas.

### COMPÁS

The compás is a predefined cyclic rhythm, which covers the time signature and the accentuation and phrasing of the piece of music. To the guitarist, compás are always played as a series of chords, but although there is considerable scope for harmonic deviation, the rhythm of the compás is strictly observed. This idea can seem a little vague if you are only familiar with the Western musical tradition.

Indeed, it has closer similarities with aspects of Indian classical music, although this may not be such as surprise as it's generally thought that Gypsy tribes originally migrated from India.

There are many different types of compás, perhaps the purest of which is the soleares. This has 12 beats in its cycle and is accented on the 3rd, 6th, 8th, 10th, and 12th beats. Try clapping out the soleares rhythm shown below. Simply clap louder on the accented beats.

### FALSETAS

Falsetas are sequences of individual notes which are inserted at appropriate times between the chords on the compás. It is here that the guitarist plays the melody of the piece, although, again, this is never fixed precisely, leaving the guitarist to improvize around the structure.

## PLAYING FLAMENCO

Here are some techniques that will help you to achieve a flavor of some of the basic flamenco techniques. Begin by checking the way you are holding the guitar. Although there are a number of flamenco players who use the classically "correct" posture of positioning the body of the guitar between the legs on the left thigh, the traditional flamenco tradition balances the instrument on the right knee, with the fingerboard angled close to the body at around 45°. Some players, such as the virtuoso Paco de Lucia, bring the guitar in a higher position by first crossing the right leg over the left.

The chords used within compás are often very simple open-string chords: tonic, subdominant and dominant chords

(I-IV-V) linked by single-note runs—often of staggering complexity—based around the Phrygian mode (see page 124). Indeed, the Phrygian mode is central to flamenco music.

Perhaps more than any other component, it is the fast strumming of chords which for many characterizes the sound of flamenco guitar. This involves the use of a right-hand playing technique referred to as "rasgueado." This frenetic strumming is sometimes complemented by the picking out of individual bass notes with the thumb.

## RASGUEADO TECHNIQUE

Here is a simple set of step-by-step instructions for playing a very basic rasgueado technique. Although the instructions are broken down into four steps, the entire process should be executed with one fast sweep of the fingers.

Begin by forming an open E major chord and then work through each step shown below. Damping can be performed by bringing the palm of the hand down on the strings immediately after the final stroke of the rasgueado.

Hold all of your fingers above and behind the 6th string.

Bring the 1st finger down and play across all six strings with the tip of the fingernail.

Bring the 2nd finger down in the same way.

Bring the 3rd finger down in the same way.    **18/4** ▶

# FLAMENCO AND LATIN RHYTHMS

## FLAMENCO RHYTHMS

Here is an extremely basic, if typically characteristic flamenco sequence. It uses the chords A minor, G major, F major, and E major. Play the A, E, and G chords on the open strings; F can be played as E-shaped barre chords. Note that the thumb plays the first note of each bar. You'll see in the notation shown below that there are several wavy lines. These are instructions to play the chords as fast arpeggios. This doesn't really do justice to the rasgueado technique or sound—the same instruction could be used to indicate playing a chord by dragging a pick across the strings—however, it is a close approximation of the effect. When the line carries on above the notes, this indicates that the arpeggio should be played from the lowest notes to the highest; the opposite could also be applied by showing the line continuing below the bottom notes.

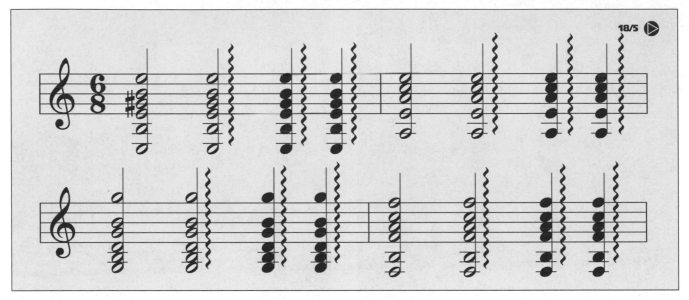

## LATIN RHYTHMS

During the Middle Ages the Spanish Empire spread its wings over much of the Central and Southern American continent. Over the years, the strong links maintained with former Spanish and Portuguese-speaking colonies brought about the evolution of new musical forms which blended Spanish influence with the colonies' own ethnic cultures. Some of these styles, such as samba from Brazil, the mambo from Central America, the tango from Argentina, the Rumba and Merengue from the Caribbean islands, have enjoyed periodic popularity in the West. Some have even crossed over into rock, jazz, and pop to produced new hybrid forms. The strong rhythms have made most of these especially popular for dancing.

## BOSSA NOVA

Of all the Latin rhythms, the most popular in the West have been those from Brazil—most notably the bossa nova. A modern development of the traditional carnival samba, the bossa nova (literally meaning "new style") evolved in the 1950s and enjoyed a strong link with the "cool jazz" movement of the period.

The acoustic guitar (like flamenco, this is nylon-strung rather than steel-strung) is a particularly important instrument for the bossa nova, as it is often used to provide an accentuated harmonic and rhythmic framework for vocal accompaniment.

Among the finest exponents of this style of playing is João Gilberto, whose gentle syncopated guitar work underpins an almost whispered vocal. His close friend and compatriot Carlos Antonio Jobim is perhaps the best-known composer of the form.

### SYNCOPATED EXERCISE

The example at the top of the opposite page gives a flavor of the rhythm of the bossa nova. As with many types of Latin guitar music, you need to pay careful attention to the syncopation between the thumb playing the bassline and the fingers playing the chords—this is what gives the bossa nova its unique feel.

As this is quite a demanding exercise, to keep things simple the example ignores the different time durations of the notes played by the thumb. For example, while the first note is shown as being a quarter note in length, in practice it will sustain until the next note is played, giving it an "actual" value of a dotted quarter note.

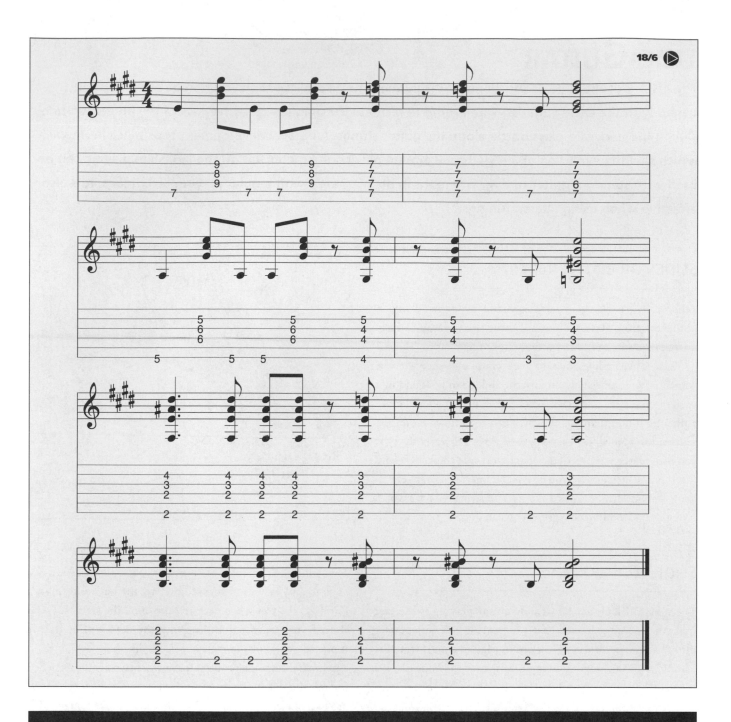

## WHERE TO NOW?

If this has whetted your apetite for flamenco or Latin music, here are a few recommended courses of action. Seek out recordings by the great artists, such as flamenco virtuosi Carlos Montoya, Paco Peña, Nino Ricardo, Sabicas, or Paco de Lucia. For Flamenco Nuevo, try out Ketama if you want to hear a modern take on the form.

To really "experience" flamenco you need to see it performed in a live setting. Watching the interaction between a group of singers, dancers, and guitarists (*a cuadro flamenco*) is quite unlike any other art form.

In terms of attaining proficiency as a flamenco or Latin guitarist, there really is no substitute for one-to-one teaching. To most Western ears, although the overall sound is an extremely pleasant one, flamenco does come from a unique musical tradition, and it really can be difficult for the novice to get to grips with what on earth is actually going on.

In short, it is in gaining an UNDERSTANDING of the form as much as being able to PLAY it that a good teacher is so useful.

# SLIDE GUITAR                    Lesson 19

**The history of the slide or "bottleneck" technique is tied closely to the evolution of blues music. It began with the early guitarists attempting to recreate the unique expressiveness of the human voice by sliding the neck of a glass bottle along the guitar strings. A parallel development took place in Hawaii, which saw the evolution of a style based around playing the guitar flat on the lap. Slide playing can be used with standard guitar tuning, where it can be integrated with regular playing techniques. It is also effective when using altered tunings.**

## SLIDES OR BOTTLENECKS?

Technically speaking, a slide is made from metal and a bottleneck from glass, but nowadays the two terms are largely interchangeable, so from now on we'll simply refer to "slides."

Rather like finding a suitable pick, choosing a slide which is comfortable is extremely important. Slides can be found in a variety of shapes and sizes. Glass produces a cleaner, more authentic sound than metal, which can sometimes produce a grazing sound as it moves along the strings. However the type you use is largely down to the effect you want to produce and the type of instrument you play. They are relatively cheap items—about the same price as a pack of strings—so it's worth trying as many different types as you can find.

## SLIDE TECHNIQUE

The most difficult aspect of slide guitar playing is the fact that you no longer have the frets to provide you with perfect intonation. Therefore, if you are to play in tune—which is usually a good thing—it is important that the slide always be positioned directly ABOVE the fret of the note required.

This will take considerable practice to get right, especially as you will be more accustomed to fitting your fingers BEHIND the fret when pressing down on the strings. If the slide is positioned behind the fret, the note will be flat; if it placed ahead of the fret, it will be sharp.

Another common problem for novice players is the tendency to press the slide too hard against the strings, which can easily produce unpleasant "buzzing" or may even cause contact with the frets. In fact, the slide needs little more pressure than its own weight against the string. Although the fingers behind the slide can be used to dampen fret rattle to a degree, if the "action" of your guitar—the height of the strings above the fretboard—is too low, buzzing may be unavoidable. To prevent this happening, some guitarists raise the action on their instrument, either by adjusting the height of the strings at the bridge, and/or increasing the height of the nut, or zero fret. Take care if trying this out—you can easily ruin the intonation of your guitar if you're not too sure what you're doing. Players who use slide as a major part of their sound usually find it easier to have a separate instrument permanently set up for slide use.

## SLIDE EXERCISE

There are a number of different ways in which slides can be indicated in written music. The most common version sees the two notes joined by a straight line with the letter "S" shown above. This is identical to the notation for regular slide performed with one of the fingers of the left hand (see page 88). Some players find it perferable simply to use curves and omit the letter.

To get your left hand accustomed to holding the slide, start off by positioning the slide above the nut. Play an open E on the 1st string, and while the string is still ringing, slide up to the octave on the 12th fret. Try the same exercise in reverse, starting on the 12th fret of the 1st string. Practice this example over all six strings.

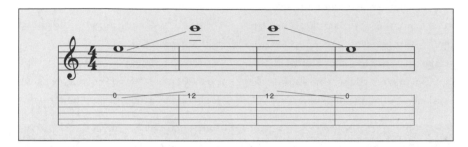

## SLIDING SCALES

The following exercises will test your intonation when playing with the slide. The first example shows a complete scale played along one string. This time, you start on the 3rd string and play a G major scale one note at a time. Again, you can try it over all six strings.

The final example shows a staggered descending major scale. Play the 12th fret; slide down to the open string; slide up to the 11th fret, then back down to the open string, and so forth until you complete the scale.

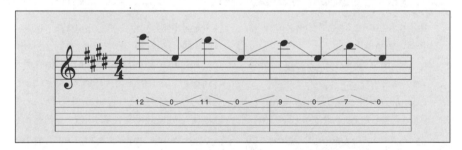

## SCALES ACROSS THE FINGERBOARD

This A minor pentatonic scale starts above the 7th fret of the 1st string and descends over two octaves to the 6th string. Trt playing this exercise descending and ascending the scales.

---

### VIBRATO

One of the most effective expressive devices associated with the slide is vibrato. You can create a vibrato with a slide by gently moving your wrist back and forth. Different effects can be produced depending on how far you move either side of the note. For a pure vibrato, a half-step (semitone) in either direction would be the absolute maximum, but other interesting effects can be produced by going further.

# SLIDES AND CHORDS

### CHORDS AND ALTERED TUNINGS

Whilst many modern players integrate slides into their regular technique, there is a strong blues and folk tradition for playing slide using altered tunings. The most common approach is to use the open tunings (see page 130). As the strings are tuned to a chord, other chords can be played simply by sliding the bottleneck along the fingerboard.

### CHORDS USING OPEN G TUNING

When you play chords using a slide, the most important consideration is that the point at which the slide touches the strings should be ABSOLUTELY parallel to the frets. If they are not, the chord will not be in tune.

On the right you will find a slide exercise that uses open G tuning. Begin by retuning the strings of your guitar—this entails lowering the pitch of the 1st, 5th, and 6th strings by a whole step. From bottom to top, your guitar strings should be tuned to D, G, D, G, B, and D. Now place the slide above the nut, and gradually move up in half-step intervals until you reach the 12th fret. Remember to keep that slide parallel to the frets—you'll soon hear how unpleasant it can sound if you don't!

---

### ALTERNATIVE SLIDES

In addition to the usual glass and metal slides, many unorthodox objects have been used as alternatives. These have included piping, glasses, screwdrivers, spray cans, spanners, penknives, and bones. In fact, anything goes—as long as it can be smoothly dragged across the strings. It is fairly simple to make your own glass slide by cutting the neck from a wine or spirit bottle. If you do this, take care to use proper glass-cutting equipment and, most important of all, make sure that the edges are sanded down, otherwise you can find yourself with an extremely painful cut.

---

### MISSISSIPPI FRED MCDOWELL

<u>Born:</u> January 12th, 1904, Rossville, Tennessee, USA
<u>Died:</u> July 3rd, 1972, Memphis, Tennessee, USA
<u>Guitars:</u> Hofner acoustic; National Resonator; Gibson "Trini Lopez"
<u>Recordings:</u> *In London*; *Sounds Of The South* (compilation)

One of the "unknown" blues pioneers, Fred MacDowell spent the first 55 years of his life working as an itinerant laborer on farms around Mississippi, occasionally playing at nights to local black audiences. It was Alan Lomax, the noted blues and folk archivist, who discovered McDowell's work, which he issued as a part of his series of field recordings made in 1959.

With the encouragement of Lomax, McDowell joined the burgeoning US folk circuit, which found itself home to so many "rediscovered" blues masters. A combination of charismatic charm and a genuine authenticity made him a popular attraction on the US college circuit. This in turn brought him to the attention of a number of prominent blues and folk labels.

His first album, *Delta Blues*, recorded in 1963—the eve of of his 60th birthday—revealed a ferocious playing technique almost entirely based around the use of a steel slide and bass-string runs executed with staggering dexterity.

McDowell's concert repertoire comprised a mix of blues standards, as well as some notable compositions of his own, such as "Write Me A few Lines."

In the mid-1960s he showed an adaptability that belied his years as he made a successful transition to the electric guitar. He gigged and recorded extensively until his death from cancer in 1972.

It was with the young white audiences that McDowell enjoyed his greatest popularity. He was also an acknowledged influence on a number of young musicians growing up through the 1960s—most notably Bonnie Raitt, herself now considered to be one of America's finest contemporary slide guitarists.

**FINGERPICKING OPEN G TUNING**
This exercise requires you to play fingerpicking with the right hand and slide chords with the left hand. With your guitar still tuned to open G, you only need to worry about three chords—D (7th fret), A (14th fret), and G (12th fret). The final chord is played as a harmonic on the 7th fret.

19/3

# ALTERNATIVE APPROACHES Lesson 20

Throughout the book, the musical styles and techniques you have encountered so far have been largely mainstream—if sometimes not quite as "by-the-book" as formal tutors might prefer. We'll finish off the playing section with a look at some alternative approaches to making music with the guitar. It's not a tutorial piece as such, just a glimpse into a world that doesn't usually get too much coverage in guitar tuition of any sort. It's a world where the fingers and picks are not the only way of striking strings, or where there are not necessarily six different strings tuned to E-A-D-G-B-E. On the following spread we'll also take a look at some hardware-based playing techniques. These are not just effects—you'll get plenty of those in Chapter 4—these are areas where the hardware drives the music and playing.

## ALTERNATIVE APPROACHES TO STRINGING AND TUNING

Although strings come in a variety of sizes (gauges) and materials, they all aim to provide the most effective means of producing a consistent sound over around four octaves of the musical spectrum. A number of experimental musicians have tried variations on the traditional approach, with varying degrees of success (depending, of course, on your musical standpoint). Perhaps the best known artist to work in this area is New York-based composer Glenn Branca, who is noted for the sounds produced by his guitar "orchestras." An awesome sound (and sight), many of Branca's works have been performed in large-group settings comprised principally of electric guitars. However, the individual instruments are either re-strung or retuned so that they can be played over a limited register or range of notes. At its most dramatic, the guitar is restrung so that ALL of the strings are identical and are tuned to the same note. Shifts in pitch are made by playing barres with the index finger. In other cases, the guitar may be strung conventionally but, again, all tuned to a single note, albeit in different registers. Various guitars in the ensemble are tuned to different core pitches. As you may well

| TUNING TO D | | |
|---|---|---|
| 1st string | D | (down 1 step) |
| 2nd string | D | (down 4 steps plus a half-step) |
| 3rd string | D | (down 2 steps plus a half-step) |
| 4th string | D | (unchanged) |
| 5th string | D | (down 2 steps plus a half-step) |
| 6th string | D | (down 1 step) |

imagine, the effect of full-six string "chords" played on a half-a-dozen or more of such instruments can be quite overwhelming.

You can try this out for yourself without having to restring your guitar—follow the retuning instructions above, tuning each string DOWN to a D. Strum across all six strings.

To hear some of the power of this approach, play a D major scale by using an index finger barre on the top three strings and treating the open bass strings as pedal tones—notes that remain "droning" beneath the scale.

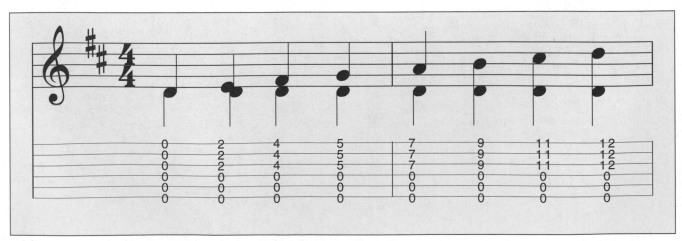

## GUITAR ORCHESTRA

Here's an interesting and enjoyable experiment you can try out for yourself. It will give you some idea of the "choral" effect of a number of guitars using the same single-note tuning shown on the previous page. All you need is access to a multitrack recorder—or, better still, convince a few friends to retune their guitars accordingly. This simple example will create D major and G major chords, each played over 24 strings. First of all, agree a rhythmic framework, perhaps each chord played as whole-note chord. Guitar 1 moves from the open string to a barre on the 5th fret; guitar 2 moves from the 4th fret to a barre on the 9th fret; guitar 3 moves from the 7th fret to a barre on the 12th fret; guitar 4 moves from the 12th fret. Try other combinations for interesting alternative sounds.

### D MAJOR

| Guitar | 1 | Open string (D) |
|--------|---|-----------------|
| Guitar | 2 | Barre on the 4th fret (F♯) |
| Guitar | 3 | Barre on the 7th fret (A) |
| Guitar | 4 | Barre on the 12th fret (D) |

### G MAJOR

| Guitar | 1 | Barre on the 5th fret (G) |
|--------|---|---------------------------|
| Guitar | 2 | Barre on the 9th fret (B) |
| Guitar | 3 | Barre on the 12th fret (D) |
| Guitar | 4 | Barre on the 17th fret (G) |

## BEYOND SIX STRINGS

Although the concept of the six-string guitar has dominated for almost 200 years, guitar makers have continued to experiment with new concepts. Some have been attempts to resolve the guitar's limited bass register. One of the more dramatic designs was the Gibson "harp-guitar" produced in the 1920s. This was a standard guitar with the headstock extended to take account of 12 dedicated bass strings, each tuned at half-step (semitone) intervals—one for each key.

Less dramatic was a seven-string design conceived by jazz guitarist George van Eps during the 1940s (and produced briefly by Gretsch in the 60s). Similarly, in the late 1980s Steve Vai collaborated with Ibanez to produce the Universe guitar. Both of these instruments featured an additional bass string which was usually tuned to a B. This is the same interval below E on the 6th string as those between the bottom four strings. Not only does this provide a significant extension to the range of available notes, but it also opens up a whole new set of chords based on the B string, or B-shaped barres.

Although seven-string guitars have their followers, it has to be said that for many, the beauty of much guitar-based music lies in its simplicity—and the fact that it is possible for a novice to learn a few open-string chords within a few days. When it comes down to it, for the vast majority of players, those extra few bass notes just don't make a whole lot of difference.

### SEVEN-STRING CHORDS

To give you an idea of the new possibilities offered by an extra seventh string, two seven-string chord diagrams are shown below. The chord on the right shows a full seven-string voicing for an open B major chord. On the left you can see how the principles of barre chords can be applied to the 7th string. This B-shaped barre from the 7th fret creates an alternative E major chord over the bottom six strings—using the bottom five strings alone creates an extremely powerful "five" chord.

In practice, when playing chords, seven-string guitars are largely used in the same way as their six-string counterparts, with the 7th string omitted. Their greatest value comes in extending the instrument's single-note range.

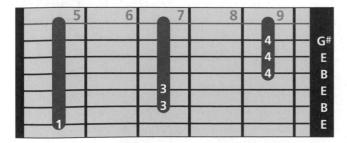

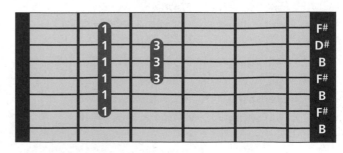

# ALTERNATIVE HARDWARE ISSUES

The variety of effects that you can get by using different amplifier settings and sound processing is covered in detail in Chapter 5; however, for some guitarists, hardware—whether using electronic sound delay, MIDI guitar synthesisers, or alternatives to the traditional pick—may be less a matter of tweaking the sound than a crucial part of creating the music itself.

## MIDI AND GUITAR SYNTHESISERS

Even though most modern guitarists are conversant with MIDI in some form, there remain few who are interested in integrating MIDI with their playing techniques. However, MIDI guitars have a lot to commend themselves, giving non-keyboard players access to a whole new sonic palette. MIDI can also be surprisingly effective in a live context, as a way of giving depth to a thin sound.

Most modern MIDI guitarists fit a specially designed bridge pickup to a guitar of their choice. This connects to a secondary unit that converts the electronic "control voltages" generated by

### FILLING THE SOUND

Guitars linked to external MIDI devices can be very effective at padding out the sound in a live situation—for example, underpinning the main guitar chords with synthesiser or organ sounds.

**20/1**

### EVERY STRING A NEW INSTRUMENT

This may seem excessive, but most MIDI guitar systems allow for the possibility of transmitting a different MIDI channel from every string. This means that if you had access to enough different pieces of equipment, you could control six independent MIDI units from a single guitar. Here is a possible example:

| | |
|---|---|
| 1st string | Synth programmed to play major triads |
| 2nd string | Ambient sustained synth tone |
| 3rd string | Synth with sustained bass tone |
| 4th string | Sample of orchestral "stab" |
| 5th string | Sampled drum loop |
| 6th string | Analog bass synth |

### ANYTHING GOES...

The strings of an amplified guitar are highly sensitive, making them responsive to the most subtle of dynamic shades. Any household object that has non-smooth surfaces can be used to vibrate the strings. Equally, some interesting percussive sounds can be achieved by striking the strings with different objects.

- Comb
- Sandpaper
- Brush
- Drum sticks
- Sliding gnarled metal
- "Bulldog" clips clamped to the string
- Paper threaded between the strings
- Cloth threaded between the strings

Of course, if it's a REAL noise you're after, then you can take the Gizmotron principle (see across) to its natural conclusion by taking the edge of a rotating sanding attachment to the strings. The results of this kind of attack can be somewhat unpredictable!

the pickups into a form that MIDI can understand, giving its own values to the pitch and duration of each note played. These signals can then be connected to external devices, such as synthesisers or samplers, where sounds of the same pitch (unless programed otherwise) are generated.

## DIFFERENT STRIKES

A variety of implements can be used to provide supplementary right-hand playing techniques, creating interesting or unexpected sounds. You can use anything you like if you think the impact will be good, but be advised that some of the ideas listed above can radically reduce the life of your strings—and your guitar.

When Led Zeppelin were performing at their peak, guitarist Jimmy Page often unleashed his very own party piece, playing the guitar with a violin bow. With care, this can produce some interesting textures that are especially effective on the bass strings, creating a cello-like effect.

During the 1970s, a pair of well-known English musicians—Kevin Godley and Lol Creme—developed a mechanical device called the Gizmotron, which fitted over the bridge. A small, lightly abrasive rotating wheel was pressed down onto the string to give a continuous bowing motion that, if played with care, could approximate the sound of a cello or violin. In spite of the great sounds it could produce, it was difficult to use.

An alternative device, and one which is slightly kinder to the strings, is the E-bow, a magnetic hand-held device which, when held close to the strings, causes them to vibrate, creating an infinitely sustainable note. This has found a sturdy, if small, following since its invention in the 1970s.

## ROBERT FRIPP

<u>Name:</u> Robert Fripp
<u>Born:</u> May 9, 1946, Wimborne, England
<u>Guitars:</u> Gibson Les Paul and customized Tokai Les Paul
<u>Recorded Highlights:</u> *The Court Of The Crimson King* (King Crimson); *No Pussyfooting* (Fripp and Eno)

Although Robert Fripp is by no means the most experimental guitarist in modern music, mainstream success has given a wider audience to some of his more esoteric work than pretty well any other "left-field" guitarist. This alone has made him a major influence on several generations of guitarists and experimental soundmakers.

Finding prominence in the late 1960s, Fripp's band King Crimson was one of the most worthwhile of the progressive rock era. It was largely the carefully balanced playing of Robert Fripp that set them apart from contemporaries, who all too often disappeared in pointlessly "technoflash" cul-de-sacs. Fripp stood out because there always seemed to be a good reason for what he was playing.

King Crimson were among the most successful British bands of the early 1970s. However, in 1973 Fripp hooked up with Brian Eno, with whom he made the ground-breaking *No Pussyfooting* album. Effectively a solo guitar work, with "processing" by Eno, the sounds were recorded in one take using a system he devised, known as "Frippertronics." This technique involved passing tape across the heads of two linked Revox tape recorders, enabling lengthy loops of sound to be layered, thus creating lush soundscapes over which Fripp could then play solo parts.

One of the few progressive rock musicians whose reputation increased throughout the New Wave era, Fripp resuscitated King Crimson in 1980 in a "supergroup" line-up featuring Adrian Belew, the two guitarists interlocking

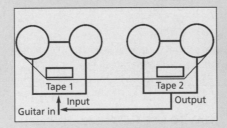

brilliantly on their "debut" album, *Discipline*. From the late 1970s, Fripp proved to be an in-demand session figure, his work finding its way onto albums by artists like David Bowie, Peter Gabriel, and David Sylvian.

Fripp has now laid his tape recorders to rest in favor of the powerful TC digital delay lines, which allow for the creation of 64-minute delays. This system allows for greater control, flexibility, and, of course, sound quality.

Aptly, Fripp refers to his new way of working as "Soundscapes." He is also one of a small band of notable guitarists to work with a MIDI guitar-synth system.

Much of the 1990s saw Fripp concentrating on his *Guitar Craft* schools, which has seen him teach an alternative philosophy of the instrument that includes altered, as well as standard, tunings. He continues to issue new recordings regularly, although his later releases, with *Guitar Craft* students, or his wife—former New Wave star Toyah Wilcox—are perhaps not among his most noteworthy.

# CHAPTER 3
## The Chord Finder

## USING THE CHORD FINDER

**An expansive chord vocabulary, and an understanding of the way in which chords are constructed, is perhaps the most useful capability that a guitarist can acquire. It provides composers and songwriters with a more sophisticated palette from which to draw. It also provides arrangers with valuable lessons, such as the importance of understanding the way different voicings and inversions work.**

The Chord Finder offers a useful reference guide for playing 33 different chord types in all twelve keys.

voicing for every key—the notes may all be there, but sometimes the effect will just sound a little bit strange.

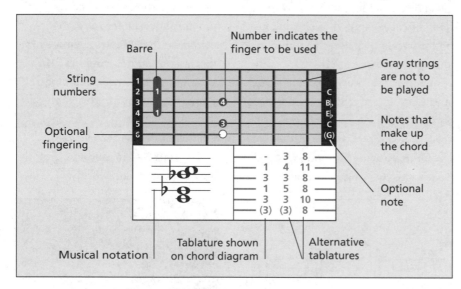

Barre

Number indicates the finger to be used

String numbers

Optional fingering

Gray strings are not to be played

Notes that make up the chord

Optional note

Musical notation

Tablature shown on chord diagram

Alternative tablatures

Each voicing appears with two alternative positions. In all, there are 1188 different chord shapes shown. Additionally, each of the main voicings can be heard on the accompanying CD. Not only does this enable you to compare your own playing of the chords, but by listening to the CD you will (hopefully) be able to place those mysterious chords that you've heard used on familiar recordings but have not been able to name or play. It will also, hopefully, get you newly acquainted with some of the more unusual or esoteric sounds. Be warned, however, that it may not be possible to produce a satisfactory

### HOW TO USE THE CHORD FINDER
The chord diagram represents an overhead view of the fingerboard. Circles indicate finger positioning. Unmarked circles indicate that the note is optional. Alongside each string you can see the name of the note being played. Where a string is gray, it should NOT be played. Finally, you will also find the standard music notation and guitar tablature for the chord: two further inversions of each chord are shown in tablature form, allowing the same chords to be played in different positions on the fingerboard.

### SCALE DEGREES
To aid your understanding of the way the chords are built, the table on the opposite page illustrates the components of each chord type. The crosses on the matrix tie up the chord names to the scale degrees used in any key.

### ENHARMONIC ISSUES

To keep things neat and tidy, the enharmonic keys—those that have two names—are identified by their most commonly used names. We therefore refer to the key of B♭ rather than A♯. Similarly, the keys of C♯, E♭, F♯, and A♭ are used instead of D♭, D♯, G♭, and G♯ respectively.

However, the notes on the chord diagrams are named so as to be enharmonically correct. This may mean that sometimes you come across a less familiar identity for a specific note. For example, the chord F 7-9 has a flattened ninth, as it is in the key of F, reduces the ninth note from G to G♭. Hence, G♭ is the correct label, even though it's far more common to refer to the note as F♯.

| Chord Type | Abbrev. | I | ii | II | iii | III | IV | v | V | vi | VI | vii | VII | I | ii | II | iii | III | IV | v | V | vi | VI |
|---|---|---|---|---|---|---|---|---|---|---|---|---|---|---|---|---|---|---|---|---|---|---|---|
| _(note)_ | | C | C♯/D♭ | D | D♯/E♭ | E | F | F♯/G♭ | G | G♯/A♭ | A | A♯/B♭ | B | C | C♯/D♭ | D | D♯/E♭ | E | F | F♯/G♭ | G | G♯/A♭ | A |
| _(interval)_ | | 1st | ♭2nd | 2nd | ♭3rd | 3rd | 4th | ♯4th or ♭5th | 5th | ♯5th or ♭6th | 6th | ♭7th | 7th | 1st | ♭9th | 9th | ♯9th | ♭11th | 11th | ♯11th | 5th | ♭13th | 13th |
| Major | maj | ● | | | | ● | | | ● | | | | | | | | | | | | | | |
| Minor | m | ● | | | ● | | | | ● | | | | | | | | | | | | | | |
| Dominant Seventh | 7 | ● | | | | ● | | | ● | | | ● | | | | | | | | | | | |
| Minor Seventh | m7 | ● | | | ● | | | | ● | | | ● | | | | | | | | | | | |
| Major Seventh | maj7 or Δ7 | ● | | | | ● | | | ● | | | | ● | | | | | | | | | | |
| Suspended Fourth | sus4 | ● | | | | | ● | | ● | | | | | | | | | | | | | | |
| Seventh Suspended Fourth | 7sus4 | ● | | | | | ● | | ● | | | ● | | | | | | | | | | | |
| Sixth | 6 | ● | | | | ● | | | ● | | ● | | | | | | | | | | | | |
| Minor Sixth | m6 | ● | | | ● | | | | ● | | ● | | | | | | | | | | | | |
| Diminished Seventh | dim7 or ° | ● | | | ● | | | ● | | | ● | | | | | | | | | | | | |
| Augmented | aug or + | ● | | | | ● | | | | ● | | | | | | | | | | | | | |
| Seventh Diminished Fifth | 7-5 | ● | | | | ● | | ● | | | | ● | | | | | | | | | | | |
| Seventh Augmented Fifth | 7+5 | ● | | | | ● | | | | ● | | ● | | | | | | | | | | | |
| Half Diminished Seventh | m7-5 or ø | ● | | | ● | | | ● | | | | ● | | | | | | | | | | | |
| Minor/Major Seventh | m/maj7 | ● | | | ● | | | | ● | | | | ● | | | | | | | | | | |
| Major Seventh Augmented Fifth | maj7+5 | ● | | | | ● | | | | ● | | | ● | | | | | | | | | | |
| Major Seventh Diminished Fifth | maj7-5 | ● | | | | ● | | ● | | | | | ● | | | | | | | | | | |
| Ninth | 9 | ● | | | | ● | | | ● | | | ● | | | | ● | | | | | | | |
| Minor Ninth | m9 | ● | | | ● | | | | ● | | | ● | | | | ● | | | | | | | |
| Major Ninth | maj9 or Δ9 | ● | | | | ● | | | ● | | | | ● | | | ● | | | | | | | |
| Seventh Augmented Ninth | 7+9 | ● | | | | ● | | | ● | | | ● | | | | | ● | | | | | | |
| Seventh Diminished Ninth | 7-9 | ● | | | | ● | | | ● | | | ● | | | ● | | | | | | | | |
| Seventh Augmented Ninth Diminished | 7+9-5 | ● | | | | ● | | ● | | | | ● | | | | | ● | | | | | | |
| Sixth/Ninth | 6/9 | ● | | | | ● | | | ● | | ● | | | | | ● | | | | | | | |
| Ninth Augmented Fifth | 9+5 | ● | | | | ● | | | | ● | | ● | | | | ● | | | | | | | |
| Ninth Diminished Fifth | 9-5 | ● | | | | ● | | ● | | | | ● | | | | ● | | | | | | | |
| Minor Ninth Diminished Fifth | m9-5 | ● | | | ● | | | ● | | | | ● | | | | ● | | | | | | | |
| Eleventh | 11 | ● | | | | ● | | | ● | | | ● | | | | ● | | | ● | | | | |
| Minor Eleventh | m11 | ● | | | ● | | | | ● | | | ● | | | | ● | | | ● | | | | |
| Eleventh Diminished Ninth | 11-9 | ● | | | | ● | | | ● | | | ● | | | ● | | | | ● | | | | |
| Thirteenth | 13 | ● | | | | ● | | | ● | | | ● | | | | ● | | | ● | | | | ● |
| Minor Thirteenth | m13 | ● | | | ● | | | | ● | | | ● | | | | ● | | | ● | | | | ● |
| Major Thirteenth | maj13 or Δ13 | ● | | | | ● | | | ● | | | | ● | | | ● | | | ● | | | | ● |

## AUGMENTED AND DIMINISHED CHORDS

There are two chord voicings whose unique features need to be pointed out. The notes of the augmented (aug or +) and diminished (dim or °) chords are related in such a way that moving the same shape along the fingerboard produces different inversions of the same chord.

The chord A diminished uses the notes A, C, E♭, and G♭. If you move the chord shape THREE frets along the fingerboard, the chord you will hear is C diminished, which comprises the same notes—C, E♭, G♭, and A. The diminished chords in G♭ and E♭ also use these four notes. Similarly, the diminished chords in B♭, D, E, and G all use the same four notes, as do those in B, D, F, and A♭.

The augmented chord is slightly different in that it only makes use of three notes. However, if you move the augmented shape FOUR frets along the fingerboard, you also create the same augmented chord. Once again, the notes that make up this chord can all be used as the root for different inversions of the same chord.

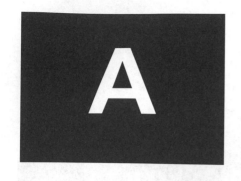

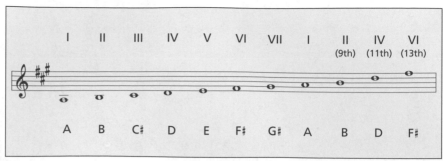

| | I | II | III | IV | V | VI | VII | I | II (9th) | IV (11th) | VI (13th) |
|---|---|---|---|---|---|---|---|---|---|---|---|
| | A | B | C# | D | E | F# | G# | A | B | D | F# |

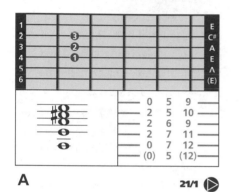

**A**    21/1 ▷

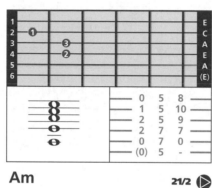

**Am**    21/2 ▷

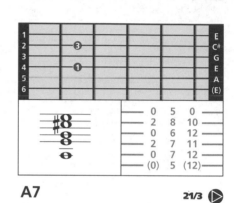

**A7**    21/3 ▷

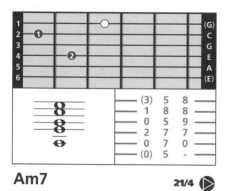

**Am7**    21/4 ▷

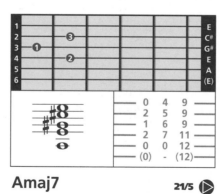

**Amaj7**    21/5 ▷

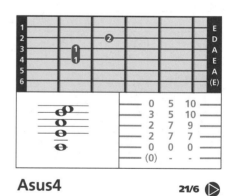

**Asus4**    21/6 ▷

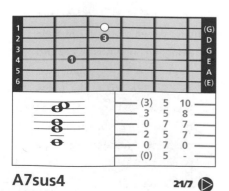

**A7sus4**    21/7 ▷

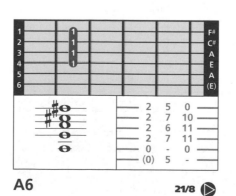

**A6**    21/8 ▷

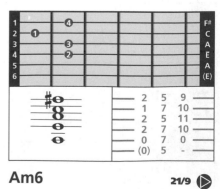

**Am6**    21/9 ▷

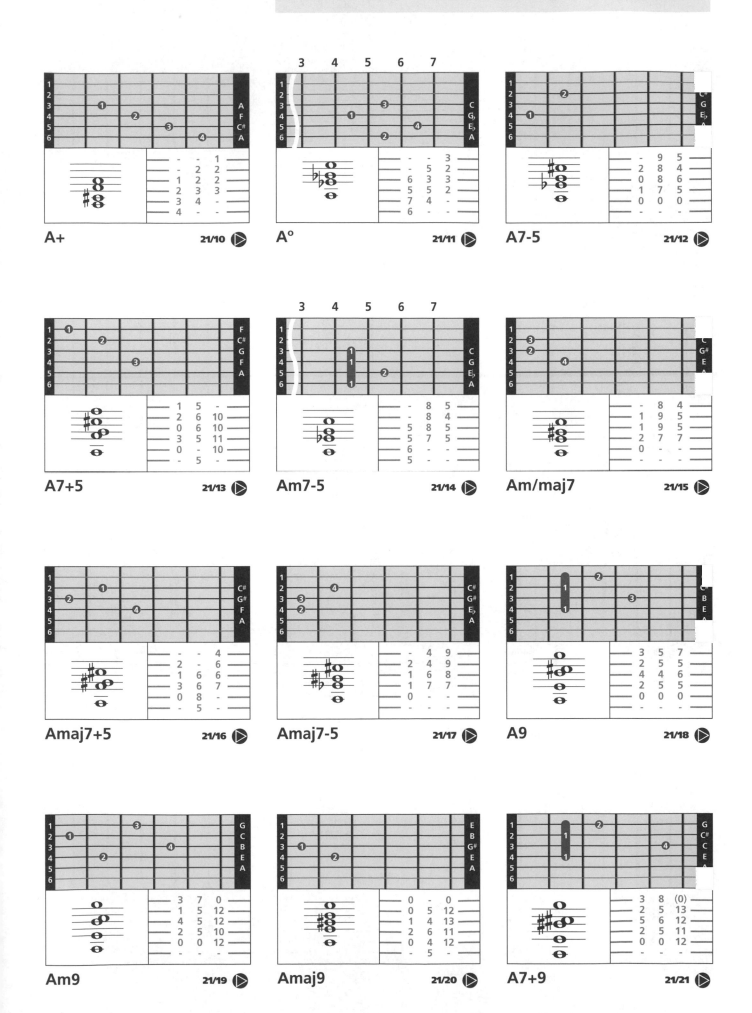

A+    21/10

A°    21/11

A7-5    21/12

A7+5    21/13

Am7-5    21/14

Am/maj7    21/15

Amaj7+5    21/16

Amaj7-5    21/17

A9    21/18

Am9    21/19

Amaj9    21/20

A7+9    21/21

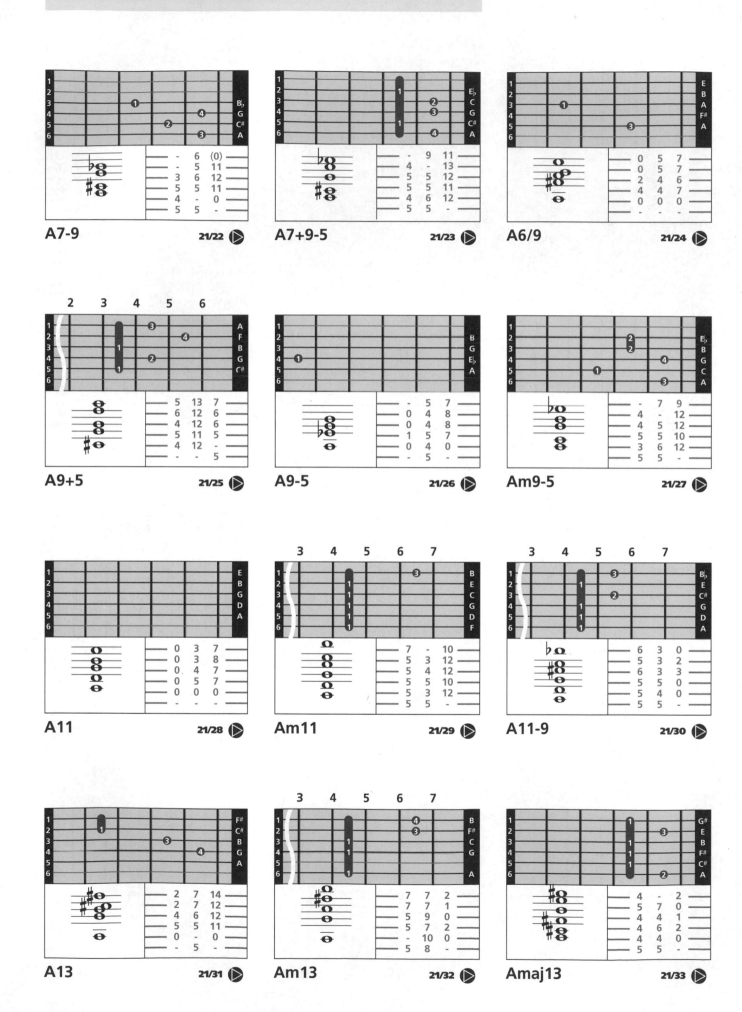

**A7-9**   21/22

**A7+9-5**   21/23

**A6/9**   21/24

**A9+5**   21/25

**A9-5**   21/26

**Am9-5**   21/27

**A11**   21/28

**Am11**   21/29

**A11-9**   21/30

**A13**   21/31

**Am13**   21/32

**Amaj13**   21/33

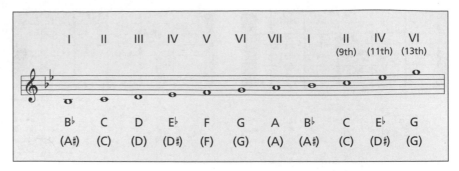

| | I | II | III | IV | V | VI | VII | I | II (9th) | IV (11th) | VI (13th) |
|---|---|---|---|---|---|---|---|---|---|---|---|
| | B♭ | C | D | E♭ | F | G | A | B♭ | C | E♭ | G |
| | (A#) | (C) | (D) | (D#) | (F) | (G) | (A) | (A#) | (C) | (D#) | (G) |

**B♭**          22/1

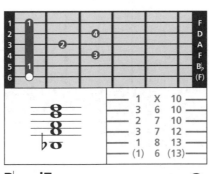

**B♭m**          22/2

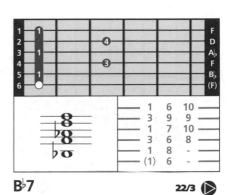

**B♭7**          22/3

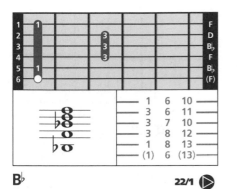

**B♭m7**          22/4

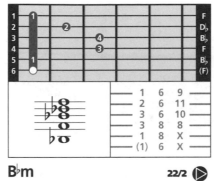

**B♭maj7**          22/5

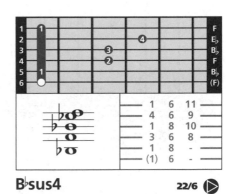

**B♭sus4**          22/6

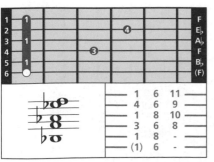

**B♭7sus4**          22/7

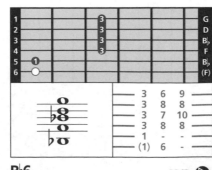

**B♭6**          22/8

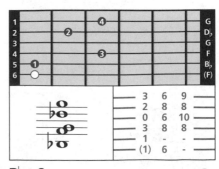

**B♭m6**          22/9

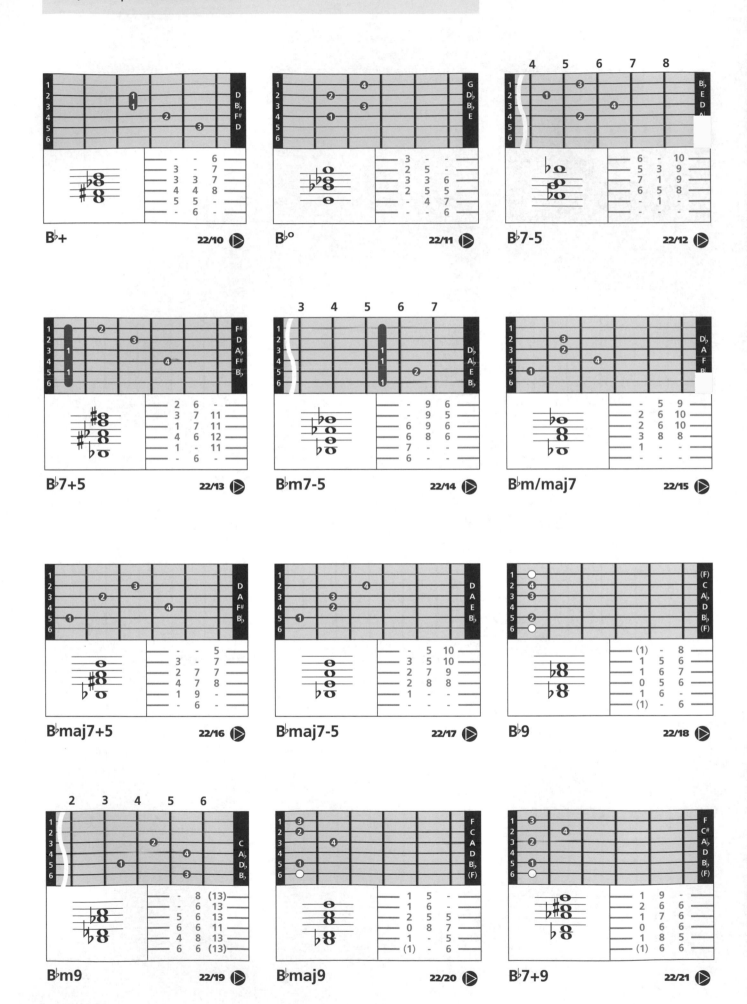

B♭+                                    22/10 ▶

B♭°                                    22/11 ▶

B♭7-5                                  22/12 ▶

B♭7+5                                  22/13 ▶

B♭m7-5                                 22/14 ▶

B♭m/maj7                               22/15 ▶

B♭maj7+5                               22/16 ▶

B♭maj7-5                               22/17 ▶

B♭9                                    22/18 ▶

B♭m9                                   22/19 ▶

B♭maj9                                 22/20 ▶

B♭7+9                                  22/21 ▶

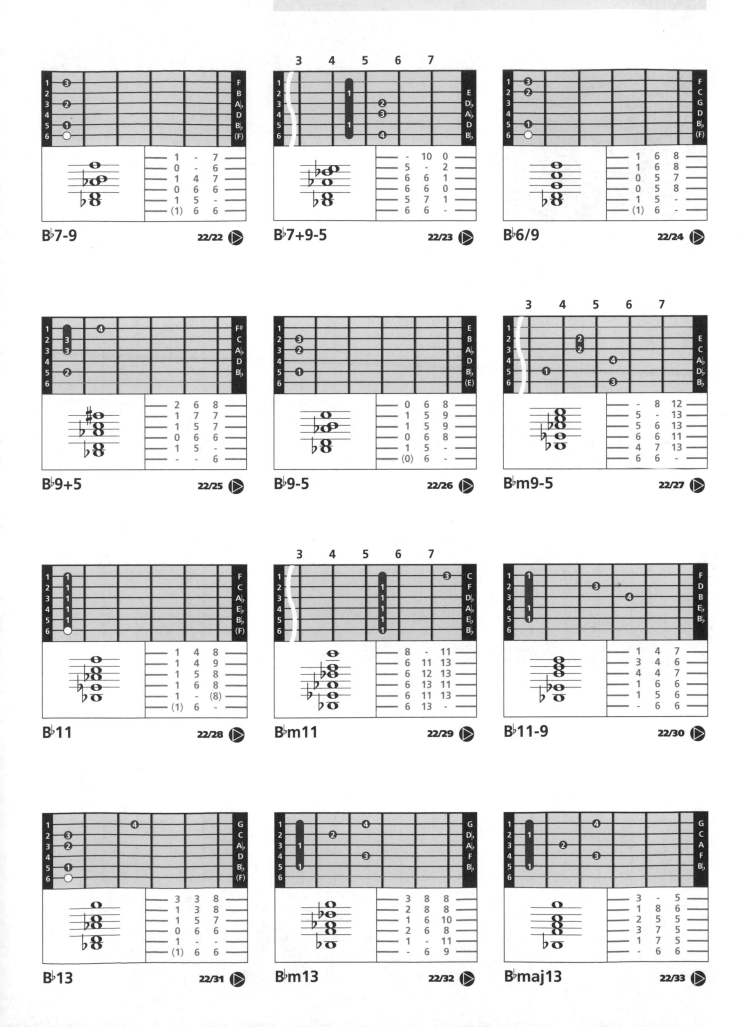

B♭7-9     22/22

B♭7+9-5     22/23

B♭6/9     22/24

B♭9+5     22/25

B♭9-5     22/26

B♭m9-5     22/27

B♭11     22/28

B♭m11     22/29

B♭11-9     22/30

B♭13     22/31

B♭m13     22/32

B♭maj13     22/33

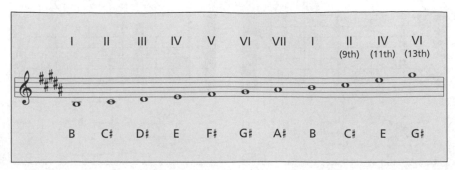

| | I | II | III | IV | V | VI | VII | I | II (9th) | IV (11th) | VI (13th) |
|---|---|---|---|---|---|---|---|---|---|---|---|
| | B | C# | D# | E | F# | G# | A# | B | C# | E | G# |

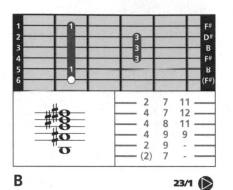

**B**   23/1

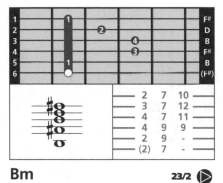

**Bm**   23/2

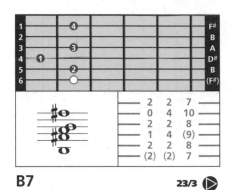

**B7**   23/3

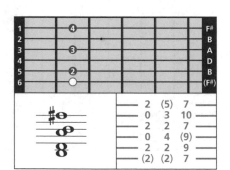

**Bm7**   23/4

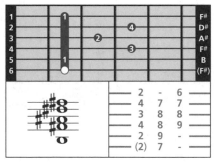

**Bmaj7**   23/5

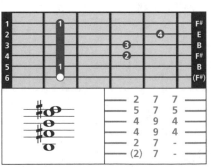

**Bsus4**   23/6

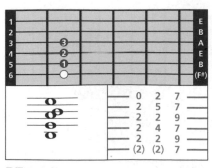

**B7sus4**   23/7

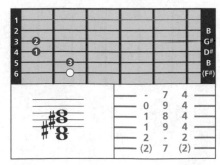

**B6**   23/8

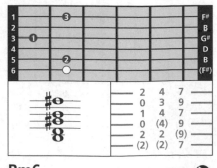

**Bm6**   23/9

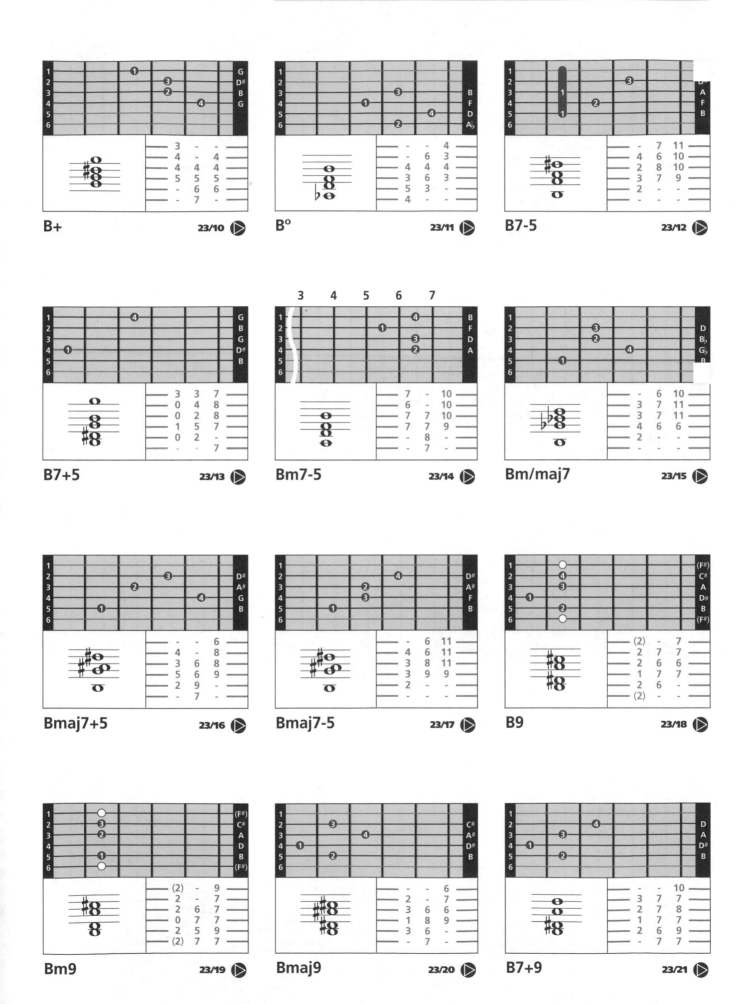

B+  23/10

B°  23/11

B7-5  23/12

B7+5  23/13

Bm7-5  23/14

Bm/maj7  23/15

Bmaj7+5  23/16

Bmaj7-5  23/17

B9  23/18

Bm9  23/19

Bmaj9  23/20

B7+9  23/21

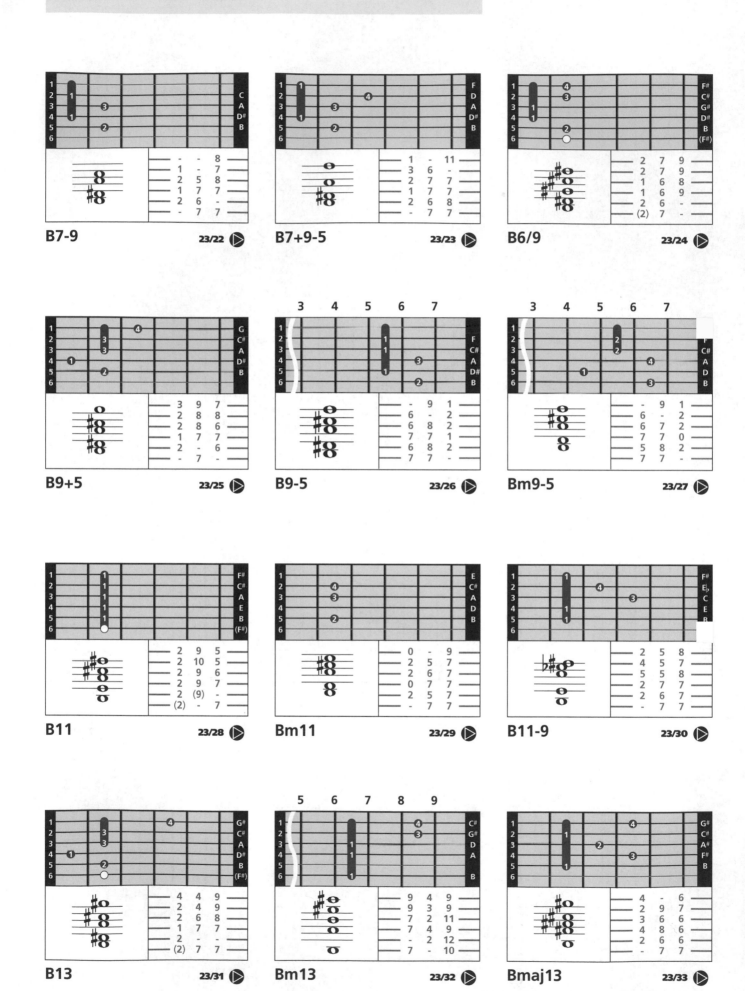

**B7-9**  23/22

**B7+9-5**  23/23

**B6/9**  23/24

**B9+5**  23/25

**B9-5**  23/26

**Bm9-5**  23/27

**B11**  23/28

**Bm11**  23/29

**B11-9**  23/30

**B13**  23/31

**Bm13**  23/32

**Bmaj13**  23/33

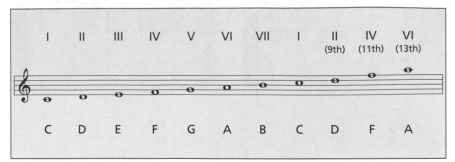

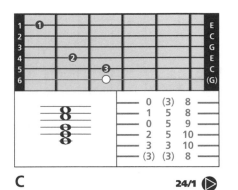

C    24/1 ▶

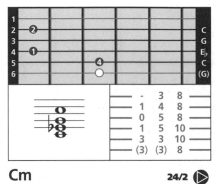

Cm    24/2 ▶

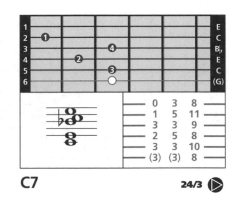

C7    24/3 ▶

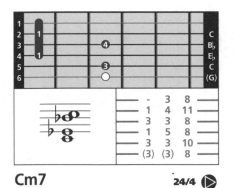

Cm7    24/4 ▶

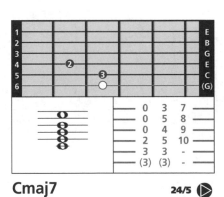

Cmaj7    24/5 ▶

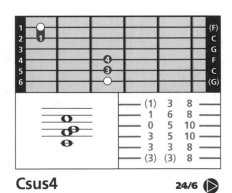

Csus4    24/6 ▶

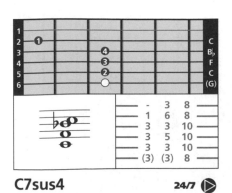

C7sus4    24/7 ▶

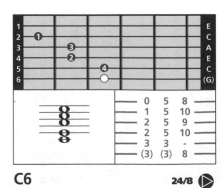

C6    24/8 ▶

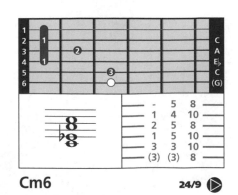

Cm6    24/9 ▶

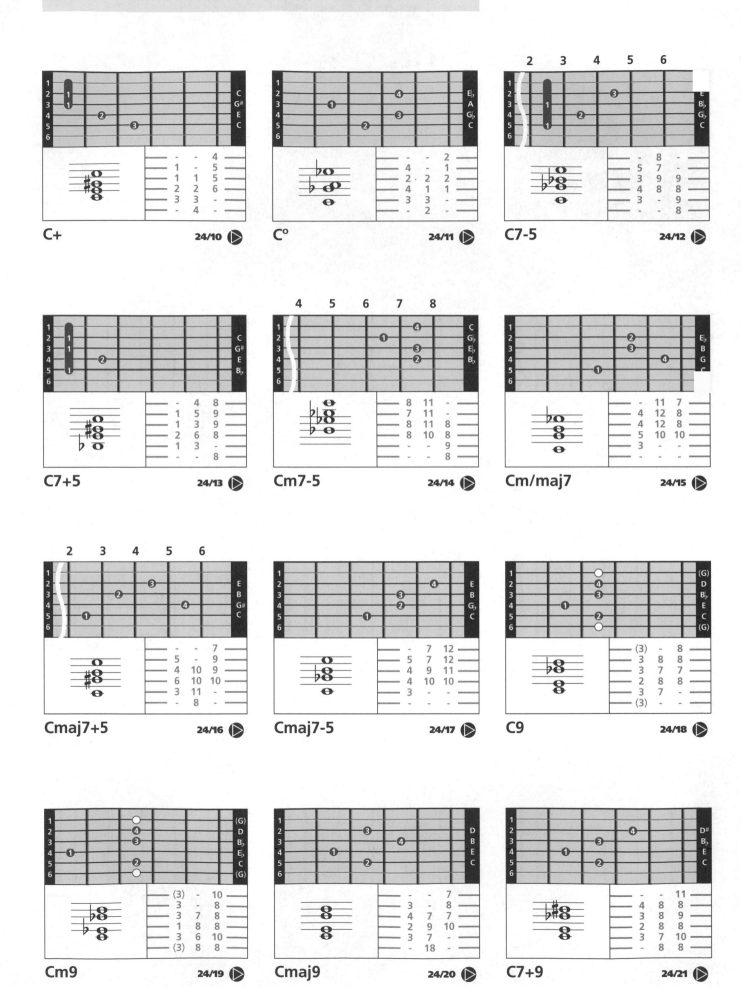

C+    24/10

C°    24/11

C7-5    24/12

C7+5    24/13

Cm7-5    24/14

Cm/maj7    24/15

Cmaj7+5    24/16

Cmaj7-5    24/17

C9    24/18

Cm9    24/19

Cmaj9    24/20

C7+9    24/21

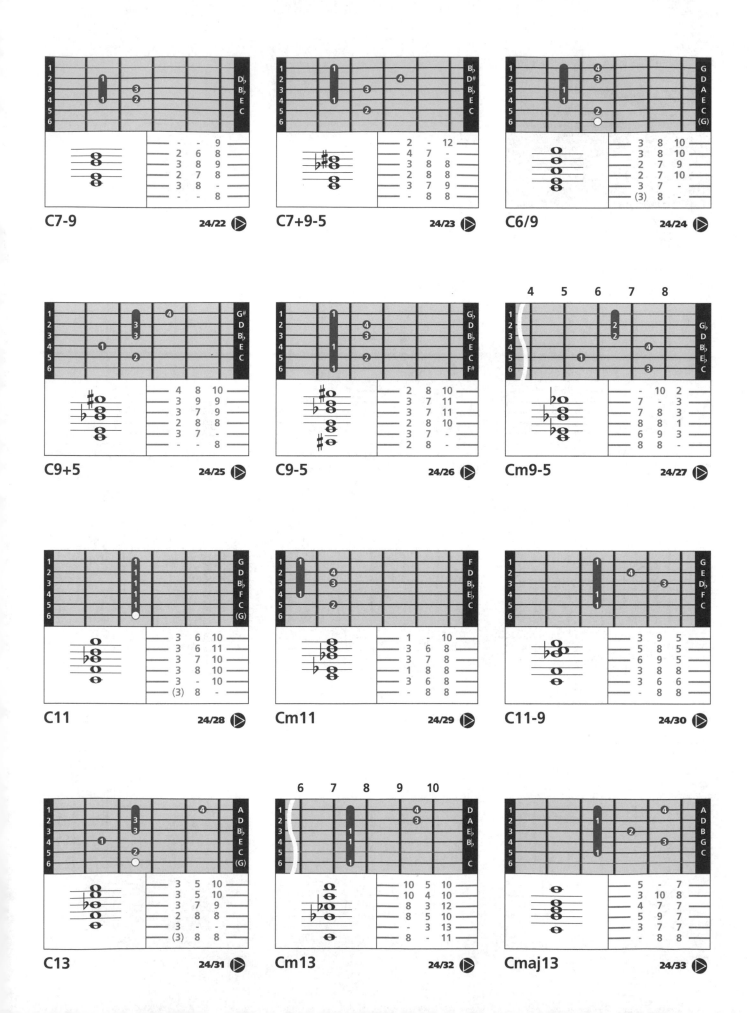

C7-9    24/22

C7+9-5    24/23

C6/9    24/24

C9+5    24/25

C9-5    24/26

Cm9-5    24/27

C11    24/28

Cm11    24/29

C11-9    24/30

C13    24/31

Cm13    24/32

Cmaj13    24/33

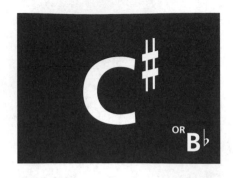

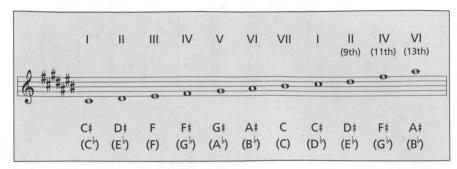

| | I | II | III | IV | V | VI | VII | I | II (9th) | IV (11th) | VI (13th) |
|---|---|---|---|---|---|---|---|---|---|---|---|
| | C# | D# | F | F# | G# | A# | C | C# | D# | F# | A# |
| | (C♭) | (E♭) | (F) | (G♭) | (A♭) | (B♭) | (C) | (D♭) | (E♭) | (G♭) | (B♭) |

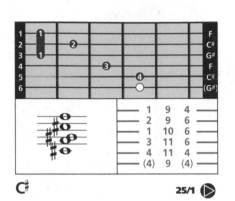

C#    25/1 ▶

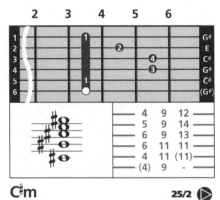

C#m    25/2 ▶

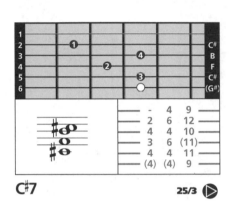

C#7    25/3 ▶

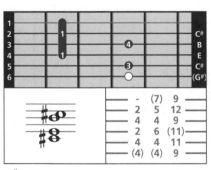

C#m7    25/4 ▶

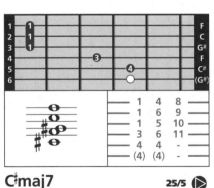

C#maj7    25/5 ▶

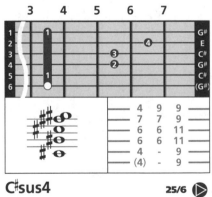

C#sus4    25/6 ▶

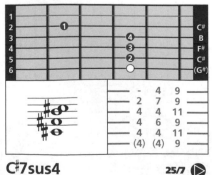

C#7sus4    25/7 ▶

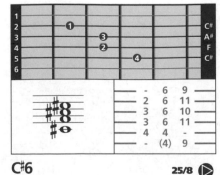

C#6    25/8 ▶

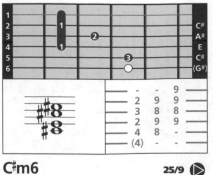

C#m6    25/9 ▶

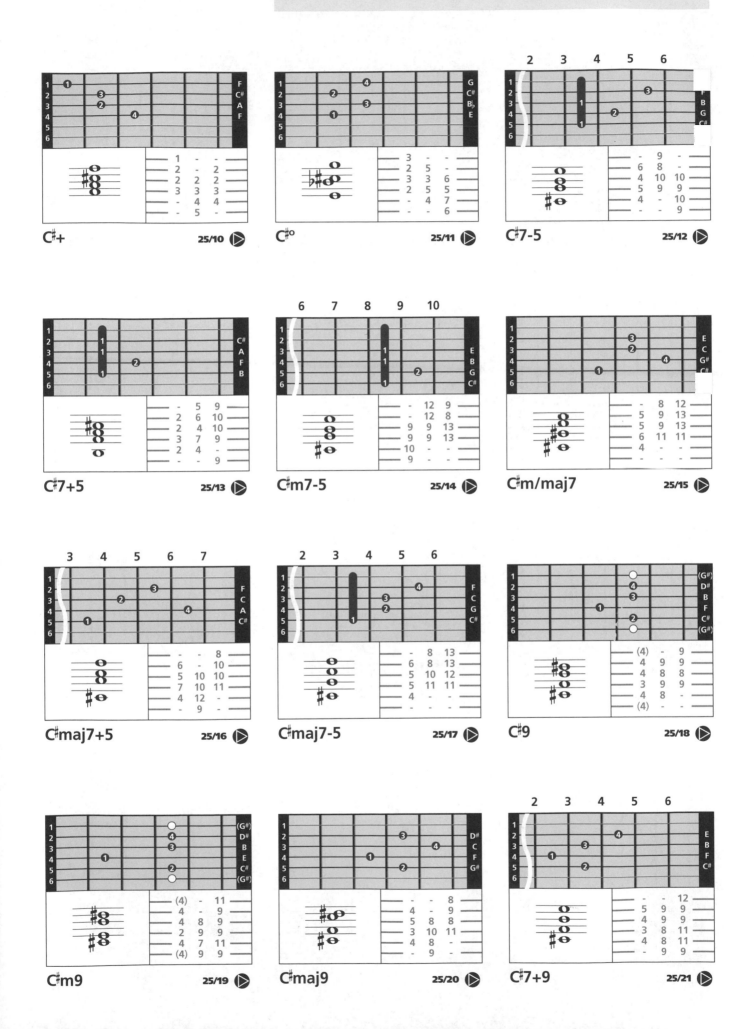

C#+    25/10 ▶

C#o    25/11 ▶

C#7-5    25/12 ▶

C#7+5    25/13 ▶

C#m7-5    25/14 ▶

C#m/maj7    25/15 ▶

C#maj7+5    25/16 ▶

C#maj7-5    25/17 ▶

C#9    25/18 ▶

C#m9    25/19 ▶

C#maj9    25/20 ▶

C#7+9    25/21 ▶

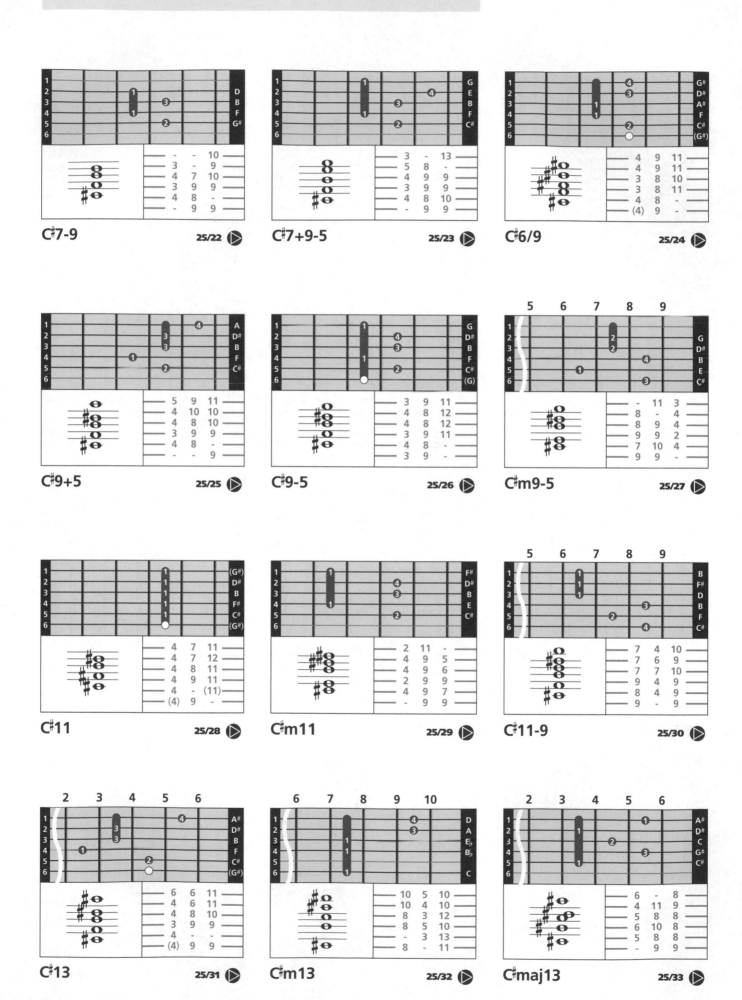

C#7-9    25/22 ▶

C#7+9-5    25/23 ▶

C#6/9    25/24 ▶

C#9+5    25/25 ▶

C#9-5    25/26 ▶

C#m9-5    25/27 ▶

C#11    25/28 ▶

C#m11    25/29 ▶

C#11-9    25/30 ▶

C#13    25/31 ▶

C#m13    25/32 ▶

C#maj13    25/33 ▶

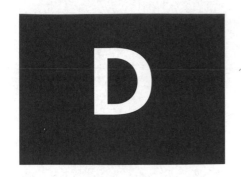

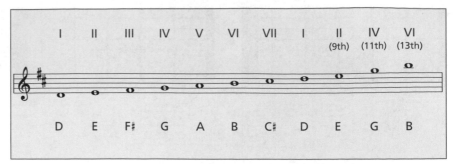

| | I | II | III | IV | V | VI | VII | I | II (9th) | IV (11th) | VI (13th) |
|---|---|---|---|---|---|---|---|---|---|---|---|
| | D | E | F# | G | A | B | C# | D | E | G | B |

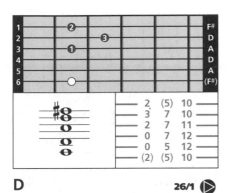

**D**  26/1 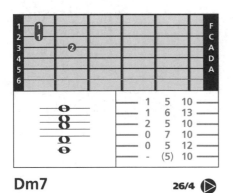 

**Dm**  26/2

**D7**  26/3

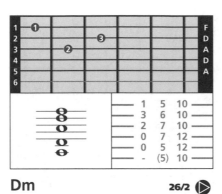

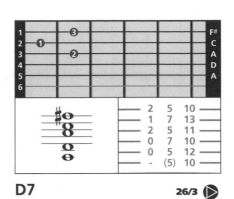

**Dm7**  26/4

**Dmaj7**  26/5

**Dsus4**  26/6

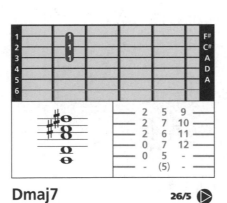

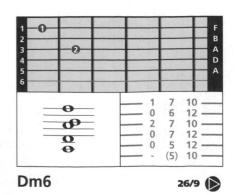

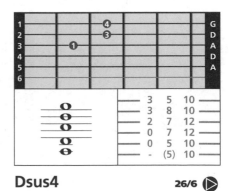

**D7sus4**  26/7

**D6**  26/8

**Dm6**  26/9

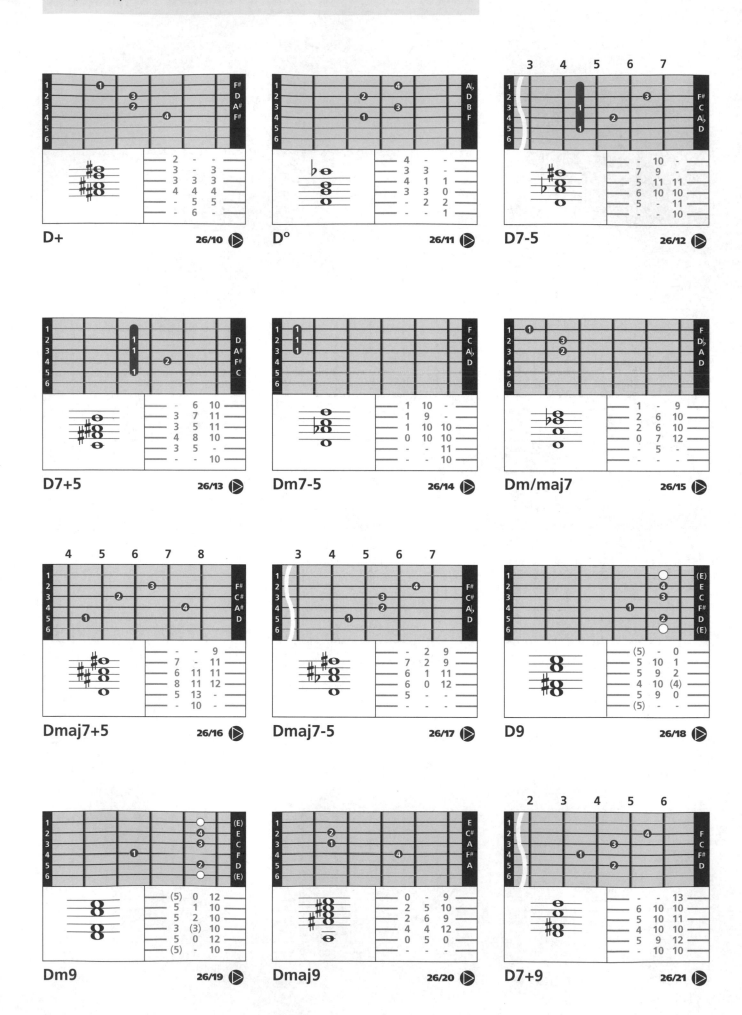

D+          26/10

D°          26/11

D7-5        26/12

D7+5        26/13

Dm7-5       26/14

Dm/maj7     26/15

Dmaj7+5     26/16

Dmaj7-5     26/17

D9          26/18

Dm9         26/19

Dmaj9       26/20

D7+9        26/21

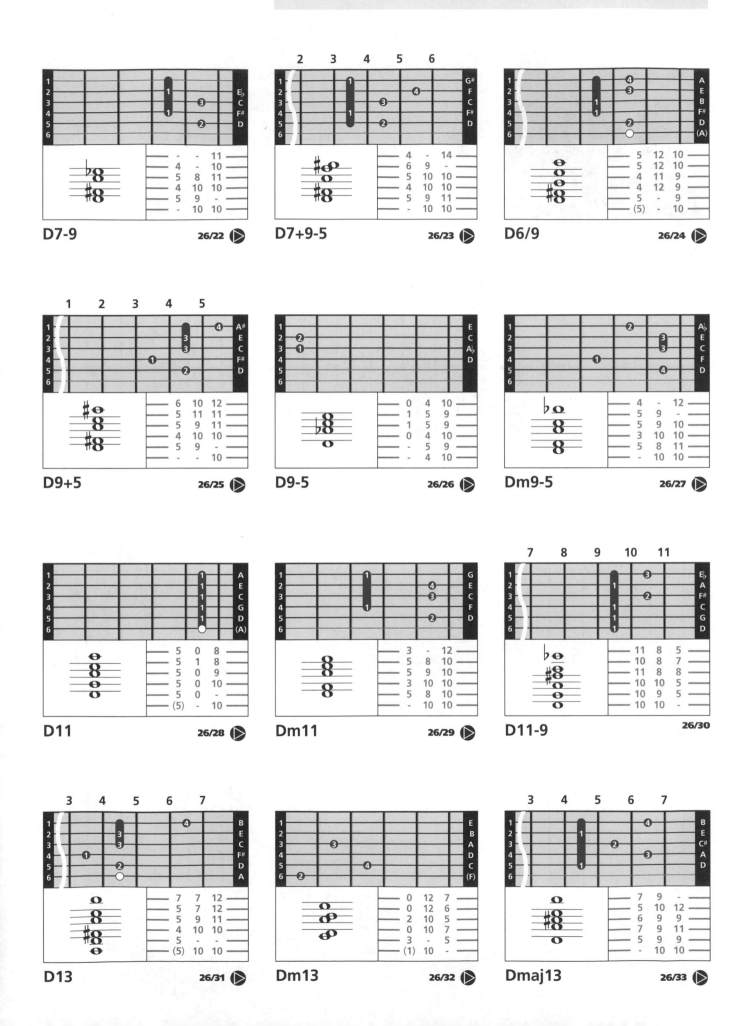

D7-9    26/22

D7+9-5    26/23

D6/9    26/24

D9+5    26/25

D9-5    26/26

Dm9-5    26/27

D11    26/28

Dm11    26/29

D11-9    26/30

D13    26/31

Dm13    26/32

Dmaj13    26/33

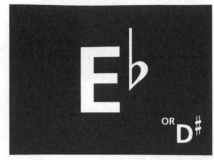

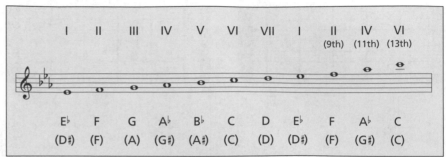

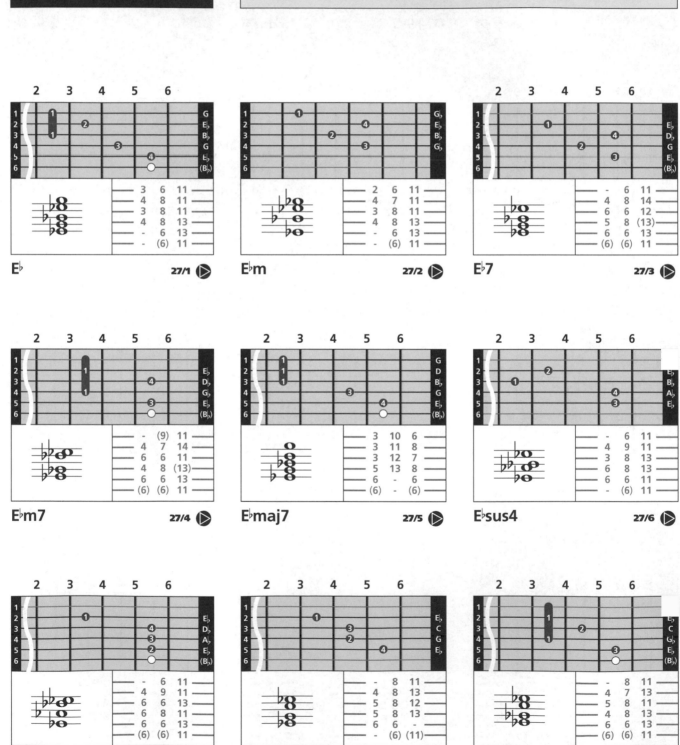

E♭                         27/1 ▶

E♭m                        27/2 ▶

E♭7                        27/3 ▶

E♭m7                       27/4 ▶

E♭maj7                     27/5 ▶

E♭sus4                     27/6 ▶

E♭7sus4                    27/7 ▶

E♭6                        27/8 ▶

E♭m6                       27/9 ▶

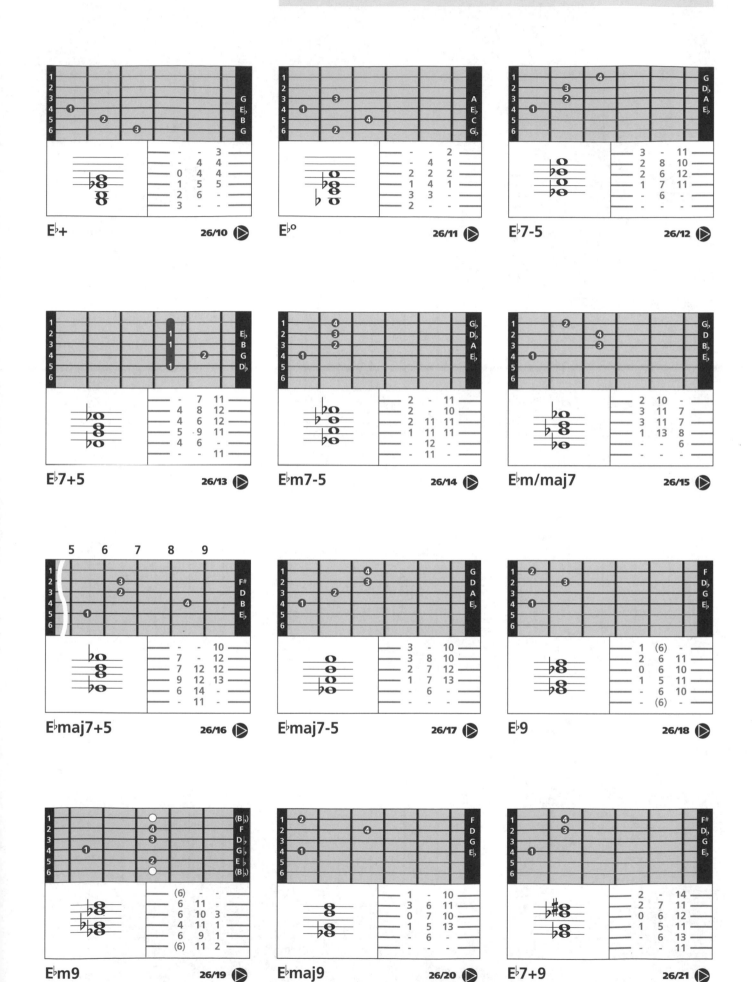

E♭+ 26/10

E♭o 26/11

E♭7-5 26/12

E♭7+5 26/13

E♭m7-5 26/14

E♭m/maj7 26/15

E♭maj7+5 26/16

E♭maj7-5 26/17

E♭9 26/18

E♭m9 26/19

E♭maj9 26/20

E♭7+9 26/21

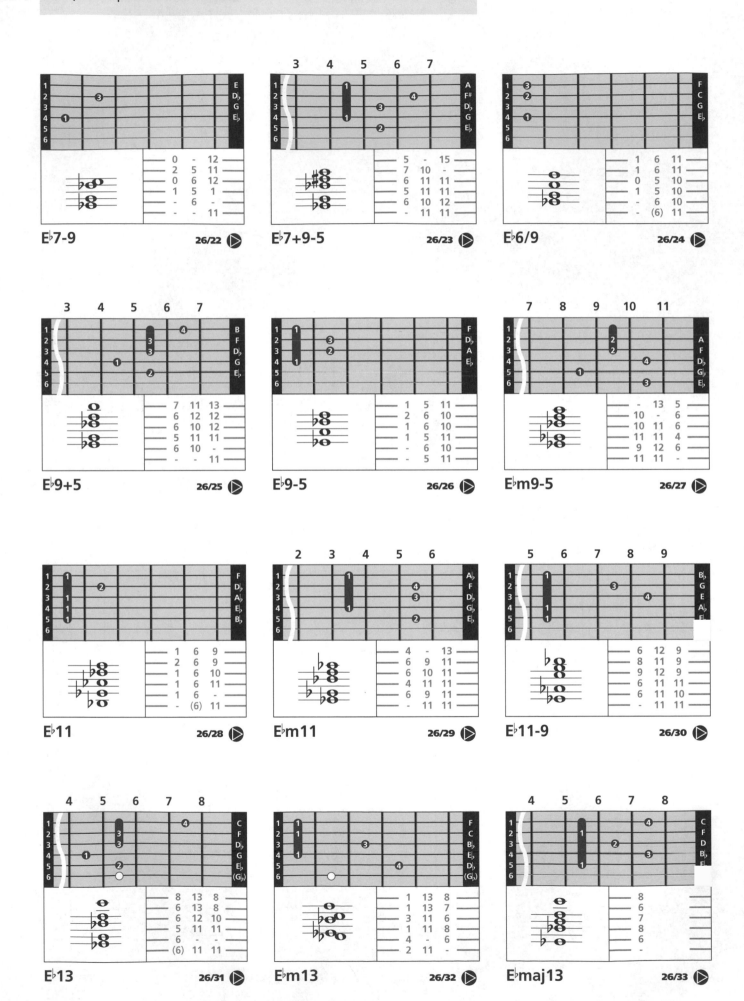

E♭7-9          26/22

E♭7+9-5        26/23

E♭6/9          26/24

E♭9+5          26/25

E♭9-5          26/26

E♭m9-5         26/27

E♭11           26/28

E♭m11          26/29

E♭11-9         26/30

E♭13           26/31

E♭m13          26/32

E♭maj13        26/33

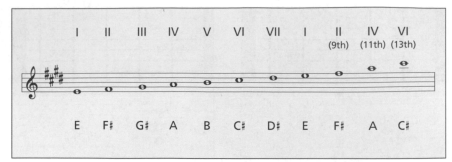

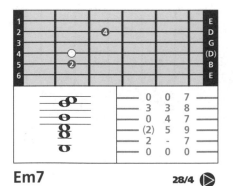

**E**    28/1 ▷

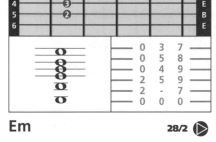

**Em**    28/2 ▷

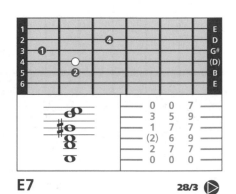

**E7**    28/3 ▷

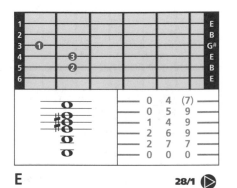

**Em7**    28/4 ▷

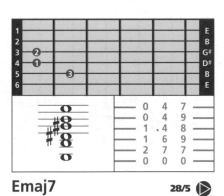

**Emaj7**    28/5 ▷

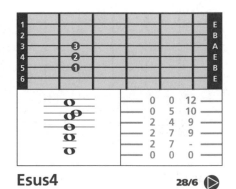

**Esus4**    28/6 ▷

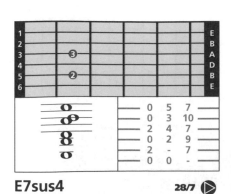

**E7sus4**    28/7 ▷

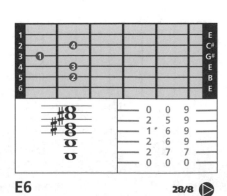

**E6**    28/8 ▷

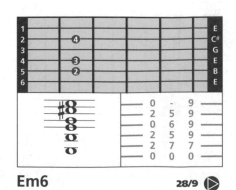

**Em6**    28/9 ▷

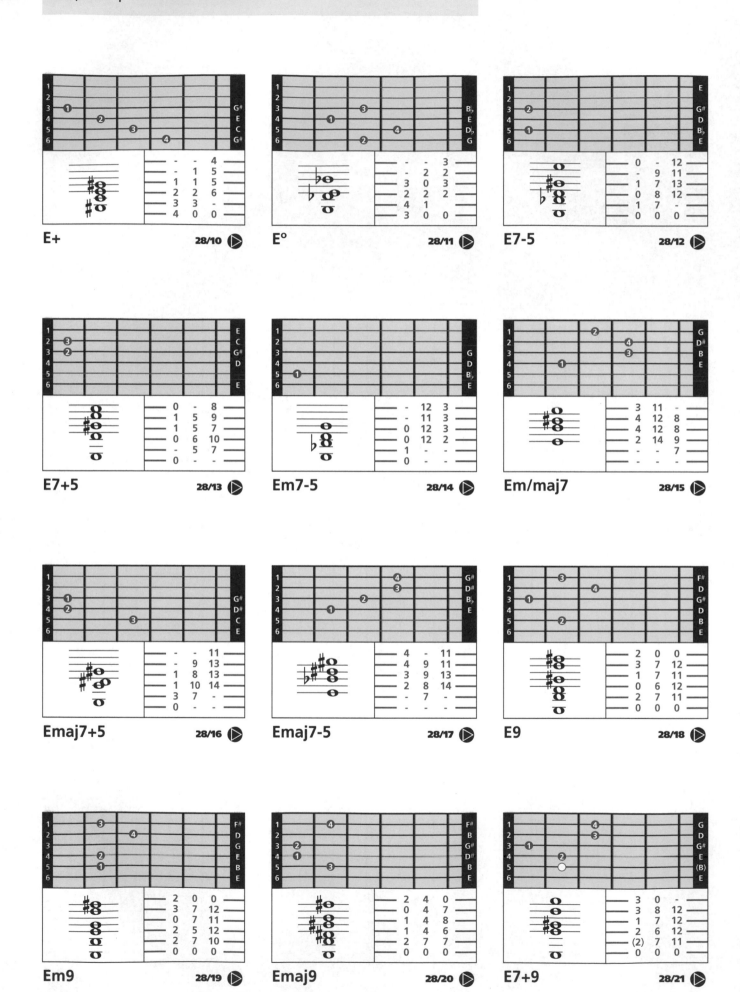

E+                28/10 ▶

E°                28/11 ▶

E7-5              28/12 ▶

E7+5              28/13 ▶

Em7-5             28/14 ▶

Em/maj7           28/15 ▶

Emaj7+5           28/16 ▶

Emaj7-5           28/17 ▶

E9                28/18 ▶

Em9               28/19 ▶

Emaj9             28/20 ▶

E7+9              28/21 ▶

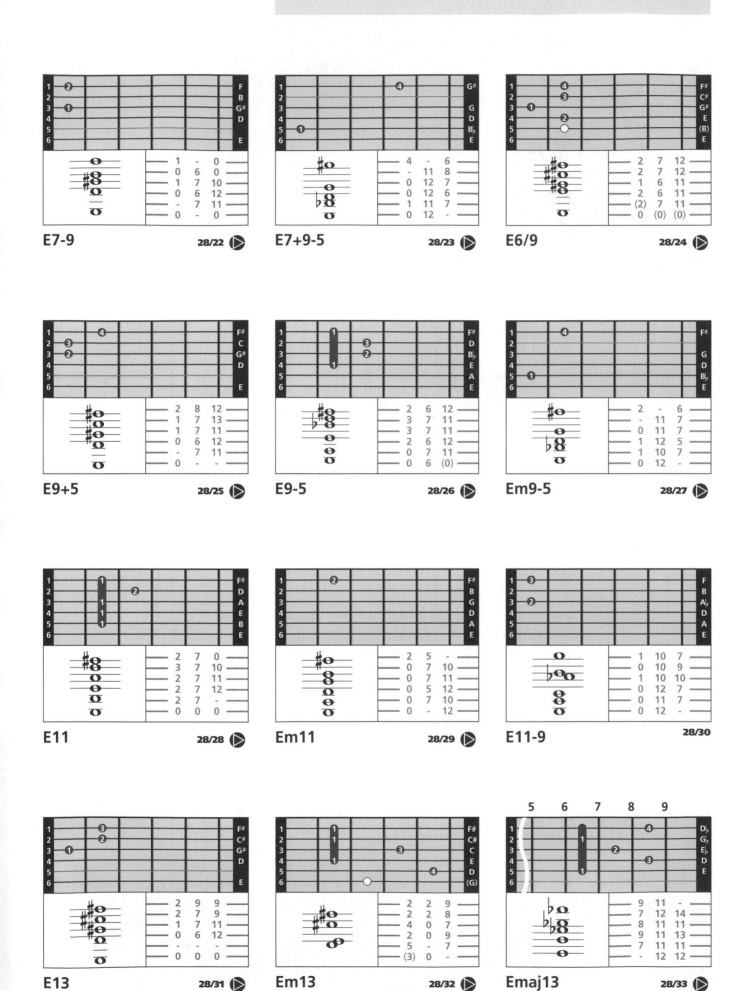

E7-9          28/22 ▶

E7+9-5        28/23 ▶

E6/9          28/24 ▶

E9+5          28/25 ▶

E9-5          28/26 ▶

Em9-5         28/27 ▶

E11           28/28 ▶

Em11          28/29 ▶

E11-9         28/30

E13           28/31 ▶

Em13          28/32 ▶

Emaj13        28/33 ▶

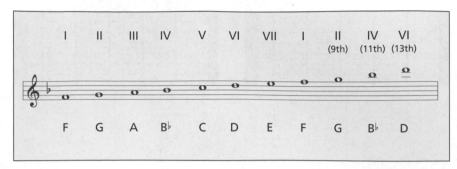

| I | II | III | IV | V | VI | VII | I | II (9th) | IV (11th) | VI (13th) |
|---|----|-----|----|---|----|----|---|---------|-----------|-----------|
| F | G | A | B♭ | C | D | E | F | G | B♭ | D |

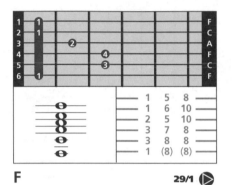

**F**                    29/1 ▶

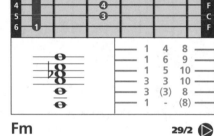

**Fm**                   29/2 ▶

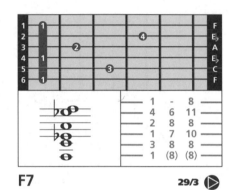

**F7**                   29/3 ▶

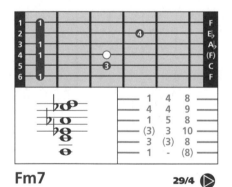

**Fm7**                  29/4 ▶

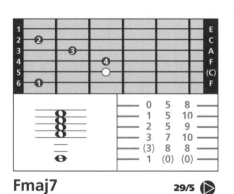

**Fmaj7**                29/5 ▶

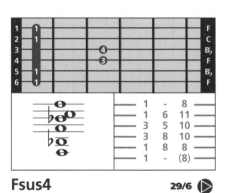

**Fsus4**                29/6 ▶

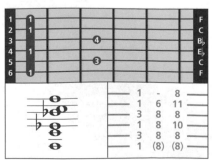

**F7sus4**               29/7 ▶

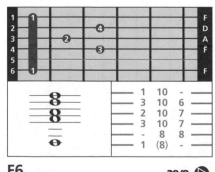

**F6**                   29/8 ▶

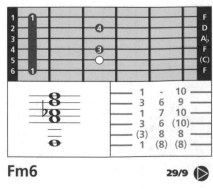

**Fm6**                  29/9 ▶

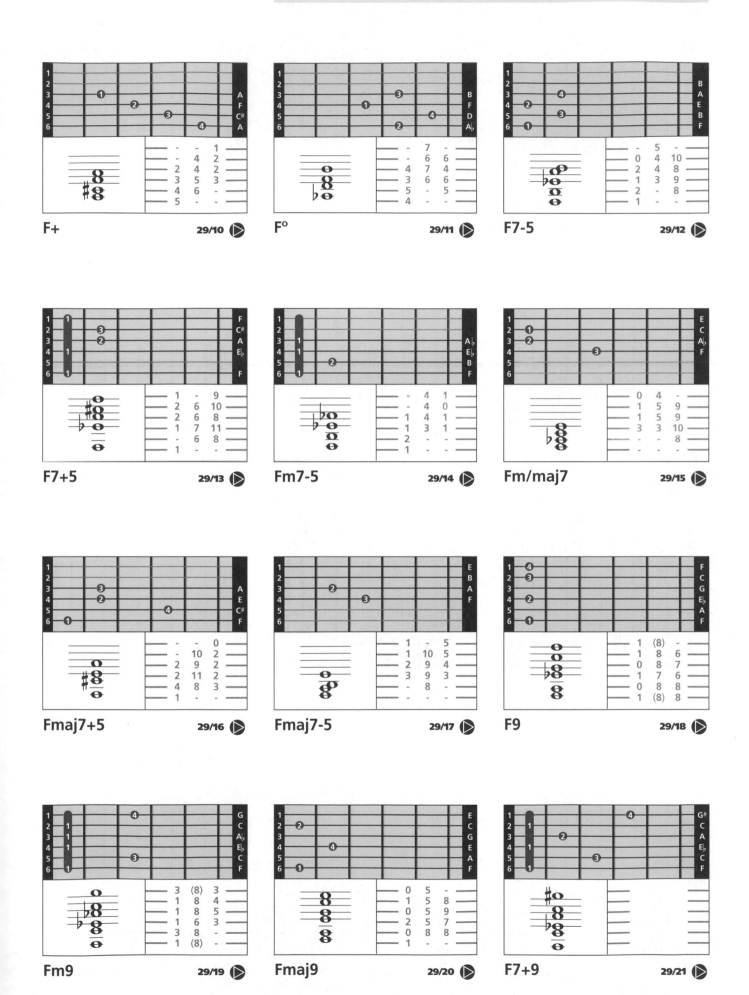

F+    29/10

F°    29/11

F7-5    29/12

F7+5    29/13

Fm7-5    29/14

Fm/maj7    29/15

Fmaj7+5    29/16

Fmaj7-5    29/17

F9    29/18

Fm9    29/19

Fmaj9    29/20

F7+9    29/21

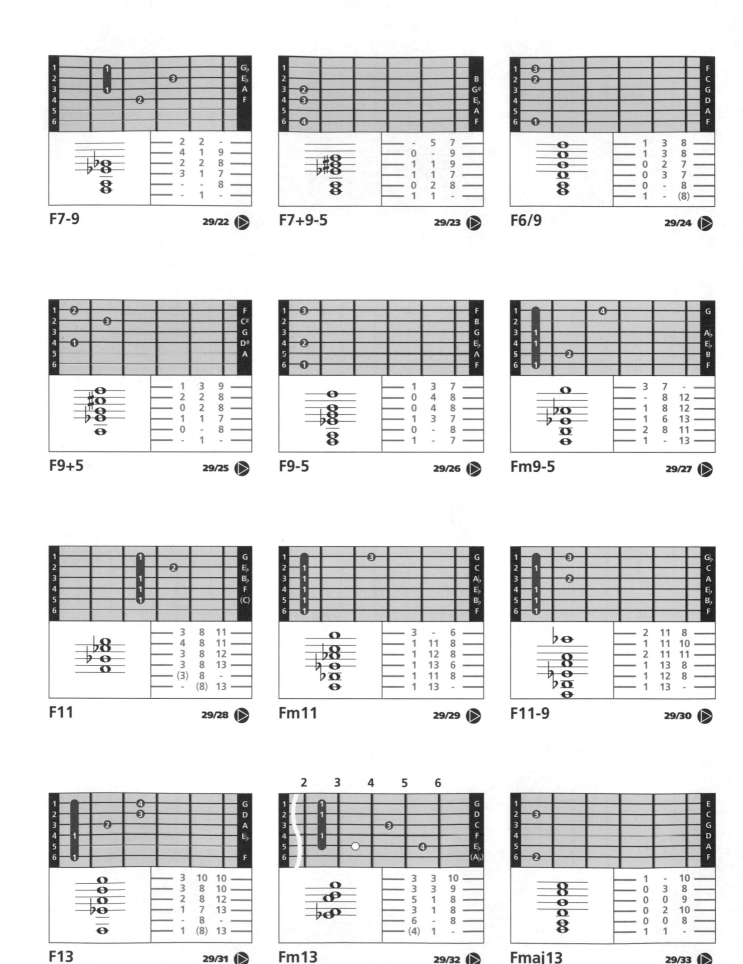

**F7-9**   29/22 ▶

**F7+9-5**   29/23 ▶

**F6/9**   29/24 ▶

**F9+5**   29/25 ▶

**F9-5**   29/26 ▶

**Fm9-5**   29/27 ▶

**F11**   29/28 ▶

**Fm11**   29/29 ▶

**F11-9**   29/30 ▶

**F13**   29/31 ▶

**Fm13**   29/32 ▶

**Fmaj13**   29/33 ▶

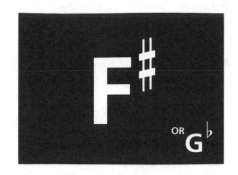

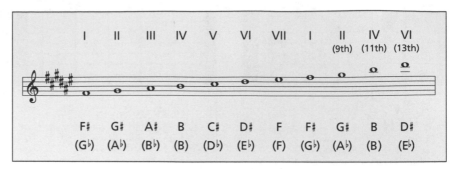

| | I | II | III | IV | V | VI | VII | I | II (9th) | IV (11th) | VI (13th) |
|---|---|---|---|---|---|---|---|---|---|---|---|
| | F# | G# | A# | B | C# | D# | F | F# | G# | B | D# |
| | (G♭) | (A♭) | (B♭) | (B) | (D♭) | (E♭) | (F) | (G♭) | (A♭) | (B) | (E♭) |

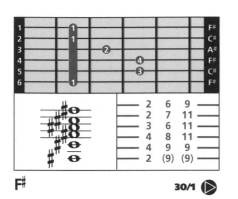

**F#**  30/1 ▶

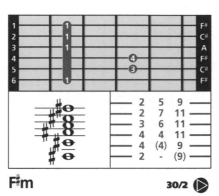

**F#m**  30/2 ▶

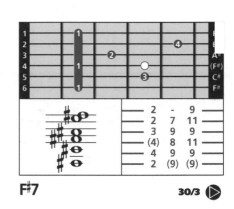

**F#7**  30/3 ▶

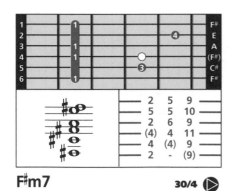

**F#m7**  30/4 ▶

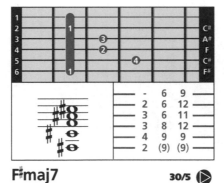

**F#maj7**  30/5 ▶

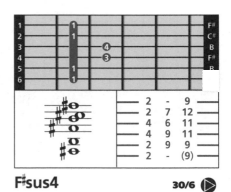

**F#sus4**  30/6 ▶

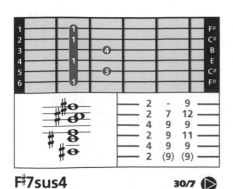

**F#7sus4**  30/7 ▶

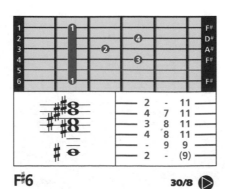

**F#6**  30/8 ▶

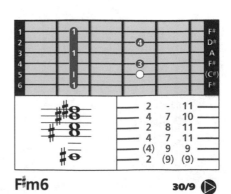

**F#m6**  30/9 ▶

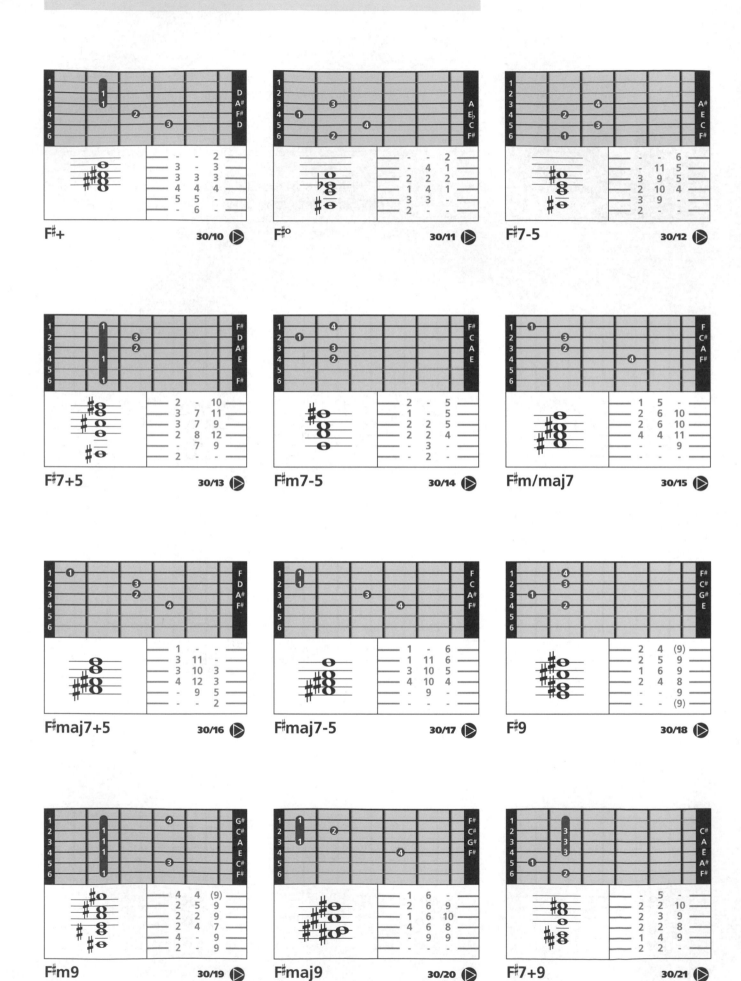

F#+ 30/10

F#o 30/11

F#7-5 30/12

F#7+5 30/13

F#m7-5 30/14

F#m/maj7 30/15

F#maj7+5 30/16

F#maj7-5 30/17

F#9 30/18

F#m9 30/19

F#maj9 30/20

F#7+9 30/21

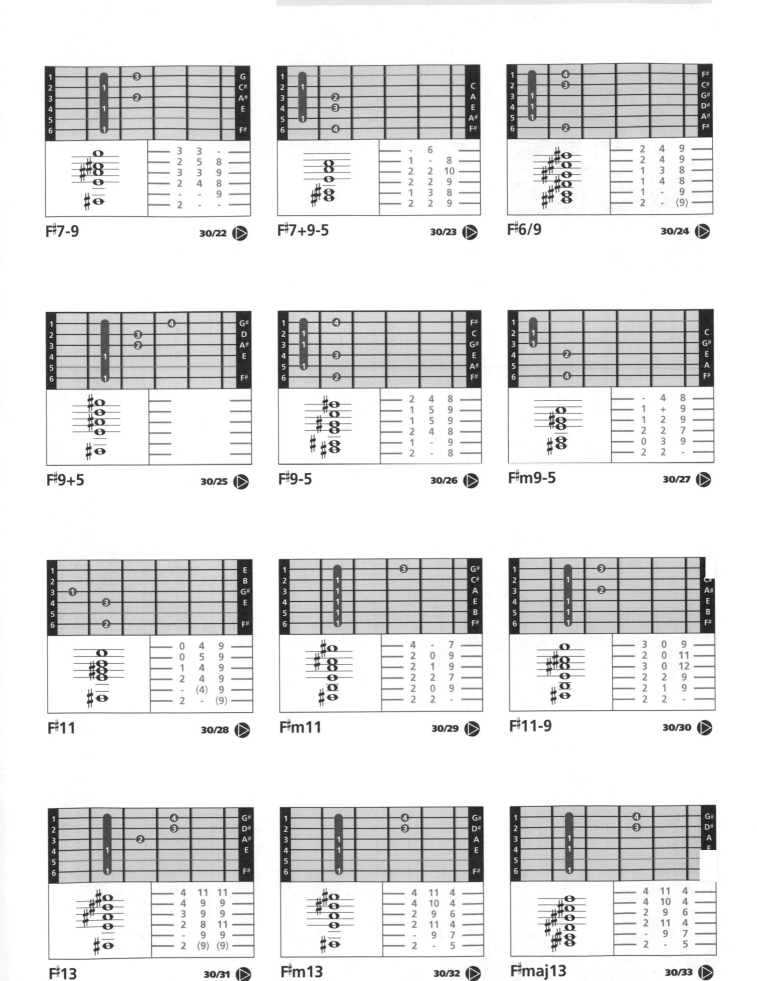

F#7-9     30/22

F#7+9-5     30/23

F#6/9     30/24

F#9+5     30/25

F#9-5     30/26

F#m9-5     30/27

F#11     30/28

F#m11     30/29

F#11-9     30/30

F#13     30/31

F#m13     30/32

F#maj13     30/33

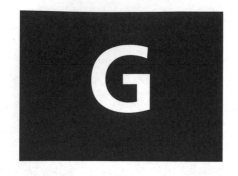

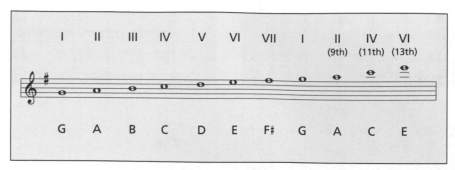

| | I | II | III | IV | V | VI | VII | I | II (9th) | IV (11th) | VI (13th) |
|---|---|---|---|---|---|---|---|---|---|---|---|
| | G | A | B | C | D | E | F# | G | A | C | E |

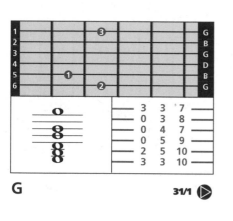

**G**  31/1

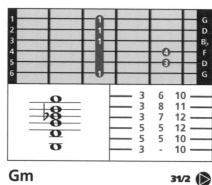

**Gm**  31/2

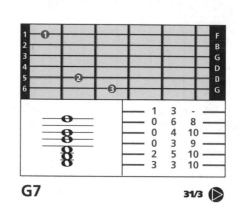

**G7**  31/3

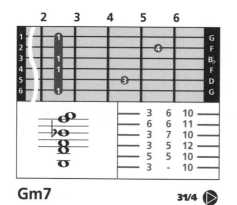

**Gm7**  31/4

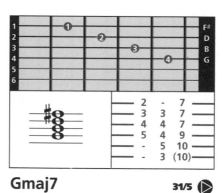

**Gmaj7**  31/5

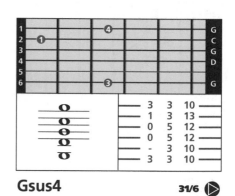

**Gsus4**  31/6

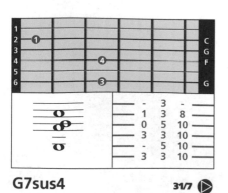

**G7sus4**  31/7

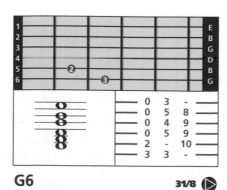

**G6**  31/8

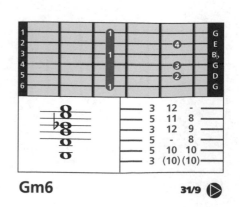

**Gm6**  31/9

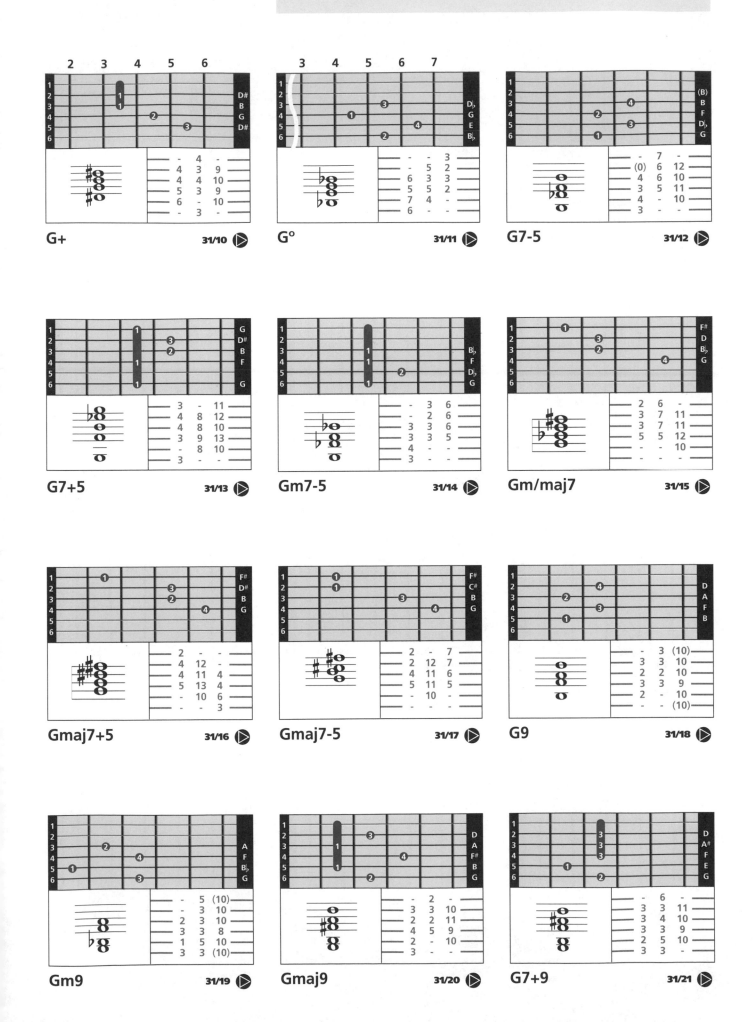

G+    31/10

G°    31/11

G7-5    31/12

G7+5    31/13

Gm7-5    31/14

Gm/maj7    31/15

Gmaj7+5    31/16

Gmaj7-5    31/17

G9    31/18

Gm9    31/19

Gmaj9    31/20

G7+9    31/21

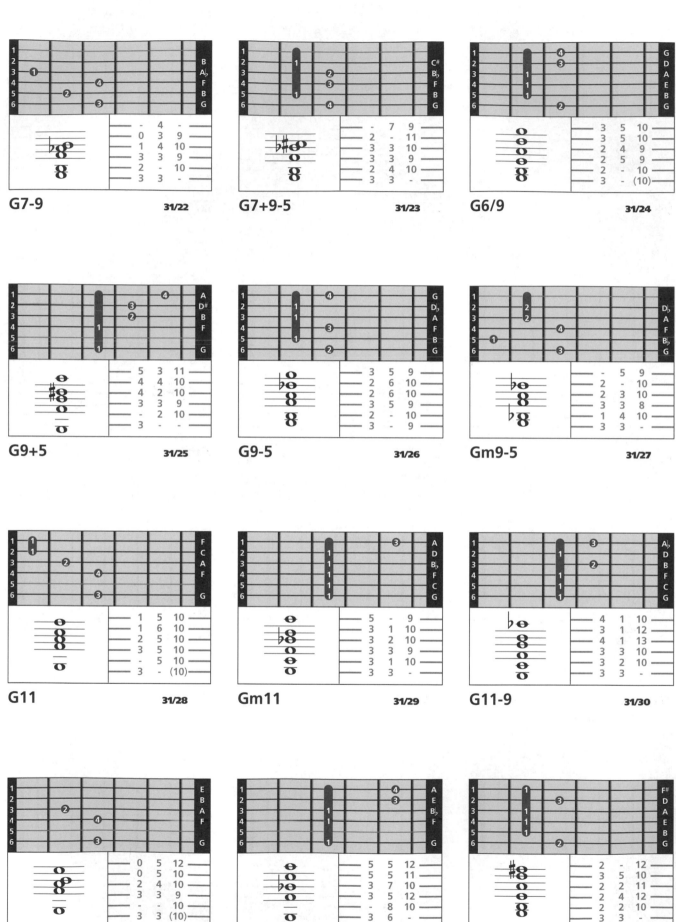

**G7-9**  31/22

**G7+9-5**  31/23

**G6/9**  31/24

**G9+5**  31/25

**G9-5**  31/26

**Gm9-5**  31/27

**G11**  31/28

**Gm11**  31/29

**G11-9**  31/30

**G13**  31/31

**Gm13**  31/32

**Gmaj13**  31/33

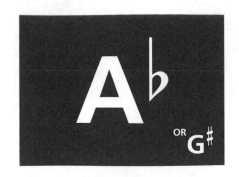

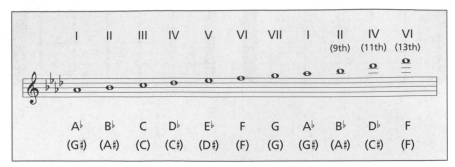

| | I | II | III | IV | V | VI | VII | I | II (9th) | IV (11th) | VI (13th) |
|---|---|---|---|---|---|---|---|---|---|---|---|
| | A♭ | B♭ | C | D♭ | E♭ | F | G | A♭ | B♭ | D♭ | F |
| | (G#) | (A#) | (C) | (C#) | (D#) | (F) | (G) | (G#) | (A#) | (C#) | (F) |

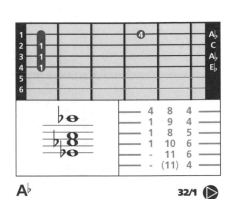

A♭    32/1

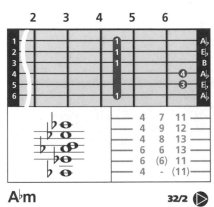

A♭m    32/2

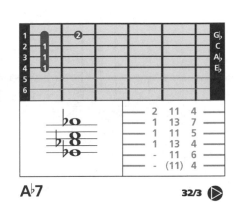

A♭7    32/3

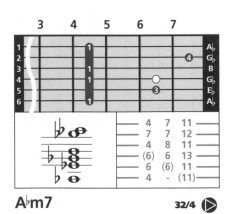

A♭m7    32/4

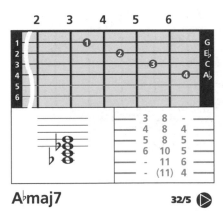

A♭maj7    32/5

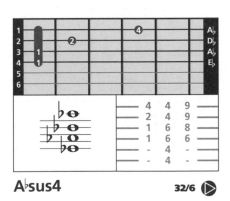

A♭sus4    32/6

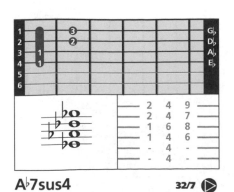

A♭7sus4    32/7

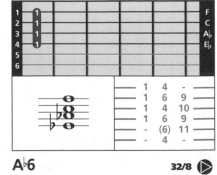

A♭6    32/8

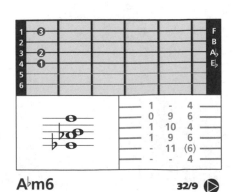

A♭m6    32/9

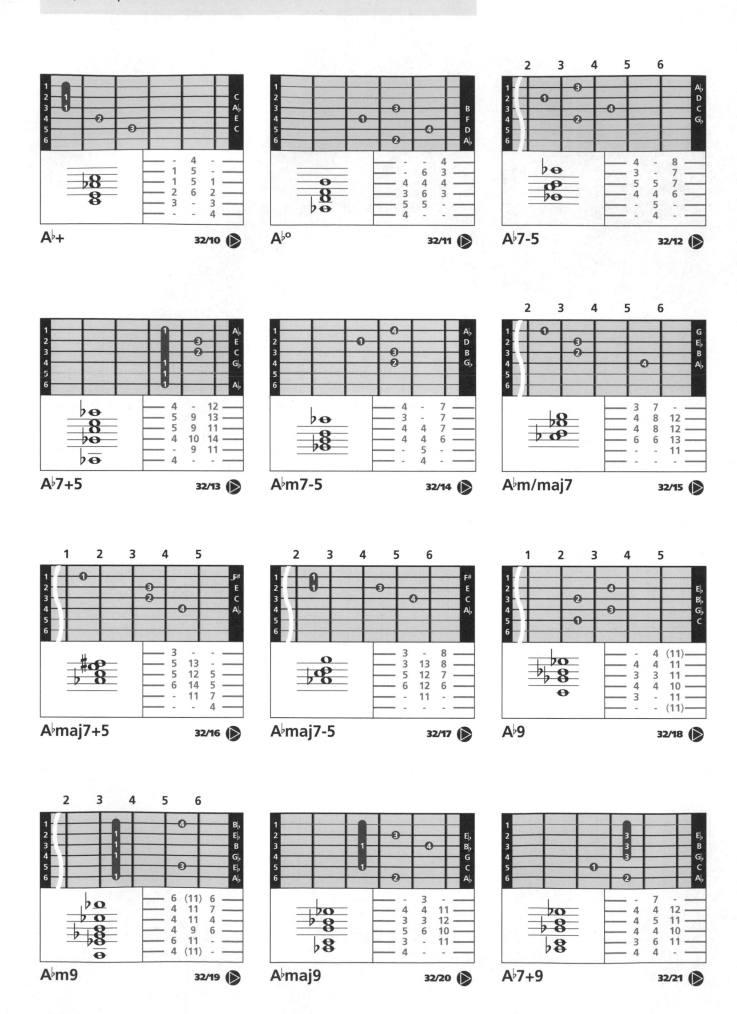

A♭+     32/10 ▶

A♭o     32/11 ▶

A♭7-5     32/12 ▶

A♭7+5     32/13 ▶

A♭m7-5     32/14 ▶

A♭m/maj7     32/15 ▶

A♭maj7+5     32/16 ▶

A♭maj7-5     32/17 ▶

A♭9     32/18 ▶

A♭m9     32/19 ▶

A♭maj9     32/20 ▶

A♭7+9     32/21 ▶

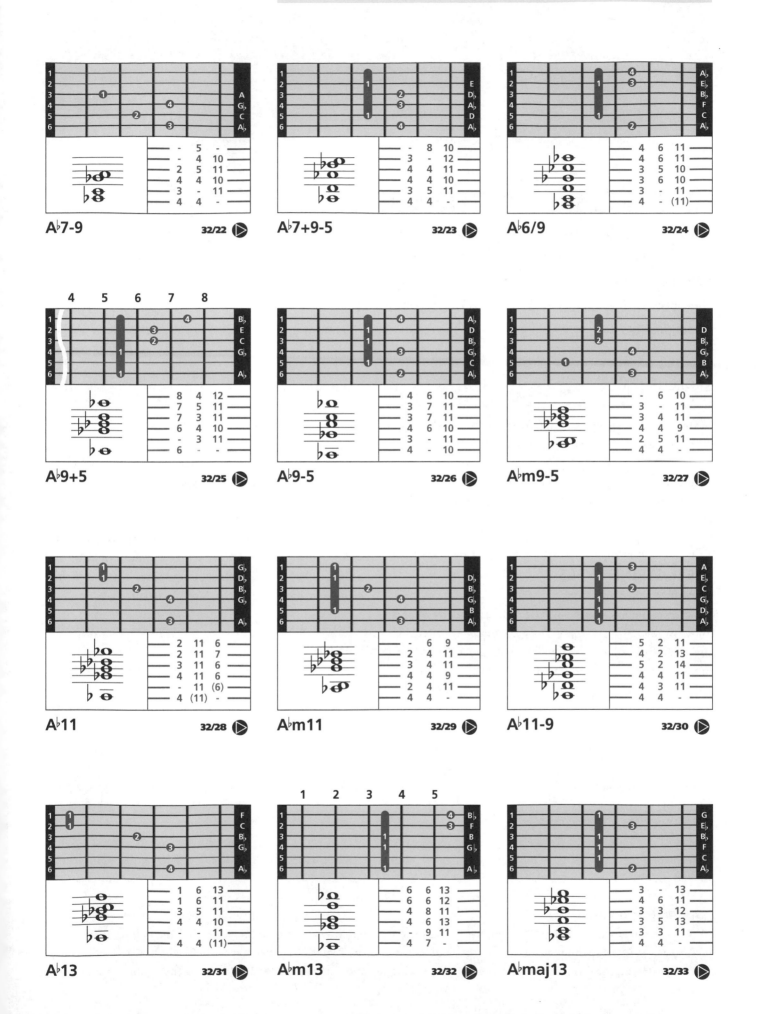

A♭7-9                                    32/22

A♭7+9-5                                  32/23

A♭6/9                                    32/24

A♭9+5                                    32/25

A♭9-5                                    32/26

A♭m9-5                                   32/27

A♭11                                     32/28

A♭m11                                    32/29

A♭11-9                                   32/30

A♭13                                     32/31

A♭m13                                    32/32

A♭maj13                                  32/33

# CHAPTER 4
## Guitar Maintenance

## TAKING CARE OF THE GUITAR

**Unlike most modern musical instruments, a high-quality guitar of any kind is likely to depreciate little in value—this is why it's always recommended to buy the best instrument you can afford. But even if you don't have a precious investment to protect, simply taking a few simple measures, such as cleaning the components, changing the strings, checking the way it's been set up, and storing or transporting it in the safest possible way, will help you to get the maximum enjoyment and playability from your guitar.**

## STRINGS

In spite of traditionally being referred to as "catgut," strings on the earliest guitars were usually made from the intestines of sheep. The innovation of steel and nylon strings did not occur until the 19th century. Steel strings are used on electric, flat-top, and arch-top acoustic instruments; nylon is used for classical and flamenco guitars.

## STEEL-STRING TYPES

Differences among steel strings are characterized by what is known as the "string wrap." Whilst the top two strings, and sometimes the 3rd when using ultra-light-gauge strings (see opposite page), are invariably a single thread of wire, the remaining strings comprise a wire inner core with an second piece of wire wound tightly around the outside. The nature of the wrapping has a direct impact on the sound and playability of the strings. There are three common types of winding: roundwound, flatwound, and groundwound, and each of these types has its own characteristics.

### ROUNDWOUND STRINGS
The most commonly used strings on electric and acoustic instruments, these strings are wound using conventionally shaped round wire, giving the characteristic ridge-like feel.

### FLATWOUND STRINGS
Most commonly used on arch-top guitars, flatwound strings feature a core enveloped by a flat ribbon of metal. When tightly wound, this gives a feel as smooth as one of the treble strings. This allows the fingers to move along the strings without creating an acoustic "squeak." They have a disadvantage in that the sound they produce is somewhat duller in tone than that found with roundwound strings, and they also have a tendency to crack, making them the least long-lasting of the three types.

### GROUNDWOUND STRINGS
An attempt to provide the tonal advantages of roundwound with the playing advantages of flatwound, groundwound strings use conventional round windings which are then ground down so that the surface is partially flat.

## STRING GAUGES

Strings not only come in variety of materials, but also in different sizes. This, too, can have a major impact on the way you play and on the sound you produce.

The different string widths are known as "gauges," and are generally expressed as decimal fractions of an inch. Weighing up the pros and cons of each type is very much a matter of personal taste. You need to balance the fact that lighter strings are easier to hold down and bend, and are less hard on the fingers, with the knowledge that they create a lower volume, shorter sustain, and the degree to which they can stretch makes them more difficult to keep in tune. Some players also maintain that heavier-gauge strings simply sound better.

Strings are most commonly sold as complete sets, grouped into various gauges from heavy (the largest) down to ultra-light (the smallest). However, they are usually available individually, and many guitarists experiment using strings from different sets—or even using different windings.

The diagram at right shows some of the most typical strings sets, although they are by no means definitive—some manufacturers have intermediate gauges. If you are an electric guitarist using extra- or ultra-light-gauge strings, it's a good idea to buy a few spares for the top two strings. Not only do they break more easily, they are also apt to lose their "ring."

## STRING WEAR

Strings don't last forever: they wear out or they break. This can be a result of applying too much tension, which can happen if you bend them a great deal, use altered tunings, or tune to above concert pitch. Your playing technique can also have an effect. Heavy right-hand strummers, like The Who's Pete Townshend, notoriously work through their strings at a considerable rate. Strings also lose their stretch with time and use. This is often caused by build-ups of salt from sweating fingers, which makes them rust.

You can make strings last longer by cleaning them after each use (see page 198). "Snapping" is also a way that some players get rid of build-ups of dirt and grime form the underside and windings of the strings. This involves pulling the string away from the fingerboard and letting it snap back into position.

One of the best-known tricks used by musicians of limited means is to remove the strings and boil them in water for around 10 minutes. This removes the grease and grime from the strings and improves the tone. The benefits, however, are temporary, and you won't get away with more than two or three boilings. Additionally, treble strings once removed are apt to kink and snap around the nut and machine head when you are trying to refit them. Boiling can be handy for bass guitarists, for whom string replacement is a more costly business, but otherwise it's usually more trouble than it's worth—better to go without a few pints of beer and buy a new set of strings!

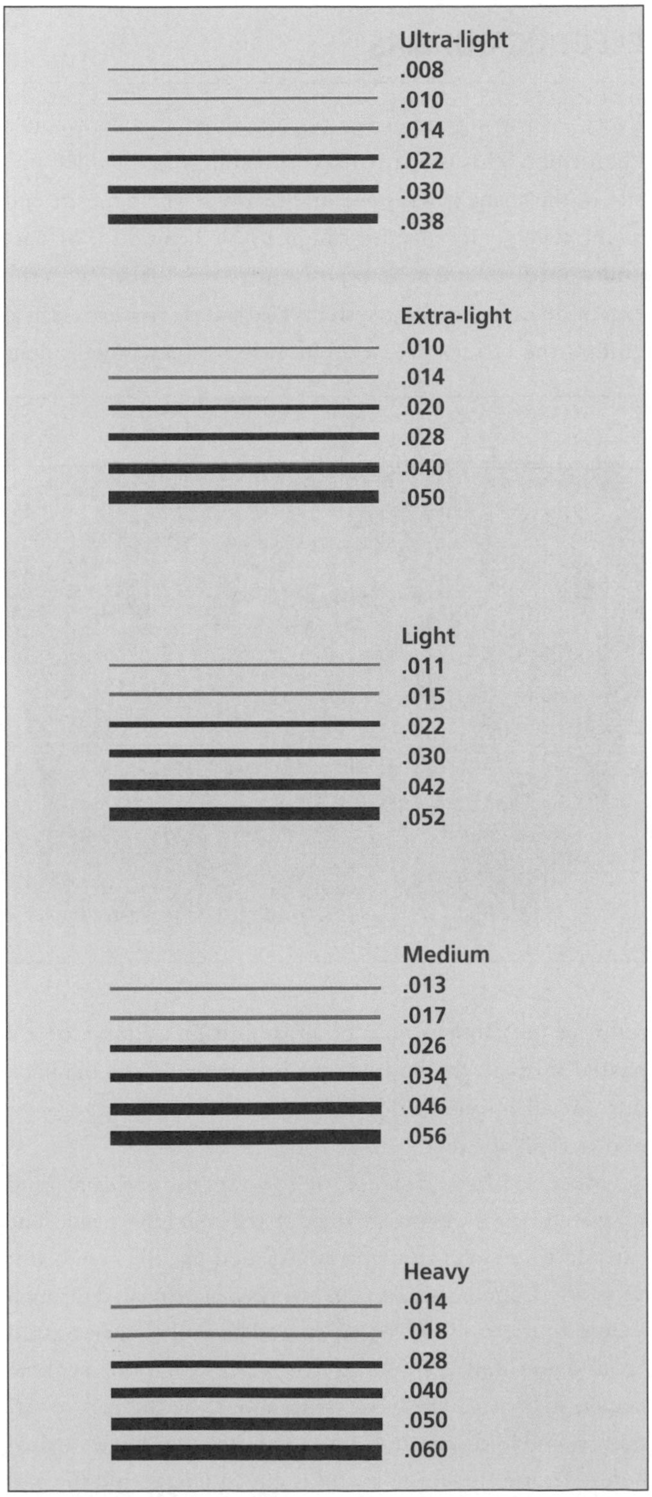

**Ultra-light**
.008
.010
.014
.022
.030
.038

**Extra-light**
.010
.014
.020
.028
.040
.050

**Light**
.011
.015
.022
.030
.042
.052

**Medium**
.013
.017
.026
.034
.046
.056

**Heavy**
.014
.018
.028
.040
.050
.060

# CHANGING STRINGS

**There are a number of alternative string-fixing mechanisms found on different guitars—both at the bridge and headstock—-all of which require slightly different string-changing techniques. In all cases, whatever type of instrument you use, whenever you fit new strings they need to be "stretched." To do this, pull the string a few inches away from the fretboard and then release it. If the pitch has dropped, retune it and repeat. Keep doing this until the string stays broadly in tune. Do this for all the strings. The techniques shown over the following two pages should equip you to restring any type of instrument.**

## ELECTRIC GUITARS

Every steel string comes equipped with what is known as a "ball end." This is a tiny disk of metal around which one end of the string is wrapped and secured. The opposite end of the string is threaded through a hole behind the bridge, pulled through and held in position by the "ball." With the exception of locking-nut systems (see right), on most electric guitars the strings are secured either by an independent

tailpiece (as can be found on most Gibson guitars), or are passed through the body of the instrument from the back into an all-in-one-bridge unit (most Fender guitars—see photograph above).

Most electric and steel-string guitars use the same kind of system for securing strings at the machine head. The capstan to which the string is attached usually stands out vertically from the headstock. Strings can be passed through a hole in the side of the capstan. The end is then passed around and under, trapping it in place when the machine head is tightened. The loose string should be cut back to less than an inch in length. Some capstans also have vertical holes. To use these, the string is cut to length and the end

inserted into the tip of the capstan. The string is then bent to one side and wound around. This method has the advantage of leaving string endings neat and tidy.

### LOCKING-NUT SYSTEMS

On locking-nut systems, such as the Floyd Rose tremolo units, changing strings can be somewhat arduous. The strings are simply clamped in place at the bridge saddle, using an Allen key. For this reason, the ball ends must be removed—they can be cut away with a pair of pliers. On tremolo systems, because the tension of ALL of the strings alters when one string is removed, it is a good idea to fix something like a block of wood or pack of cards in place beneath the bridge mechanism, to prevent it from rocking back and forth.

At the other end of the guitar, the strings are wound onto the machine heads in the same way as with any other electric guitar. Once the strings are all in place, the block supporting the bridge should be removed. It's important that you don't overtighten the string prior to this point, otherwise when you move the block you may find that the string snaps. The strings are then tuned with the machine heads in the usual way. Afterwards, they are locked in place at the nut with an Allen key. Fine tuning is undertaken using the individual adjusters on each bridge saddle.

## STEEL-STRING ACOUSTIC GUITARS

Most steel-string guitars feature vertical bridge pins that go into the bridge itself. The ball end of the string is passed through the hole behind the saddle. The pin is then inserted firmly into the hole, trapping the strings in place.

## CLASSICAL GUITARS (BRIDGE)

Nylon strings do not have ball ends, they are fitted using a tied loop. The end of the string is passed through the bridge hole, passed back over the bridge, knotted behind the saddle, and then the slack is passed under the string on the bridge. When the other end of the string is pulled the loop behind the bridge tightens, thus holding the string in place.

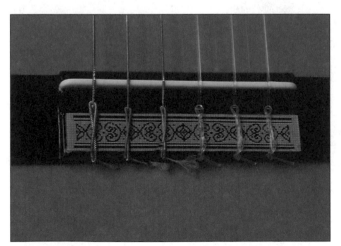

### HOW OFTEN?

How often you should change your strings is a matter of personal taste. Some professional players restring every time they perform or record. And yet there are others who leave strings in place for years, or until they break. If you put on a new set of strings, they do need to be "worn in"—a few hours of playing should do this nicely.

## CLASSICAL GUITARS (HEADSTOCK)

Pass the string over the nut and insert it through the hole in the capstan. Bring the end of the string over the capstan and pass it underneath itself. When you begin to tighten the machine head, the end of the string will be trapped in place.

### SAVING TIME AND ENERGY

Turning machine heads until a string becomes tight can be a tedious task. To save yourself time and energy, you can use a plastic or wooden string winder which fits over the machine head, allowing you to turn it that much more quickly. A more advanced alternative is to take the end of the string winder—the piece which comes into contact with the machine head—saw it away, and fix it to the bit of an electric screwdriver. This will allow you to wind on your strings at the press of a button.

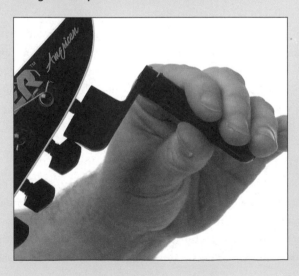

# SETTING UP

**The following two pages show the kind of alterations that can be made to any guitar, to suit the preferences or playing style of any particular player, or if things go wrong with the guitar. Some of these changes can be made by the ordinary player; the more complex work is best left to the skilled specialist. Professional guitar technicians and makers of custom instruments will often spend time watching their client play before assessing how the guitar would best be set up.**

## ACTION

The simplest modification a guitarist can make is to adjust the "action" of the guitar. This refers to the height of the strings above the frets. The further away they are, the more pressure needs to be applied by the left hand to fret the notes—this is a high action, and is usually deemed undesirable. For fast solo work, a low action is more suitable; however, setting the action too low will result in fret buzz. Some players whose playing incorporates bottlenecks compromise by raising the action higher than they would prefer for normal playing, so that the slide doesn't scrape against the frets.

To measure the action, take a steel rule with fine gradations and place it on top of the 12th fret. Measure the distance to the bottom of the string. Setting the action is not usually conducted with scientific precision—more often than not, guitarists choose the lowest action possible without causing fret buzz. This is achieved by a matter of trial and error. Nonetheless, average figures are likely to be between 0.05–0.09 inches for an electric guitar and 0.08–0.12 inches for an acoustic instrument.

### CHANGING THE ACTION

The height of the strings is altered by changing the height of the bridge. On most electric guitars, each string has its own saddle which can be raised by turning a small screw in a clockwise direction.

Acoustic guitars usually have a bridge saddle made from bone. On some models, screws at the side can be used to raise the entire platform at either edge, which may be sufficient for your needs. However, to make adjustments to specific strings, the saddle must be filed down. This kind of alteration is most definitely best left to the experts.

### INTONATION

If you make a dramatic alteration to the action, you are effectively changing the distance between the nut and the bridge. However small this adjustment is, it can have widespread implications on the intonation of your guitar. Indeed, without making further changes your guitar may not play in tune across the entire fingerboard. This discrepancy occurs because the distance between the nut and the 12th fret must be IDENTICAL to the distance between the 12th fret and the point at which the string touches the bridge saddle.

You can test the intonation of your guitar by playing an open string and then comparing it to the note played on the 12th fret. If the latter is not EXACTLY one octave above the open string, your guitar will go out of tune the further you play along the fretboard. An effective alternative is to compare the open string to the harmonic on the 12th fret. These two notes should be identical.

If the note at the 12th fret is sharp, the string is too short and must be lengthened by moving the saddle back. Most electric guitars have individually adjustable string saddles which are usually controlled by an Allen key or small screwdriver. In most cases, turning the screw clockwise will move the saddle closer to the nut.

## ADJUSTMENTS BEST LEFT TO THE EXPERTS

There are some jobs which are really not worth the time, effort, or potential risk. These are skilled activities which only the most cavalier should attempt.

### NECK PROBLEMS

All necks have a very slight curve, usually centered around the 7th or 8th fret. This is a result of the tension caused by the strings, and the curve can become further exaggerated with the use of heavy strings, which in turn makes the action around the middle of the fingerboard noticeably higher than at either end of the fingerboard, making the strings more difficult to press down onto the frets.

The curve of the neck is controlled by a "truss rod"—an adjustable metal bar that passes through the length of the neck. It can be adjusted using a small spanner or screwdriver (turning it clockwise tightens the truss rod, and reduces the curve).

If the curving becomes too extreme or the fingerboard begins to warp or twist, the problem is likely to need more serious attention, and the entire neck may need to be removed, refitted, or even in the worst cases, replaced.

### FRETS

Although most parts of the guitar, if cared for, can last for a lifetime, frets can wear out and grooves will appear where the strings have worn away the nickel. If the grooves become too pronounced, the result will be fret buzz. Removing and replacing a fret may be relatively straightforward, but the fine tuning required to bring it down to the correct height is best left to the specialist. A well-worn instrument can be given a new lease of life with a set of replacement frets.

## ELECTRICS

It's very rare indeed for the simple circuitry in an electric guitar to "break down" as such. The most likely problems you will come across are crackling potentiometers (tone and volume controls) and pickup switches, or a loose jack socket. The former can often be solved simply by spraying switch-cleaning fluid along the contact points.

If the worst comes to the worst, however, you may have to replace the component. Most electric guitars feature relatively simple electronic circuitry, so anyone who can use a soldering iron should be able to replace any of the individual parts.

Even if you have little understanding of basic electronics, there are so few components to worry about (typically, two pickups, a switch, a socket, four potentiometers, and two capacitors) that it's a simple matter of marking the wires so as to make sure that they are soldered to the same points on their replacement parts.

Access to the circuitry is usually gained by removing a perspex panel at the back of the guitar, although on some models the entire circuitry is fitted behind a front panel which can be unscrewed and lifted off the body of the guitar.

# CLEANING AND STORAGE

**Your guitar is not only a tool for your personal creativity, it can represent an investment which, if cared for, will increase in value over the years. The best way of keeping your guitar clean and safe is to store it in a specially made case when it's not being used. Moving the guitar around can also be a perilous task, so you must ensure that it is suitably protected, not only from physical damage, but from the effects of a change in climate or environment.**

## CLEANING THE BODY AND OTHER PARTS OF THE GUITAR

The different parts of the guitar can be cleaned using a wide variety of agents. Most modern guitars are finished in cellulose or other kinds of synthetic varnishes, and as such can be cleaned with care, using any regular household sprays or creams. However, it's a good idea to avoid those cleaning agents that contain silicone or wax, as they can sometimes cause discoloration to the finish and give the instrument an unpleasant, sticky feel. Under NO circumstances should you use abrasive cleaning fluids, as these will damage the finish. Most music stores sell a variety of specialized cleaning fluids, so if in doubt it is advisable to use one of these.

**Specially made cleaning agents are widely available: string-cleaning fluid (left); body-cleaning fluid (right).**

Additional care needs to be taken when dealing with high-quality classical guitars, many of which have a French-polished finish, rather than a synthetic varnish. These instruments should NEVER be treated with regular polishes. Surfaces should simply be regularly wiped down with a lightly damped cloth and then buffed with a dry cloth.

## CLEANING THE STRINGS

Keeping your strings clean not only makes the guitar feel more pleasant to play, but it can make the strings last a good deal longer. The most effective cleaning method is to take a dry, lint-free cloth, pass it between the strings and fingerboard, and drag it the full length of the strings between the bridge and the nut. Some players favor the use of string-cleaning fluids, although these should not be used on nylon strings.

Ideally, steel strings should be wiped down as soon after you finish playing as possible—this will prevent the salt that you naturally produce in your sweat from reacting with the string, thus creating rust.

## CLEANING THE FINGERBOARD

Fretboards with a synthetic varnish can be cleaned in the same way as the body. Many guitars have oiled ebony or rosewood fingerboards. These should be given a thorough cleaning every time you change the strings. A neat trick here is to apply some lemon oil to the wood and leave it for around five minutes. This should then be cleaned off using a dry cloth. Apart from cleaning the fingerboard and maintaining its feel, lemon oil also feeds the wood, preventing it from drying out.

## CLEANING THE FRETS

Dirt from the fingers often builds along the edge of the frets. This should be removed with a gently pointed object, such as a nail file or toothpick. The grime should come away quite easily, so don't scratch too hard, otherwise you will damage the fingerboard.

## HARDWARE

Keeping the guitar's metal parts—such as machine heads, pickups, bridges, and tremolo arms—clean is the most effective way of preventing rusting or other tarnishing effects. A regular domestic chrome-cleaning agent will be sufficient for most of these items.

Switch-cleaning sprays should be used on the pickup or polarity switches, to prevent them sticking or clicking. It can also be used to clean the tone and volume controls, keeping their operation smooth.

## STORAGE

If your guitar is not going to be used for any length of time, you should pay some attention to the way in which you keep it stored. Apart from protecting the instrument from knocks and scrapes, the main consideration is to avoid the instrument being exposed to wide variations in temperature or humidity. This is especially important for delicate acoustic instruments, where a sudden change of climate can alter the action, distort the woods used, damage glue joints, and cause cracks in the finish. For this reason alone, guitars shouldn't be stored in lofts or basements, or close to radiators or other hot water pipes.

It's always a good idea to store your guitar in a sturdy case (see right), although some guitarists favor hanging their instruments from walls. This is less recommended, as it will inevitably suffer from heavy build-up of dust. If you insist on hanging your guitar (and it can admittedly be convenient, especially where shortages of floor space are concerned), it's a good idea to buy specially made fixtures and fittings. Finally, never hang your guitar in direct sunlight—this can damage the bodywork, causing the color to fade and wood to distort.

Befor storing the instrument, always give it a thorough cleaning, to prevent tarnishing or rusting of the metal parts. Always detune the strings so that there is no tension stress placed on the joints between the neck and the body.

## TRAVEL PLANS

If you intend transporting your guitar in a car, van, or by rail, your instrument is at all kinds of risk. You should ALWAYS keep your guitar in its case and lay it down longways, either on its back or side. This will prevent it falling over. Avoid placing heavy items on top—such as amplifiers, PA systems, or drum kits. Even the sturdiest of flight cases has its limits.

Traveling by air poses enormous potential risks. Although regulations will vary from one airline to another, if at all possible, arrange in advance to take your guitar onboard as hand luggage. Whatever you do, however, DON'T EVEN CONSIDER putting it the cargo hold without a sturdy, metal flight case—you can be guaranteed that a standard plywood case will be smashed, and your guitar badly damaged. Even though some airlines offer a separate hold for delicate items, the above warning still applies.

If you travel around with your guitar on a regular basis, you should give serious thought to obtaining insurance cover. This is expensive, though—insurance companies usually let out a loud shriek the moment a musician walks through their doors—but it can help to protect your investment.

To give your guitar even the most basic protection, it should have its own flight case. These come in a wide variety of shapes and sizes. The most basic cases are made from padded plastic or fabric, and zip around the outside of the guitar. They are very cheap and offer you the barest minimum of protection—to be honest, it is just as effective to wrap your guitar up in an old thick blanket, if less neat and tidy.

The sturdiest cases have a hard shell, usually made from plywood or a strong plastic. The insides are padded to keep the instrument in place, and lined with fake fur to protect the body finish. These cases are usually ideal for most everyday protection.

If you are playing in a touring group or regularly traveling with your guitar, a metal flight case is a necessity. Such cases are fitted with aluminum side panels and thick metal corner units. While they offer great protection, they can be very expensive, sometimes costing as much as a guitar itself, and usually triple the weight of the entire package. They also invariably cause damage to any thing or body with which they accidentally come into contact.

# CHAPTER 5
## Sound and Effects

## AMPLIFICATION

**If you are using an electric guitar, you need a combination of an amplifier and a loudspeaker to produce any sound. Apart from simply boosting the volume of the guitar, amplifiers are also capable of producing a variety of different sounds and effects in their own right. Indeed, your choice of amplifier can in some ways be as important as your choice of guitar, in the overall impact it has on your sound.**

### THE HISTORY OF THE AMPLIFIER

The first amplifiers were built in the 1930s. They allowed guitars fitted with pickups to be heard over the louder acoustic instruments found in typical dance bands. By today's standards, their output was very low—no more than 10 watts—and they used the valve radio and hi-fi technology of the day to produce sounds through a small loudspeaker. As popularity of electrified acoustic guitars rose during the 1940s, a demand grew for higher volumes. The first dedicated maker of guitar amplifiers was Leo Fender. In 1949, he and his engineer Don Randall produced their own Super Amp model. With the development of their own famous range of solid-body guitars, the overall demand exploded. This period also saw the output pushed up to a respectable 50 watts and the speaker size increase to 12 inches, which remains the norm for guitar amplifiers. Towards the end of the 1950s, the British Vox company produced the AC30, which remains as much a classic of its type as the Fender Twin. Such models were popular with blues and early rock musicians, not only because of the warmth of their tone, but also because of the way in which they sounded when the valves were overdriven. This latter feature was by no means a deliberate design feature at the time, but a happy accident that helped to define much of the classic rock guitar sound.

During the early 1960s, as rock music became more popular and was played in larger venues, power once again became a problem. The solution was developed by British engineer Jim Marshall who produced a 100-watt amplifier which was connected to a stack of four 12-inch speakers. This allowed the sound characteristics of the lower-rated models to be used in much larger venues, and guitarists like Jeff Beck actively started using distortion and feedback (two of the engineers' traditional enemies) in their playing style. The "Marshall stack" became the norm throughout the heavy rock era.

By the 1970s, valve technology was already deemed 20 years out of date by radio and hi-fi manufacturers, who had all began to use cheaper and more predictable transistors. Therefore the traditional guitar amplifier manufacturers followed suit, producing "solid-state" transistor amps. This cheaper technology quickly became extremely popular, especially among beginners and semi-professional users. However, the problem with transistors was that when they overloaded, the tone they produced was made up of unpleasant harmonics—if they fed back, the result was an terrible "howl." Designers tried to compensate by introducing analog distortion circuitry, but it just wasn't as effective as the real thing. It was clear that the old-fashioned valve sound was an important part of the electric guitar

sound. Nonetheless, solid-state circuitry found its following, and remains popular with bass guitarists, who traditionally prefer the cleaner sound that valves offer. The 1980s and onwards saw a widespread return to valves, and many companies produced "hybrid" models which featured valve pre-amplifiers and solid-state power amplifiers—for some, the best of both worlds.

## VALVE, SOLID STATE, OR HYBRID?

Most guitarists favor the classic valve amplifier sound, characterized by a warmth and smoothness of tone. Valves also produce a pleasant distortion as the volume increases. Unlike solid-state circuitry, valves can come loose, or may need periodic replacement. Different valves can produce different sounds, therefore some guitarists experiment endlessly with different combinations.

Solid-state "transistor" amplifiers have a sharper, brittle characteristic. They are favored by players who value a cleaner tone. Transistors are capable of dealing with a wider range of frequencies than valve amplifiers. They also distort less at higher volumes, making them more suited to pure amplification purposes, such as PA systems or studio monitors. A fact of life is that solid state is more consistent, meaning that any two similar models will always sound identical, although this is another reason why some players regard them lacking character.

A popular alternative which has emerged over the past decade is to use a hybrid of both systems, typically a valve amplifier or pre-amplifier to provide the basic sound, which is then amplified using an independent solid-state power amplifier.

## COMBOS, STACKS, AND RACKS

The traditional guitar amplifier combines an amplifier and loudspeaker in a single unit. These are called "combos." They are compact and easy to transport.

The vogue for separate amplifier and loudspeakers grew during the 1960s. In this combination, the amplifier is usually referred to as the "head" and the speakers as the "stack." This can potentially produce greater volume than a combo, although in a small venue it can be difficult to produce a high-quality distortion sound at a low enough volume. However, separate components allow the player the advantage of choosing their own combination of amp and speaker cabinet.

Some manufacturers now produce pre-amplifiers and power amplifiers that fit into standard 19-inch rack units. This can simply be viewed as an alternative way of storing the amplifier "head", although in recent years MIDI has been used to allow different settings to be stored, and controlled from a footswitch, or external sequencer or computer.

# AMPLIFIERS IN PRACTICE

In order to produce a sound, the guitar has to be connected to one of the input sockets of an amplifier using a "lead"—a piece of screened cable with jack plugs at either end. Although amplifiers come in many shapes and forms, and their specific features differ, there are a number of functions that are common to nearly all models. These are input sockets, channel input level, tone controls (usually bass, mid-range, and treble), and a master volume control.

## STAGES OF AN AMPLIFIER

Guitar amplifiers work in a variety of different ways, but irrespective of whether they are combos or heads and stacks, or whether they use valve or solid-state circuitry, there are a number of common operations that every amplifier has to be able to perform.

This pre-amplifier stage boosts the signal, which is then passed through to the equalization stage.

### TONE CONTROLS ("EQ")

At its simplest, this part of the process can consist of just a single bass and treble control. More sophisticated models often feature a mid-range control. Some, like the advanced

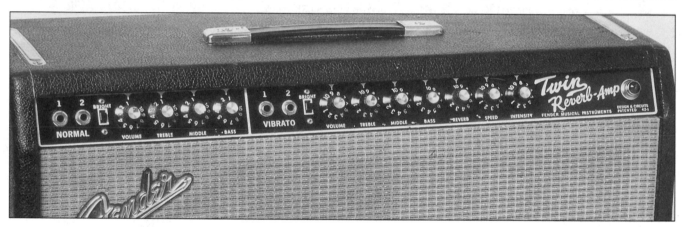

There are two fundamental stages: the pre-amplifier (usually termed the "pre-amp") controls the input volume and tone, while the power amplifier controls the overall volume. Most of the tonal coloration takes place during the crucial pre-amp stage.

### INPUT SOCKET

The process begins with an input signal from a guitar. This is invariably a jack socket. Some amplifiers feature more than one input channel. This can sometimes be used to allow a second guitar or other electronic instrument to be plugged in. It can also be used to switch between different settings—this can be extremely useful when deciding on the different volumes needed for playing, for example, lead and rhythm guitar.

### CHANNEL INPUT VOLUME

Although the level and tone of this signal can be altered on the guitar itself (see page 205), the volume of the initial signal is determined by the input channel volume control.

Mesa Boogie combos, feature a graphic equalizer instead of conventional tone controls. This splits the sound spectrum into five or more bands, and allows for very precise tonal programming at the amplifier stage.

### OUTPUT VOLUME

The final stage of the process sees the output signal from the pre-amplifier passed through to the power amplifier. The master volume is the final control before the signal is output to the loudspeaker. The master volume governs the overall output of the amplifier, irrespective of how many input channels exist, or how they are set.

### VARIATIONS

The more expensive or sophisticated valve amplifiers often have a number of intermediary stages. Some classic amplifiers have built-in sound effects, such as reverberation, or even tremolo in the case of some vintage Vox AC30s. Many amps also feature "lead" or "overdrive" channels that are separate from the standard volume ones.

## LOUDSPEAKERS

At some point, a guitar amplifier must be connected to a loudspeaker in order for the sound coming from the the output of the guitar to be heard. Speakers come in a wide range of sizes, and can be linked together to produce different kinds of sound.

### HOW IT WORKS

A loudspeaker is superficially a microphone in reverse. When an electric guitar string is struck, it creates a disturbance within the magnetic field around the pickup. This generates a low-level electrical signal, which is output from the guitar and then boosted and tonally adjusted by an external amplifier. The final signal from the amplifier is passed to a "voice coil" that is connected to a large diaphragm, which forms the heart of the speaker cone. The voice coil sits between the poles of a large magnet. When it receives the signal from the amplifier, the coil generates a magnetic field of its own, causing the diaphragm and cone to vibrate. This disturbs the surrounding air, simulating the soundwaves that were originally generated by striking the guitar string in the first place.

### IMPEDANCE AND SIZE

Loudspeakers are referred to in terms of their "impedance value." This is measured in units of electrical resistance known as ohms (or the Greek symbol $\Omega$). Although many different impedances are available, the kinds of speakers normally used with guitar amplifiers are rated as 8 ohms or 15–16 ohms. These values are crucial to the sound and volume produced by an amplifier, and it is important that amplifier output ratings and loudspeaker impedances are understood for the purposes of correct matching. Most standard guitar amplifiers use 8-ohm speakers, but if you use a higher rating (15–16 ohms), the higher resistance will reduce the overall output volume. It may also reduce the level and nature of the amplifier's distortion.

For the purposes of the majority of guitar amplifiers, speakers are usually a standard 12 inches in diameter, although 10-inch and 15-inch speakers are favored by some. It is possible to connect the output of an amplifier to speakers linked together in pairs or quads, although the way in which they are connected will determine their output.

## PRACTICE IN THE HOME

For the electric guitarist, practicing in the home can be a bit of a nightmare. The main problem involves finding a satisfactory balance between volume and sound: if you have a 100-watt valve head and a four-by-twelve stack

sitting in the corner of your bedroom, it simply won't be feasible to drive it at a sufficient volume to create a decent sound—crank it up, and you risk alienating your family and neighbors (and damaging your hearing). One solution is to use a practice amplifier: a small combo—usually of less than 5 watts in power—that has the features of a standard guitar amplifier. The best-quality models are designed to create an excellent sound at low volumes.

Another popular solution is to practice using headphones. This can be done in several different ways. A number of multi-effect guitar pedals are nowadays equipped with headphone sockets, so you don't even necessarily need an amplifier for this reason—the sound won't be particularly great, but you'll still be able to hear yourself. More satisfactory is the use of a speaker simulator or direct injection (DI) box. These allow you to plug the speaker output of your amplifier into a line input on a mixing desk or hi-fi. However, NEVER take the speaker output and plug it DIRECTLY into your hi-fi amp—if you ever want to listen to another CD, anyway!

# FINDING THE RIGHT SOUND

**With such a wide range of sonic possibilities, it is clearly important that you should be able to produce the kinds of sound appropriate to the kind of music you are playing. With a thorough understanding of the way your equipment works, you should be able to produce any kind of sound that you need.**

## SETTINGS

Six different but widely used amplifier settings are shown below for you try out for yourself. Although they won't necessarily sound the same from one model to another, the fundamental principles will apply to most types of valve

amplifier. As always, though, you should spend some time experimenting for yourself until you find settings that are best suited to your own playing and music. In the examples below, the letters on the knobs represent the following: I—input volume; B—bass; M—mid-range; T—treble; O—output (master) volume.

### 1. NEUTRAL SETTINGS     33/1

All of the controls are all set in a central position, producing a clean sound, with little or no distortion. Such a sound would be appropriate for straightforward rhythm or chord work in most styles of music. You can use the master volume control to alter the volume without changing the nature of the sound.

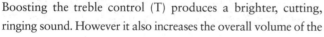

### 2. TREBLE-HEAVY SETTINGS     33/2

Boosting the treble control (T) produces a brighter, cutting, ringing sound. However it also increases the overall volume of the sound, so the master volume (O) needs to be reduced to compensate. Adding treble (and a touch of mid-range) may be needed to create a flat sound in a heavily sound-absorbent atmosphere, or when using certain types of humbucking pickup.

### 3. BASS-HEAVY SETTING     33/3

Boosting the bass control (B) produces a deeper, fuller sound. Again, you may need to compensate by reducing the master level (O). Bass levels vary depending on the kind of loudspeakers you use. Smaller speakers with a limited low-frequency response can benefit from extra bass, although too much can cause distortion.

### 4. GENTLE DISTORTION     33/4

In valve pre-amplifiers, boosting the input volume (I) will cause a gradual distortion of the sound. As this boosts the overall volume, the master volume (O) will have to come down to compensate. With the tone controls even, this usually makes a good, general lead-guitar setting.

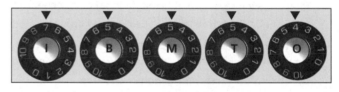

### 5. CRUNCH     33/5

With the input volume (I) on high, the pre-amplifier distorts. The increase in treble (T) produces a cutting sound. This kind of effect only really works when using a valve amplifier—solid-state models will require an external effect unit. This setting can also create feedback, whether you want it or not. This can sometimes be controlled by cutting back the treble on the guitar's control panel.

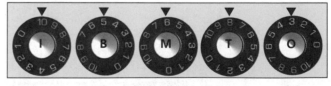

### 6. MUTE DISTORTION     33/6

With the input volume (I) still set to the maximum, reducing the treble (T) and mid-range (M) creates a "muffled" sound which can provide an extremely effective "bluesy" lead effect when played with valve overdrive and possibly also using the rhythm pickup (see across the page).

## PICKUPS AND SOUND

The amplifier and effects are not the only major considerations when discussing the sound produced by an electric guitar. Also significant are the pickups. Different kinds of pickup, and the way they are positioned on the body of the instrument, play a significant role in the overall sound. Magnetic pickups fall into two broad categories—single-pole and twin pole or humbucking (see picture below). Each has its own type of sound.

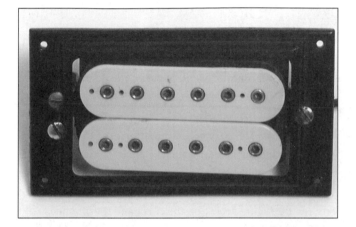

All of the original pickups were single-pole in nature. Twin-pole pickups were first produced by engineers at Gibson in the 1950s as a way of cutting down electrical hum, hence their name—"humbuckers".

Because the string vibrates in different ways along its axis, the sound amplified will alter depending on where the pickup is positioned. Most electric guitars have two or three pickups. The one positioned closest to the bridge produces the brightest sound, and is best for lead work—indeed, it is often known as the "lead" pickup. The one closest to the fingerboard creates a mellower, less cutting tone, best suited for rhythm work (although it is commonly used by jazz musicians for playing lead). If a third pickup exists, it is positioned between the lead and rhythm pickups. A mechanical switch on the body of the guitar allows one or a combination of both pickups to be heard.

You may notice that some pickups on a number of well-known guitars (Telecasters and Stratocasters, for example) feature a lead pickup angled so that the poles on the top strings are closer to the bridge than those of the bass strings. This alters the tonal balance so that the top strings produce a more biting, treble sound.

## GUITAR CONTROLS

Most electric guitars are equipped with at least a volume and tone control. Some models (such as the classic Gibson Les Paul) have a volume and tone control for each pickup. This allows the player to switch between settings easily. In practice, however, many players rarely touch the controls, leaving them permanently on "full", and making any tonal changes on the amplifier. However, it is always worth experimenting with the guitar settings. Heavy valve distortion, for example, can sound sweeter with the treble tone on the guitar set to a minimum value.

The controls can also be used to produce a variety of playing effects, such as playing a note or chord with the volume turned off, and then fading the volume up while the note is sustaining.

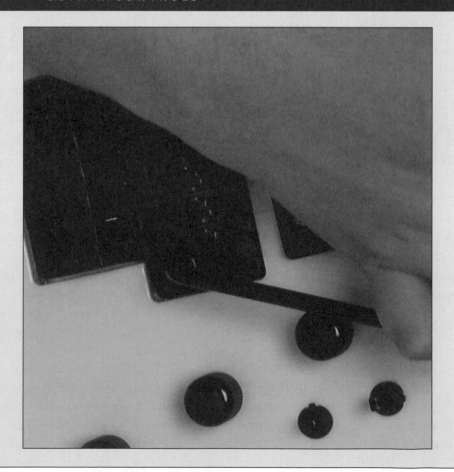

# ALTERING THE SOUND

Electronic effects units—whether they are simple foot pedals or costly digital multi-effect units—enable the guitarist to produce a vastly greater range of sounds than could previously be achieved with just an amplifier and guitar. It's fair to say that numerous sounds which are now taken for granted as a standard part of the modern music repertoire can only be achieved with some sort of add-on unit. Quite simply, for most types of music, effects are now a necessity.

## EFFECT PEDALS

If you plug your guitar straight into an amplifier, by the time the signal emerges from the loudspeaker, it will already have gone through a wide range of tonal coloration in the amplifier itself, such as alterations in equalization, or deliberate distortion created by overloading the preamplifier. There are a great number of other electronic processing effects that can be used to further alter the nature of the sound.

The earliest electronic sound processing effects were created in the 1950s and 1960s. They were either mechanical or used, by today's standards, crude analog electronics. In the modern era, even the simplest and cheapest effects tend to be either digital simulations of natural acoustic phenomena, such as reverberation and echo, or completely artificial effects based largely on changes in pitch or the distortion of the original signal.

### PLUGGING IN

The simplest and cheapest way of obtaining an electronic effect is to buy a plug-in foot pedal. Most of the commonly heard effects—delay, chorus, phasing, flanging, etc.—can be created using dedicated foot pedals.

Foot pedals are extremely straightforward to use. All you need is an additional guitar lead. The effect is inserted between the guitar and amplifier, the guitar is plugged into the "In" socket on the effect, using one lead, and the second lead is connected between the "Out" socket on the effect and the amplifier.

### POWERING EFFECTS

The majority of footpedals are powered by a standard 9-volt battery. Most modern units also provide the option of using a mains converter unit, although it's always a good idea to use transformers supplied by the effects manufacturers specifically the job—"unregulated" units may not work, can create unwanted hum, and, at worst, may damage the foot pedal.

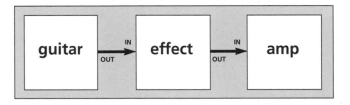

## REVERBERATION

Reverberation is a natural effect caused by a sound bouncing off the surrounding environment, such as walls, ceilings, and objects, before fading away. It is heard as a part of the original sound—you can hear the effect immediately if you shout in a large, empty room. When added to a guitar signal, "reverb" produces a warm, ambient effect of the sound spreading out

Simulated reverb effects were originally created by the use of a small spring that was vibrated by the guitar signal. This "clunking" sound can be heard on numerous classic, twangy rock-and-roll instrumentals.

Studios throughout the 1960s tended to produce natural reverb in acoustic chambers with microphones placed at different intervals from the sound source. This idea is still used for recording in some modern studios (see page 224).

During the 1970s, some manufacturers attempted analog recreations of the sound, but these were largely unsuccessful, and spring reverb remained the norm until it was replaced by high-quality, electronic digital units in the 1980s. Nowadays, even the most basic reverb unit allows you the luxury of programming parameters, based on the attributes of natural reverberation, such as the size, shape, and sound-damping features of an imaginary room.

As far as the guitarist is concerned, there are two distinct uses for reverberation. In a studio situation—whether at home or in the most professional setting—high-quality reverb is easily the most essential effect. It is reverb that breathes life into "dead" sounds. Lead vocals and drums are rarely mixed down without some reverberation—although in some cases, it may be natural rather than electronically supplied. On the other hand, the quality of the effect found in the form of pedals or, to a lesser extent, in multiple effect units (see page 210) tends to be considerably lower, their aim being more for playing live.

# DELAY EFFECTS

A significant proportion of the most popular electronic effects used by guitarists are produced by repeating a delayed signal. Like reverberation, delay is a natural effect produced by a sound reflected from a distant surface.

Delay effects were originally produced by mechnical means. Using a cut-down version of a reel-to-reel tape recorder, a loop of quarter-inch tape passed across a series of heads: the signal was created by a record head, and then replayed by a series of playback heads. The best known early model was the Watkins Copycat, first produced in 1954. Although these units suffered the same problems as any lo-fi tape recorder—namely, a poor signal-to-noise ratio and limited frequency response—they remained popular until well into the 1980s. Hi-tech versions are still produced today, with some guitarists resolute that the effect of a signal saturating the magnetic tape cannot be duplicated.

Delay is now almost entirely produced digitally. Different effects are created depending on the length of the delay. They are shown below measured in milliseconds (note: 500 milliseconds equals half a second).

## PHASING (7–12 MS) AND FLANGING (12–20 MS)

The effect of phasing occurs when the same signal is played back from two different sources at the same time. Every sound comprises a soundwave which passes from peaks to troughs. When two identical signals are slightly out of alignment and the peaks on one signal tie up with the troughs on another, the effect is known as "phase cancellation," producing a "sweeping" sound. If the delay is greater, the sweep becomes more dramatic and "metallic"—this is known as flanging.

## CHORUS AND ADT (20–35 MS)

Delay effects were originally created by recording a signal on two tape machines, and then playing them back at the same time. The inconsistencies in speed and pitch between machines helped to create the overall sound. Electronic emulates of these effects are created by adding pitch modulation and speed controls to disturb the delayed signal. ADT—"automatic double tracking"—and "chorus" are two such effects. Adding variations in pitch to a delayed signal can create the effect of doubling up the performance. It's usually employed to beef up vocals or a "thin" guitar sound, and is an effective alternative to recording the same part twice on separate multitrack channels. If used over a rhythm guitar part, it is especially effective when the original signal and the effect are panned to extremes in the stereo spectrum.

Chorus extends this approach, modulating a number of repeats. As the delay is so fast, this creates a full-bodied, rich, and sustained sound which is especially effective on chord work.

## ECHO (OVER 35 MS)

When a delay is of a sufficient length that the repeated signal can be heard as a distinct sound in its own right isolation, this is an echo. A single fast repeat played back at the same volume as the original signal is known as "slap-back" echo—this sound was used extensively by early rock and rollers, both on guitar and vocals. In recent years, guitarists like Queen's Brian May or folk-rock musician John Martyn have used delays of several seconds to build up, and play over, thick layers of sound. This approach reached a natural conclusion with Robert Fripp, who used two tape recorders linked together by one spool of tape to create soundscapes built from delays of 10 seconds or more.

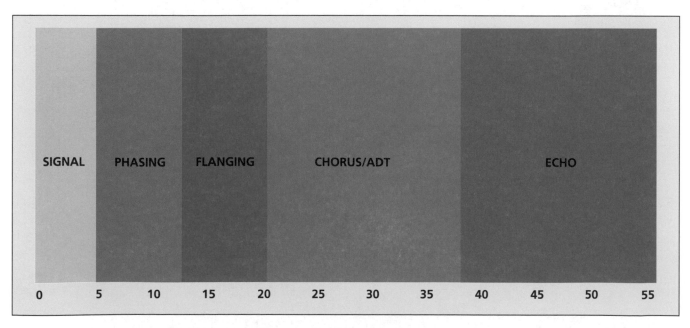

# PITCH, VOLUME, AND TONE EFFECTS

Besides delay and reverberation, a number of other commonly used effects have evolved out of making alterations to the pitch, volume or tone of the original signal.

## ALTERING THE PITCH

Pitch effects—a relatively recent development—are a byproduct of digital delay. The principle is simple—the original signal is delayed by shortest possible time it takes to turn a sound into a digital sample and replay it at a different speed. Such units are usually called "pitch shifters," and they allow the guitarist to generate harmony lines automatically. Most units have a range of one octave above and below the original signal, with half-step "click-stops" in between. For example, if you set the unit to play major 3rds, every sound that goes into the unit will come out a major 3rd higher.

Some of the more sophisticated units are capable of generating multiple harmonies of up to four or five parts. Again, these can either be set manually, or in some cases, they can create "intelligent" harmonies, allowing the chord types to alter, depending on the notes which are being played to generate the signal.

The repeated signal is a heavily processed digital sample, so the sound quality can deteriorate badly. It can create tracking problems for digital technology, because the original signal has to be processed and appear to be replayed simultaneously with no delay. This can result in an unpleasant effect known as "glitching." This usually happens when processing moves the pitch downwards—such units work more effectively in the treble register than the bass.

## DISTORTION

Distorted sound is one of the most famous of all effects. Although it can be produced in numerous different ways—you have already seen how amplifiers can be used in this way on page 204—the principle is largely the same. The signal is fed into a low-output pre-amplifier, where the volume is boosted to the point of distortion; the treated signal is then boosted by a "clean" power amplifier.

Fuzz pedals were first produced in the 1960s for guitarists who liked the effect of valve distortion, but wanted to be able to produce a similar effect at much lower volumes. The claimant for the title of first fuzz box was the one designed by Gary Hurst for the British Sola Sound company. Called the Tone Bender, it was first used by Jeff Beck on the Yardbirds' single "Heart Full Of Soul." Further popularized by Jimi Hendrix and Eric Clapton, by the 1970s all manner of sophisticated overdrive units were available, many aimed at providing not only distortion but a simulated valve sound for those using solid-state amplifiers.

## COMPRESSION

Compression is hardly a sound effect in its own right, but it is often used with fuzz and distortion effects to make the guitar sound sustain for a longer period, especially when playing a solo. Compression units reduce the volume of sounds above a pre-defined threshold, smoothing out the overall dynamics. Compression is discussed in more detail on page 213.

## RELICS FROM A BYGONE ERA?

Just like music itself, guitar-processing effects go in and out of fashion. Indeed, some of these sounds are so strongly linked to a certain time as to restrict their usage to the deliberately retro-minded.

One of the most famous (and earliest) guitar-based effects is the wah-wah pedal. This unit is essentially a tone filter which is rocked back and forth inside a foot pedal. It can be used to create a variety of different effects. Perhaps more than anyone else, Jimi Hendrix was responsible for popularizing the wah wah pedal, his album *Electric Ladyland* providing some of the most expressive uses ever heard—in some cases, using the effect to imitate the nuances of the human voice. Frank Zappa often used the wah-wah as an additional tone control, finding a setting that he liked and leaving the pedal permanently in that position—the filter in most units providing greater resosonance (or "Q") than the tone controls that any amplifier could manage. Funk guitarists in the early 1970s also used the effect heavily; muting the strings and strumming a rhythm whilst rocking the footpedal produces a sound characterized by Isaac Hayes' music for the film "Shaft." In the past, manufacturers have also produced automatic wah-wah effects. These are "envelope filters," whose tonal characteristics are controlled by the volume of the incoming signal—the harder you play, the more "wah" you create. The wah-wah pedal fell almost entirely from grace at the end of the 1970s. Around 1990, British indie-dance bands like the Stone Roses and Happy Mondays brought them back into fashion. Since then, the wah-wah pedal has remained popular among a younger generation of players.

Another interesting relic from the 1970s, which will doubtless find a vogue in the future, is the voice box. These units were used to create literally "talking guitar" effects. Most famously used by Peter Frampton on his mid-70s hit "Show Me the Way," the sound created a minor sensation back then, even though it was pretty much the same effect as that which had been used on the "Sparky's Magic Piano" children's records of the 1950s. To create the effect, the guitar was plugged into a unit which fed a low-volume signal along a plastic tube, which was attached to the microphone stand. Placing the end of the tube in the mouth, the guitarist could modulate the sound, which would then be picked up by the microphone.

# COMBINING EFFECTS

**Many of the effects that can be heard used by guitarists are a result of two or more different types of processing taking place at the same time. This can be done by linking together two or more effects; a more modern approach is to use a multi-effects unit—a single box that can produce effects simultaneously.**

## DAISYCHAINING

Effects pedals can be linked together in a "daisychain." By that, we mean simply that the output from one unit can be input directly into another. To all intents and purposes, any number of effects can be joined together in this way.

The overall sound produced can alter radically, depending on the sequence in which you link the different units together. Try to think logically what is happening at each point along the chain. In the diagram below, if effect A was echo-generating four delays, and effect B was distortion, all of the delays would be distorted; if they were the other way round, a single distorted signal would be delayed—the harmonic content produced would therefore be quite different in each case.

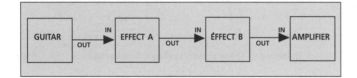

## MULITIPLE DAISYCHAIN

By inserting a switching unit—whether a crude pedal (which can be home-built extremely cheaply) or a sophisticated MIDI-controlled foot pedal—between the guitar and the front of the chain, it is possible to channel the signal through different kinds of effect.

The very simple example shown below shows a two-way switching mechanism. With the switch in one position, the output from the guitar is passed through to the amplifier via units A and B. With the switch in the second position, the signal can be heard from the same amplifier, but this time via effect units C and D.

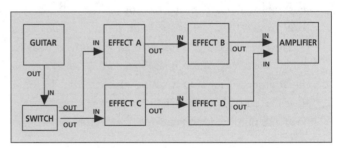

## MULTIPLE-EFFECTS PEDAL

Single-effects pedals, such as those featured on the last few pages, are a relatively cheap and efficient way of changing a basic guitar sound. However, a major drawback of their use is that complex set-ups involving a large number of pedals can become unwieldy to operate, especially when playing on stage. Additionally, many pedals have a great number of parameters that can be changed, making it difficult to store precise settings without recourse to written documentation—again, hardly practical in the middle of a concert!

A modern solution to this quandary has come in the development of the multiple-effects module. Often specially designed with the guitarist in mind, these are usually high-quality, digital units capable of producing at the very least, reverb, a full range of delays, distortion, and compression effects at the same time. The greatest advantage, apart from doing away with the need for a tangle of cables, is that all of the individual parameters can be stored and recalled either by a footswitch (as in the Zoom 503, shown on the right), or rack-mounted and recalled by a MIDI foot pedal or sequencer.

## VOLUME PEDALS

A volume pedal can be inserted between the guitar and amplifier to provide foot control of the signal entering the amplifier. This can be useful when switching between playing lead and rhythm guitar without having to manually alter the volumes on the amplifier's control panel. If a series of effects are being daisychained, it should appear as the final element before the signal enters the amplifier.

Volume pedals can also be used as playing effects, providing a rich "swell" when used in conjunction with echo and reverb effects—when used in this way, the pedal should be connected AT THE FRONT of the chain, allowing the effects to treat the "faded-in" signals.

### RELATIVE VOLUMES

If you use any guitar effect you create two distinct signals, the original, clean sound and the new, "effected" sound. The way they are mixed together can have a considerable impact on the final sound. Most effects have some kind of in-built mixing control, which lets you set the proportions of each sound that is output—some even provide independent output sockets. If you are using delay effects and the treated signal is louder than the original source, it may make it difficult for you to play in time. As always, there are no fixed rules here, but it's always worth bearing in mind that this balance is yet another sound parameter under your control.

### USING EFFECTS

If you read guitar and technology magazines, you will have seen the plethora of glossy adverts imploring you to buy the latest state-of-the-art processing. As tempting as this can be, think carefully about its application before you shell out your hard-earned cash. Here are some considerations to bear in mind, and some practical tips on using effects:

- Take great care with effects that are too gimmicky. Sounds that leap out of the speakers and scream "I AM AN EFFECT" are not usually very versatile. Any effect that becomes fashionable WILL DATE. Do you want your recordings to be tied to a specific era?

- When you first buy an effect, spend time working through all the possible sound permutations its parameters will allow. Units can sometimes generate interesting noises that you didn't expect (or that they were not even intended to create).

- Work it to death before you consider using it live or on a recording. However great the sound, the novelty WILL wear off, so it's better to discover this before you cover an entire set's worth of songs with your flavor of the moment.

- If you use effects pedals live, invest in a suitable transformer. They are cheap and will save you a fortune in batteries in the long run—after all, the venue usually pays for the electricity! Otherwise, ALWAYS keep a good supply of spare batteries in your guitar case—it's a good idea to do this anyway, in case your transformer packs up.

- Take the time to make up (or buy, if you prefer) a series of small six-inch patch-bay leads for daisychaining effects. If you use regular-length guitar leads, you will find yourself with a mess of cables all over the stage or studio.

- EFFECTS ARE NOT AN END IN THEMSELVES. A BAD IDEA OR PERFORMANCE RARELY MAGICALLY BECOMES GOOD BY APPLYING AN EFFECT.

# TABLE OF EFFECTS

The following two pages show you how you can achieve 33 different sound-processing effects. Some may have little practical use, but are nonetheless presented to show the kinds of sounds that some can make when pushed to their extremes. The final 12 are multiple effects—combinations of one or more already shown. Multiple-effects units are becoming increasingly common, both as dedicated guitar effects and in studio racks. All of these sounds are offered only as possibilities—each effect unit is different—and it is only by exploring the extent of each parameter that you will be able to gauge its full potential.

### 1. CLEAN SIGNAL

For the purposes of comparison, this is a straight, "clean" signal from valve amplifier—no sound-processing effects can be heard.

34/1

### 2. REVERB (SHORT DECAY)

Set the reverb to a decay time of around 2 seconds. The ratio between original signal and effect should be around 4:1.

34/2

### 3. REVERB (MEDIUM DECAY)

Set the reverb to a decay time of around 5 seconds. The ratio between original signal and effect should be around 4:1.

34/3

### 4. REVERB (HEAVY DECAY)

Set the reverb to a decay time of around 10 seconds. The ratio between original signal and effect should be around 2:1.

 34/4

### 5. SLAP-BACK DELAY

Set a delay time of around 35 milli-seconds. Feedback should be at a minimum. The signal-to-effect ratio should be around 1.5:1.

34/5

### 6. MEDIUM DELAY

Set a delay time of around 75 milli-seconds. Feedback should be set to provide about four repeats. The signal-to-effect ratio should be around 3:1.

 34/6

### 7. LONG DELAY

Set a delay time of over one second. Feedback should provide two or three repeats. The ratio between original signal and effect should be around 2:1.

 34/7

### 8. TAPE DELAY

Different sound characteristics can be achieved by using tape delay units, although they provide less flexibility in altering parameters.

34/8

### 9. PHASING (GENTLE)

Speed and modulation parameters both on low settings. The ratio between original signal and effect should be around 2:1.

34/9

### 10. PHASING (EXTREME)

Speed and modulation parameters both on high settings. The ratio between original signal and effect should be around 1.5:1.

34/10

### 11. FLANGING (GENTLE)

Speed and modulation parameters both on low settings. The ratio between original signal and effect should be around 2:1.

34/11

### 12. FLANGING (EXTREME)

Speed and modulation parameters both on high settings. The ratio between original signal and effect should be around 1.5:1.

34/12

### 13. CHORUS (GENTLE)

Both the speed and modulation controls are kept to low settings. The ratio between original signal and effect is 2:1.

 34/13

### 14. CHORUS (EXTREME)

Both the speed and modulation controls are set to a maximum. The ratio between original signal and effect is 2:1.

 34/14

### 15. AUTOMATIC DOUBLE TRACKING (ADT)

For the best results (in recording, at least), clean and effected signals can be panned to extremes.

 34/15

### 16. COMPRESSION

Heavily compressed signal with no other effects in the chain—effective with distortion. The ratio between original signal and effect is 1:1.

**34/16**

### 17. "FUZZ BOX"

A classic 1960s-style distorting, pre-amplifier sound. The ratio between the original signal and the effect is 1:1.

**34/17**

### 18. DISTORTION (LIGHT)

Gentle solid-state distortion (less warmth than that produced using a valve amplifier). The ratio between original signal and effect is 3:1.

**34/18**

### 19. DISTORTION (HEAVY)

Heavy solid-state distortion: these effect units are favored by heavy- and speed-metal players. The ratio between original signal and effect is 1:1.

**34/19**

### 20. OVERDRIVE UNIT

Synthetic copy of a classic overdriven valve sound. Harsher and more clinical than the real thing, but highly usable nonetheless.

**34/20**

### 21. WAH-WAH PEDAL (MOVEMENT)

The tonal characteristics of the clean signal can be heard to shift as the position of the pedal changes.

**34/21**

### 22. WAH-WAH PEDAL (MOVEMENT WITH DISTORTION)

The wah-wah sound is particularly effective when it is combined with distortion.

**34/22**

### 23. WAH-WAH PEDAL (NO MOVEMENT WITH DISTORTION)

Holding the pedal in one fixed position is a very extreme form of tone control.

**34/23**

### 24. ELECTRONIC TREMOLO

Another classic sound of the 1950s and 60s. Altering the level of modulation determines how far the pitch moves either side of the note.

**34/24**

### 25. PITCH SHIFT (INCREASED BY MAJOR 3RD)

The pitch is increased by "+3"—an interval of a major 3rd. The ratio between effect and signal is 1:1.

**34/25**

### 26. PITCH SHIFT (DECREASED BY PERFECT 5TH)

The pitch is lowered by "-5"—an interval of a perfect 5th. The ratio between effect and signal is 1:1.

**34/26**

### 27. PITCH SHIFT (INCREASED BY OCTAVE)

The pitch is raised by "+12"—an interval of an octave. The ratio between effect and signal is 1:1.

**34/27**

### 28. DISTORTION, DELAY (LONG), AND REVERB (LONG DECAY)

Distortion, delay, and reverb effects can be used together to create extremely "big" sounds.

**34/28**

### 29. DELAY (SHORT) AND REVERB (LONG DECAY)

Combination of a short delay (less than 30 milliseconds) with a slow-decaying reverb.

**34/29**

### 30. OVERDRIVE, DELAY (MEDIUM), AND REVERB (MEDIUM DECAY)

Although similar to 28, reducing the length of delay and reverb decay produces a tighter sound.

**34/30**

### 31. REVERB (LONG DECAY) AND CHORUS (GENTLE)

The impact of combining chorus and reverberation effects creates a fuller, luscious sound.

**34/31**

### 32. DISTORTION, PITCH SHIFT (INCREASED BY PERFECT 5TH), AND REVERB (MEDIUM DECAY)

Distortion and pitch shift together create an "extreme" metal sound.

**34/32**

### 33. DISTORTION WITH DELAY AND VOLUME CONTROL "SWELL"

The volume pedal can also be used as a playing effect. For this purpose, it should be used at the front of the chain, so that it controls the signal entering the effect.

**34/33**

# CHAPTER 6
# Performing and Recording

## THE RECORDING STUDIO

The first tape recorders appeared in the 1930s; before that time, the only way of capturing a sound permanently was to "cut" a record. A great achievement though this was, it didn't allow for the sound to be altered after it had been recorded, nor could the disc be used again. The early tape machines set a pattern which would become standard throughout the recording industry for the next 60 years. Spools of tape coated with a magnetic-oxide surface were passed over a series of record and playback "heads" on the tape machine. This captured the sound, which could be retained until the tape was erased, after which it could be recorded over again.

In the 1940s, multi-channel tape recorders were developed for the first time. These machines allowed for a basic rhythm track to be recorded on one channel, and for other sounds to be "overdubbed" afterwards on separate channels. The balance between all of the sounds could then be balanced using a mixing console, and "mastered" on a separate tape recorder.

The greatest revolution to hit the recording industry in the 1950s was the creation of stereophonic sound. Until that time, all recordings had been made in "mono," so when played back on a radio, tape recorder, or record player, the overall sound could be heard from a single loudspeaker. By adding a second speaker with an independent amplifier, it became possible to pass different levels of sound through each speaker. This created the illusion of positioning each instrument within the stereo spectrum, giving the same kind of effect as listening to an orchestra in an auditorium. This was initially thought to be the only real use for stereo.

During the 1960s, rock music appropriated stereo to create an entirely new sonic palette, which had nothing to do with recreating an authentic listening experience. The psychedelic era saw the development of all manner of studio effects, which were often used as a way a simulating the effects of hallucinogenic drugs. During this time, the multitrack recorders became more flexible, allowing for the recording of up to 16 individual channels. To accommodate this increase in the number of tracks, the width of the magnetic tape was increased—various machines used everything from the standard quarter-inch tape, right up to the two-inch tape used on the largest machines.

The 1970s saw studio machines equipped with up to 24 individual tracks, and the widespread use of analog studio effects, such as delay and reverberation. Also significant was the birth of the Philips cassette, a low-quality, high-convenience format which signaled the death of the domestic reel-to-reel machine. The same decade also saw the development of quadraphonic sound, an extension of stereo in which the listener was positioned at the center of four loudspeakers. Largely viewed as a fad, quadraphonic failed to capture the imagination of mainstream listeners, and by the end of the decade was all but forgotten. Interestingly, the concept has been revived in recent years, as "surround-sound" home entertainment systems become increasingly popular.

By the end of the 1980s, digital technology had finally caught up with the recording world. Small, rack-mounted DAT (digital audio tape) recorders gradually replaced the larger analog two-track reel-to-reel machines, and the best-equipped studios now accommodated digital multitrack recorders. The greatest advantage of digital equipment was that it offered no background tape hiss of its own, and could be copied (theoretically) as many times as necessary, without the original signal being degraded.

It was a decade that also saw a proliferation of the home recording market. For producing the most basic of multitrack recordings, the four-track Portastudio cassette units sold millions of units all over the world. For the more ambitious, high-quality digital studio effects became increasingly affordable for the masses.

The most radical technical departure of the 1980s can truly be said to have altered the way musical was written, recorded, and performed. It was a systems protocol called MIDI—"Musical Instrument Digital Interface"—a system of coding which enabled computers, synthesizers, drum machines, sequencers, and digital effects to communicate with one another. Its existence enabled home recordists to produce professional-sounding music quickly and cheaply. MIDI was directly responsible for the development of the entire dance music boom. New musical genres, such as hip-hop, electro, and acid house, using digital sampling techniques, were being created by a new generation for whom musical expertise was not a prerequisite for producing a creative and challenging sound. Many of these genres later evolved into newer forms, such as garage, and drum and bass.

The last decade has seen some interesting evolutions in the field of digital multitrack recording—the Alesis ADAT format has become something of a semi-professional standard. However, the greatest developments have been made in the area of computer hard-disk recording. Software-based solutions like Digidesign's ProTools systems enabled high-quality multitrack recording to be performed on an Apple Macintosh or PC. The soundwaves could then be edited on-screen, allowing for a degree of flexibility that would have been unthinkable even a decade earlier. Until this time, there was only one possibility for editing a piece of music—you had to physically cut up the tapes with a razor blade.

The capabilities now open to even the most basic home recording artists would have seemed to most engineers of the 1960s as an impossible dream. And the developments in digital recording look set to continue, as recordable and rewritable CDs become increasingly mainstream, and the Sony Minidisk format looks as if the analog cassette may finally have met its match.

# WHERE TO BEGIN?

**The desire to bare their soul for the world to hear is a natural one for most musicians at some stage in their lives, irrespective of whether they are looking to "make it" or play it to their friends. However, the disciplines needed to record successfully are very different to performing live. Many musicians who seem to "come to life" when they are on stage find that the restrictions of the studio prevent them from giving their usual electric performance. In short, they just can't cut it.**

Having decided that the time is right to capture your performance, there are several different options that you can consider. If you are working in a really hot live band, you might be better off having one of your gigs recorded—although, be warned, it can be really difficult to capture a good live recording. The more feasible option you need to consider is recording in a studio, at home, or using a combination of both environments.

For most bands, especially those using a "real" drummer (rather than drum sequencers or samples), the most practical solution is to hire a studio. The advantages over a home set-up are plain to see—any studio offering its services professionally

should be better equipped than the average home studio, both in terms of hardware and acoustic treatments. The downside to using a professional studio is that it costs money—sometimes a great deal of money—and it can also be a nerve-wracking experience, especially if you've never done it before.

Before you can go any further, you have to decide how many songs you want to record, and how much money you want to spend. These two questions will be strongly interconnected: your budget will not only dictate how many songs you can complete, but how you go about recording. A 24-track recording involving a lot of overdubs will not only take longer than a stereo recording cut "live" in the

studio, but the hourly or daily rates charged for the higher-specification professional studio equipment will undoubtedly be a great deal higher.

Here are some (very) approximate guidelines to how much you are likely to be able to achieve during the course of different types of recording session. Naturally, such a figure will depend on factors such as the competency of the musicians. In addition, if you are trying to integrate your sound with sequencing and samples, this can push your session times upwards.

### DIRECT TO TWO-TRACK—NO OVERDUBS
Allow up to three hours to get the basic sound right, and then aim for one hour per song thereafter. This can be a very intense way of working—everyone is on the go the whole time—so make sure that you take regular breaks and that you don't forget to take refreshments.

### MULTITRACK—NO OVERDUBS
Allow two hours for the basic set-up—this should be less difficult than before, because the final mix is done at the end of the session. Allow an hour for every song, and at least another hour for every mix.

### MULTITRACK WITH OVERDUBS
The conventional way to record in a multitrack studio is to record the rhythm section—the drums, bass, and second guitar—playing together. This is the only way of guaranteeing a tight sound. Afterwards the solo instruments and vocals can be added separately. As a rule of thumb, the more tracks you have to play with, the longer the session will take to record and mix. To be honest, if you are working in a 24-track studio, you will be doing extremely well to get more than one song finished in a ten-hour session.

## WHO'S WHO IN THE STUDIO?

If you use a top-of-the-range recording studio, you will find that individual tasks are made the responsibility of individuals. In a small-budget studio, ALL of these jobs may well be done by just one person.

The engineer is responsible for getting the sound sources down onto tape in the best possible way. A typical engineer will be well versed in microphone techniques, with a good understanding of which type of equipment is best suited to an individual voice or instrument. Most engineers will have graduated from working as a "tape op"—usually, frankly, a studio dogsbody who does everything that the engineer or musicians don't want to do. It is from this menial position that most of the world's best-known engineers and producers have developed. There is a growing trend among some studios—mostly those specializing in classical recording—to employ "tonmeister" engineers, who have formally been taught the principals of recording on a university course.

The term "producer" can mean many different things. However, the principal role is quite simply to help the artist achieve the results they are looking for. The most famous producer of them all is probably Sir George Martin, whose groundbreaking work with the Beatles led many to refer to him as the 5th member of the band. By understanding the kinds of ideas that Lennon and McCartney were trying to bring to their music, he was able to use his extensive knowledge as a trained classical musician to introduce new aspects, of which the band themselves had little previous knowledge. Imagine "Yesterday" without the string quartet, or "A Day in the Life" or "Strawberry Fields Forever" without the orchestral elements, and you can see how important Martin has been to the history of popular music.

This is not to say that every producer seeks to achieve such an impact—many are simply responsible for creating the final mixes. The advent of dance music and DJs actively involved in creating music has added a new dimension to studio work. Indeed, some of the most successful producers working now may know little or nothing about recording instruments. During the 1990s, a growing trend has seen the birth of a new kind of producer, who may be an expert in sampling and sequencing. Such producers may be called upon to build up a new soundscape with only a vocal track to work from.

So, do you need a producer? Frankly, sessions at every level benefit from having experienced personnel on hand. If you are already signed to an established record label, the chances are that your management wouldn't even dream of letting you in a studio without someone overseeing your work. But in practical terms, experienced producers are a very expensive luxury that few first-time bands can afford. One alternative may be to seek out an engineer or established musician who is trying to make the transition to producer. Ask around local studios and rehearsal rooms—if you're lucky, you may get someone prepared to work just for the experience.

# PREPARING TO RECORD

No matter how experienced you are as a musician, working in a studio for the first time can be daunting, not least of all in deciding how to choose which studio to hire. The kinds of studios accessible to the pockets of most semi-professional musicians are likely to be owned or run by engineer/producers, so you won't usually need to worry about hiring extra hands. Studios should be chosen with great care, because the recording process can be greatly aided if the environment is pleasant and you have a sympathetic engineer. It helps to understand a little about the recording process, so that you can use your time more effectively. Here are some basic guidelines on using professional or semi-professional studios.

- Audition the studio as if it were a new member of your band. Pay a visit, and ask to hear examples of what they have already done. Check out the condition of the equipment—if faulty or poor-quality, it can not only result in a poorer sound, but can waste valuable time—that you are paying for.

- Quiz the engineer/producer. What kind of music is he or she experienced in producing? It may seem obvious, but different types of music require different production techniques. A country and western producer may have problems understanding the needs of a thrash metal band.

- Know EXACTLY what you are getting for your money. The studio rates that you see advertised may not necessarily include: engineer, producer, purchase or hiring of multitrack tape, mixdown tape, copies of mixes, use of studio-owned instruments, or other amenities that might be at hand.

- Rehearse your music. Many great albums have been put together in a studio by musicians jamming or coming up with ideas on the spur of the moment. This is all well and good if you have an unlimited budget. Studio hire is expensive. The better prepared you are, the more efficiently you can use that time. Try out different arrangements during rehearsals, rather than on the day.

- Be prepared. Make sure that all equipment you are taking is in the best possible condition. As a guitarist, this ALWAYS means changing your strings for a session and bringing along several sets of spares. You should also try to bring spare leads, picks, and batteries (if you use foot pedals).

- Be punctual. Musicians have an appalling reputation for reliability. If you or members of your band arrive late for the session, you'll probably still be charged for the time. If you arrive early, you can do useful things like setting up drum kits or tuning instruments, or warm-up exercises.

- Don't be over-ambitious. It's better to create one well-produced track than rushing through a handful songs which you end up discarding when you decide that they are not good enough to use.

- Plan ahead. If you are recording a handful of songs, record ALL of the rhythm tracks at the same time. Getting a good drum sound is the most time-consuming problem in a small studio. If you record and complete tracks one at a time, you will have to go through this process every time.

- Studio recording is stressful. Everyone involved needs maximum concentration. The last thing you need is interruption from friends or other hangers-on. You should seriously consider barring EVERYBODY who is not directly involved in the band from attending the session.

- Take a balanced approach to your performance. The type of music you play will depend on how much latitude you have to work within. For some, a slight error in an otherwise passionate take might be acceptable (or even preferable), but NEVER let anything go that you are just not happy with. It will ALWAYS be there, and every time you hear it you can be guaranteed that it will just keep getting louder and louder in your head. Consider shooting any engineer or producer who says, "I can fix it in the mix!"

- Try to agree some kind of mixdown protocol. This is a really tough one. If you are not working with a producer who has been hired to oversee your session, it is liable to become a committee event, in which the various members of the band control their own volume faders on the desk. BE WARY OF THIS APPROACH. In these situations, even the most pleasant, self-effacing individual can turn into the original ego monster. Quite simply, everyone will be focusing closely on their own performance, rather than the overall sound. If you're not careful, the most persuasive voice may end up with their own instrument leaping out of the mix. The more inexperienced the band, the more likely this is to happen. One idea might be to give the engineer the final say in the event of dispute. To be honest, for many bands there may be no real solution to this problem—after all, if everyone is paying for the session, then they deserve to have their say. It is, however, an aspect of basic human psychology, and everyone should be aware that this is a common occurrence.

- Learn to let go. A mixing session offers an infinite number of possibilities. Some studio novices completely overlook this part of the session, imagining it to be a few minutes' work at the end of the day. The corollary to this is the indecisive school, who are never quite happy that they have achieved the perfect mix. In such cases, it is a good idea to record a number of mixes and decide in your own time which you want to choose. In fact, many musicians prefer to take some time out between the recording and the mixing. If you have three days budgeted for, think about spending two days together recording, and taking a break for a week before you approach the mixdown. This will give you allow you to approach the mixdown with fresh ears.

# UNDERSTANDING THE STUDIO

The first time you walk into a studio, you may well be overwhelmed by the racks of flashing lights and rows of knobs on the mixing console. An understanding of what the different components that are found in most studios can help you to get a lot more out of the session, and also give you a better idea of possibilities that you might not have ever considered. The basic components of a recording studio are the same from a $1000 home set-up right up to a multi-million-dollar complex, albeit of very different size, flexibility, and quality. Nonetheless, every studio will comprise a mixing desk, multitrack recorder, digital or analog effects, a monitoring system, and mastering recorder.

## THE MIXING DESK

The heart of even the most modest of recording studios, the mixing desk is essentially an sophisticated patch bay where signals from a microphone or musical instrument are input, altered, re-routed, and then output. The desk is used for two distinct but equally crucial functions: recording and mixing.

### RECORDING

At the start of the session, the microphones or instruments are connected into the mixing console, where the sounds can be individually altered, either by using the features that are built into the desk—typically volume, gain, or equalization (tone control)—or by patching in external digital or analog effects, such as compression or delay. The signals are then routed into one or more of the channels of a multitrack recorder.

### MIXING

After the initial recording has been completed, each channel of the multitrack requires connection to an individual channel of the desk. Here the signal can be altered as before or positioned differently within the stereo spectrum. The sounds from the different channels are then played together and "balanced" to produce the final stereo "mixdown." In practice, most reasonable modern mixing desks are sufficiently flexible to allow both the recording and mixing phases to be carried out without the need for extensive repatching.

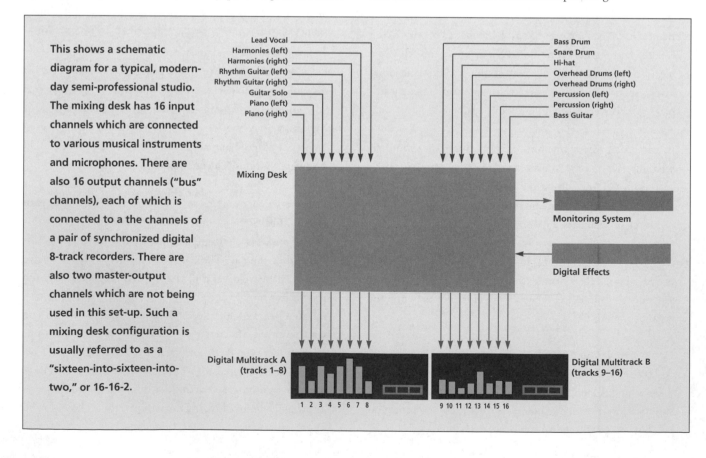

This shows a schematic diagram for a typical, modern-day semi-professional studio. The mixing desk has 16 input channels which are connected to various musical instruments and microphones. There are also 16 output channels ("bus" channels), each of which is connected to a the channels of a pair of synchronized digital 8-track recorders. There are also two master-output channels which are not being used in this set-up. Such a mixing desk configuration is usually referred to as a "sixteen-into-sixteen-into-two," or 16-16-2.

Lead Vocal
Harmonies (left)
Harmonies (right)
Rhythm Guitar (left)
Rhythm Guitar (right)
Guitar Solo
Piano (left)
Piano (right)

Bass Drum
Snare Drum
Hi-hat
Overhead Drums (left)
Overhead Drums (right)
Percussion (left)
Percussion (right)
Bass Guitar

Mixing Desk

Monitoring System

Digital Effects

Digital Multitrack A (tracks 1–8)

Digital Multitrack B (tracks 9–16)

1 2 3 4 5 6 7 8        9 10 11 12 13 14 15 16

The signal routing for the mixing session, using the same set-up shown at left, looks like this. Each output from the multitrack is now connected to an input channel on the mixing desk. The master output passes the final stereo mix into the mastering 2-track machine, typically a DAT recorder. Digital effects can also be applied to individual signals. In fact, they also could have been during the recording session, although most professionals prefer to record dry, unaffected signals, as this allows for greater flexibility during the mixdown—you can always add an effect, but if the original signal has been recorded with an effect, it CANNOT be removed afterwards.

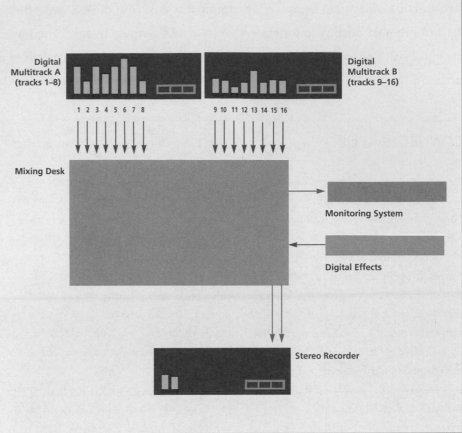

Digital Multitrack A (tracks 1–8)

Digital Multitrack B (tracks 9–16)

1 2 3 4 5 6 7 8        9 10 11 12 13 14 15 16

Mixing Desk

Monitoring System

Digital Effects

Stereo Recorder

## CONSOLE TYPES

All mixing desks fall into two main categories—they are referred to as being "in-line" or "split-console." These features describe the way in which the desk deals with the different aspects of recording. A "split-console" desk invariably has a set of inputs on one side of the desk and a set of output channels on the other side. The output channels are used for recording onto the multitrack recorder. The "in-line" console has switching that allows both functions to be performed by a single channel.

## CHANNEL GROUPING

Mixing desks also have facilities for grouping together different input channels. This can be used for several different purposes. When a mix has been decided for a "set" of instruments, they can be routed away from their individual volume faders and sent to a pair of grouped channels. For example, a complete drum track might be made up from six individual signals. Once they have been EQ'd and relative levels set, all six channels can be patched through to a stereo group. Thereafter, the overall volume of the drums can be controlled as a whole. Other common uses include vocal tracks and string parts.

# CONNECTING TO THE DESK

Irrespective of its size, expense, or complexity, a mixing desk is essentially a series of input channels linked to a number of output channels via what are known as "buses." The basic contents of a typical input channel will be largely the same, concentrating on matching impedances of incoming equipment, and altering the tonal qualities of the sound (known as "EQ") or volume.

## CONNECTING UP

Input connections to mixing desks are usually by way of jack plugs or XLR plugs. Some of the cheaper models may also use phono plugs.

Connections are termed either "balanced" or "unbalanced." Phono plugs used on domestic hi-fi and mono jack plugs are always unbalanced. These are the simplest types of connection, where the signal is carried by a single "hot" wire surrounded by earthed screening. Guitar and effects leads are also unbalanced. Balanced connections comprise two "hot" wires that carry "out of phase" signals. Microphone signals and connections to and from high-quality components are usually balanced. Where you have a choice, select balanced connections—they will give you a cleaner signal.

## MICROPHONE/LINE INPUTS

The output of any electrical signal is governed by what is termed the "impedance." The unit of measurement covering impedance is the same for any form of electrical resistance—the ohm.

This is signified by the Greek letter omega($\Omega$).

Although every piece of equipment will have a different impedance, they fall into two broad categories: microphone levels and line levels. Microphones are low-impedance devices, usually operating at around 250$\Omega$. Standard line outputs from other pieces of equipment, such as effects units or electronic keyboards, operate at a much higher level—so high, in fact, that they are measured in thousands of ohms, or kilo-ohms.

All mixing desks have a method for matching these different impedances with the input of the desk. These usually take two forms, one that switches between the two (typically a "mic/line" switch), and a variable "gain" control to fine-tune. This is sometimes also referred to as a "trim pot." The variable controls can be used in conjunction with the volume fader to set signal levels correctly (see "Volume fader" on the right).

## EQUALIZATION

The term "EQ" simply refers to the alteration of the tone of the signal, which is much the same as altering the bass and treble controls on a hi-fi system. However, on most desks the potential for altering the EQ is more dramatic. The sound spectrum—the range of audible signal—is usually split into separate bandwidths. Within each grouping, the specific frequencies can be cut or boosted according to your tastes. Equalization systems where the specific frequency

can be fine-tuned before cutting or boosting are referred to as "parametric equalization." Those where the frequency bands are preset or fixed are known as "shelved" systems.

Use of EQ is one of the subtle arts of the recording engineer. It's easy to get carried away when given the opportunity to radically alter a sound, but most professionals use EQ in a more practical way, to "tighten" the sound of some instruments, or in extreme cases to "remove" irritating signal deficiencies.

### AUXILIARIES

Whilst some of the top-flight desks incorporate built-in effects such as compression or noise gates, for most, patching in external units is the way to add traditional effects such as reverberation and delay. The principal is a simple one. Each desk is equipped with a set of auxiliary "sends" and "returns." Each pair can be patched up to an external effect—the send and return being connected to in

and out sockets respectively. By rotating the auxiliary knob on the desk clockwise, increasing amounts the signal are "sent" through to the effects unit. The output of the effect is "returned" to the desk, where the original clean signal and the new "effected" signal are brought together. The diagram below shows a system where there are two auxiliaries—the first is connected to a digital delay; the second to a reverberation unit.

There are a variety of different viewpoints on how effects should be used. Which method you prefer may well be dictated by your own system. Generally speaking, in an ideal world, signals should be recorded clean and effects added during the final mixdown. This gives you maximum flexibility. That's all well and good if you only need one or two different effects. But if you have only a single multi-effects unit, then you're likely to find yourself forced to record the effects onto the multitrack master. If you have spare channels on the master tape, you could

consider recording the clean signal on one and the effect on another. However, sometimes there will be no alternative to laying down the full signal on one track. When you do this, just make sure you REALLY mean it!

### PAN

The "pan" control determines where the signal will be positioned in the stereo spectrum: if the control is panned to the far left, ALL of the signal will come from out of the left-hand speaker. If you have a stereo signal coming into two separate channels, they must be panned in extreme direction to achieve their true stereo effect. If both signals are panned in the center, a monophonic effect will be created.

### VOLUME FADER

This is a sliding potentiometer that governs the overall volume of the track. The higher it is pushed, the higher the volume.

The volume fader is used in conjunction with the gain controls to set levels over individual tracks. If the incoming signal is too high, it will cause distortion. Reducing the volume fader will not help—it will simply lower the overall volume of the distorted signal. To prevent this happening, the levels for signals on every channel should be set. This is a simple process which needs to be done while the signal is being played.

- Set the volume fader to 0dB
- Turn the gain control at the top of the channel until the VU or bargraph meter also shows a reading of 0dB. Those desks that don't have metering on every channel usually have "peak overload indicators." These are lights which flash red each time a signal exceeds 0dB.

The signal entering the desk is now at its optimum level, and ONLY the volume fader should be used to balance the levels going into the overall mixdown.

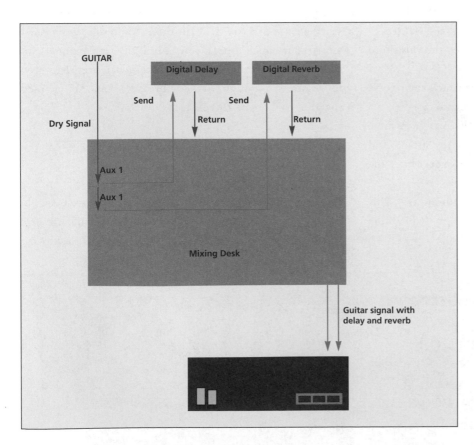

# STUDIO EFFECTS

Many of the most commonly heard effects used in the studio are similar to those used by guitarists, even if they are usually of a much higher sound quality. Reverberation and delay, which have already been covered in some detail in Chapter 5, are the most significant of these effects. Every studio should be in possession of at least one high-quality reverb and delay unit. In recent years there has been a trend towards the production of multi-effects—digital units that are capable of simultaneously creating and linking together a number of different reverb or delay effects. These offer fantastic value for those with a limited budget. There are also a number of other less glamorous, but nonetheless essential, effects that even the humblest domestic studio needs.

## COMPRESSION

The term "dynamic range" refers to difference between the maximum and minimum volumes levels for any signal. Some instruments, typically the guitar, possess a very wide dynamic range. This means that in the course of mixdown (or, for that matter, playing live) at various times the overall signal will be too loud, and at other times it will disappear from the mix. To prevent this from happening, engineers use a piece of equipment called a "compressor."

The main controls on a typical compressor are marked "threshold" and "ratio." The threshold control dictates the level of volume above which the compression takes effect—when the overall signal stays below that level, it is left untouched. The ratio control sets the degree to which the signal is to be compressed once the threshold figure has been breached.

Most decent compressors also include attack and release controls. The act of suddenly limiting a signal can create a unnecessarily dramatic effect, or even distortion in some cases. To smooth out these occurrences, the attack and release controls set the amount of time over which the compression effect can be "faded" in or out.

Many compressors also double up as "limiters." This is a cruder form of compression, which simply reduces the gain when a signal exceeds a preset threshold.

## PRACTICAL USES FOR COMPRESSION

Undervalued by many home recordists—perhaps because it doesn't radically alter sound in the same way as, for example, a digital multi-effects unit—compression can be used both in the recording and mixing processes. As such, it's worth spending a significant amount of money on a professional model.

Vocals, guitars, and bass invariably benefit from being compressed while they are being recorded on the multitrack. It is extremely difficult for all but the most highly trained "clean" vocals to cut through a mix. Without compression, you are likely to spend the entire mix "chasing" the vocal fader at key moments.

There is also a good case for compressing an entire mix. Certainly most modern-sounding mixes can be tightened up when a ratio of 1.5:1 or 2:1 is used. To do this, you need a stereo unit which allows you to link the two channels, so that exactly the same processing takes place over the stereo mix. Many monophonic compressors can be chained together to work in this way.

## NOISE GATES

Another "dull," but vital, studio effect, a noise gate is simply used to shut out unwanted signals. Working rather in the reverse way to a limiter, a threshold setting on the noise gate dictates the

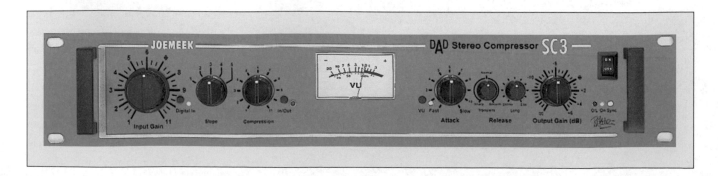

level at which the signal can be heard. Until the signal reaches that point, nothing at all can be heard.

The noise gate is at its most valuable in the recording chain. If you imagine a typical multitrack recording, there are likely to be many moments during the course of a song when a particular track is silent—the lead vocal track during a solo; solo tracks during the rest of the song. If you listen to these in isolation, you will surprised how much noise you hear. Apart from hiss generated by electronic equipment, there is likely to be anything from gentle electronic buzzing to the occasional cough or audible breathing. Although you would be hard-pressed to pick any

of these out of the mix, they all contribute "noise" which can help to "muddy" the total sound.

By recording through a noise gate you can avoid all of the above occurrences. Sometimes a particularly raw, heavily effected, solo guitar sound can produce an unavoidable degree of buzzing when the guitar is not being played. If you set the noise gate threshold above the buzz it will not be heard—no signal will pass through the gate until the first note of the guitar is struck.

Noise gates will not make your recordings sound different as such, but they will improve the sound quality, which is clearly a good thing.

## ENHANCERS

Emerging in the early 1980s, enhancers (also known as aural exciters) are among the more mysterious of the studio effects. Indeed, some of the early manufacturers of enhancer units chose to encase the entire printed circuit board inside the unit within a black resin, making it impossible for other manufacturers to glean the secrets of their operation. Nowadays, such units are among the cheapest rack-mounted modules.

The effects created by an enhancer are not alsways easy to explain—indeed, a number of fundamentally different systems are employed.

However, using "harmonic regeneration" and/or phase shifting, the impact of playing a dry signal through an enhancer is to provide depth, clarity, and "sparkle," either to an individual signal or over an entire mix.

Some enhancers use additional valve circuitry to provide warmth to the overall sound. Enhancers can also be used to breath new life into old tapes, especially those which have been copied several generations over. Be warned, however, that these effects are very easy to overuse, and can be very "fatiguing" to the ears.

## RECORDING STUDIO EFFECTS

Like the twin functions of the mixing console, studio effects can be used both in the recording and mixing chain. The traditional "pure" approach of the professional studio engineer has tended to be to lay tracks down as cleanly as possible—this generally means using little EQ and no external effects. Therefore, during the mixdown process each of the original signals can be processed in any possible way. If, for example, you record a vocal part with heavy slap-back digital delay, the delay will always be there;

record it clean, and it can be processed in the mixdown in any way you like.

The disadvantage of leaving the effect processing to the final stages of mixing is that if you want to put different effects on different channels (or more than one effect on a single channel, for that matter) you need a separate unit for each different effect. One of the reasons that multi-effects units have become so popular among budget or project home studios is that one effect can be used to record a signal, and then the same unit can be used to provide a different effect during the final mix.

# MICROPHONES

**Although many modern electronic instruments can be recorded simply by plugging them into a mixing desk and setting the levels, the fundamental art of recording still revolves around the use of the microphone. The vast majority of microphones fall into two categories: dynamic and condenser.**

### DYNAMIC MICROPHONES

Dynamic microphones (or "moving coils" as they have also been known) comprise a coil joined to a diaphragm which is set around a magnetic cap. When a sound—which is essentially a movement of air waves—hits the diaphragm, the coil moves. This produces a voltage output.

Dynamic microphones are widely favored for their robustness in a live situation, being capable of handling particularly high levels without their coils becoming damaged, but they are also often used in the studio for miking up instruments.

### CONDENSER MICROPHONES

The majorityy of the best-known and most expensive models, such as the classic Neumann U87, are condenser microphones. The diaphragm in these models is coated with a thin layer of metal with an separate backing plate. A high "polarizing" voltage is contained between the two pieces of metal, which fluctuates

according to pressure changed by movement in the diaphragm.

All condenser microphones have a built-in pre-amp which boosts the level of the output. It is powered either by batteries, or by the "phantom" power supply built into most mixing desks.

### PRESSURE-ZONE MICROPHONES

Not fitting easily into either of the traditional categories, pressure-zone microphones (or "PZMs" as they are usually known) are what is referred to generically as "ambient" microphones. Each unit consists of a transducer attached to a metal plate which can be fixed to a wall or other alternative

upright surfaces. PZMs are most effective when they are used in pairs, and panned at extremes to produce stereo ambience—the characteristics of the surrounding space. These sounds are then mixed in with the original, "dry" signals.

## POP SHIELDS

A pop shield is a piece of foam which covers the head of the microphone. It is used to prevent the first syllable of "P" words causing a sudden jerk in the diaphragm, which results in a loud popping sound. When vocal "pops" are recorded they are very difficult to mask—it's possible to "ride" the fader momentarily, but this will usually result in the loss of the first syllable.

On particularly sensitive microphones, placing a thick pop shield over the head can have the effect of muting the overall sound. Therefore, in studio situations it's more satisfactory to use a windscreen. This is a layer of thin material placed between the microphone and the vocalist. You can model a simple windscreen by stretching a nylon stocking over a coathanger. This can then be fixed with duct tape to the microphone stand.

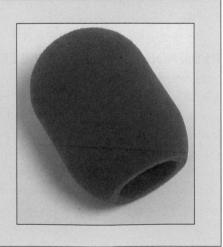

## PICK-UP PATTERNS AND CHARACTERISTICS

Irrespective of its characteristics, every type of microphone has what is termed a "pick-up pattern." From this it is possible to discern the area around the microphone that will be picked up when the microphone is connected. Some models have the facility for switching between different pick-up patterns.

Omnidirectional microphones are designed to able to pick up signals equally from any direction. As you can see from the left-hand diagram on the right, irrespective of the way the microphone is facing, the signal is equally good from all directions. Such a pick-up pattern (or "polar response") is usually found in general recording microphones, and is best suited to recording sources which involve some degree of movement.

Directional microphones are designed to pick up sound predominantly from one direction. The most common polar response for

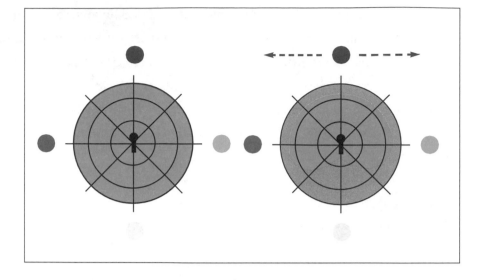

directional microphones is termed a "cardioid" pattern—so called because its resemblance to the shape of a heart. As you can see from the diagram above on the right, the strongest signal is picked up from the front; a greatly reduced signal is picked up from the rear. A number of other types of cardioid shapes can be found, but the principle that applies to them is exactly the same.

The use of cardioid microphones is vital when trying to prevent sound spillage from other sources. This could mean a vocal microphone cutting down on ambiance from the back and sides, or those surrounding a drum kit where each individual drum is being miked up.

To work properly, however, cardioid mikes do require the sound source to remain broadly still. If, for example, a vocalist moves to the left or right of the optimum position, the most sensitive cardioid microphones will register a significant variation in volume.

### STANDS AND MOUNTINGS

If you use a microphone, then you also need a microphone stand—it's not really a good idea to use hand-held microphones when recording in a studio. The most versatile type of stand is the "boom," which will allow for movement in any direction. When you buy a stand, ensure that it has a sturdy vertical frame and feet that are sufficiently wide so that the whole thing won't topple over.

Microphones are held in place by a fixture to a mounting. Most instrumental microphones are slotted into a sliding mounting. The larger condenser microphones, such as the Neumann "U" range or the popular budget Rode models, are a good deal heavier and require the use of a "shock" mounting. On such systems, the microphone is clamped into a central unit which is held in position by a thick elastic belt. This provides the microphone with an in-built suspension system, making it less sensitive to floor movement.

If you find that you need to get a microphone into a particularly tricky close position, it may be worth acquiring a "goose-neck" extension.

# RECORDING THE GUITAR

**If there is one subject guaranteed to cause heated debate among recording engineers, it is the issue of recording with microphones. Most engineers have their own personal favorite microphones and their own views on the most appropriate ways to position them. The fact that there is such widespread disagreement on the matter emphasizes the point that—just like playing the guitar—there are no hard-and-fast rules. The ideas shown below can largely be categorized as good, sensible practice, but the only way you can ever get the sound that YOU want is by experimentation.**

### CLOSE-MIKING

Different effects can be produced, depending on how far away the microphone is away from the sound source. In a studio situation it is most common to use "close-miking" techniques. Positioning a microphone between 2 and 18 inches away from the instrument or voice produces the most detailed sound. This is because the signal captured is predominantly the sound of the instrument and less the ambiance of the room—the natural effect of soundwaves reflecting off walls and ceilings. For this reason, close-miked recordings can sound unnatural, because they contain little or no ambient reverberation. As such, artificial studio digital reverb is usually added to make it sound "real" again.

As you will find out for yourself as you experiment, and your hearing becomes more sensitive to the subtle characteristics of a sound, the way an instrument is recorded can sound vastly different simply by repositioning the microphone by a few inches. Simply moving a microphone closer or further away from a source can have unpredictable results, although there are a couple of rules that you should bear in mind when placing microphones. The first is that moving a microphone away from the source not only reduces the volume but reduces the bass response; the second is that in the same situation, the volume does not decrease in an consistent fashion. depending on the sensitivity of the microphone, the relative signal may drop off dramatically between the space of 12 to 24 inches.

### DISTANCE MIKING

This refers to the deliberate placement of microphones at a distance of a meter or further away from the sound source. Recordings made at between 1 and 3 meters away from the source provide a natural balance between the sound of the instrument and the characteristics of the surrounding room; this effect can be magnified by using omni-directional microphones.

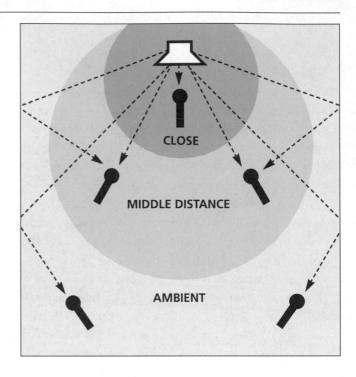

### AMBIENT MIKING

The signal achieved by placing microphones at a distance further than 3 meters from the source will largely comprise ambient room reflections.

The most effective guitar sounds can often be achieved by recording microphones positioned in a combination of all three modes, as shown above.

## MIKING AN ACOUSTIC GUITAR

The character of the acoustic guitar sound is extremely subtle, and always difficult to capture with a microphone. The traditional position for miking an acoustic guitar is around the soundhole—this is the loudest point on the guitar. Moving the microphone along the strings to the bridge will alter the tonal balance, increasing the bass; moving it toward the top of the fingerboard will boost the treble. The positioning of the microphone will to some extent depend on the type of music being played.

One major difficulty that arises, however, is that of dealing with variations in volume. Many novices have a limited understanding of dynamics, and working in a studio calls for a more delicate and accurate touch than in live performance. Whilst few decent engineers would presume to have a musician alter his or her playing style to make a recording easier, knowledge of which playing techniques are most appropriate to a given situation can make life a good deal easier all round.

## RECORDING AN ELECTRIC GUITAR

Given that a guitar fitted with a pickup has an electrical signal just like any other piece of equipment, it should be possible to plug the guitar directly into the mixing console. This approach is referred to as "DI-ing" (direct injection), and suggesting recording this way is probably the easiest short-cut to antagonizing a guitarist in the studio. Most guitarists rightly consider their amplifier as a part of their overall sound, and so it is usual to mike up the

loudspeaker. However, there are alternatives and compromises, as you'll see shortly.

The simplest recording set-up is to position a single directional microphone at the same height as the center of the loudspeaker, at a distance of between 2 and 6 inches. If the signal varies in its dynamic content, try inserting compression into the recording chain: a ratio of around 2:1 will help level out a clean sound; for a heavily distorted sound, you can go as far as 8:1.

A two-microphone alternative sees a second microphone placed above the first and pointing downwards at a 45° angle. The slightly different sounds can then be mixed together on the desk before being recorded on a single track. If you have enough spare channels on the recorder, you could record them on separate tracks, and balance them during the mixdown.

Many guitarists and producers have experimented with unusual ways of capturing a guitar sound in the studio. It is not uncommon for microphone signals from close, natural, and ambient positions to be mixed together, or the sound from the louspeaker to be chaneled through acoustic tunnels created by baffle screens. Perhaps one of the most extreme approached was used by producer Mutt Lange, who while working with the rock band Def Leppard evidently recorded the notes of some of the heavy power chords one string at a time—rumors circulated that it was taking weeks of studio time to record a single guitar part! Presumably everyone involved felt it worthwhile when the resulting album, *Hysteria*, became one of the biggest sellers of the 1980s.

### SPEAKER SIMULATORS

Although few serious guitarists would be happy to have their signal plugged directly into the mixing desk, technology has brought about an increasingly popular alternative—the speaker simulator. This is a processing effect which is connected between the speaker output of the amplifier and mixing desk. Some models even have additional onboard processing to create the effect of different types of speaker configuration.

There are some significant advantages to using a speaker simulator, especially in home-studio situations, not least of which is the reduction of excess noise. Powerful valve amplifiers need to be played at high volumes to achieve their characteristic overdrive. In an enclosed environment, this may not only result in deafening volume, but may also result in unwanted feedback. By recording via a speaker simulator you not only bypass these problems, but you can also accurately monitor the sound going down onto tape.

# HOME RECORDING FORMATS

**Home recording has become an ever more significant part of the music world. Gone are the days when band members innocently trooped into a big recording studio, waiting to be told what to do. Knowledge of studio techniques has empowered the musician, resulting in a generation of techno-literate musicians capable of using the recording studio not only as means to document their work, but also as a creative tool every bit as important to the compositional process as a conventional musical instrument.**

## ANALOG SYSTEMS

Compared to even a decade ago, the modern home recordist is spoilt for choice. When Teac introduced the first Portastudio in 1979, it revolutionized the home recording market. Up until that time, reel-to-reel multitrack home recording had required a basic investment roughly the equivalent to buying a small new car. The Portastudio was an affordable unit which combined a four-track cassette recorder and mixing desk, and was about the same size as a modern fax machine. Musicians quickly discovered what a useful medium it was for composition and working out arrangements, even if the sound quality may not have been generally considered good enough to produce releasable results (not that it stopped some indie artists from doing just that).

Since then, the Portastudio idea has developed in both directions. At one end, cheap "pocket-sized" models with in-built microphones allow musicians to lay down ideas as the muse hits

them. Alternatively, high-end digital models can, with care, be used to create professional, releasable recordings.

## DIGITAL SYSTEMS

The majority of musicians buying new recording systems now go for digital sound, even if some still hanker after the "warmth" of analog recording, or the unique sounds created by tape compression. Digital systems come broadly in three different forms: dedicated real-time tape machines; dedicated hard-disk recording systems; or systems that can be run from a computer. Each one offers the user flexibility and an exceptionally high sound quality.

### REAL-TIME DIGITAL TAPE MACHINES

Digital multitrack tape recorders largely captured the semi-professional market during the 1990s. The most widespread format is the ADAT system, developed by Alesis and also used by Fostex machines. Appearing as a standard, three-unit-high, rack-mounted item, the ADAT allows eight tracks to be recorded either individually or together on SuperVHS video tape. A similar system has been developed by Tascam, though this is not directly compatible with the ADAT format. Although less popular, it is widely considered to be of higher quality and more reliable.

Another area where digital machines generally supersede their analog predecessors is in their synchronization capabilities. It is possible for pretty well any number of these machines to be linked together and controlled from a single source, or one machine controlling a number of "slaves" Recorders using different formats can even be linked together. With a suitable interface unit, it is even possible to control a recorder from an external MIDI sequencer or drum machine.

## HARD-DISK RECORDING

There are two distinct types of hard-disk system. Less popular, (if very flexible) are dedicated hardware units which allow the user to record directly onto an external hard drive. More common are systems operated by a personal computer—most of which are aimed at the popular PC market, although professional users still favor the Apple Macintosh. The advantage of hard-disk systems is that they can be edited very easily. For example, song sections can be repeated or sounds "cut-and-pasted" as easily as moving text around in a word processor. Additionally, recordings can be sequencer-based, which means that tracks of digital sounds can be integrated with MIDI tracks.

## WHICH FORMAT?

Apart from the issue of expense, the choice of format might come down to the kind of music you play, and the way in which you're most comfortable working. If you only want your machine to capture audio performances, then real-time systems, be they

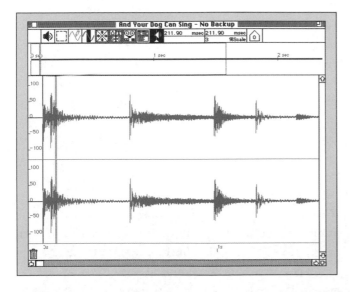

analog or digital, are probably the most suitable. If your music integrates MIDI and sampling a computer-based system will be more suitable. However, such is the flexibility of modern technology that there is no reason why, expense allowing, you cannot have a single system that integrates both.

## ANALOG PORTASTUDIO MULTITRACK

For:
- Cheap to buy
- Built in mixing facilities
- Portable
- Cassette tape is the cheapest

Against:
- Poor sound quality
- Limited on-board facilities
- Multitrack tapes are impossible to edit

## REAL-TIME DIGITAL SYSTEMS

For:
- Excellent sound quality
- Easy to synchronize with other machines
- Tapes are relatively inexpensive

Against:
- Impossible to edit tapes without hard-disk facilities
- Formats are not all compatible

## COMPUTER SYSTEMS

For:
- Superb sound quality
- Matchless editing capabilities
- Seamless integration with MIDI
- Different sound-file formats can easily be converted

Against:
- Storage is expensive
- Can be mentally taxing to work
- Can be time-consuming
- Reduce spontaneity
- Computer systems can be volatile
- Software and hardware date at an absurd rate

## REEL-TO-REEL R.I.P?

Can it really be true that a discussion of multitrack recording ignores the traditional analog tape recorder? For most home systems the answer is, sadly, yes. Whilst there are numerous musicians still using old systems, few—other than those with an appetite for "retro" sounds—would consider buying such machines new. However, if you imagine that EVERY great record made before the mid-1980s used such a system, then analog studios still clearly have a lot going for them—indeed, there are some studios that now specialize in vintage analog equipment. Additionally, the speed at which many have sought to convert to digital has meant that some extremely high-quality analog equipment has found its way onto the secondhand market at almost give-away prices.

Strangely, at the top end of the professional scale, the matter is less clear-cut, with extremely high-spec, half-inch, two-track, analog machines often being used in the mastering process. It would seem that some artists, having recorded in a 100% digital environment, are only truly happy with their stereo master once it has passed through some kind of analog stage.

# PUTTING TOGETHER A PROJECT HOME STUDIO

When a professional recording studio is being designed, you might think that pretty much the entire budget goes on buying equipment. What is less apparent when you enter a studio is the amount of time and expense that have gone into producing an acoustically ideal environment. The "live" room—where the music is recorded—will have been prepared to fulfill certain acoustic characteristics; the control room—where the mixing takes place—will be as "dead" as possible, so that the sound coming from the monitor speakers is not colored by other items in the room. These effects are not produced by trial and error, but by the scientific knowledge of highly qualified acoustic specialists. When you record at home, no matter how good your equipment, you are unlikely to achieve acoustic perfection.

Another, often overlooked, issue is that of the surrounding environment. Top studios spend a fortune hiring interior designers to come up with a pleasant and creative environment in which musicians feel relaxed and happy to work. Again, this is a luxury that few home recordists can enjoy, such matters being largely dictated by what they have available.

There are two major problems to consider when putting a studio together. The first is the two-way problem of noise. To make the best possible recordings, you have to prevent noise from outside, such a traffic, from being picked up by your microphone; equally, if you live in a one-bedroom apartment, your neighbors will quickly become intolerant when you record a drum kit in the early hours of the morning.

The second difficulty is the quality of the acoustics. Every characteristic of a room—from its shape to its contents—will in some way affect the sound you hear. You will almost certainly have experienced the difference that occurs in sound when a carpet has been taken up in room—all of a sudden, the sound of voices can be heard resonating around the room. When you record in such an environment, this will affect everything, from the sound of a microphone that goes down on the multitrack to the way a final mix sounds.

## CREATING A SUITABLE ACOUSTIC ENVIRONMENT

Before you seriously consider putting a studio of any sort together, you need to ask yourself some basic questions. The first is to decide exactly what do you want to be able to produce. If your project studio is intended principally as a musical notebook and no more, a small Portastudio system might well be sufficient. You don't need too much space to work in, and when you've finished you unplug everything and put it away in a cupboard. However, for anything more demanding you need to be prepared for

a considerable investment of time and energy before you even lay down a single note.

The ultimate acoustic environment is outside in the open, where there are no objects for the soundwaves to bounce off: it is the ideal "dry" sound. But this is an option that few, if any, will be able to consider. Professional studios have multi-layered wall structures which are treated with fiberboard and other absorbent materials to soak up different areas of the sound spectrum. Whilst this is probably unfeasible for all but the most serious home users, even the simplest kinds of alternative acoustic treatment will require time, money, and ingenuity. Indeed, home studio recording will provide you with an endless succession of quandaries to think your way out of.

## REFLECTING SURFACES

The major problem faced in recording in any domestic room is that of dealing with the reflective surfaces, from which the sounds will bounce back and forth. The aim is to get the room sounding as "dead" or "dry" as possible. The first option is to cover every reflective surface, principally walls, floors, and ceilings, with an absorbent material. Here you can do a lot worse than simply covering the ENTIRE room with thick carpet. Most carpet stores sell offcuts at a reduced rate, so this is an economical way of improving room acoustics.

Another cheap, and commonly used, acoustic trick is to glue cardboard egg-cartons to the surrounding walls. This type of material is very effective for absorbing sound, but there is little point in trying this out with the increasingly common styrofoam alternatives.

If your recording room still has to double for regular domestic use, making permanent fixtures in it may not be desirable. Less effective, temporary alternatives include hanging an absorbent cloth, such as canvas.

## SEEPAGE

If you want to record more than one instrument at a time in a home studio, you may need to look into the idea of acoustic separation—preventing the signals from one instrument seeping into a microphone intended for another. In large studios, this can sometimes be achieved by having different instruments played in isolated booths. A more common alternative is to mask the different instruments by using thick padded screens known as "baffles." These can be moved around depending on what instrument is being played. In a home environment, baffles can rarely succeed in providing total isolation, but will give you a greater level of control over the sound. The diagram above shows how baffles can be used to isolate several different instruments.

A simpler, if less attractive, alternative to making baffles is to fit curtain rails to the ceiling, to hang thick material which can then be used to envelop an instrument.

One advantage that most homes have over semi-professional studios is that they are already divided off into a number of small rooms. Therefore, as long as your microphones and headphone monitors are on sufficiently long leads, there is no reason why you could not record instruments simultaneously in different rooms of the house, which will each have different acoustic properties.

## ISOLATION

These suggestions may make your room a drier place in which to record. However, they won't help in solving the issue of external noise. If you live in an apartment with neighbors in surrounding rooms, there really is NO WAY to avoid noise, without literally building a new room within your existing room. Unless you have extremely understanding neighbors, there are only two solutions—keep the noise down or move!

### WHAT THE HELL!

Don't be put off by what you've just read. What we've been discussing here are ways to improve an inherently flawed alternative to hiring a recording studio. In fact, it's absolutely true to say that many home recordists simply piece together their recording equipment in a spare bedroom and power it up without giving a thought to acoustic matters. And they are perfectly happy with the results they achieve. To be brutally honest, as long as the room you choose is carpeted, and the windows can be covered by reasonably thick curtains, with care (and a limited desire to mike up acoustic instruments) it IS possible to achieve some very satisfactory results.

# LAYING OUT THE STUDIO

**The ergonomic positioning of your studio equipment is a critical concern which can have a major impact on the way you work, the way you enjoy working, your sound, and your efficiency. Frankly, for most users this is an evolutionary process—most of us don't know the way we want to work until we've experienced methods that don't work. That said, there are very few solid rules that dictate where items should be situated, although one aspect that shouldn't be overlooked is the positioning of the monitoring loudspeakers.**

The "soundfield" is a term given to listening area between the two loudspeakers. For monitoring a stereo mixdown, you MUST position yourself in the center of the field. The speakers should ideally be at ear-level height. However, if they are positioned higher, you can still achieve the right effect by pointing the speakers in a downward position. For monitoring during the recording process, being within the soundfield is less important—in fact, you can stand or sit wherever you like, as long as you can hear satisfactorily. In the diagram at right, the area shaded in yellow represents the soundfield. Seating is positioned in the optimum listening point within the soundfield—the mixing engineer shouldn't drift too far from this position.

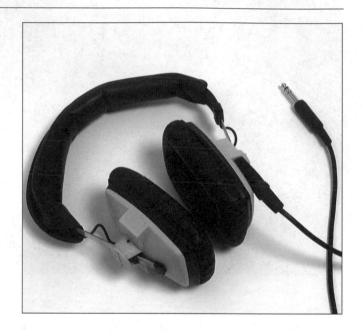

## MONITORS

The quality of monitor speakers should be regarded as a critical issue for home recordists. Many on a small budget will simply use hi-fi speakers. These may be adequate for monitoring recordings, but they are largely misleading for mixing a stereo master. The main difference between hi-fi speakers and dedicated studio monitors is one of basic functionality: hi-fi speakers are designed to make your pre-recorded music sound as good as possible; monitor speakers aim to provide a "flat" response which is level across the audible sound spectrum, meaning that, in theory, mixes should sound clear on any system.

Even if you work in a professional studio with ten-foot-high stacks in front of the mixing desk, you may be surprised to see how much work is done using small "near-field" monitors placed only a few feet away from the desk. No matter how many sets of speakers you have at your disposal—and it IS useful to switch between different sizes and types, especially if your music is aimed at specialist locations, such as television or clubs—every home studio should be equipped with good pair of near-field monitors. These will give you the clearest indication of how your mix is likely to sound in general. Headphones can also be used as an occasional mix monitor, as they provide a clear view of the stereo positioning.

If you mix over headphones or cheap hi-fi speakers there is every possibility that your mixes will be fine, but you leave an AWFUL LOT to chance. For example, a mix made on (unknowingly) bass-deficient speakers will probably result in your overcompensating on the "bottom end." When your master recording is played back over an average, decent hi-fi system, you may be horrified to find a VERY heavy bass sound leaping from the speakers.

## RACKING UP

Increasing amounts of home studio equipment, not only digital effects, but recorders, guitar amplifiers, loudspeakers, and MIDI expanders are designed to be fitted into the industry standard 19-inch rack. Such equipment is described in terms of its width in units (or "U's"); the racks themselves are sized according to how many "U's" they can hold. Rack-mounting equipment is the neatest way to operate a home studio. Racks can be bought to hold between 6 and 20 units of space, but if you plan on filling up one of the larger racks, make sure that you fit castors first, otherwise you will never be able to move it.

Pay special attention to where you position rack equipment. Banks of flashing lights fitted neatly flush against a wall may look very impressive, but the rack becomes less useful if you can't get easy access to the connections at the back.

If you plan to move equipment around frequently—for example, if you want to make on-location recordings—then you should seriously consider buying flight-cased racks. These can be stacked up neatly in the studio, and just as easily

packed away and moved. A word of warning, though— it is difficult for a single person to move anything heavier than a 6U rack without additional help.

## STUDIO PLAN

The studio plan shown below is a compact layout designed for use by one person. The revolving stool gives easy access to the mixing desk, effects rack, keyboards, and computer. The monitoring equipment is positioned between the two loudspeakers. A 2-meter-high, 19-inch rack contains ADAT, DAT, compressors, noise limiters, digital effects, guitar amplifier, speaker simulator, eight-channel digital hard-disk system, two samplers, and MIDI expansion units. The A-frame holds a MIDI "mother" keyboard, drum machines, and computer keyboard and mouse.

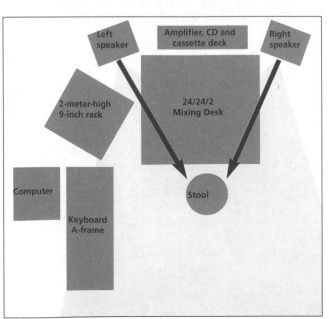

If the contents of the previous few pages are making you wonder whether it's all worth bothering with, here is a checklist of tips that might help you through the maze of problems faced by the novice home recordist.

- Restrict your recording to "respectable" hours.

- Work at low volumes.

- Keep all of the windows and doors in the studio closed.

- Consider using drum sequencers. There is no question that for most types of music, using a programmed drum machine is a poor second best to recording real drums. But they do allow you to record in near silence.

- Direct inject ("DI") as much as possible. Most instruments can be plugged directly into the mixing desk. If you don't like the over-clean sound, you can add effects at the same time (although recording clean does give you more options for the mixdown).

- For guitars, consider buying a speaker simulator; this is an electronic device which is connected between the speaker output of an amplifier and the mixer insert. It is especially effective with valve amplifiers, which normally require "cranking up" to get their sound at its best. Using a speaker simulator allows you to drive the amplifier at an unfeasibly high volume and monitor at a very low volume.

- Work over headphones as much as possible. It may not be ideal for the final mixing, but it's a fine way of monitoring yourself while recording.

- If you are using a "standard" multitrack format like ADAT, why not consider doing your final mixes in a professional studio? This gives you many of the advantages of both worlds—you create your work in an environment free of time, and mix it down in an environment which has better outboard equipment (desk and effects)—and no limits on how much noise you can make.

# COMPUTERS AND MIDI

**Once you have a satisfactory studio set-up, and understand how to use the different pieces of equipment, the recording process is usually straightforward. You record the different instruments on the multitrack and mix them down to produce a stereo master recording. However, there are number of other alternatives to this traditional approach which have emerged in recent years.**

Probably the most revolutionary technical advance of the past 15 years has been the development and evolution of MIDI (Musical Instrument Digital Interface). This is a computer language which enables computers, synthesizers, drum machines, sequencers, and digital effects to communicate with one another. The first dedicated MIDI recorders appeared in the mid-1980s, allowing complete multitrack performances of songs to be "recorded" without storing the sounds themselves on tape or hard disk. More recently, MIDI recording has more commonly taken place using computer software packages.

The principles of MIDI recording are relatively simple. The sequencer (or computer software) records an incoming MIDI signal, usually from suitably equipped keyboard. The information about the performance is then stored—for example, the pitch of the note, its duration, and its volume. To play back the recorded part, a MIDI out signal is sent to an external sound module. It can then be heard using whatever type of sound is currently programmed into the module. In this way, any piece of music recorded via MIDI can be played back using the sounds of ANY MIDI module. Furthermore, once it has been recorded, any MIDI data can be edited, so that correcting errors of playing, or any other alterations, can be easily made.

A MIDI recorder works much in the same way as a regular multitrack recorder. To differentiate between tracks, each separate performance can be allocated one of 16 channels. Therefore, 16 different MIDI modules can be played back at the same time—assuming that you have that many external MIDI devices. A major advantage of this approach over other systems is that the outputs from each module can be connected directly to the mixing desk, without ever having been consigned to a multitrack tape. This is known as "first-generation" sound—which is as "pure" as it possibly could be.

### EXTENDING TRACKS
Using only MIDI to record, you are largely limited to the number of sound modules you have at your disposal. However, MIDI sequencing can also be used in conjunction with tape-based systems, and can therefore be integrated

with conventional audio recordings. There are many different options, but most require some kind of synchronization interface. Some digital multitracks can be "slaved" to a computer, so that their transport controls (play, record, fast forward, etc.) are overridden by those of the computer. Alternatively, SMPTE synchronization units can be used. These can be used to record a signal onto one of the audio tracks, which is then used to control the MIDI recorder. These approaches allow for considerable track expansion without having to upgrade the multitrack. The diagram below shows how the combination of an eight-track tape machine and MIDI recorder can easily fill up all 24 channels of a mixing desk.

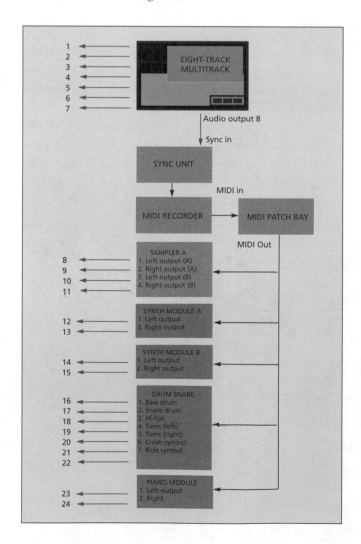

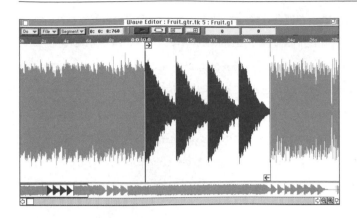

This computer screen image shows an enlarged view part of the guitar section of a recording being selected.

## GUITARS AND SAMPLING

For guitarists working in a studio, recording is no longer a matter of necessarily playing through an entire song. More and more guitarists are experimenting with the techniques of sampling and hard-disk editing. Imagine, for example, that have just played a particularly good part throughout one chorus of a song—using digital sampling or digital editing, you can simply "cut" the part you like out of the overall performance and "paste" it so that it plays throughout every chorus.

Sampling and hard-disk editing share some similarities. Sampling is a technique in which a sound is recorded digitally, after which it can be manipulated and played back from a MIDI keyboard or sequencer. Digital samples can be looped, played back in different keys, or "stretched" so that they last for different lengths of time. This process is performed on an external device called a "sampler," or alternatively on a computer using sampling software.

In many repects, hard-disk recording is quite a similar technique—a sound is recorded digitally, after which the sound-waves can be edited and then repositioned using a computer sequencer. The main difference between the two methods is that samples created by hard-disk recording are not triggered to play via MIDI.

Computer-based sequencing software, such as the Steinberg Cubase system, that were once MIDI-only recorders, are now

### DRUM MACHINES

One of the biggest problems of home recording is that most of us simply don't have suitable facilities for recording drums. This is where drum machines (or MIDI sequencers/recorders playing back drum samples) can be most useful. Such equipment is simple to program, although if you are not a drummer a brief lesson on drum patterns may be useful. As a very simplistic rule of thumb, in a four-four time signature the bass drum plays on the first beat of the bar, the snare drum on the third, and the hi-hat plays on every beat, or in double time. Typically, every four bars, or in keeping with the song structure, each new phrase is signaled by a "fill," which is usually an embellishment on the snare drum or toms.

equipped to deal with real-time hard-disk recording. Both MIDI and digital sounds appear alongside one another.

In the example being shown in the computer images on this page, a two-minute guitar part has been recorded. A small section has then been edited out (top left) so that it can be repeated at the start of each bar. Because the cut-and-paste features of such sequences can be set to lock to the start of any bar, the sound can easily be duplicated and then the sample can be locked to the start of the bar (below). The equivalent procedure using a sampler would be to edit the sound on an external device and then set it up in such a way that the sound is triggered each time a specific MIDI note is played on the sequencer.

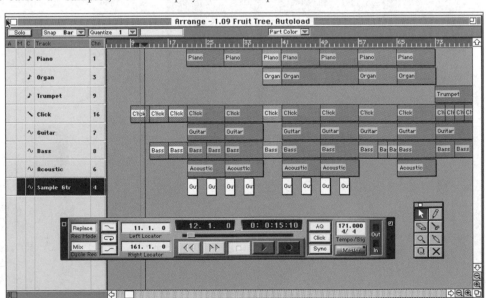

The selected section of guitar music is now pasted into each bar.

# TAKING TO THE STAGE

**The last three decades have seen recorded music—in particular, the album format—seemingly viewed as the benchmark of an artist's capabilities. For many musicians, however, performing live is a far more meaningful way of communicating with an audience. For the novice, taking to the stage for the first time can be a daunting prospect that throws up a whole host of new issues. Indeed, being a good performer is not necessarily the same thing as being a good musician, or for that matter being effective in the studio. Apart from having to come to terms with using different technology in alien surroundings, the stage rookie has to face the same issues that affect performers in any discipline, such as confidence, projection of an image, and, of course, the dreaded stage nerves.**

## WHAT DO YOU NEED?

The type of equipment you will need if you are to perform in public depends on a number of factors, principally the nature of your music and the size of the venue. For all but the smallest of club or bar settings, the central requirement is for a PA (public address) system. At its most basic, it may consist of little more than an amplifier and speaker, with a single microphone for vocals. At the opposite end of the scale, a major artist is likely to require a PA system which bears a closer resemblance to a digital recording studio.

## SMALL CLUB SET-UP

For performing in a very small club or bar, it's not uncommon for each of the musicians to provide their own amplification, which they control from the stage. Drums and brass instruments in small venues tend to be more than loud enough without needing to be miked up. If your music requires a singer, an additional amplifier and microphone will most likely be needed, although it may be possible to get away with simply plugging a microphone into a spare channel on the guitarist's amplifier, although it probably won't sound too great! To be honest, with no mixing desk and no external engineer in control of the overall sound, the balance between the instruments is certain to be, at best, hit-and-miss. If you use such a set-up, you probably won't be able to hear yourself playing very well either, but whatever you do, DON'T turn your own volume to compensate—you can be guaranteed that everyone else will copy you, and that your audience will be deafened!

Although there is undoubtedly some appeal in the raw simplicity of this way of working, it's worth trying to produce something a little more controllable. Start by looking for someone who would be interested in acting as your sound engineer—in fact, new young bands often seem

to have extras who tag along to rehearsals and gigs, waiting to be asked to get involved in some way. It's possible to put together a reasonable-quality PA system for very little money. All it takes is a simple six-channel mixing desk, a reasonably powerful stereo amplifier (500 watts per channel should be ideal for small venues), bass speakers, horns and crossovers, and a few microphones. Buy as many of these components as you can secondhand. As well as making you self-sufficient when playing gigs, your own PA system will also be a boon when rehearsing—there's no bigger motivation than hearing yourself sounding good.

In live situations, learn to trust your sound engineer. Give him or her as much control as possible, so that the band concentrates only on performing. Consider using DI boxes or speaker simulators (see page 222), so that the overall volumes of the bass, guitars, keyboards, and vocals are balanced by the engineer. A good, sympathetic sound engineer who knows your material is a valuable member of the band, even if this is unknown to the audience.

## MONITORING IN LARGER VENUES

In most professional venues, the front-of-house PA system is likely to be either hired in for the occasion, or a permanent fixture. Such systems will use a lot of standard recording studio technology, such as multiple speaker and amplification systems and rack-mounted digital effects. All of the instruments, as well as the drums, will have their own dedicated inputs or microphones. The individual sound levels of each instrument are controlled by an engineer at a large mixing desk, usually positioned behind the audience at the back of the hall.

Naturally, the larger the venue, the more power is needed to fill the space. It is at this point that the problems of allowing the musicians to hear themselves clearly become more critical. A professional PA system invariably incorporates monitoring facilities, which allow the musicians to hear a special mix of the overall sound via one or more speakers positioned on the floor in front of them on the stage. More up-market venues will often use a completely independent PA system for monitoring. This usually comprises a mixing desk and engineer positioned at the side of the stage, providing individual mixes of the overall sound tailored to the needs of each musician.

The diagram below shows a typical, large, concert PA system. The red items are all a part of the monitoring system; the gray items are connected to the main front-of-house PA system, and are controlled by a mixing desk at the back of the auditorium.

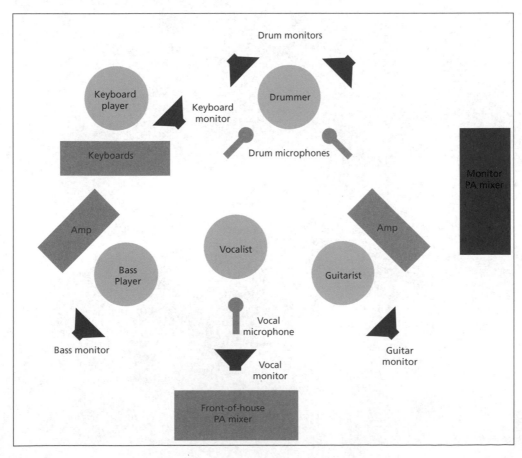

# THE LIVE GUITAR

**Once upon a time, playing an electric guitar on stage was a straightforward business—players turned up at the gig, switched on their amplifiers and plugged in. Whilst many of the possibilities are still based around this principle, there are several other options that the modern day guitarist can consider. The issue of making a acoustic (as distinct from an electro-acoustic guitar) heard, remains a challenge.**

## USING A BACKLINE SYSTEM

Even at the highest level, many guitar-based bands still prefer to work with "backline" amplification—that is, retaining control of their own amplifier settings and having the signal reach the front-of-house PA via microphone. Although the more sophisticated DI solutions can retain amplifier characteristics and allow a greater degree of external control, there are some playing effects which are impossible to achieve without a backline system. Perhaps the best known effect is the acoustic phenomenon of feedback.

### SUSTAIN AND FEEDBACK

If it is loud enough, the sound coming from the amplifier's loudspeaker will cause the strings of harmonically related notes on the guitar to vibrate in "sympathy." This creates a continuous loop of never-ending sustain known as feedback. The early electric guitars were, in essence, electrified acoustic models, which meant that the resonating body exacerbated the feedback problem. It was this, as much as anything else, that resulted in the likes of Les Paul and Merle Travis experimenting with solid bodies.

However, during the late 1950s and early 1960s some electric blues players realized that this sustained overdrive could be used as an interesting effect in its own right, and began to integrate it into their sound. Using controlled feedback takes considerable skill in understanding the volumes and EQ to set up on specific configurations of guitar and amplifier. It can also require considerable taste when integrating it within a general playing technique—especially

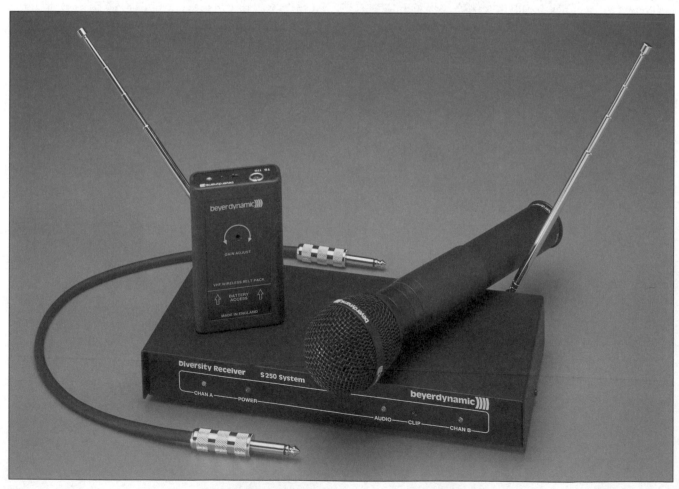

## YOUR GOOD HEALTH

Most of the time, playing the guitar is a relatively safe pursuit. However, there are a number of health risks which you should at least be aware of. The first one is the potential damage that may result from too much noise. So much research has now been done on the subject that there really can be no doubt that prolonged exposure to extremely loud music—the kind of volumes that you would experience in an average gig situation—is likely to damage your hearing. There is no

easy answer to this, although avoiding your ears being too close to loudspeakers may help. If you suffer with persistent hearing problems, such as a "ringing" noise for days after you have performed, you should treat this as a serious warning sign and consult your doctor.

Another area to treat with the utmost seriousness is electricity. Numerous musicians have been harmed—some fatally—after receiving electric shocks while performing or recording. Such tragedies are usually a result of faulty earthing on electrical

equipment. Frustratingly, in almost all of these occurrences, problems can invariably be avoided by regular servicing of equipment, and checking leads, plugs, and fuses. Your amplifier will usually give out clues when it is becoming faulty—listen out for excessive buzzing, especially when your hand comes into contact with the strings, or other metal parts on the guitar. As should ALWAYS be the case with all electrical matters, if you have any doubts seek qualified help.

important is muting strings, to prevent unwanted notes also feeding back.

You will find that the effectiveness of the sustain will depend on your position on stage in relation to the amplifier. This will vary from stage to stage, depending on the acoustics of the surrounding area. Players who are serious about controlled feedback sometimes find it effective to move around the stage during a soundcheck to find the optimum feedback spots. They then mark these positions with chalk or tape.

## TRANSMITTER SYSTEMS

The use of radio or "wireless" transmitters on stage is becoming more and more popular, even among semi-professional guitarists. Instead of plugging the guitar directly into an amplifier, a transmitter, which is worn on the guitarist's belt or strap, is plugged into the guitar. The signal from the guitar is picked up by a VHF receiver, which is positioned alongside and plugged into the amplifier or mixing desk. This allows the player to move around the stage without having to worry about tripping over guitar leads.

The early transmitters acquired something of a dubious reputation for being subject to Spinal Tap-style radio interference; however, sophisticated frequency-switching has now all but illuminated this problem. Similarly, radio systems are also commonly used in on-stage monitoring, allowing mixes to be heard by the performers using earpieces specially molded to the contours of the player's ear.

## ACOUSTIC GUITARS

Since the evolution of electrical instruments and amplification, the issue of mixing electronic and acoustic instruments together on stage has been one the the greatest banes in the life of any sound engineer.

The principal difficulty of working with acoustic guitars on stage stems from the problem of controlling the volume and sound. If an acoustic guitar is miked up using regular studio techniques, the player MUST remain in the same position if a consistent signal is to be heard—movement away from the microphone not only changes the volume but the tonal balance. This is all well and good for most classical, folk, or flamenco performances, but more difficult to achieve in a rock or pop setting. It can also be extremely difficult to prevent external sounds from drifting into the microphone, causing a muddy sound, or, indeed, the microphone picking up its own sounds from the PA, resulting in high-pitched feedback.

There is no easy solution to this problem, although careful use of compressors and noise gates can help. Some musicians overcome this problem by using electro-acoustic instruments. These are straightforward acoustic guitars with built in pickups: they can used acoustically, or plugged into an amplifier. For most uses, in a group context, at any rate, they provide a sufficiently authentic acoustic sound, although they are weaker when heard in isolation. A similar alternative, with largely the same pros and cons, is to fit a magnetic pickup or transducer microphone to the soundhole of a regular acoustic guitar.

# SELLING YOUR SOUL

Although for many musicians it may be enough to perform live to small audiences, or make recordings for their own sake, or to play to friends and family, some will have greater ambitions. At some stage, most will feel an urge to commit their work to posterity—to have a REAL record, cassette, or CD of their music. This is becoming increasingly common as high-quality home recording equipment becomes more and more affordable, as does the bulk manufacture of a medium like the compact disc. In fact, it seems odd to relate that, even ignoring general inflation, it now costs little more to produce a small run of, say, 1000 CDs than it did to produce the same number of vinyl LPs a decade ago.

## THE WHYS AND WHEREFORES...

When it comes down to it, once you've made the decision that you want to make your recordings available to the world, there are two stark possibilities that will govern your next move: you either release your own music, or get somebody else to do it for you.

### GO WITH THE INDUSTRY

The latter of the two options is not really worth dwelling on here. With the mainstream music industry increasingly concentrating on a small number of artists selling larger amounts of "product," the likelihood of a new band getting a record deal with a major, multi-national label is very slim indeed. The amount of investment involved in launching a new artist nowadays means that risks have to minimized, which, for the serious musician, almost inevitably means the dreaded "C" word—compromise. Indeed, evidence would seem to suggest that success is more often than not likely to be just as much a result of peripheral matters, such as image, as the quality or originality of your music.

Nonetheless, excellent bands like Nirvana, R.E.M., Pearl Jam, and Radiohead have managed to creep through the gaps, but these are surely the exceptions to the rules. And in any case, artists such as these usually graduate from cult success on an independent label. It is here that more specialized types of music have a better chance of thriving. Indeed, the independent world, especially in the US, can generate a good deal of sales—the larger labels often acting as unpaid A&Rs for the majors—and have enough financial backing to "push" a cult band.

If your music falls outside of the commercial mainstream, this line might well be worth your consideration, although you have the best chance of being taken seriously if you have an already established live reputation, and you have already got releases under your belt—even if you've put them out yourself.

Otherwise, there is very little practical advice to give on this matter, although anyone who has worked in the mainstream music business will tell you that nowadays pretty well nobody gets signed up to a major label by sending out endless streams of "demo" cassettes.

If this is a serious aim, you would probably be better off channeling your energy into finding a good manager, whose job it would be to deal with such matters. You can then get on with the serious business of getting out there and making music. Good luck—you'll need it!

## DO IT YOURSELF

The principal advantage of pressing up your own music is that you get to present yourself EXACTLY the way you want it. You don't have to make any compromises at all. The downside, of course, is that you have to pay for the privilege. And then you have to try to sell it yourself.

The first decision you need to make is to choose your format. This may well come down to the nature of your music. There are four principal formats for pre-recorded music—compact disc, vinyl, cassette, and latterly mini-disk. The first two are by some distance the most common formats used by the independent market.

### CHOOSING A FORMAT

Cassette and mini-disk have an inherent advantage over the other formats in that, if you have the time and inclination, they can be mass-duplicated in real-time using domestic equipment. Unfortunately, they are also by far the hardest formats to sell en masse.

In spite of their unnecessarily high costs in the shop, CDs are the most cost-effective format to produce in small quantities. Also, they are popular with music stores because they take up such little space. Their size and weight also makes them cheaper to send through the mail than the traditional vinyl format.

## HOW MUCH TIME?

Here is a table of the maximum times available using each format. Note that when cutting vinyl, the width of the groove has an impact on the overall sound. To fit more music on, the groove must be shallower. This compresses the frequency range and reduces the volume, making surface noise (crackles and clicks) more audible. For regular cassettes, longer times mean using thinner tape. This doesn't affect sound quality too much, but makes them less robust and long-lasting. No such compromises are necessary with other formats.

**Vinyl (per side)**

| | | |
|---|---|---|
| Single @ 45 rpm | 6:30 (max) | 4:00 (optimum) |
| Single @ 33 rpm | 8:00 (max) | 5:30 (optimum) |
| 10-inch @ 33 rpm | 18:00 (max) | 15:00 (optimum) |
| 12-inch @ 45 rpm | 15:00 (max) | 10:00 (optimum) |
| 12-inch @ 33 rpm | 30:00 (max) | 20:00 (optimum) |
| **Compact disc** | 74:00 | |
| **Cassette** | 120:00 | |
| **Minidisk** | 120:00 | |
| **DAT** | 120:00 | |

Recordable CD has also taken off in recent times. If you have suitable hardware for your computer, it is possible to bulk record large numbers of blank CD-Rs. This has two excellent advantages: blank CD-Rs are now almost as cheap as high-quality cassette tapes, and they are not recorded in "real-time". This means that if you have, say, a "four-times record" CD-R unit you should be able to record a full-length CD in something like 20 minutes. It's fair to say, however, that most music shops and distributors would be wary of selling CD-Rs. In addition, the format does have a reputation for being a little unreliable.

### VINYL SOLUTIONS

Against music industry predictions (and its hopes, judging by the outrageous profit margins achieved by CD pricing), the traditional vinyl format has enjoyed something of a renaissance in recent years. Although albums by most major artists are only given very limited releases on vinyl, the 12-inch single remains the most popular format among dance music producers and club DJs. In other specialized independent markets—such as punk and garage pop—the 7-inch single and EP, and 12-inch album forms are often more popular in their vinyl versions. But in spite of the fact that some purists still prefer the sound of vinyl, mainstream music buyers seem nowadays highly reluctant to buy "old-fashioned" vinyl records.

## FINDING A MANUFACTURER

Whichever format you choose, the manufacturing process is broken down into separate stages, most of which are performed by an entirely different set of people (see page 244) or companies. Therefore, if time is a major consideration to you, it's a good idea to find a broker—a go-between who looks after every stage of the production. In fact, the ability to strike bulk deals with their sub-contractors often means that brokers can offer a better deal than if you took care of each stage yourself. Also, they take responsibility for the inevitable problems that occur during the different stages of manufacture.

Manufacturing brokers often advertize in the back pages of music and technology magazines, or can usually be found in music-industry directories. It's always sensible to get quotes from a number of different sources—you may well find that even over a run of 500 CDs, there is a variance of up to 30% between one company and another. As in most other areas, it's always better to get recommendations from other satisfied customers.

A final word of warning: ALWAYS know exactly what you're getting for your money—it's no fun driving 50 miles to collect a couple of thousand albums from a pressing plant, just because you hadn't realized that the manufacturer's costs excluded delivery!

# MASS PRODUCTION

It can be an unpredictable experience the first time you make an record or CD. You can never quite tell how the finished article is going to look or sound. But the experience of opening up a box to see a copy of your own work for the first time is a pretty major thrill. More nerve-wracking is when you flip the disc onto the turntable or CD player for the first time. This is when it will dawn on you exactly what you've done: every last blemish or element of dissatisfaction will remain there FOREVER—and this is exactly what the rest of the world will be hearing, too!

## MAKING A COMPACT DISC

Although scientifically the most complex manufacturing process, from the user's point of view, producing a CD is a relatively straightforward process. Your original stereo recording will be digitally remastered so that the PQN codes are added—these are the codes that provide the CD with information that the player needs to be able to function, such as track numbers, index points, start times, and durations. From this new master copy a "glass master" is produced—this is the template from which all your final CDs will emanate.

You can master a compact disc from any other format—cassette, reel-to-reel, minidisk—although the most commonly used these days is DAT (digital audio tape). Some mastering suites may even be able to deal with digital soundfiles (such as AIF, WAV, or Sound Designer II files) on a computer hard disk, although these will generally require playback or sequencing software, such as Digidesign's MasterList.

If your own master copy has track pointers already recorded—and if it is been recorded on DAT or minidisk, then this is likely—you can simply hand over the tape or disk with your artwork and sit back to wait for the finished articles to arrive! However, there are some further possibilities which are worth considering.

### MASTERING

You should not ignore the possibilities offered by the "mastering room," especially if your recordings were made in "lo-fi" surroundings. The mastering suite is a deliberately "dead"-sounding room equipped with professional sound-processing equipment. By attending the mastering, you can get a clear picture for yourself of how your music is going to sound on other systems. Here you also have the option of making final alterations to your mixed tape. These can include the following types of feature:

- Adding compression to "tighten" up the sound.
- Taking advantage of the professional equalization facilities that the mastering desk can offer.
- Altering EQ between tracks.
- Matching relative volumes between tracks.
- Tidying up ("chasing") fades.

All of these features can be used to help your final product sound more polished. The mastering engineer can also act as a useful set of ears, recommending possible courses of action. Don't expect miracles, though—mastering can NEVER magically transform a poor original.

### PRESENTATION FORMATS

With vinyl formats, the types of jacket possible were largely predetermined. With CDs, there are options that cater for different tastes and pockets.

Whether you love it or hate it, the plastic "jewel" case is the packaging of choice for the vast majority of CDs. Because they are so widely used, they are the cheapest. The jacket sleeve is usually the front page of a small booklet which slots into the front of the case.

The simplest package features a basic, cardboard "record"sleeve; however, these are unpopular, as they are too thin to show information on a spine. An increasingly popular compromise is the "Digipack," which features a cardboard flap that, when opened, reveals the disc inside.

## MECHANICAL COPYRIGHT

If you record a cover version of someone else's music and manufacture a record, tape, or CD, you are legally obliged to pay a small fee to the publisher and/or composer of the music. This cost is known as "mechanical copyright," and is usually charged or at least registered by the pressing plant, based on the number of units you have pressed. When budgeting, bear in mind that mechanical payments can push up the cost of manufacture by between 5 and 10%—another incentive to compose your own material.

# MANUFACTURING A VINYL ALBUM, 12-INCH, OR SINGLE

The mastering stage of producing a vinyl recording is similar to that for producing a CD, in that it offers the same kind of scope for alteration. However, one further aspect of control that you have (and that will dictate your costs) is in your choice of vinyl quality. "Classical" pressings cost the most, and use virgin vinyl; other options use combinations of recycled vinyl, which can produce a higher level of surfece noise. Pressing your record on colored vinyl, or as a picture disc (which a few plants can still do) may look attractive, but this nearly always results in a surfeit of crackles and clicks.

## THE CUT

The mastering process for vinyl is known as "the cut." Your original tape is played back through a mixing console, which is linked to a lathe mechanism that cuts the groove into a blank lacquer disc. If you pay extra, you can get a reference lacquer cut first. This can be played like a normal record, to help you judge how the recording will transfer to vinyl. This is one of the unpredictable areas of vinyl. With the digital CD format, you theoretically get back EXACTLY what goes in; this is not so with vinyl, where different sounds transfer in different ways. For example, sibilant vocals can easily become exaggerated on vinyl.

## THE LACQUERS

After the lacquer has been produced, it is sent off for plating. The lacquer is coated with a thin layer of silver and electro-plated in a solution of nickel. When the nickel plating is stripped away, it holds a negative impression of the original lacquer. This is used to make the "mother" mold, from which the final "stamper" is produced. The stamper holds a negative impression of the original lacquer, which is then used to press the vinyl. A pair of stampers can press between 1500–2000 records before they wear out and a new set has to be made from the mother molds.

## PRESSING

The pressing process sees molten vinyl compressed hydraulically between the stampers to create the finished record. Before you give the go-ahead for the complete pressing, you MUST listen to a test pressing. This will sound identical to the final record, so any problems that may have occurred in the cutting and plating processes will become apparent.

## ARTWORK

After the amount of work you've put into creating the music in the first place, you owe it to yourself to present the finished product in a way which is suitable to the music. Also, the way you present your music to the outside world will have some impact on the way it's received—by reviewers, buyers, and distributors alike.

Whether, like many independent artists, you choose to create your own sleeve and label designs, or hand the work over to a professional designer, the costs will be dictated by how many colors you decide to use in the printing process. Using just one color will cost the least money, but is usually less interesting. The cheapest single colors to use are known as "process" colors. These are black, cyan (pale blue), magenta (dark red), and yellow. These four colors are known to printers as CMYK—combinations of these four colors are used to create every other color possibility. You will usually be charged extra if you request a specific tint—either by providing a swatch or a reference, such as a Pantone.

To achieve a full-color effect, your original artwork has to be converted to CMYK—this produces four pieces of film which are converted into lithographic plates, each of which generates a single color.

The cheapest way to create artwork, which is increasingly common as technology continues to fall in price, is to do it yourself using graphics or desktop publishing software. The film can then be generated by a typesetting company. The manufacturing costs for a CD or vinyl usually drop considerably if you provide the film yourself.

If you create your own "camera-ready" artwork, consisting of, say, a finished painting, this can be a more costly process, because the artwork has to undergo high-quality computer scanning to separate the colors—using a domestic scanner will usually give less than impressive results for very detailed work.

# SPREADING THE WORD

So, you've taken the plunge, and your garage is now filled with boxes of CDs or records. What do you have to do to prevent them from staying there forever? The first time you release something, you'll almost certainly have some support from your friends and family, all of whom will eagerly dip into their pockets to buy your lovingly crafted epic. If you play live on a regular basis, you should also be able to sell copies at your gigs. However, if you want to reach a wider audience there is no alternative to getting a distributor involved. Without a distributor you will not be able to get your music into the shops, which is, after all, where nearly all music is bought. Then there is the issue of finding yourself an audience—without promotion, you will be invisible to the world.

## DISTRIBUTION

At the simplest level, a distributor is simply a middle-man who steps in between you and the music store. In short, he buys from you and sells your products on to shops at a higher price. But if all he is doing is taking a cut of your profits, why do you need a distributor? Can't you do it yourself?

The answer to that question has to be "quite possibly"—you may be able to devote more time to selling your own material that a distributor could afford to. However, what you won't have straightaway is market knowledge and connections. You might be able to sell a few copies to a local, independent music shop, or ones that specialize in your particular type of music, but it simply isn't practical to do this for every outlet in the country. And as for dealing with overseas (even the humblest DIY indie band has a potential global audience), just compiling a list of stores to approach could take months.

Any decent distributor (and beware, there are a whole lot of very poor distributors, too) will have links to a whole array of music stores, not to mention distributors in other countries. Your distributor will be responsible for letting these outlets know that your recording exists, and offering it to them. If successful, they do the selling, posting, and packaging.

You may be able to sell small quantities directly to a single distributor; however, most will want exclusive rights for a particular territory. In these cases, like most distribution networks in the independent world operate, they work on a sale-or-return basis. The harsh reality of this system is that if, after a period of time, your records or CDs remain unsold, they will be returned to you.

### FINDING A DISTRIBUTOR

When the independent music scene really took off during the early 1980s, it seems to have been relatively easy to turn up at a distributor's warehouse with a carfull of albums to sell. These days, with more people making and releasing their own music,

and, frankly, less people buying their endeavors, distributors are now a little more choosy about who they take on. For this reason, it's always a good idea to try to find a distributor for your music before you have it pressed up. It will give you a feel for how the industry will respond to what you're doing, and will also allow your music to hit the streets at the earliest opportunity. Distributors very often specialize in particular types of music, so it's always a good idea to find out who distributes the artists or groups that you most resemble.

### MAIL-ORDER NETWORKS

The past decade has also seen a major growth in the development of small mail-order outlets. These operations are usually fan-based, and are geared towards certain types of music and artist. They have the advantage that if you can get on their lists, you become associated with similar more successful artists. This can help to build up a following—especially if you don't perform live. People who buy via mail-order are often the most fanatical, and when "captured," they usually remain loyal to your cause.

### PERFORMANCE RIGHTS

If your music is played on TV, radio, or in a film (or, theoretically, anywhere in public), the composer or publisher of the composition is entitled to a performance fee. Reputable television and radio stations fill out returns forms, which are then logged with a performing right society. The only practical way of collecting the royalties to which you are entitled is to register with one of these societies. The principal organizations are ASCAP and BMI in the USA, PRS in Britain, and GEMA in central Europe. These organizations are non-profit-making, although you will usually have to pay a small fee to join.

## THE INTERNET

No matter how strange and obscure your music might be, you can be guaranteed that somebody somewhere will be interested and "understand" what you're getting at. The easiest way to find such an audience these days is to use the Internet. Indeed, the Internet is fast-becoming a vital promotional tool for all musicians and artists. If you're serious about reaching an audience, you really ought to consider getting your own web page. This will allow anyone in the world with access to the Internet to read about—and even listen to—your music.

There are a number of good reasons for considering the Internet—in fact, there are many music-industry analysts who believe that in the near future a significant proportion of all music sales will take place over the Internet.

• Your presence is there for anyone to find. Make sure that you've registered your site with the major search engines, such as Lycos and Altavista. Look out for "index" sites—these are simply world-wide web signposts—that deal with your kind of music. Try to get your own site hotwired to as many like-minded pages as you can.

• You can include snatches of your music, which allows the end-user to sample your work from their own home computer. It's advisable to keep samples down to around 20 seconds, as most people don't have the capability of dealing with on-line streaming, where while the music is playing, the next section is already downloading. Most machines simply download the whole soundfile before it can be played.

• You also get to communicate with your audience. At best, you can sell your music directly to the customer, cutting out the shops and distributors. Some cult artists, whose music sales would rarely reach the mainstream, use this system to increase their own profitability. When you build up a substantial mailing list, it's easy to keep your audience informed of new developments, recordings, or live performances.

## PROMOTION

Far and away the most difficult aspect of DIY music, promotion is critically important: the biggest labels wouldn't devote millions of dollars to marketing a new album by a major artist if it weren't. The simple truth is that if you don't promote yourself, few will know you exist, and few will buy your music. Here are some very basic guidelines to DIY promotion:

• Be prepared to give away your CD or record to ANYONE who might be useful, or who might know somebody useful.

• Try to back up your new releases with as many live performances as possible.

• Put together a press pack. This should at the very least include the music and a basic press release. Photographs and other promotional aids can be effective, but are not worth doing unless they're done professionally.

• Build up your own list of music journalists and radio DJs who might be interested in your work. Keep them informed of your activities—anything that helps to imbed your name in the music industry's collective brain.

• Follow up your mail-outs. Many music journalists and DJs get hundreds of new releases sent to them every week, and even if they like your music, they're probably not going to call you to let you know. If you don't hear anything, hassle them for a response.

• Begin by targeting locally or, if your music is in a specialist field, clubs and societies. Many colleges have their own radio and TV stations; try to push for coverage, offering yourself for interviews or live performances.

## A FINAL THOUGHT

If you think all of this a little bleak—it's supposed to be. For most musicians with little or no interest in business matters, recording the music is the easy bit. Selling yourself to the world is hard work, and can be a thoroughly depressing experience. But you WILL find people who are interested in what you are doing. On the plus side, the costs of manufacture ARE very cheap nowadays, and if you pay to press up 1000 CDs, you only need to sell around 200 to a distributor, or 100 directly to the public, to recoup your money. Anyone with a good product and a bit of energy should be able to do that. Good luck!

# GLOSSARY

**ACCENT**

A dynamic playing effect that places an emphasis on specific notes or chords within a sequence, making them louder or creating rhythmic effects.

**ACCIDENTALS**

Symbols used in written music to raise or lower the pitch of a note: the sharp (#) raises the pitch by a half-step or semitone; the flat (♭) lowers the pitch by a half-step or semitone; the double sharp (##) raises the pitch by a step or tone; the double flat (♭♭) lowers the pitch by a step or tone; the natural (♮) is used to cancel a previous accidental.

**ACOUSTIC GUITAR**

Guitar which can be played without using amplification.

**ACTION**

The height between the strings and the frets on the fretboard. The higher the action, the harder it becomes to fret notes.

**ADAT**

Popular digital multitrack recording format created by US company Alesis. The system uses standard Super-VHS video format cassettes.

**ADT**

Automatic Double Tracking. An electronic delay effect that simulates the sound of two instruments playing the same part.

**APPOGGIATURA**

An ornamental note used to indicate a bend in pitch.

**ARCH-TOP**

Steel-string acoustic guitar with an arched top.

**BOTTLENECK**

A glass or metal bar dragged along the strings to alter the pitch. Also the name given to the technique and style of for playing with a bottleneck.

**BRIDGE**

A mechanical device fitted to the body of an electric guitar which supports the strings and controls their height and length. On an acoustic guitar, the part into which the strings are set.

**CAPO**

A movable nut or zero fret which can be clamped at different positions along the fingerboard, allowing open strings to be played in alternative keys.

**CHORD**

The sound of three or more notes played at the same time. Two notes played simultaneously can create a chordal effect. although this is technically known as an interval.

**CHORUS**

Electronic delay effect that simulates more than one instrument playing the same part. Variations in pitch and time can be used to create a richer, thicker effect.

**COMPRESSION**

Electronic processing effect that equalises the dynamic range of sounds passing through it by increasing the volume of quiet notes and reducing the volume of loud notes.

**DAMPING**

Playing technique which mutes one or more strings by deadening the natural ring with either of the hands. The opposite of accenting.

**DAT**

Digital Audio Tape. Universal two-track mastering standard which has largely replaced analog reel-to-reel format.

**DELAY**

Digital simulation of natural reflected sounds, such as echo.

**DISTORTION**

Electronic effect created by heavily boosting the volume in the preamp stage of the amplifier. Can also be achieved using external effects units.

**DREADNOUGHT**

A large-bodied, steel-string acoustic guitar.

**ELECTRO-ACOUSTIC GUITAR**

A guitar that can be played acoustically or plugged into an external amplifier.

**FEEDBACK**

A sound produced when amplified sound from a loudspeaker causes a string to vibrate.

**FINGERPICKING**

Right-hand playing technique where the strings are plucked by individual fingers.

**FLAT-TOP GUITAR**

A steel-string guitar with a flat soundboard.

**FRET**

Metal strips placed at intervals along the fingerboard.

**FRET TAPPING**

Playing technique where both left and right hands are used to fret notes on the fingerboard. Sometimes referred to as finger tapping.

**FUZZ BOX**

See distortion.

**GUITAR SYNTHESIZERS**

Guitars with in-built synthesizer systems for dramatically altering the sound, or equipped with MIDI to control external synthesizers, drum machines, or processing effects.

**HEADSTOCK**

The uppermost part of the guitar neck, where the machine heads are mounted.

**HUMBUCKERS**

Twin-coil electronic pickups that produce a thick or "fat" sound favored by many rock guitarists.

**MACHINE HEAD**

Mechanical device for controlling the tension, and therefore pitch, of a string.

**MIDI**

Musical Instrument Digital Interface. Electronic protocol language that allows computers, synthesizers, drum machines, sequencers, and other suitably equipped electronic units to communicate with one another.

**NOISE GATE**

Electronic effect which cuts out all noise until it receives a signal passing a preset threshold.

**NUT**

The string supports positioned at the top of the fingerboard.

**OCTAVE**

An interval of 12 half-steps (or semitones). Doubling the sound frequency of any note has the effect of increasing the pitch by an octave.

**P A SYSTEM**

Stands for Public Address system. Amplification system used when performing to an audience.

**PEDALS**

Foot-controlled electronic units placed between the output of the guitar and the input of the amplifier, which can be used to process the sound in a variety of different ways.

**PICK**

Object used for striking the guitar strings—usually made from plastic. Also known as a plectrum.

**PICKUPS**

Electro-magnetic transducers that convert string vibration into electrical impulses, which are then amplified and played back through a loudspeaker. Pickups are either single-pole or twin-pole; the latter are also known as "humbuckers".

**PLECTRUM**

See pick.

**RESONATOR**

Type of acoustic guitar with in-built metal resonator which increases volume and sustain. Also known as a Dobro.

**RIFF**

A repeated sequence of notes.

**SCRATCHPLATE**

A plastic plate fitted to the soundboard to protect the guitar body. Also known as a pickguard.

**SOUNDBOARD**

The front of the guitar on which the bridge is mounted

**TEMPO**

The speed at which a piece of music is played. Usually measured in beats per minute (bpm).

**TIME SIGNATURE**

Two numbers shown at the beginning of a piece of music, indicating both the number of beats, and their value, within a bar.

**TREMOLO ARM**

See vibrato.

**TRUSS ROD**

Metal rod that passes beneath the fingerboard of the guitar and prenets the neck from being distorted by natural string tension.

**VIBRATO ARM**

Mechanical device that can alter the pitch of a string while playing—sometimes wrongly referred to as a "tremolo arm". Vibrato is also a playing technique where a finger of the left hand is used to create a minor fluctuation in pitch.

**VOLUME PEDAL**

Foot pedal connected between the guitar and amplifier, allowing the volume to be altered without using the controls on the guitar.

**WAH-WAH PEDAL**

Foot-operated effect unit that can either be rocked back and forth to produce a "wah" sound, or fixed in one position as a tone control.

**ZERO FRET**

Fret found on some guitars directly in front of the nut, controlling the action—the height of the strings—at the top of the neck.

# INDEX

## A

## B

## C

# BIBLIOGRAPHY

Craig Anderton—*Home Recording For Musicians* (AMSCO, 1978)

Tony Bacon—*The Ultimate Guitar Book* (Dorling Kindersley, 1991)

Derek Bailey—*Improvisation* (Moorland, 1980)

Terry Burrows—*The Complete Encyclopedia Of The Guitar* (Carlton, 1998)

Terry Burrows—*Play Rock Guitar* (Dorling Kindersley, 1995)

Terry Burrows—*Play Country Guitar* (Dorling Kindersley, 1995)

Richard Chapman—*The Complete Guitarist* (Dorling Kindersley 1993)

Ralph Denyer—*The Guitar Handbook* (Pan, 1992)

Chris Everard—*The Home Recording Handbook* (Virgin, 1985)

Hugh Gregory—*1000 Great Guitarists* (IMP, 1992)

Mark Hanson—*The Alternate Tuning Guide For Guitar* (AMSCO, 1991)

Juan Martín—*El Arte De Flamenco De La Guitarra* (United Music, 1982)

Fred Miller—*Studio Recording For Musicians* (AMSCO, 1981)

Don Randall—*The New Harvard Dictionary Of Music* (Harvard University Press, 1986)

Darryl Runswick—*Rock, Jazz and Pop Arranging* (Faber and Faber, 1992)

Erik Satie—*A Mammal's Notebook: Collected Writings...* (Atlas, 1996)

Aaron Shearer—*Classic Guitar Technique* (Franco Colombo, 1963)

Nicolas Slonimsky—*Thesaurus of Scales and Melodic Patterns* (Scrivener's, 1947)

Happy Traum—*Flat-pick Country Guitar* (Oak, 1973)

Harvey Turnbull—*The Guitar* (Bold Strummer, 1991)

Jason Waldron—*Progressive Classical Guitar* (Koala, 1992)

# ACKNOWLEDGMENTS

In addition to everyone at Carlton Books and The Design Revolution, Terry Burrows would like to thank the following people for their help with this book: Jim Barber for his expertise on guitar hardware; The Guitar, Amp and Keyboard Centre, Brighton; Dan Burgess at Sound Valley; Richard Chapman; Chrys&themums; Jerome Davies; S.J.Deg; Ralph Denyer; Los Bros Dillingham; Mike Flynn; Flamingo Records; Vic Flick; Robert Fripp; Fred Frith; David Gross and Rene Deformeaux (Electric Snake productions); Julia Honeywell (Ace Records); Nick Kaçal for helping out with queries relating to music theory and for the loan of studio equipment; The Lovely Nay; Harvey Mandel; Helen Martín; R. Stevie Moore; Joachim Rheinbold at JAR Music; Andy Ward for his usual drumming expertise.

This book is dedicated to R.F. Burrows (1920–1997).

# PICTURE CREDITS

The publishers would like to thank the following sources for their kind permission to reproduce the pictures in this book:

AKG London
Arbiter Group plc
Steve Barber
Beyer Dynamic (GB) Ltd
Bridgeman Art Library/Bonhams, London UK *Flamenco guitar made by Manuel Ramirez/Santos Hernandes, Madrid c.1916 (wood, mother of pearl, ebony)*
Terry Burrows
Corbis/Asian Art & Archaeology, Inc.
Justin Downing
et archive
Exclusive Distribution
Focusrite Audio Engineering Ltd
Gibson
KGa
The Image Bank/Archive Photos
The Kobal Collection
The Lebrecht Collection
London Features International Ltd/Simon Fowler/Lawrence Maranao/David McGough
Mackie
Marshall Amplification plc
CF Martin Guitar & Co Inc.
Osborne Creative Services
Performing Arts Library/Clive Barda
Pictorial Press Ltd/Rob Verhorst/Combi Press
Sylvia Pitcher Photo Library/Sylvia Pitcher
Redferns/Geoff Dann/Outline/Ebet Roberts
Rex Features Ltd
Rickenbacker
SIN/Kim Tonelli
Solid State Logic/Richard Davies
Sound Technology plc
Sound Valley Distribution
Eva Vermandel

Every effort has been made to acknowledge correctly and contact the source and/copyright holder of each picture, and Carlton Books Limited apologises for any unintentional errors or omissions which will be corrected in future editions of this book.